The British Battle-Fleet

TO THOSE

WHO IN ALL AGES BUILT THE SHIPS OF

THE BRITISH NAVY

AND TO THE UNKNOWN MEN

WHO HAVE WORKED THOSE SHIPS

AND SO MADE POSSIBLE THE

FAME OF MANY ADMIRALS

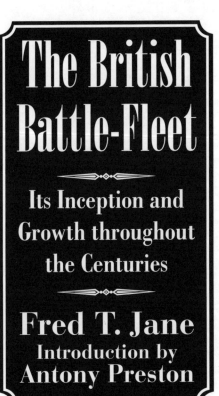

The British Battle-Fleet

Its Inception and Growth throughout the Centuries

Fred T. Jane
Introduction by
Antony Preston

With twenty-four
illustrations in colour
from the original
water-colour drawings by

W. L. Wyllie, RA

and numerous plans
and photographs

CONWAY CLASSICS

First published by S.W. Partridge & Co, Ltd, Old Bailey, London,
1912

This edition published in Great Britain in 1997 by
Conway Maritime Press
an imprint of Brassey's (UK) Ltd
33 John Street, London WC1N 2AT

Tel: 0171 753 7777   Fax: 0171 753 7795
E-mail: brasseys@dial.pipex.com
Web: http://www.brasseys.com

This edition © Conway Maritime Press, 1997
The Paintings by W L Wyllie, RA (1851-1931)
are reproduced by kind permission of Mr John Wyllie.

British Library Cataloguing in Data
is available from the British Library on request.

Library of Congress Cataloguing in Publication Data available.

ISBN 0 85177 723 6

Printed in Hong Kong by Midas Printing Ltd

CONTENTS

v

LIST OF ILLUSTRATIONS
IN COLOUR
FROM PICTURES BY W. L. WYLLIE, R.A.

THE "KING EDWARD VII" AS SHE WAS IN HER FIRST COMMISSION
     AS LORD CHARLES BERESFORD'S FLAGSHIP
SIR PHILIP WATTS
GENERAL CUNIBERTI
THE "LION"

MAPS, PLANS, DIAGRAMS, etc.

INTRODUCTION
TO THIS EDITION

Today the name Fred T Jane is widely associated with the naval and aviation reference books which he founded, but in his day he was known as a journalist, a prolific writer of books (including novels), an illustrator, and even an early motor-racing enthusiast.

Born in 1865 to the wife of a young curate in Richmond, Surrey, John Frederick Thomas Jane had to make his own way in the world. At school he published what today would be called an "underground" magazine as an alternative to the official school magazine. In 1882, inspired by the Royal Navy's spirited bombardment of Alexandria, the 17 year-old compiled a book of sketches of the major warships of the world's navies under the title *Ironclads of the World*. Despite living in a garret and selling his pen-and-ink sketches for almost nothing, by the 1890s he had become a special correspondent and was associating with the leading naval commentators of the day, notably William Laird Clowes, naval correspondent of *The Times* and Charles N Robinson, a leading contributor to the prestigious *Brassey's Naval Annual*.

What was to make Jane's reputation was his perception that the combination of rising literacy and affluence, the advent of cheap newspapers, and a growing public awareness of the vulnerability of the British Empire to attack, had created a market for much greater knowledge about the Royal Navy and its rivals. He soon ran into opposition from naval officers, who criticised him, both for expressing opinions on naval matters and for "giving away" valuable information to potential enemies. In 1997 little has changed, and Fred's rebuttal could be cited all too easily by naval commentators today. He defended himself by reminding his critics that he was forced to spend "hours and days" on the study of topics to which the average naval officer devotes "only minutes".

The gamble on selling "naval awareness" to the educated public paid off, and he was able to launch an illustrated guide to the navies of the world entitled *All the World's Fighting Ships* in 1897. This was followed in 1909 by a companion volume, *All the World's Airships (Aircraft & Dirigibles)*. In addition he produced two books for the naval market, *The Imperial Japanese Fleet* and *The Imperial Russian Fleet*, to exploit the interest aroused by the Russo-Japanese War, the first major naval war involving modern ships since the Battle of Lissa nearly 40 years earlier.

Inevitably the series was extended, and the result was *The British Battle-Fleet*. Undoubtedly Fred T Jane would have gone on to cover the French and American fleets at the very least, but time was running out. It was 1912, only two years before the Royal Navy was engulfed in a war of survival matched in its scale only by the great war against the French Revolution and Napoleon in 1793-1815. Time was running out for Jane in another sense; his health was failing, and he died in 1916.

Fred Jane was hardly the first to attempt a general history of the Royal Navy, but *The British Battle-Fleet* differed in one important respect; it was a history of the efforts to create and maintain a seagoing fleet as an instrument of national policy. He was well aware of the importance of seamanship and training in getting warships to function effectively in battle, but he drew on his experience to provide an insight into the process of what might be called "warship-creation". This process of framing requirements, designing and constructing men o'war was never fully understood by previous historians, who tended to emphasise battles, tactics and strategy. Jane's approach was a novelty in 1912, but today's audience will be more sympathetic, having been brought up to ask how things work.

What the book achieves is a chronicle of the slow evolution of a fleet which was at best "useful" in repelling an invasion or projecting power over short distances, into an instrument of national policy. This transition was very slow indeed. Even a leader as powerful as Queen Elizabeth I lacked strategic vision, and allowed her ministers to get rid of the navy which had humbled the sea power of Spain in 1588. The notion of building a navy to seize commercial advantage did not begin to take tangible form until the Dutch Wars of the 17th Century, and finally came to fruition in the Seven Years War in the following century. In the Great War against France in 1793-1815 the Royal Navy could be said to have turned itself into a "killer organisation" which ruthlessly captured or sank enough enemy ships to make up a significant second-rank navy. This tradition of seeking battle has lasted surprisingly well, and was demonstrated as recently as 1982, during the Falklands War.

Naturally some assumptions made by Jane sound dated. He lived in the age of *Pax Britannica* and was strongly influenced by the teachings of Alfred Mahan. Although he was aware of the increasingly complex problems of defending the Empire, he could hardly conceive of that Empire declining so rapidly despite being undefeated in two world wars. Yet his comments made before and after the outbreak of war in 1914 reveal a shrewd grasp of reality. He foresaw that a war between Great Britain and Germany would ruin Britain, even if the Royal Navy was victorious. He also warned of the disastrous consequences of neglecting defence, warnings which were ignored in the euphoria of post-war pacifism and the misplaced faith in "collective security" in the years after the Treaty of Versailles. "The price of peace is preparedness for war", he wrote. He was no mindless jingoist, though, referring to "the music hall twaddle that makes decent men sick". His weekly column on the war at sea in the journal *Land and Water* cautioned against excessive public optimism and corresponding pessimism at minor reverses. Almost alone among the analysts of his day, he predicted a long war without a quick Trafalgar-style battle of annihilation.

Like Mahan, he died too soon, before the traumatic experience of the First World War could be analysed properly and used to test the late Victorian and Edwardian assumptions about future naval warfare. Fred T Jane died at the age of 50, two months before the titanic clash of battle fleets at Jutland. Given the effort put into this book, it must be regretted that he did not survive to play a leading role in the post-1918 debate on the lessons of the war. What is certain is that he would have recognised the flaws in the system of selecting and training senior officers which robbed the Grand Fleet of its only chance to annihilate the German High Seas Fleet.

The British Battle-Fleet would not meet the stringent criteria of the current generation of naval historians, who have the enormous benefit of wider perspectives such as economic analysis and a better understanding of the implications of contemporary technology. Ship-historians also have the benefit of full access to official records and technical papers. All this means that some aspects of policy and true fighting potential were simply not available. But Fred Jane never claimed to be a historian; he was a journalist who was able to translate the bewildering technical changes in progress into simple language which the interested layman could understand. The studies of "branch" history in recent years have thrown up many challenges to the old orthodoxy, but Jane made a serious effort to take into account contemporary historical views when writing of ancient times. His text contains references to "modern scholars' scepticism" about certain cherished traditions.

Inevitably he is at his best when writing about the great transition of the sailing Navy to steam and the subsequent hurricane of technical advance which swept away the legacy of the Victorian Navy. His contacts with the Navy in the 1890s had put him in touch with veterans whose experience went back to the 1860s, and he took frequent counsel of engineering officers to get a clearer idea of the performance of various designs. Even today the "plumbers" are likely to have a clearer impression of the virtues and vices of the ships in which they serve. Seamen officers in particular often have only a hazy notion of the compromises embodied in all warship designs.

Nobody appreciated the full import of the "second industrial revolution" which happened in the 1880s and 1890s almost unnoticed. In the words of the modern historian Andrew Gordon, "technology passed beyond the understanding of well-educated people, and became the exclusive realm of highly trained specialists". What made the second industrial revolution different from the original eighteenth-century upheaval was that its benefits were now available to all Britain's major European rivals, as well as the sleeping giant America.

It is inevitable that Fred Jane believed implicitly in the future of the "capital ship", which by 1912 embraced the newly re-named battle-cruiser category as well the traditional battleship. But it is hard to fault his prediction that some sort of capital ship would always be required as the backbone of a fleet. Today the term is used to describe aircraft carriers and powerful missile-armed cruisers and destroyers, all many times more powerful than the dreadnoughts of 1912.

His net was cast wide when defining the "battle fleet". Jane saw the Fleet as the sum of its component parts, down to torpedo boats and submarines. Clearly he did not subscribe to the widespread fixation with numbers of dreadnoughts favoured by the Edwardian public and its opinion-formers in Parliament and the press. He predicted, for example, that submarines would play an increasingly important role in naval warfare, and rightly said that the potential of aircraft had scarcely begun to be realised. He also predicted that a naval war would be a long one, and the burden of it would be borne by the minor war vessels.

The Royal Navy in 1912 was not yet at its full strength, but it reflected the massive changes wrought by "Jacky" Fisher and his fellow-zealots. Despite the flaws at command level, it had been strengthened by HMS *Dreadnought* and nine derivatives, dictating a new division of battle-fleet strength into "pre-dreadnoughts", "semi-dreadnoughts" and "dreadnoughts". Even as this book was published, the Royal Navy was about to raise the stakes with a new class of "super-dreadnoughts" and a corresponding class of battle-cruisers which some would mistakenly regard as fast battleships. Although time was to show that these ships were not as well protected as their German counterparts, they followed a pattern established in the eighteenth century; there were always more of them than their opponents.

Moving down the scale, the Navy was beginning to reverse Fisher's disdain for light cruisers. The first of the "Town" series were in service, the forerunners of the sturdy light cruisers which always outclassed their German equivalents. Even more significant, an old cruiser, HMS *Hermes* would be converted a year later to operate seaplanes during the Annual Manoeuvres.

The situation with torpedo craft was even better. After a misguided attempt by Fisher to build large high-speed destroyers had proved unsuccessful, since the 1908-1909 Programme a series of sturdy and seaworthy vessels had been built, providing a sound basis for successful future development. In combat they would always prove superior to their German counterparts, and one of the few positive points which emerged from Jutland was the way in which Grand Fleet destroyers repeatedly defeated German torpedo boats trying to attack the battle line.

The Royal Navy's submarine force was larger than any other navy's, but despite Fisher's enthusiasm for the new "weapon of stealth", he had saddled the Navy with small boats suitable only for coastal and harbour defence. Not until 1908 did the submariners get the first of a new type of submarine intended for long patrols. In 1912 the first of the "E" class was launched, the type which bore the brunt of wartime patrols in the North Sea and the Mediterranean.

The Royal Navy had learned some lessons from the Russo-Japanese War and from 1909 converted a number of old Victorian torpedo gunboats to minesweepers. In addition the foundations were laid for a Trawler Reserve, with equipment stockpiled and a register compiled of fishing vessels suitable for conversion to minesweepers. But this promising initiative was matched by a disastrous policy on offensive mine warfare. No attempt was made to develop an efficient mine, and the Navy was content with a licence-made version of a foreign weapon. This was to prove a serious handicap in 1914, and the Navy lacked an efficient mine until 1916, the year of Jane's death.

In contrast, the Royal Navy enjoyed the benefits of an immensely successful armaments industry. In 1912 its guns were excellent and about to get even better, with a shift to a higher calibre. Its torpedoes were also reliable and as good as any foreign equivalents. What was not suspected was poor quality-control over the manufacture of armour-piercing shells and cordite propellant, an oversight which contributed to the deaths of over 3000 sailors at Jutland. In part this can be blamed on the lack of a Naval Staff; in today's Navy faults in weapon systems still occur, but the Staff and the relevant technical departments have the responsibility of monitoring the projects. Although the energetic new First Lord of the Admiralty, Winston Churchill, had taken office with specific instructions to establish a proper Naval Staff it was far too early to expect results from the shakeup.

One important aspect of the Fleet's efficiency was almost certainly not fully known to Fred Jane. Since 1905 the Royal Navy's gunnery branch had been experimenting with Captain Percy Scott's Director system of fire control. The first director went to sea in 1907 and a much improved version was being prepared for sea trials in HMS *Thunderer* in mid-1912. Here was a truly secret weapon offering decisive superiority in action by permitting British capital ships to "hit first, hit hard and keep hitting". Its intricacies were known only to a very small circle of specialists, and it seems improbable that anyone outside that circle would have been able to explain it to Jane, although its principles were well-known. Sadly the Pollen range prediction system was dropped in favour of the inferior Dreyer system, thanks to Captain Dreyer's manipulation of the evaluation and trials.

Even with these flaws the British Battle Fleet of 1912 was a formidable force, one which would preserve the nation in its terrible agony between 1914 and 1918. A later generation of leaders would learn the lessons, allowing the Navy to play a major role in the Allies' victory over the Axis in 1945. What Fred T Jane has given us is a remarkable and unique snapshot of the Royal Navy, laden with an ancient tradition of victory but shortly to demonstrate that it was still the best in the world.

Antony Preston

PREFACE
TO THE FIRST EDITION

This book is not intended to be a "history" of the British Navy in the generally accepted sense of the term. For this reason small space is devoted to various strategical and tactical matters of the past which generally bulk more largely in more regular "naval histories"—of which a sufficiency already exist.

In such histories primary interest naturally attaches to what the admirals did with the ships provided for them. Here I have sought rather to deal with how the ships came to be provided, and how they were developed from the crude warships of the past to the intricate and complicated machines of to-day; and the strictly "history" part of the book is compressed with that idea principally in view. The "live end" of naval construction is necessarily that which directly or indirectly concerns the ships of our own time. The warships of the past are of special interest in so far as they were steps to the warships of to-day; but, outside that, practical interest seems confined to what led to these "steps" being what they were.

Thus regarded, Trafalgar becomes of somewhat secondary interest as regards the tremendous strategical questions involved, but of profound importance by reason of the side-issue that the *Victory's* forward bulkhead was so slightly built that she sustained an immense number of casualties which would never have occurred had she been designed for the particular purpose that Nelson used her for at Trafalgar. The tactics of Trafalgar have merely a literary and sentimental interest now, and even the strategies which led to the battle are probably of little utility to the strategists of our own times. But the *Victory's* thin forward bulkhead profoundly affected, and to some extent still affects, modern British naval construction. Trafalgar, of course, sanctified for many a year "end-on approach" and so eventually concentrated special attention on bulkheads. But previous to Trafalgar, the return of the *Victory* after it for refit, and Seppings' inspection of her, the subject of end-on protection had been ignored. The cogitations of Seppings helped to make what would have very much influenced history had any similar battle occurred in the years that followed his constructional innovations.

Again, at an earlier period much naval history turned upon the ventilation of bilges. Improvements in this respect (devised by men never heard of to-day) enabled British ships to keep the seas without their crews being totally disabled by diseases which often overmastered their foes. The skill of the admirals, the courage of the crews, both form more exciting reading. Yet there is every indication to prove that this commonplace matter of bilges was the secret of victory more than once!

Coming back to more recent times, the loss of the *Vanguard*, which cost no lives, involved greater subsequent constructional problems than did the infinitely more terrible loss of the *Captain* a few years before. Who shall say on how many seeming constructional failures of the past, successes of the yet unborn future may not rest?

A number of other things might be cited, but these suffice to indicate the particular perspective of this book, and to show why, if regarded as an orthodox "history" of the British Navy, it is occasionally in seemingly distorted perspective.

To say that in the scheme of this book the shipbuilder is put in the limelight instead of the ship-user, would in no way be precisely correct, though as a vague generalisation it may serve well enough. In exact fact each, of course, is and ever has been dependent on the other. Nelson himself was curtailed by the limitations of the tools provided for him. Had he had the same problems one or two hundred years before he would have been still more limited. Had he had them fifty or a hundred years later—who shall say?

With Seppings' improvements, Trafalgar would have been well-nigh a bloodless victory for the British Fleet. It took Trafalgar, however, to inspire and teach Seppings. Of every great sea-fight something of the same kind may be said. The lead had to be given.

Yet those who best laboured to remove the worst disabilities of "the means" of Blake, contributed in that measure to Nelson's successes years and years later on. Their efforts may surely be deemed worthy of record, for all that between the unknown designer of the *Great Harry* in the sixteenth century and the designers of Super-Dreadnoughts of to-day there may have been lapses and defects in details. There was never a lapse on account of which the user was unable to defeat any hostile user with whom he came into conflict. The "means" provided served. The creators of warships consistently improved their creations: but they were not without care and thought on the part of those who produced them.

To those who provided the means and to the rank and file it fell that many an admiral was able to do what he did. These admirals "made history". But ever there were "those others" who made that "history making" possible, and who so made it also.

In dealing with the warships of other eras, I have been fortunate in securing the co-operation of Mr. W. L. Wyllie, R. A., who has translated into vivid pictorial obviousness a number of details which old prints of an architectural nature entirely fail to convey. With a view to uniformity, this scheme, though reinforced by diagrams and photographs, has been carried right into our own times.

Some things which I might have written I have on that account left unrecorded. There are some things that cold print and the English language cannot describe. These things must be sought for in Mr. Wyllie's pictures.

In conclusion, I would leave the dedication page to explain the rest of what I have striven for in this book.

Fred T Jane, 1912

THE BRITISH BATTLE FLEET.

I.

THE BIRTH OF BRITISH NAVAL POWER.

THE birth of British naval power is involved in considerable obscurity and a good deal of legend.

The Phœnicians, and the Romans have both been credited with introducing nautical ideas to these islands, but of the Phœnicians there is nothing but legend so far as any " British Navy " is concerned. That the Phœnicians voyaged here we know well enough, and a " British fleet " of the B.C. era *may* have existed, a fleet due to possible Phœnicians who, having visited these shores remained in the land. Equally well it may be mythical.

Whatever share the ancient Britons may have had in the supposed commercial relations with Gaul, it is clear that no fleet as we understand a fleet existed in the days of Julius Cæsar. Later, while England was a Roman Province, Roman fleets occasionally fought upon British waters against pirates and in connection with Roman revolutions, but they were ships of the ruling power.

Roman power passed away. Saxons invaded and remained ; but having landed they became people of the land—not of the sea. Danes and other seafarers pillaged English shores much as they listed till Alfred the Great came to the throne.

Alfred has been called the " Father and Founder of the British Fleet." It is customary and dramatic

A

to suppose that Alfred was seized with the whole modern theory of "Sea Power" as a sudden inspiration—that "he recognised that invaders could only be kept off by defeating them on the sea."

This is infinitely more pretty than accurate. To begin with, even at the beginning of the present Twentieth century it was officially put on record that "while the British fleet could prevent invasion, *it could not guarantee immunity from small raids* on our great length of coast line." In Alfred's day, one mile was more than what twenty are now ; messages took as many days to deliver as they now do minutes, and the "raid" was the only kind of over-sea war to be waged. It is altogether chimerical to imagine that Alfred "thought things out" on the lines of a modern naval theorist.

In actual fact,* what happened was that Alfred engaged in a naval fight in the year 875, somewhere on the South Coast. There is little or no evidence to show where, though near Wareham is the most likely locality.

In 877 something perhaps happened to the Danes at Swanage, but the account in Asser is an interpolated one, and even so suggests shipwreck rather than a battle.

In 882 (possibly 881) two Danish ships sank: "the rest" (number not recorded) surrendered later on.

In 884 occurred the battle of the Stour. Here the Saxon fleet secured a preliminary success, in which thirteen Danish ships were captured. This may or may not have been part of an ambush—at any rate the final result was the annihilation of King Alfred's fleet.

In 896 occurred the alleged naval reform so often alluded to as "the birth of the British Navy"—those ships supposed to have been designed by Alfred, which according to Asser† were "full nigh twice as

* All statements as to King Alfred's navy are taken directly from the Anglo-Saxon Chronicle, Asser, and Florence of Worcester.
† An interpolated passage.

long as the others . . . . shapen neither like Frisian nor the Danish, but so as it seemed to him that they would be most efficient."

Around these "early Dreadnoughts" much has been weaved, but there is no evidence acceptable to the best modern historians that Alfred really built any such ships—they tend to reject the entire theory.

The actual facts of that "naval battle of the Solent" in 897 from which the history of our navy is popularly alleged to date, appear to be as follows :

There were nine of King Alfred's ships, manned by Frisian pirates, who were practically Danes. These nine encountered three Danish vessels in a land-locked harbour—probably Brading—and all of them ran aground, the Danish ships being in the middle between two Saxon divisions. A land fight ensued, till, the tide rising, the Danish ships, which were of lighter draught than the Saxon vessels, floated. The Danes then sailed away, but in doing so two of them were wrecked.

All the rest of the story seems to be purely legendary. Our real "island story"—as events during the next few hundred years following Alfred clearly indicate—is not that of a people born to the sea ; but the story of a people forced thereto by circumstances and the need of self-preservation.

It is a very unromantic beginning. There is a strange analogy between it and the beginning in later days of the Sea Power of the other "Island Empire" —Japan. Japan to-day seeks—as we for centuries have sought—for an historical sequence of the "sea spirit" and all such things as an ideal islander should possess. Neither we nor they have ever understood or ever properly realised that it was the Continentals who long ago first saw that it was necessary to command the sea to attack the islanders. The more obvious contrary has always been assumed. It has never been held, or even suggested that the Little Englander protesting against "bloated naval armaments," so far

from being a modern anachronism, an ultra-Radical
or Socialist exotic, may really claim to be the true
exponent of " the spirit of the Islanders " for all
time.   That is one reason why (excluding the mythical Minos of Crete) only two island-groups have ever
loomed big in the world's history.

When Wilhelm II of Germany said : *"Unsere Zukunft
liegt auf dem Wasser,"* he uttered a far more profound
truth than has ever been fully realised. Fleets came
into being to attack Islanders with.

The Islanders saw the sea primarily as a protection
existing between them and the enemy.   To the
Continental the sea was a road to, or obstacle between
him and the enemy, only if the enemy filled it with
ships. The Islanders have ever tended to trust to the
existence of the sea itself as a defence, except in so far
as they have been taught otherwise by individuals who
realised the value of shipping. Those millions of British
citizens who to-day are more or less torpid on the
subject of naval defence are every whit as normal as
those Germans who, in season and out, preach naval
expansion.

The explanation of all this is probably to be found
in the fact that the earliest warfare known either to
Continentals or to Islanders was *military warfare*. The
ship as at first employed, was used entirely as a means
of transport for reaching the enemy—first, presumably,
against outlying islands near the coast, later for more
over-sea expeditions.

Ideas of attack are earlier than ideas of defence,
and the primary idea of defence went no further than
the passive defensive. King Alfred, merely in realising
the offensive defensive, did a far greater thing than any
of the legendary exploits associated with his history.
The idea was submerged many a time in the years
that followed, but from time to time it appeared and
found its ultimate fruition in the Royal Navy.

Yet still, the wonder is not that only two Island
Empires have ever come into existence, but that any

should have come into existence at all. The real history of King Alfred's times is that the Continental Danes did much as they listed against the insular Saxons of England, till the need was demonstrated for an endeavour to meet the enemy on his own element.

In the subsequent reigns of Athelstan and Edmund, some naval expeditions took place. Under Edgar, the fleet reached its largest. Although the reputed number of 3,600 vessels is, of course, an exaggerated one, there was enough naval power at that time to secure peace.

This "navy" had, however, a very transient existence, because in the reign of Ethelred who succeeded to the Throne, it had practically ceased to exist, and an attempt was made to revive it. This attempt was so little successful that Danish ships had to be hired for naval purposes.

A charter of the time of Ethelred II exists which is considered by many to be the origin of that Ship Money which, hundreds of years later, was to cause so much trouble to England. Under this the maintenance of the Navy was made a State charge on landowners, the whole of whom were assessed at the rate of producing one galley for every three hundred and ten hides of land that they possessed.

This view is disputed by some historians, who maintain that the charter is possibly a forgery, and that it is not very clear in any case. However, it does not appear to have produced any useful naval power.

That naval power was insufficient is abundantly clear from the ever increasing number of Danish settlements. In the St. Bride's Day massacre, which was an attempt to kill off the leading Danes amongst the recent arrivals, further trouble arose ; and in the year 1013, Swain, King of Denmark, made a large invasion of England, and in the year 1017, his son Canute ascended to the Throne.

Under Canute, the need of a navy to protect the coast against Danish raids passed away. The bulk of the Danish ships were sent back to Denmark, forty vessels only being retained.

Once or twice during the reign of Canute successful
naval expeditions were undertaken, but at the time of
the King's death the regular fleet consisted of only
sixteen ships. Five years later, an establishment was
fixed at thirty-two, and remained more or less at about
that figure, till, in the reign of Edward the Confessor
trouble was caused by Earl Godwin, who had created
a species of fleet of his own. With a view to suppressing
these a number of King's ships were fitted out ; but
as the King and Godwin came to terms the fleet was not
made use of.

Close following upon this came the Norman invasion,
which of all the foolhardy enterprises ever embarked
on by man was theoretically one of the most foolish.
William's intentions were perfectly well known. A
certain " English fleet " existed, and there was nothing
to prevent its expansion into a force easily able to
annihilate the heterogeneous Norman flotilla.

How many ships and men William actually got
together is a matter upon which the old chroniclers
vary considerably. But he is supposed to have had
with him some 696 ships*; and since his largest ships
were not over twenty tons and most of them a great
deal smaller, it is clear that they must have been
crowded to excess and in poor condition to give battle
against anything of the nature of a determined attack
from an organised fleet.

No English fleet put in appearance, however.
Harold had collected a large fleet at Sandwich, but
after a while, for some unknown reason, it was
dispersed, probably owing to the lateness of the season.
The strength of the fleet collected, or why it was dispersed, are, however, immaterial issues ; the fact of
importance is that the fleet was " inadequate " because
it failed to prevent the invasion. A neglected fleet
entailed the destruction of the Saxon dominion.

* Wace.

II.

THE NORMAN AND PLANTAGENET ERAS.

WILLIAM the Conqueror's first act on landing was to burn all his ships—a proceeding useful enough in the way of preventing any of his followers retiring with their spoils, but inconvenient to him shortly after he became King of England. Fleets from Denmark and Norway raided the coasts and, though the raiders were easily defeated on shore, the pressure from them was sufficient to cause William to set about recreating a navy, of which he made some use in the year 1071. In 1078 the Cinque Ports were established, five ports being granted certain rights in return for policing the Channel and supplying ships to the King as required. But the amount of naval power maintained was very small, both in the reign of William the First and his successors.

Not until the reign of Henry II was any appreciable attention paid to nautical matters. Larger ships than heretofore were built, as we assume from records of the loss of one alleged to carry 300 men. It was Henry II who first claimed the " Sovereignty of the British Seas" and enacted the Assize of Arms whereby no ship or timber for shipbuilding might be sold out of England.

When Richard I came to the throne in 1189, fired with ambition to proceed to the Crusades, he ordered all ports in his dominions to supply him with ships in proportion to their population. The majority of these ships came, however, from Acquitaine. The fleet thus collected is said to have consisted of nine large ships, 150 small vessels, thirty galleys, and a number of transports.   The large ships, which have also been given as thirteen in number, were known at the time as "busses."   They appear to have been three-masters.   The fleet sailed in eight divisions. This expedition to the Holy Land was the first important over-sea voyage ever participated in by English ships, the greatest distance heretofore traversed having been to Norway in the time of Canute.   This making of a voyage into the unknown was, however, not quite so difficult as it might at first sight be supposed to be, because there is no doubt whatever that the compass was by then well-known and used.   Records from 1150 and onwards exist which describe the compass of that period.   A contemporary chronicler* wrote of it :—

" This [polar] star does not move.   They [the seamen] have an art which cannot deceive, by virtue of the *manite*, an ill brownish stone to which iron spontaneously adheres.   They search for the right point, and when they have touched a needle on it, and fixed it to a bit of straw, they lay it on water, and the straw keeps it afloat.   Then the point infallibly turns towards the star ; and when the night is dark and gloomy, and neither star nor moon is visible, they set a light beside the needle, and they can be assured that the star is opposite to the point, and thereby the mariner is directed in his course.   This is an art which cannot deceive."

The compass would seem to have existed, so far as northern nations were concerned, about the time of William the Conqueror.   Not till early in the Fourteenth Century did it assume the form in which we now know it, but its actual antiquity is considerably more.

In connection with this expedition to the Holy Land, Richard issued a Code of Naval Discipline, which has been described as the germ of our Articles of War. Under this Code if a man killed another on board ship, he was to be tied to the corpse and thrown into the sea.   If the murder took place on shore, he was to be buried alive with the corpse.   The penalty for drawing a knife on another man, or drawing blood from him in any manner, was the loss of a hand.   For

*Guyot de Provins *ex* Nicholas.

"striking another," the offender was plunged three times into the sea. For reviling or insulting another man, compensation of an ounce of silver to the aggrieved one was awarded. The punishment for theft was to shave the head of the thief, pour boiling pitch upon it and then feather him. This was done as a mark of recognition. The subsequent punishment was to maroon a man upon the first land touched. Severe penalties were imposed on the mariners and servants for gambling.

Of these punishments the two most interesting are those for theft and the punishment of "ducking." This last was presumably keel-hauling, a punishment which survived well into the Nelson era. It is to be found described in the pages of Marryat. It consisted in drawing the offender by ropes underneath the bottom of the ship. As his body was thus scraped along the ship's hull, the punishment was at all times severe; but in later days, as ships grew larger and of deeper draught, it became infinitely more cruel and heavy than in the days when it was first instituted.

The severe penalty for theft is to be noted on account of the fact that even in these early times, theft, as now, was and is recognised as a far more serious offence on ship board than it is on shore—the reason being the greater facilities that a ship affords for theft.

On his way to the Holy Land, Richard had a dispute at Sicily with the King of France, out of which he increased his fleet somewhat. Leaving Sicily, somewhere between Cyprus and Acre he encountered a very large Saracen ship, of the battle with which very picturesque and highly coloured accounts exist. There is no doubt that the ship was something a great deal larger than anything the English had ever seen heretofore, although the crew of 1,500 men with which she is credited by the chroniclers is undoubtedly an exaggeration.

The ship carried an armament of Greek fire and "serpents." The exact composition of Greek fire is unknown. It was invented by the Byzantines, who by means of it succeeded in keeping their enemies at bay for a very long time.   It was a mixture of chemicals which, upon being squirted at the enemy from tubes, took fire, and could only be put out by sand or vinegar. "Serpents" were apparently some variation of Greek fire of a minor order, discharged by catapults.

In the first part of the attack the English fleet was able to make no impression upon the enemy, as her high sides and the Greek fire rendered boarding impossible.   Not until King Richard had exhilarated his fleet by informing them that if the galley escaped they "should be crucified or put to extreme torture," was any progress made.   After that, according to the contemporary account, some of the English jumped overboard and succeeded in fastening ropes to the rudder of the Saracen ship, "steering her as they pleased."   They then obtained a footing on board, but were subsequently driven back.   As a last resource King Richard formed his galleys into line and rammed the ship, which afterwards sank.

The relation of Richard's successor, King John, to the British Navy, is one of some peculiar interest. More than any king before him he appears to have appreciated the importance of naval power, and naval matters received more attention than heretofore. In the days of King John the crews of ships appropriated for the King's service were properly provisioned with wine and food, and there are also records of pensions for wounds, one of the earliest being that of Alan le Walleis, who received a pension of sixpence a day for the loss of his hand.*

King John is popularly credited with having made the first claim to the "Sovereignty of the Seas" and of having enacted that all foreign vessels upon sighting an English one were to strike their flags to her, and that if they did not that it was lawful to destroy them.   The authenticity of this is, however, very doubtful; and it is more probable that, on account

* *ex* Nicolas.

of various naval regulations which first appeared in the reign of King John, this particular regulation was fathered upon him at a later date with the view to giving it an historical precedent.

In the reign of King John the " Laws of Oberon" seem to have first appeared, but it is not at all clear that they had any specific connection with England. They appear rather to have been of a general European nature. The gist ,of the forty-seven articles of the " Laws of Oberon," of which the precise date of promulgation cannot be ascertained, is as follows :—*

" By the first article, if a vessel arrived at Bordeaux, Rouen, or any other similar place, and was there freighted for Scotland, or any other foreign country, and was in want of stores or provisions, the master was not permitted to sell the vessel, but he might with the advice of his crew raise money by pledging any part of her tackle or furniture.

"If a vessel was wind or weather bound, the master, when a change occurred, was to consult his crew, saying to them," Gentlemen, what think you of this wind ? " and to be guided by the majority whether he should put to sea. If he did not do this, and any misfortune happened, he was to make good the damage.

"If a seaman sustained any hurt through drunkenness or quarrelling, the master was not bound to provide for his cure, but might turn him out of his ship ; if, however, the injury occurred in the service of his ship, he was to be cured at the cost of the said ship. A sick sailor was to be sent on shore, and a lodging, candles, and one of the ship's boys, or a nurse provided for him, with the same allowance of provisions as he would have received on board. In case of danger in a storm, the master might, with the consent of the merchants on board, lighten the ship by throwing part of the cargo overboard ; and if they did not consent, or objected to his doing so, he was not to risk the vessel but to act as he thought proper ; on their arrival in port, he and the third part of the crew were to make oath that it was done for the preservation of the vessel ; and the loss was to be borne equally by the merchants. A similar proceeding was to be adopted before the mast or cables were cut away.

" Before goods were shipped the master was to satisfy the merchants of the strength of his ropes and slings ; but if he did not do so, or they requested him to repair them and a cask were stove, the master was to make it good.

" In cases of difference between a master and one of his crew,

* *ex* Nicolas.

the man was to be denied his mess allowance thrice, before he was turned out of the ship, or discharged; and if the man offered reasonable satisfaction in the presence of the crew, and the master persisted in discharging him, the sailor might follow the ship to her place of destination, and demand the same wages as if he had not been sent ashore.

"In case of collision by a ship undersail running on board one at anchor, owing to bad steering, if the former were damaged, the cost was to be equally divided; the master and crew of the latter making oath that the collision was accidental. The reason for this law was, it is said, "that an old decayed vessel might not purposely be put in the way of a better." It was specially provided that all anchors ought to be indicated by buoys or 'anchor-marks.'

"Mariners of Brittany were entitled only to one meal a day, because they had beverage going and coming; but those of Normandy were to have two meals, because they had only water as the ship's allowance. As soon as the ship arrived in a wine country, the master, was, however, to procure them wine.

"Several regulations occur respecting the seamen's wages, which show that they were sometimes paid by a share of the freight. On arriving at Bordeaux or any other place, two of the crew might go on shore and take with them one meal of such victuals as were on board, and a proportion of bread, but no drink; and they were to return in sufficient time to prevent their master losing the tide. If a pilot from ignorance or otherwise failed to conduct a ship in safety, and the merchants sustained any damage, he was to make full satisfaction if he had the means to; if not, he was to lose his head; and, if the master or any one of the mariners cut off his head, they were not bound to answer for it; but, before they had recourse to so strong a measure, " they must be sure he had not wherewith to make satisfaction.

"Two articles of the code prove, that from an 'accursed custom' in some places, by which the third or fourth part of ships that were lost belonged to the lord of the place,—the pilots, to ingratiate themselves with these nobles, "like faithless and treacherous villains," purposely ran the vessel on the rocks. It was therefore enacted that the said lords, and all others assisting in plundering the wreck, shall be accursed and excommunicated, and punished as robbers and thieves; that "all false and treacherous pilots should suffer a most rigorous and merciless death," and be suspended to high gibbets near the spot, which gibbets were to remain as an example in succeeding ages. The barbarous lords were to be tied to a post in the middle of their own houses, and, being set on fire at the four corners, all were to be burned together ; the walls demolished, its site converted into a marketplace for the sale only of hogs and swine, and all their goods to be confiscated to the use of the aggrieved parties.

"Such of the cargoes as floated ashore were to be taken care of for a year or more ; and, if not then claimed, they were to be sold by the lord, and the proceeds distributed among the poor, in marriage portions to poor maids and other charitable uses. If, as often happened, 'people more barbarous, cruel, and inhuman than mad dogs,' murdered shipwrecked persons, they were to be plunged into the sea till they were half-dead, and then drawn out and stoned to death."

These laws, unconnected though they appear to be with strictly naval matters, are none the less of extreme interest as indicating the establishment of "customs of the sea," and the consequent segregation of a "sailor class." It has ever to be kept very clearly in mind that there was no such thing as a "Navy" as we understand it in these days. When ships were required for war purposes they were hired, just as waggons may be hired by the Army to-day ; nor did the mariners count for much more than horses. The "Laws of Oberon," however, gave them a certain general status which they had not possessed before ; and the regulations of John as to providing for those engaged upon the King's service—though they in no way constituted a Royal Navy—played their part many years later in making a Royal Navy possible, or, perhaps, it may be said, "necessary." Necessity has ever been the principal driving force in the naval history of England.

To resume. The limitations of the powers of the master (*i.e.* captain) in these "Laws of Oberon" deserve special attention. "Gentlemen, what think you of this wind?" from the captain to his crew would be considered "democracy" carried to extreme and extravagant limits in the present day ; in the days when it was promulgated as "the rule" it was surely stranger still! Little wonder that seamen at an early stage segregated from the ordinary body of citizens and became, as described by Clarendon in his "History of the Rebellion" a few hundred years later, when he wrote :—

"The seamen are a nation by themselves, a humorous and fantastic people, fierce and rude and resolute in whatsoever they resolve or are inclined to, but unsteady and inconstant in pursuing it, and jealous of those to-morrow by whom they are governed to-day."

To this, to the earlier things that produced it, those who will may trace the extreme rigour of naval discipline and naval punishments, as compared with contemporaneous shore punishments at any given time, and the extraordinary difference at present existing between the American and European navies. The difference is usually explained on the circumstance that " Europe is Europe, and America, America." But " differences " having their origin in the " Laws of Oberon" may play a greater part than is generally allowed.

The year 1213 saw the Battle of Damme. This was the first real naval battle between the French and English. The King of France had collected a fleet of some " seventeen hundred ships " for the invasion of England, but having been forbidden to do so by the Pope's Legate, he decided to use his force against Flanders. This Armada was surprised and totally destroyed by King John's fleet.

After the death of John the nautical element in England declared for Henry III, son of John, and against Prince Louis of France, who had been invited to the throne of England by the barons. Out of this came the battle of Sandwich, 1217, where Hubert de Burgh put into practice, though in different form, those principles first said to have been evolved by Alfred the Great—namely, to attack with an assured and complete superiority.

Every English ship took on board a large quantity of quick-lime and sailed to meet the French, who were commanded by Eustace the Monk. De Burgh manœuvred for the weather guage. Having gained it, the English ships came down upon the French with the wind, the quick-lime blowing before them, and so secured a complete victory over the tortured and blinded French. This is the first recorded instance of anything that may be described as " tactics " in Northern waters.

The long reign of Henry III saw little of interest

in connection with nautical matters. But towards the end of Henry's reign a private quarrel between English and Norman ships, both seeking fresh water off the Coast of Bayonne, had momentous consequences. The Normans, incensed over the quarrel, captured a couple of English ships and hanged the crew on the yards interspersed with an equal number of dead dogs. Some English retaliated in a similar fashion on such Normans as they could lay hands on, and, retaliation succeeding retaliation, it came about that in the reign of Edward I, though England and France were still nominally at peace, the entire mercantile fleets of both were engaged in hanging each other, over what was originally a private quarrel as to who should be first to draw water at a well.

Ultimately the decision appears to have been come by "to fight it out." Irish and Dutch ships assisted the English. Flemish and Genoese ships assisted the Normans and French. The English to the number of 60 were under Sir Robert Tiptoft. The number of the enemy is placed at 200, though it was probably considerably less. In the battle that ensued the Norman and French fleets were annihilated.

This battle, even more than others of the period, cannot be considered as one of the battles of " the British fleet." It is merely a conflict between one clique of pirates and traders against another clique. But it is important on account of the light that it sheds on a good deal of subsequent history; for the fashion thus started lasted in one way and another for two or three hundred years.

Nor were these disputes always international. Four years later than the fight recorded above, in 1297, the King wished to invade Flanders with an army of 50,000 men. The Cinque Ports being unable to supply the requisite number of ships to transport this army, requisitions were also made at Yarmouth. Bad blood soon arose between the two divisions, with the result that they attacked each other. Thirty of the Yarmouth ships with their crews were destroyed and the expedition greatly hampered thereby.

Two events of importance in British naval history happened in the reign of Edward I. The first of these, which took place about the year 1300, arose out of acts of piracy on foreigners, to which English ships were greatly addicted at that time. In an appeal made to Edward by those Continentals who had suffered most from these depredations, the King was addressed as "Lord of the Sea." This was a definite recognition of that sea claim first formulated by Henry II and which was afterwards to lead to so much fighting and bloodshed.

The second event was the granting of the first recorded "Letters of Marque" in the year 1295. These were granted to a French merchant who had been taking a cargo of fruit from Spain to England and had been robbed by the Portuguese. He was granted a five year license to attack the Portuguese in order to recoup his loss.

In the reign of Edward II the only naval event of interest is, that when the Queen came from abroad and joined those who were fighting against the King, the nautical element sided with her.

The reign of Edward III saw some stirring phases in English history. With a view to carrying on his war against France, Edward bestowed considerable attention on naval matters, and in the year 1338, he got together a fleet stated to have consisted of 500 vessels. These were used as transports to convey the Army to France, and are estimated to have carried on the average about eighty men each.

Meanwhile, the French had also got together a fleet of about equal size, and no sooner had the English expedition reached the shores of France than the whole of the south coast of England was subjected to a series of French raids. Southampton, Plymouth and the Cinque Ports were sacked and burned with practical impunity. These raids continued during 1338 and 1339; the bulk of the English fleet still lying idle on transport service at Edward's base in Flanders. A certain number of ships had been sent back, but most of these had been as hastily sent on to Scotland, where their services had been urgently needed. Matters in the Channel culminated with the capture of the two largest English ships of the time. A fleet of small vessels hastily fitted out at the Cinque Ports succeeded in destroying Boulogne and a number of ships that lay there, but generally speaking the French had matters very much their own way on the sea.

Towards the end of 1339, Edward and his expedition returned to England to refit, with a view to preparing for a fresh invasion of France in the following summer.

As Edward was about to embark, he learned that the French King had got together an enormous fleet at Sluys. After collecting some additional vessels, bringing the total number of ships up to 250 or thereabouts, Edward took command and sailed for Sluys, at which port he found the French fleet. He localised the French on Friday, July 3rd, but it was not until the next day that the battle took place.

The recorded number of the enemy in all these early sea fights requires to be accepted with caution. For what it is worth the number of French ships has been given at 400 vessels, each carrying 100 men. The French, as on a later occasion they did on the Nile, lay on the defensive at the mouth of the harbour, the ships being lashed together by cables. Their boats filled with stones, had been hoisted to the mast-heads. In the van of their fleet lay the *Christopher*, *Edward*, and various other " King's ships," which they captured in the previous year.

The English took the offensive, and in doing so manœuvred to have the sun behind them. Then, with their leading ships crowded with archers they bore down upon the main French division and grappled with them.

The battle, which lasted right throughout the

B

night, was fought with unexampled fury, and for a long time remained undecisive, considerable havoc being wrought by the French with the then novel idea of dropping large stones from aloft. The combatants, however, were so mixed up that it is doubtful whether the French did not kill as many of their own number as of the enemy ; whereas, on the other side, the use of English archers who were noted marksmen told only against those at whom the arrows were directed. Furthermore, the English had the tactical advantage of throwing the whole of their force on a portion of the enemy, whom they ultimately totally destroyed.

This Battle of Sluys took place in 1340. In 1346, after various truces, the English again attacked France in force, and the result was the Battle of Cressy. A side issue of this was the historic siege of Calais, which held out for about twelve months.   738 ships and 14,956 men are said to have been employed in the sea blockade.

Up to this time the principal English ship had been a galley, *i.e.*, essentially a row boat. About the year 1350 the galley began to disappear as a capital ship, and the galleon, with sail as its main motive power, took its place. Also a new enemy appeared ; for at that time England first came into serious conflict with Spain.

To a certain extent the galleon was to the fleets of the Mid-Fourteenth Century much what the iron-clad was to the last quarter of the Nineteenth Century, or " Dreadnoughts " at the end of the first decade of the Twentieth Century.

The introduction of this type of vessel came about as follows :—

A fleet of Castillian galleons, bound for Flanders, whiled away the monotony of its trip by acts of piracy against all English ships that it met. It reached Sluys without interference. Here it loaded up with rich cargoes and prepared to return to Spain. The

English meanwhile collected a fleet to intercept it, this fleet being in command of King Edward himself, who selected the "cog *Thomas*" as his flagship.

The English tactics would seem to have been carefully thought out beforehand. The Castillian ships were known to be of relatively vast size and more or less unassailable except by boarding. The result was that when at length they appeared, the English charged their ships into them, sinking most of their own ships in the impact, sprang aboard and carried the enemy by boarding. The leading figure on the English side was a German body-servant of the name of Hannekin, who distinguished himself just at the crisis of the battle by leaping on board a Castillian ship and cutting the halyards. Otherwise the result of the battle might have been different, because the Castillians, when about half only of the English ships were grappled with them, hoisted their sails, with the object of sailing away and destroying the enemy in detail. Hannekin's perception of this intention frustrated the attempt.

The advantages of the galleons (or carracks as they were then called), must have been rendered obvious in this battle of "Les Espagnols-sur-Mer," as immediately afterwards ships on the models of those captured began to be hired for English purposes.

Concurrent, however, with this building of a larger type of ship, a decline of naval power began ; and ten years later, English shipping was in such a parlous state, that orders were issued to the effect that should any of the Cinque Ports be attacked from the sea, any ships there were to be hauled up on land, as far away from the water as possible, in order to preserve them.

In the French War of 1369, almost the first act of the French fleet was to sack and burn Portsmouth without encountering any naval opposition.

In 1372 some sort of English fleet was collected, and under the Earl of Pembroke sent to relieve La Rochelle, which was then besieged by the French and

Spanish. The Spanish ships of that period had improved on those of twenty years before, to the extent that (according to Froissart), some carried. guns. In any case they proved completely superior to the English, whose entire fleet was captured or sunk.

This remarkable and startling difference is only to be accounted for by the difference in the naval policy of the two periods. In the early years of Edward III's reign, when a fleet was required it was in an efficient state, and when it encountered the enemy, it was used by those who had obviously thought out the best means of making the most of the material available. In the latter stage, there was neither efficiency nor purpose. The result was annihilation.

How far the introduction of cannon on shipboard contributed to this result it is difficult to say exactly. In so far as it may have, the blame rests with the English, who were perfectly familiar with cannon at that time. If, therefore, the very crude stone-throwing cannon of those days had any particular advantages over the stone-throwing catapults previously employed, failure to fit them is merely a further proof of the inefficiency of those responsible for naval matters in the closing years of Edward III's reign. Probably, how- ever, the cannon contributed little to the result of La Rochelle, for like all battles of the era, it was a matter of boarding—of "land fighting on the water."

The reign of Richard II saw England practically without any naval power at all. The French and Spaniards raided the Channel without interference worth mention. Once or twice retaliatory private expeditions were made upon the French coast ; but speaking generally the French and Spaniards had matters entirely their own way, and the latter penetrated the Thames so far as Gravesend.

In the year 1380, an English army was sent over to France, but this, as Calais was British, was a simple operation, and although two years later ships were collected for naval purposes, English sea impotence remained as conspicuous as ever. In 1385, when a French armada was collected at Sluys for the avowed purpose of invading England on a large scale, no attempt whatever seems to have been made to meet this with another fleet. Fortunately for England, delays of one kind and another led to the French scheme of invasion being abandoned.

Under Henry IV, matters remained much the same, until in the summer of 1407, off the coast of Essex, the King, who was voyaging with five ships, was attacked by French privateers, which succeeded in capturing all except the Royal vessel.

This led to the organisation of a " fleet " and a successful campaign against the privateers. The necessity of Sea Power began to be realised again, and this so far bore fruit that in the reign of Henry V, no less than 1,500 ships were (it is said) collected in the Solent, for an invasion of France. But since some of these were hired from the Dutch and as every English vessel of over twenty tons was requisitioned by the King, the large number got together does not necessarily indicate the existence of any very great amount of naval power. This fleet, however, indicated a revival of sea usage.

In 1417, large ships known as " Dromons " were built at Southampton, and bought for the Crown, but these were more of the nature of " Royal Yachts " than warships. The principal British naval base at and about this period was at Calais, of which, at the time of the Wars of the Roses, the Earl of Warwick was the governor.

The first act of the Regency of Henry VI was to sell by auction such ships as had been bought for the Crown under Henry V. The duty of keeping the Channel free from pirates was handed over to London merchants, who were paid a lump sum to do this, but did not do it at all effectively.

Edward IV made some use of a Fleet to secure his accession, or later restoration. Richard III would seem to have realised the utility of a Fleet, and during his short reign, he did his best to begin a revival of " the Navy " by buying some ships, which, however, he hired out to merchants for trade purposes ; and so, at the critical moment, he had apparently nothing available to meet the mild over-sea expedition of Henry of Richmond. So—right up to *comparatively* recent times—there was never any Royal Navy in the proper meaning of the word, nor even any organised attempt to create an equivalent, except on the part of those two Kings who we are always told were the worst Kings England ever had—John and Richard III. Outside these two, there is not the remotest evidence that anyone ever dreamed of " naval power," " sea power," or anything of the sort, till Henry VII became King of England, and founded the British Navy on the entirely unromantic principle that it was a financial economy.

Such was the real and prosaic birth of the British Navy in relatively recent times. It was made equally prosaic in 1910 by Lord Charles Beresford, when he said, " Battleships are cheaper than war."

There is actually no poetry about the British Navy. There never has been—it will be all the better for us if there never is. It is merely a business-like institution founded to secure these islands from foreign invasion. Dibden in his own day, Kipling in ours, have done their best to put in the poetry. It has been pretty and nice and splendid. But over and above it all I put the words of a stoker whose name I never knew, " It's just this—do your blanky job ! "

That is the real British Navy. Henry VII did not create this watch-word, nor anyone else, except perhaps Nelson.

III.

THE TUDOR PERIOD AND BIRTH OF A REGULAR NAVY.

THAT Henry VII assimilated the lesson of the utility of
naval power is abundantly clear. Henry VII it was
who first established a regular navy as we now understand it. Previous to his reign, ships were requisitioned
as required for war purposes and, the war being over,
reverted to the mercantile service. The liability of the
Cinque Ports to provide ships when called upon
constituted a species of navy, and certain ships were
specially held as "Royal ships" for use as required,
but under Henry ships primarily designed for fighting
purposes appeared. The first of these ships was a
vessel generally spoken of as the " *Great Harry*," though
her real name seems to have been *The Regent*, built in
1485. Incidentally this ship remained afloat till 1553,
when she was burned by accident. She has been
called "the first ship of the Royal Navy"; and though
her right to the honour has been contested, she appears
fully entitled to it. The real founder of the Navy as
we understand a navy to-day was Henry VII.

Another important event of this reign is that
during it the first dry dock was built at Portsmouth.
Up till then there had been no facilities for the under-
water repair of ships, other than the primitive method
of running them on to the mud and working on them
at low tide. While ships were small this was not a
matter of much moment, but directly larger vessels
began to be built, it meant that efficient overhauls
were extremely difficult, if not impossible.

Yet another step that had far reaching results was the granting of a bounty to all who built ships of over 120 tons. This bounty, which was "per ton" and on a sliding scale, made the building of large private ships more profitable and less risky than it had been before, and so assisted in the creation of an important auxiliary navy as complement to the Royal Navy.

The bounty system did more, however, than encourage the building of large private ships. The loose method of computing tonnage already referred to, became more elastic still when a bounty was at stake; and even looser when questions of the ship being hired per ton for State purposes was at issue. Henry VII, who was nothing if not economical, felt the pinch; the more so, as just about this time Continentals with ships for hire became alarmingly scarce. Something very like a "corner in ships" was created by English merchants.

Henry VII was thus, by circumstances beyond his own control, forced into creating a permanent navy in self defence. He died with a "navy" of eighteen ships, of which, however, only two were genuinely entitled to be called "H.M.S." He had to hire the others!

This foundation of the "regular navy" is not at all romantic. But it is how a regular navy came to be founded—by force of circumstances. Henry VII, "founder of the Royal Navy," undoubtedly realized clearer than any of his predecessors for many a hundred years, the meaning of naval power. But—his passion for economy and the advantage taken by such of his subjects as had ships available when hired ships were scarce, had probably a deal more to do with the institution of a regular navy than any preconceived ideas. In two words—"Circumstances compelled." And that is how things stood when Henry VIII came to the throne.

The nominal permanent naval power established by Henry VII consisted of fifty-seven ships, and the crew of each was twenty-one men and a boy, so that the *Great Harry*, which must have required a considerably larger crew, would seem to have been an experimental vessel. The actual force, however, was but *two* fighting ships proper.

Under Henry VIII, however, the policy of monster ships was vigorously upheld, and one large ship built in the early years of his reign—the *Sovereign*—was reputed to be "the largest ship in Europe." In 1512 the King reviewed at Portsmouth "twenty-five ships of great burthen," which had been collected in view of hostilities with France. These ships having been joined by others, and amounting to a fleet of forty-four sail, encountered a French fleet of thirty-nine somewhere off the coast of Brittany.

This particular battle is mainly noteworthy owing to the fact that the two flagships grappled, and while in this position one of them caught fire. The flames being communicated to the other, both blew up. This catastrophe so appalled the two sides that they abandoned the battle by mutual consent ; from which it is to be presumed that the nautical mind of the day had, till then, little realised that risks were run by carrying explosives.

The English, however, were less impressed by the catastrophe than the enemy, since next day they rallied and captured or sank most of the still panic-stricken French ships.

Henry replaced the lost flagship by a still larger ship, the *Grace de Dieu*, a two-decker with the lofty poop and forecastle of the period. She was about 1,000 tons. Tonnage, however, was so loosely calculated in those days that measurements are excessively approximate.

When first cannon were introduced, they were (as previously remarked) merely a substitute for the old-fashioned catapults, and discharged stones for some time till more suitable projectiles were evolved. Like the catapults they were placed on the poop or forecastle, as portholes had not then been introduced.

These were invented by a Frenchman, one Descharges, of Brest. By means of portholes it was possible to mount guns on the main deck and so increase their numbers.

Although the earliest portholes were merely small circular holes which did not allow of any training, and though the idea of them was probably directly derived from the loopholes in castle walls, the influence of the porthole on naval architecture was soon very great indeed. By means of this device a new relation between size and power was established, hence the " big displacements" which began to appear at this time. The hole for a gun muzzle to protrude through, quickly became an aperture allowing of training the gun on any ordinary bearing in English built ships. The English (for a very long time it was English only) realisation of the possibilities of the porthole in Henry VIII's reign contributed very materially to the defeat of the Spanish Armada some decades later. Indeed, it is no exaggeration to say that the porthole was to that era what the torpedo has been in the present one. Introduced about 1875 as a trivial alternative to the gun, in less than forty years the torpedo came to challenge the gun in range to an extent that as early as 1905 or thereabouts began profoundly to affect all previous ideas of naval tactics, and that by 1912 has changed them altogether !

Another great change of these Henry VIII days was in the form of the ships.* At this era they began to be built with " tumble-home" sides, instead of sides slanting outwards upwards, and inwards downwards as heretofore. With the coming of the porthole came the decline of the cross-bow as a naval arm. In the pre-porthole days every record speaks of " showers of arrows," and the gun appears to have been a species of accessory. In the early years of the Sixteenth century it became the main armament, and so

---

* Henry VIII introduced a new form of warship in the " pinnaces," which were, to a certain extent, analogous to the torpedo craft of to-day.

remained unchallenged till the present century and the coming of the long-range torpedo.

Henry VIII's reign is also remarkable for the first institution of those "cutting out" expeditions, which were afterwards to become such a particular feature of British methods of warfare. This first attempt happened in the year 1513, when Sir Edward Howard, finding the French fleet lying in Brest Harbour refusing to come out, "collected boats and barges" and attacked them with these craft. The attempt was not successful, but it profoundly affected subsequent naval history.

Therefrom the French were impressed with the idea that if a fleet lay in a harbour awaiting attack it acquired an advantage thereby. The idea became rooted in the French mind that to make the enemy attack under the most disadvantageous circumstances was the most wise of policies. That "the defensive is compelled to await attack, compelled to allow the enemy choice of the moment" was overlooked!

From this time onward England was gradually trained by France into the rôle of the attacker, and the French more and more sank into the defensive attitude. Many an English life was sacrificed between the "discovery of the attack" in the days of Henry VIII, and its triumphant apotheosis when centuries later Nelson won the Battle of the Nile; but the instincts born in Henry's reign, on the one hand to fight with any advantage that the defensive might offer, on the other hand to attack regardless of these advantages, are probably the real key to the secret of later victories.

The Royal ships at this period were manned by voluntary enlistment, supplemented by the pressgang as vacancies might dictate. The pay of the mariners was five shillings a month; but petty officers, gunners and the like received additional pickings out of what was known as "dead pay." By this system the names of dead men, or occasionally purely fancy names, were on the ship's books, and the money drawn for these was distributed in a fixed ratio. The most interesting feature of Henry VII and Henry VIII's navies is the presence in them of a number of Spaniards, who presumably acted as instructors. These received normal pay of seven shillings a month plus " dead pay."

The messing of the crews was by no means indifferent. It was as follows per man :—

Sunday, Tuesday, Thursday : $\frac{3}{4}$ lb. beef and $\frac{1}{2}$ lb. bacon.

Monday, Wednesday, Saturday : Four herrings and two pounds of cheese.

Friday : To every mess of four men, half a cod, ten herrings, one pound of butter and one pound of cheese.

There was also a daily allowance of one pound of bread or biscuit. The liquid allowance was either beer, or a species of grog consisting of one part of sack to two of water. Taking into account the value of money in those days and the scale of living on shore at the time, the conditions of naval life were by no means bad, though complaints of the low pay were plentiful enough. Probably, few received the full measure of what on paper they were entitled to.

Henry VIII died early in 1547. In the subsequent reigns of Edward VI and Mary, the Navy declined, and little use was made of it except for some raiding expeditions.

When Elizabeth came to the throne the regular fleet had dwindled to very small proportions, and, war being in progress, general permission was given for privateering as the only means of injuring the enemy. It presently degenerated into piracy and finally had to be put down by the Royal ships.

No sooner, however, was the war over than the Queen ordered a special survey to be made of the Navy. New ships were laid down and arsenals established for the supply of guns and gunpowder, which up to that time had been imported from Germany. Full advantage was taken of the privateering spirit, the erstwhile pirates being encouraged to undertake distant voyages. In many of these enterprises the Queen herself had a personal financial interest. She thus freed the country from various turbulent spirits who were inconvenient at home, and at one and the same time increased her own resources by doing so.

There is every reason to believe that this action of Elizabeth's was part of a well-designed and carefully thought out policy. The type of ship suitable for distant voyages and enterprises was naturally bound to become superior to that which was merely evolved from home service. The type of seamen thus bred was also necessarily bound to be better than the home-made article. Elizabeth can hardly have failed to realise these points also.

To the *personnel* of the regular Navy considerable attention was also given. Pay was raised to 6/8 per month for the seamen, and 5/- a month with 4/- a month for clothing for soldiers afloat. Messing was also increased to a daily ration of one pound of biscuit, a gallon of beer, with two pounds of beef per man four days out of the seven, and a proportionate amount of fish on the other three days. Subsequently, and just previous to the Armada, the pay of seamen rose to 10/- a month, with a view to inducing the better men not to desert.

The regular Navy was thus by no means badly provided for as things went in those days; while service with "gentlemen adventurers" offered attractions to a very considerable potential reserve, and so England contained a large population which, for one cause and another, was available for sea service. To these circumstances was it due that the Spanish Armada, when it came, never had the remotest possibility of success. It was doomed to destruction the day that Elizabeth first gave favour to the "gentlemen adventurers."

Of these adventurers the greatest of all was Francis Drake, who in 1577 made his first long voyage with five

ships to the Pacific Ocean. Drake, alone, in the *Pelican,*
succeeded in reaching the Pacific and carrying out his
scheme of operations which—not to put too fine a point
on it—consisted of acts of piracy pure and simple
against the Spaniards. He returned to England after
an absence of nearly three years, during which he
circumnavigated the globe.

There is little doubt that Drake in this voyage,
and others like him in similar expeditions, learned a
great deal about the disadvantages of small size in
ships. Drake, however, learned another thing also.
Up to this day the crew of a ship had consisted of
the Captain and a certain military element; also the
Master, who was responsible for a certain number of
"mariners." The former were concerned entirely with
fighting the ship—the latter entirely with manœuvring it.

This system of specialisation, awkward as it appears
thus baldly stated, may have worked well enough in
ordinary practice. It did not differ materially from the
differentiation between deck hands and the engineering
departments, which to a greater or less extent is very
marked in every navy of the present day.

Drake, however, started out with none too many
men, and it was not long before he lost some of those
he had and found himself shorthanded. His solution of
the difficulty is in his famous phrase, "I would have the
gentlemen haul with the mariners." How far this was a
matter of expediency, how far the revelation of a new
policy, is a matter of opinion. It must certainly have been
outside the purview of Elizabeth. But out of it gradually
came that every English sailor knew how to fight his ship
and how to sail her too, and this amounted to doubling
the efficiency of the crew of any ship at one stroke.

Of Drake himself, the following contemporary pen-
picture, from a letter written by one of his Spanish victims,
Don Franciso de Zarate,* explains almost everything :—

"He received me favourably, and took me to his room, where
he made me seated and said to me : 'I am a friend to those who
* Records of the Drake family.

speak the truth, that is what will have the most weight with me. What silver or gold does this ship bring ? '

" . . . . We spoke together a great while, until the dinner-hour. He told me to sit beside him and treated me from his dishes, bidding me have no fear, for my life and goods were safe ; for which I kissed his hands.

" This English General is a cousin of John Hawkins ; he is the same who, about five years ago, took the port of Nombre de Dios ; he is called Francis Drake ; a man of some five and thirty years, small of stature and red-bearded, one of the greatest sailors on the sea, both from skill and power of commanding. His ship carried about 400 tons, is swift of sail, and of a hundred men, all skilled and in their prime, and all as much experienced in warfare as if they were old soldiers of Italy. Each one, in particular, *takes great pains to keep his arms clean ;** he treats them with affection, and they treat him with respect. I endeavoured to find out whether the General was liked, and everyone told me he was adored."

Less favourable pictures of Drake have been penned, and there is no doubt that some of his virtues have been greatly exaggerated. At the present day there is perhaps too great a tendency to reverse the process. Stripped of romance, many of his actions were petty, while those of some of his fellow adventurers merit a harsher name. Hawkins, for instance, was hand-in-glove with Spanish smugglers and a slave trader. Many of the victories of the Elizabethan " Sea-Kings " were really trifling little affairs, magnified into an importance which they never possessed.

But, when all is said and done, it is in these men that we find the birth of a sea spirit which still lingers on, despite that other insular spirit previously referred to—the natural tendency of islanders to regard the water itself as a bulwark, instead of the medium on which to meet and defeat the enemy.

The Spanish, already considerably incensed by the piratical acts of the English " gentlemen adventurers," presently found a further cause of grievance in the assistance rendered by Elizabeth to their revolting provinces in the Netherlands. Drake had not returned many years from his famous voyage when it became

* The italics are mine.—F. T. J.

abundantly clear that the Spaniards no longer intended quietly to suffer from English interference.

Spain at that time was regarded as the premier naval power of Europe. Her superiority was more mythical than actual, for reasons which will later on be referred to: however, her commercial oversea activities were very great. The wealth which she wrung from the Indies—though probably infinitely less than its supposed value—was sufficient to enable her to equip considerable naval forces, certainly larger ones numerically than any which England alone was able to bring against them.

Knowledge of the fact that Spain was preparing the Armada for an attack on England, led to the sailing of Drake in April, 1587, with a fleet consisting of four large and twenty-six smaller ships, for the hire of which the citizens of London were nominally or actually responsible. His real instructions are not known, but there is little question that, as in all similar expeditions, he started out knowing that his success would be approved of, although in the event of any ill-success or awkward questions, he would be publicly disavowed.

Reaching Cadiz, he destroyed 100 store ships which he found there; and then proceeding to the Tagus, offered battle to the Spanish war fleet. The Spanish admiral, however, declined to come out—a fact which of itself altogether discredits the popular idea about the vast all-powerful ships of Spain, and the little English ships, which in the Armada days, could have done nothing against them, but for a convenient tempest. On account of this expedition of Drake's, the sailing of the Armada was put off for a year. So far as stopping the enterprise was concerned, Drake's expedition was a failure. Armada preparations still went on.

It is by no means to be supposed that the Armada in its conception was the foolhardy enterprise that on the face of things it looks to have been. The idea of it was first mooted by the Duke of Alva, so long ago as 1569. In 1583 it became a settled project in the able hands of the Marquis of Santa Cruz, who, alone among the Spaniards, was not more or less afraid of the English. In the battle of Tercera in 1583, certain ships, which if not English were at any rate supposed to be, had shown the white feather. Santa Cruz assumed therefrom that the English were easily to be overwhelmed by a sufficiently superior force, and he designed a scheme whereby he would use 556 ships and an army of 94,222 men.

Philip of Spain had other ideas. Having a large army under the Duke of Parma in the Netherlands, he proposed that this force should be transported thence to England in flat-bottomed boats, while Santa Cruz should take with him merely enough ships to hold the Channel, and prevent any interference by the English ships with the invasion.

Before the delayed Armada could sail Santa Cruz died ; and despite his own protestations Medina Sidonia was appointed in Santa Cruz's place to carry out an expedition in which he had little faith or confidence. His total force at the outset consisted of 130 ships and 30,493 men. Of these ships not more than sixty-two at the outside were warships, and some of these did not carry more than half-a-dozen guns.

The main English fighting force consisted of forty-nine warships, some of which were little inferior to the Spanish in tonnage, though all were much smaller to the eye, as they were built with a lower freeboard and without the vast superstructures with which the Spaniards were encumbered. As auxiliaries, the English had a very considerable force of small ships ; also the Dutch fleet in alliance with them.

The guns of the English ships were, generally speaking, heavier, all their gunners were well trained, and their portholes especially designed to give a con- siderable arc of fire, whereas the Spanish had very indifferent gunners and narrow portholes. The Spaniards themselves thoroughly recognised their inferiority in the matter of gunnery, and the specific instructions

c

of their admiral were that he was to negative this inferiority by engaging at close quarters, and trust to destroying the enemy by small-arm fire from his lofty superstructures.

The small portholes of the Spanish ships, which permitted neither of training, nor elevation, nor depression, are not altogether to be put down to stupidity or neglect of progress, for all that they were mainly the result of ultra-conservatism. The gun—as Professor Laughton has made clear—was regarded in Spain as a somewhat dishonourable weapon. Ideals of "cold steel" held the field. Portholes were kept very small, so that enemies relying on musketry should not be able to get the advantage that large portholes might supply. To close with the enemy and carry by boarding was the be-all and end-all of Spanish ideas of naval warfare. When able to employ their own tactics they were formidable opponents, though to the English tactics merely so many helpless haystacks.

On shore, in England, the coming of the Armada provoked a good deal of panic; though the army which Elizabeth raised and reviewed at Tilbury was probably got together more with a view to allaying this panic than from any expectations that it would be actually required. The views of the British seamen on the matter were entirely summed up in Drake's famous jest on Plymouth Hoe, that there was plenty of time to finish the game of bowls and settle the Spaniards afterwards!

Yet this very confidence might have led to the undoing of the English. The researches of Professor Laughton have made it abundantly clear that had Medina Sidonia followed the majority opinion of a council of war held off the Lizard, he could and would have attacked the English fleet in Plymouth Sound with every prospect of destroying it, because there, and there only, did opportunity offer them that prospect of a close action upon which their sole chance of success depended. Admiral Colomb has elaborated the point still further, with a quotation from Monson to the effect that had the Armada had a pilot able to recognise the Lizard, which the Spaniards mistook for Ramehead, they might have surprised the English fleet at Plymouth. This incident covers the whole of what Providence or luck really did for England against the Spanish.

To a certain extent a parallel of our own day exists. When Rodjestvensky with the Baltic fleet reached Far Eastern waters, there came a day when his cruisers discovered the entire Japanese fleet lying in Formosan waters. The Russian admiral ignored them and went on towards Vladivostok. The parallel ends here because the "Japanese fleet" was merely a collection of dummies intended to mislead him.*

The first engagement with the Spanish Armada took place on Sunday, June 21st. It was more in the nature of a skirmish than anything else. The Spaniards made several vain and entirely ineffectual attempts to close with the swifter and handier English vessels. They took care, however, to preserve their formation, and so to that extent defeated the English tactics, which were to destroy in detail what could not be destroyed without heavy loss in the mass. So the Spaniards reached Calais on the 27th with a loss of only three large ships.

They there discovered that Parma's flat-bottomed boats were all blockaded by the Dutch, and that any invasion of England was therefore entirely out of the question. It must have been perfectly obvious to the most sanguine of them by this that they could not force action with the swifter English ships, while they could not relieve the blockaded boats without being

---

* So far as I am aware nothing about this appears in any official account. I have no Japanese confirmation, but accounts gleaned at the time from the Russian auxiliaries—who, being foreigners had no object in lying—make it perfectly clear to my mind that the Russian admirals believe that the Japanese were astern of them till they met them at Tsushima. It is the only logical explanation of why Rodjestvensky essayed the narrow passage with his best ships, when he could equally well have gone round Japan with them unopposed, and so secured at Vladivostok that refit of which he was so much in need.

attacked at the outset. In a word, the Armada was
an obvious failure.

On the night of the 28th, fire ships were sent into
the Spanish fleet by the English. This, though the
damage done was small, brought the Spanish to sea,
and the next morning they were attacked off Gravelines
by the English. The battle was hardly of the nature
of a fleet action, so much as well-designed tactical
operations intended to keep the enemy on the move.
It resulted in the Spaniards losing only seven ships in
a whole day's fighting. The only really serious loss
that the Spaniards sustained was that they were driven
into the North Sea, with no prospect of returning
home except by way of the North of Scotland.

Followed for awhile and harried by a portion of the
English fleet, which fell upon and destroyed stragglers,
the Spaniards were driven into what to most of them
were unknown waters and uncharted seas. To the
last the retreating fleet maintained a show of order.
Fifty-three ships succeeded in returning to Spain.

Stripped of romance this is the real prosaic history
of the defeat of the Spanish Armada. The wonder is
not that so few Spanish ships returned, but that so
many did! The loss in Spanish warships proper
appears to have been little over a dozen all told, and
of these not more than three at the outside can be
attributed to "the winds."

Havoc was undoubtedly wrought, but the "galleons"
which "perished by scores" on the Scotch and Irish
coasts were mainly the auxiliaries, transports, and
small fry; the battle fleet proper kept together all the
time, and with a couple of exceptions the ships
reached home together as a fleet.*

At no time in the advance of the Spanish—probably
at no time in the retreat either—could the English
have engaged close action with any certainty of
success. Victory was attributable solely and entirely to

* It was badly weather-beaten, of course, and in sore straits on account of its
lengthy voyage.

the evolution of a type of ship, fast, speedy and handy, able to hit hard, and which had been more or less specially designed with an eye to offering a small target to the clumsily designed Spanish style of gun mounting.

It was "history repeating itself" in another way. As Alfred overcame the Danes by evolving something superior to the Danish galleys; so, in Elizabethan days, there was evolved a type of warship meet for the occasion.

From the defeat of the Armada and onwards, English naval operations were mainly confined to raiding expeditions against the Spanish coast, with a view to checking the collection of any further Armadas. These operations were chiefly carried out by the "gentlemen adventurers;" but the real Navy itself was maintained and added to, and at the death of Elizabeth in 1603, it consisted of forty-two ships, of which the 68-gun *Triumph* of 1,000 tons was the largest. This Navy was relied upon as the premier arm in case of any serious trouble.

IV.

THE PERIOD OF THE DUTCH WARS.

WITH the accession of James I peace with Spain came about, but the Dutch being ignored in the transaction, out of this there arose that ill-feeling and rivalry which was later on to culminate in the Dutch wars.

In James I's reign no naval operations of great importance took place, but considerable interest attaches to the despatch of eighteen ships (of which six were "King's Ships"), to Algiers in 1520. This was the first appearance of an English squadron in the Mediterranean.

Under James I the numerical force of the Navy declined somewhat. The art of ship-building, however, made considerable advance. * A Shipwrights' Company was established in 1656, and Phineas Petts, as its first master, built and designed a 1,400 ton ship named the *Prince Royal*. Pett introduced a variety of novelties into his designs, and the *Prince Royal* and her successors were esteemed superior to anything set afloat elsewhere at the time.

Here it is desirable to turn aside for a moment in order to realise the influences at work behind Phineas Pett. It has ever been the peculiar fortune of the Royal Navy—and for that matter of the inchoate "Navy" which preceded its establishment—to have had men capable of "looking ahead" and forcing the

* In 1620 the first submarine appeared. It was invented by a Dutch physician, C. Van Drebel; and James I went for a lengthy underwater trip in a larger replica.—See *Submarine Navigation*, by Alan H. Burgoyne.

pace in such a way that new conditions were prepared for when they arrived.

Of such a nature, each in his own way, were King Alfred, King John, Richard III, and Henry VII, but greater than any of these was Sir Walter Raleigh, whose vision in the days of Elizabeth and James I ran so clearly and so far that even now we cannot be said to have left him behind where "principles" are concerned. Drake was the national hero of Elizabethan days, but in utility to the future, Raleigh was a greater than he, albeit his best service was of the "armchair" kind.

The following extracts from Raleigh's writings, except for geographical and political differences, stand as true to-day as when he wrote them about 300 years ago. The idea of a main fleet, backed up by smaller vessels, the idea of meeting the enemy on the water and so forth, are commonplaces now, but in Raleigh's time they were quite otherwise. The italicised portions in particular indicate quite clearly in Elizabethan words the naval policy of to-day.

"Another benefit which we received by this preparation was, that *our men were now taught suddenly to arm, every man knowing his command, and how to be commanded,* which before they were ignorant of; and who knows not that sudden and false alarms in any army are sometimes necessary? To say the truth, the expedition which was then used in drawing together so great an army by land, and rigging so great and royal a navy to sea, in so little a space of time, was so admirable in other countries, that they received a terror by it ; and many that came from beyond the seas said *the Queen was never more dreaded abroad for anything she ever did.*

"Frenchmen that came aboard our ships did wonder (as at a thing incredible) that Her Majesty had rigged, victualled, and furnished her royal ships to sea in twelve days' time; and Spain, as an enemy, had reason to fear and grieve to see this sudden preparation.

"It is not the meanest mischief we shall do to the King of Spain, if we thus war upon him, to force him to keep his shores still armed and guarded, to the infinite vexation, charge and discontent of his subjects; for no time or place can secure them so long as they see or know us to be upon that coast.

"The sequel of all these actions being duly considered, we may be confident that *whilst we busy the Spaniard at home, they dare not think of invading England or Ireland;* for by their absence their fleet from the Indies may be endangered* and in their attempts they have as little hope of prevailing.

"Surely I hold that the *best way is to keep our enemies from treading upon our ground; wherein, if we fail, then* must we seek to make him wish that he had stayed at his own home.   In such a case, if it should happen, our judgments are to weigh many particular circumstances, that belongs not to this discourse.   But making the question general, *the position, whether England, without that it is unable to do so;* and, therefore, I think it most dangerous to make the adventure.   For the encouragements of a first victory to an enemy, and the discouragement of being beaten to the invaded, may draw after it a most perilous consequence.

"Great difference, I know there is, and diverse consideration to be had, between such a country as France is, strengthened with many fortified places, and this of ours, where our ramparts are but the bodies of men.   But I say that an army to be transported over sea, and to be landed again in an enemy's country, and the place left to the choice of the invader *cannot be resisted on the coast of England without a fleet to impeach it; no, nor on the coast of France, or any other country, except every creek, port, or sandy bay had a powerful army in each of them to make opposition . . . . . For there is no man ignorant that ships, without putting themselves out of breath, will easily outrun the soldiers that coast them.*†

"Whosoever were the inventors, we find that every age hath added somewhat to ships, and to all things else.   And in mine own time the shape of our English ships hath been greatly bettered.   It is not long since the striking of the topmast (a wonderful ease to great ships, both at sea and in harbour) hath been devised, together with the chain pump, which takes up twice as much water as the ordinary did.   We have lately added the Bonnet and the Drabler. To the courses we have devised studding-sails, topgallant-masts, spritsails, topsails.   The weighing of anchors by the capstone is also new.   We have fallen into consideration of the length of cables, and by it we resist the malice of the greatest winds that can blow. Witness our small Millbroke men of Cornwall, that ride it out at anchor half seas over between England and Ireland, all the winter quarter.   And witness the Hollanders that were wont to ride before Dunkirk with the wind at north-west, making a lee-shoar in all weathers.   For true it is, that the length of the cable is the life of the ship, riding at length, is not able to stretch it; and nothing

---

* In this connection, *see* The First Dutch War, a few pages further on.

† It is interesting to note that this particular argument, seemingly rather hyperbolical to-day on account of railways, is so *only if the hostile ships can be kept under observation.*

breaks that is not stretched in extremity. We carry our ordnance better than we were wont, because our nether over-loops are raised commonly from the water, to wit, between the lower part of the sea.

"In King Henry VIII time, and in his presence at Portsmouth, the Mary Rose, by a little sway of the ship in tacking about, her ports being within sixteen inches of the water, was overset and lost.

"We have also raised our second decks, and given more vent thereby to our ordnance lying on our nether-loop. We have added cross pillars† in our royal ships to strengthen them, which be fastened from the keels on to the beam of the second deck to keep them from setting or from giving way in all distresses.

"We have given longer floors to our ships than in elder times, and better bearing under water, whereby they never fall into the sea after the head and shake the whole body, nor sink astern, nor stoop upon a wind, by which the breaking loose of our ordnance, or of the not use of them, with many other discommodities are avoided.

"And, to say the truth, a miserable shame and dishonour it were for our shipwrights if they did not exceed all others in the setting up our Royal ships, *the errors of other nations being far more excusable than ours.* For the Kings of England have for many years *being at the charge to build and furnish a navy of powerful ships for their own defence, and for the wars only. Whereas the* French, the Spaniards, the Portuguese, and the Hollanders (till of late) *have had no proper fleet belonging to their Princes or States.* Only the Venetians for a long time have maintained their arsenal of gallies. And the Kings of Denmark and Sweden have had good ships for these last fifty years.

"I say that the aforenamed Kings, especially the Spaniards and Portugals, have ships of great bulk, but fitter for the merchant than for the man-of-war, for burthen than for *battle.* But as Popelimire well observeth, ' the forces of Princes by sea are marques de grandeur d'estate—marks of the greatness of an estate—for *whosoever commands the sea, commands the trade ; whosoever commands the trade of the world commands the riches of the world, and consequently the world itself.'*

"Yet, can I not deny but that the Spaniards, being afraid of their Indian fleets, have built some few very good ships ; *but he hath no ships in garrison,* as His Majesty hath ; and to say the truth, no sure place to keep them in, but in all invasions he is driven to take up of all nations which come into his ports for trade. . . . .

*   *   *   *

"But there's no estate grown in haste but that of the United Provinces, and especially in their sea forces, and by a contrary way to that of Spain and France ; the latter by invasion, the former by

† This practice appears to have been allowed to die out. At anyrate it was re-introduced in the time of Queen Anne

oppression. For I myself may remember *when one ship of Her Majesty's would have made forty Hollanders strike sail and come to an anchor*. They did not then dispute de Mari Libero, but readily acknowledged the English to be Domini Maria Britannici. That we are less powerful than we were, I do hardly believe it ; for, although we have not at this time 135 ships belonging to the subject of 500 tons each ship, as it is said we had in the twenty-fourth year of Queen Elizabeth ; at which time also, upon a general view and muster, there were found in England of able men fit to bear arms, 1,172,000, yet are our merchant ships now far more warlike and better appointed than they were, and the Navy royal double as strong as it then was. For these were the ships of Her Majesty's Navy at that time :—

1. The Triumph	8. The Revenge
2. The Elizabeth Jonas	9. The Hope
3. The White Bear	10. The Mary Rose
4. The Philip and Mary	11. The Dreadnought
5. The Bonadventure	12. The Minion
6. The Golden Lyon	13. The Swiftsure
7. The Victory	

to which there have been added :—

14. The Antilope	20. The Ayde
15. The Foresight	21. The Achates
16. The Swallow	22. The Falcon
17. The Handmaid	23. The Tyger
18. The Jennett	24. The Bull
19. The Bark of Ballein	

"We have not, therefore, less force than we had, the fashion, and furnishing of our ships considered, for there are in England at this time 400 sail or merchants, and fit for the wars, which the Spaniards would call galleons ; to which we may add 200 sail of crumsters, or hoys of Newcastle, which, each of them, will bear six Demi-culverins and four Sakers, needing no other addition of building than a slight spar deck fore and aft, as the seamen call it, which is a slight deck throughout. . . . . . .

"I say, then, if a vanguard be ordained of those hoyes, who will easily recover the wind of any other sort of ships, with a battle of 400 other warlike ships, and a rear of thirty of His Majesty's ships to sustain, relieve, and countenance the rest (if God beat them not) I know not what strength can be gathered in all Europe to beat them. And if it be objected that the States can furnish a far greater number, I answer that His Majesty's forty ships, added to the 600 beforenamed, are of incomparable greater force than all that Holland and Zealand can furnish for the wars. As also, that a greater number would breed the same confusion that was found in

Xerxes' land army of 1,700,000 soldiers; *for there is a certain proportion, both by sea and land, beyond which the excess brings nothing but disorder and amazement.*"

I have quoted from Raleigh at considerable length—a length which may seem to some out of all proportion to the general historical scheme of this work. But of the three possible "founders of the British Navy," King Alfred by legend, King Henry VII by force of circumstances, and Sir Walter Raleigh, Knight, by his realisation of certain eternal verities of naval warfare, the palm goes best to Raleigh, to whose precepts it was mainly due that England did not succumb to Holland in the days of the Dutch wars. Compared to the struggle with the Dutch, neither the Spanish wars, which preceded them, nor the great French wars which followed, were of any like importance as regarded the relative risks and dangers. And the interest is the greater in that where the United Provinces were, about and just after Raleigh's time, Germany stands towards the British Navy to-day.

In 1618 the Duke of Buckingham was appointed Lord High Admiral and continued in that position after the accession of Charles I. Of the incapacity of the Duke much has been written, but whatever may be said in connection with various unsuccessful oversea enterprises, for which he was officially responsible, naval shipbuilding under his régime made very considerable progress.

Things were quite otherwise, however, with the *personnel*. Abuses of every sort and kind crept in unchecked, and the men were the first to feel the pinch. The unscrupulous contractor appeared, and with him the era of offal foods and all kinds of similar abuses, of which many have lasted well into our own time, and some exist still. The money allotted for the men of the fleet became the prey of every human vulture, the officers, as a rule, being privy thereunto. Besides food, clothing also fell into the hands of contractors, who supplied shoddy at ridiculously high prices, with the commission to officers stopped out of the men's pay.

Pay, nominally, rose a good deal, and in 1653 reached twenty-four shillings a month for the seaman, but the figures (approximately equal in purchasing value to the pay of to-day) convey nothing. The men were half-starved, or worse, on uneatable food, and their clothing was such that they went about in rags and died like rats in their misery.

The first naval event in Charles I's reign is mainly of interest because of the peculiar personal circumstances that attended it. One King's ship and six hired ships were despatched, nominally to assist the French against the Genoese. On arriving at Dieppe, however, the English officers and men discovered that they were really to be used against the revolted French Protestants of La Rochelle. This being against their taste, they returned to the Downs and reported themselves to the King. They were ordered to sail again for La Rochelle. One captain, however, point blank refused to do so. The other ships went, but the officers and men, with a single exception, having handed their ships over to the French, returned to England.

Little or nothing seems to have been done in the way of punishment to the mutineers (possibly on account of public opinion). But the incident sheds an interesting sidelight on the state of the Navy at the time. It is hardly to be conceived that the Army at the same period could have acted in similar fashion with equal impunity.

The history of the British Navy of this period is the history of a navy lacking in discipline, and its officers divided against each other. Such expeditions as were undertaken against France and Spain signally failed. It is usual to attribute these failures to the mal-administration of the Duke of Buckingham, an unpopular figure. But whether this is just or not is another matter. The entire Navy was rotten to the core in its *personnel*. But Buckingham's share in it would seem to have been inability to understand rather than direct carelessness.

Under the Duke's régime the building of efficient warships continued to progress. The "ship money," which was to cause so much trouble inland later, is outside the scope of this work, save in so far as its direct naval aspect is concerned. This, of course, was the principle that inland places benefited from sea defence quite as much as seaside districts. A great deal of the money was undoubtedly spent on ship-building, indeed, some of the trouble lay over alleged (and seemingly obvious) excessive expenditure on the "Dreadnought" of the period, Phineas Pett's *Royal Sovereign*, a ship altogether superior to anything before built in England, and the first three-decker ever constructed in this country. She was laid down in 1635 and launched in 1657. An immense amount of gilding and carving about her irritated the economically minded, but it is questionable whether the objections were well informed.

Just about this time elaborate ornamentations of warships was the "vogue," and it carried moral effect accordingly. What to the uninitiated landsmen merely spelt "waste of money on unnecessary display" spelt something else to those who went across the seas. Even in our own present utilitarian days a fresh coat of paint to a warship has been found to have a political value; and fireworks and illuminations (seemingly pure waste of money) have played their share in helping to preserve the peace.

John Hampden, according to his lights, was a patriot, and according to the purely political questions with which he was concerned he may also have been ; but on the naval issue of Ship Money he was little more or less than the First Little Englander, and hampered by just that same inability to see beyond his nose which characterises the modern Little Englander who protests against "bloated naval expenditure" to-day. The intentions are excellent—the intelligence circumscribed.

A contemporary account of the *Royal Sovereign* is as follows :—

" Her length by the keele is 128 foote or thereabout, within some few inches ; her mayne breadth or wideness from side to side, 48 foote ; her utmost length from the fore-end to the stern, *á prova ad pupin*, 232 foote.   Shee is in height, from the bottom of her keele to the top of her lanthorne, 76 foote ; she beareth five lanthornes, the biggest of which will hold ten persons to stand upright, and without shouldering or pressing one on the other.

" Shee hath three flush deckes and a forecastle, an halfe decke, a quarter-decke, and a round house.   Her lower tyre hath thirty ports, which are to be furnished with demi-cannon and whole cannon, throughout being able to beare them ; her middle tyre hath also thirty ports for demi-culverin and whole culverin ; her third tyre hath twentie sixe ports for other ordnance ; her forecastle hath twelve ports, and her halfe decke hath fourteen ports ; she hath thirteene or fourteene ports more within board for murdering-pieces, besides a great many loope-holes out of the cabins for musket shot. Shee carrieth, moreover, ten pieces of chase ordnance in her right forward, and ten right off, according to lande service in the front and the reare.   Shee carrieth eleven anchores, one of them weighing foure thousand foure hundred pounds ; and according to these are her cables, mastes, sayles, cordage."

It remains to add that the ship was extraordinarily well built.   She fought many a battle and survived some fifty years, and then only perished because, when laid up for refit in 1696, she was accidentally burned.   And about sixty years ago (1852) naval architects still alluded to her with respect, nor did their designs differ from her very materially.

Wherever and however Charles I and the Duke of Buckingham failed, their shipbuilding policy cannot but command both respect and admiration.   It is the curious irony of fate that—excepting King Alfred, and also Queen Elizabeth—it is the Sovereigns of England with black marks against them who ever did most for the Navy or understood its importance.   And understanding what the Navy meant, generally secured these marks at the hands of some quite well meaning, but intellectually circumscribed prototype or successor of John Hampden, to whom " meeting the enemy on the water " was an entirely indigestible theory, and a waste of money into the bargain. There is no question whatever that to them the sea appeared a natural rampart and ships upon it pure superfluity, save in so far as inconvenience to the shore counties might result. Later on, Cromwell, of course, acted on a different principle—but Cromwell was an Imperialist. Hampden was merely the "Insular Spirit" personified.

In 1639, a naval incident occurred which goes to discredit the popular idea of the impotence of the British Navy under Charles I, whatever its internal condition. Naval operations were in progress between Holland and France on the one side, and Spain on the other. The British fleet was fitted out under Sir John Pennington (that same Pennington who had commanded the squadron which refused to attack La Rochelle) with orders to maintain British neutrality.

The Spanish fleet took refuge from the Dutch in the Downs, whereupon Pennington informed the rival admirals that he should attack which ever of them violated the neutrality of an English harbour. The Spanish having fired upon the Dutch, the Dutch Admiral Van Tromp applied to Pennington for permission to attack in the Downs. This was given, and the bulk of the Spanish fleet destroyed. The incident suggests that the English fleet was recognised as a neutral able to enforce its orders against all and sundry.

In connection with this, it is interesting to record the existence of a naval medal of the period, bearing the motto : "*Nec meta mihi quae terminus orbi*"—a free translation of which would be, "Nothing limits me but the size of the World." However short practice may have fallen, Charles and his advisers had undoubtedly grasped the theory of "Sea Power."

THE CIVIL WAR.

When the Civil war began in 1642, the regular fleet consisted of forty-two ships. It was seized by the Parliamentarians and put under the Earl of Warwick,

who held command for six years. With his fleet he
very effectually patrolled the Channel, rendering abortive
all over-sea attempts to assist the King with arms and
ammunition.

On Warwick being superseded in 1648, the fleet
mutinied, and seventeen ships sailed for Holland to join
Prince Charles; but upon Warwick being reinstated
the bulk of the fleet returned to its allegiance to the
Parliamentarians. That the Parliamentarians were fully
alive to the importance of naval power is evidenced by
the fact that they seized every opportunity to lay down
new ships ; and " Parliament " once in power made it
very clear indeed that the Sovereignty of the Seas
would be upheld at all costs.

THE FIRST DUTCH WAR.

Some forty years before, Sir Walter Raleigh, discussing the rise of the Dutch United Provinces, remarked:
" But be their estate what it will, let them not deceive
themselves in believing that they can make themselves
masters of the sea." He advised the Dutch to remember
that their inward and outward passages were through
British seas. There were but two courses open to the
Dutch : amity with England or destruction of English
naval power.

Since both nations had large commercial fleets,
rivalries were inevitable ; and for some long while
previous to 1652, both sides were ready enough for a
quarrel. Minor acts of hostility occurred. The Dutch
failed to pay the annual tax for fishing in British
waters. In May, 1652, a Dutch squadron refused to
pay respect to the English flag. It was fired on accordingly, and after some negotiations, war was declared
two months later.

The war is interesting because it saw an end to
the old ideas of cross-raiding with ships regarded
primarily as transports in connection with raids or to
cover such. In this war fighting on the sea for the
command of the sea first made a distinct appearance.

PHINEAS PETT, 1570-1647.

From the contemporary portrait by William Dobson in the National Portrait Gallery.

THE "ROYAL SOVEREIGN."

The dotted lines represent a ship of the time of 1850.

Ex. Fincham.

ANTHONY DEANE.

GENERAL BENTHAM.

"SALAMANDER" PADDLE WARSHIP.

From the original negative in the possession of W. A. Bieber, Esq.

THE "LONDON."—TWO DECKER WOODEN CONVERTED SCREW SHIP OF THE LINE.

Designed by Sir William Symonds. Launched 1840. Damaged at the bombardment of Fort Constantine, Sevastopol, 1854. Turned into a hulk at Zanzibar, 1874.

From the original negative in the possession of W. A. Bieber, Esq.

JOHN SCOTT RUSSELL.

THE "WARRIOR," as completed, 1861.

From the original negative in the possession of W. A. Bieber, Esq.

THE "ACHILLES" AS A FOUR-MASTER. Photographed about 1866.

From the original negative in the possession of W. A. Bieber, Esq.

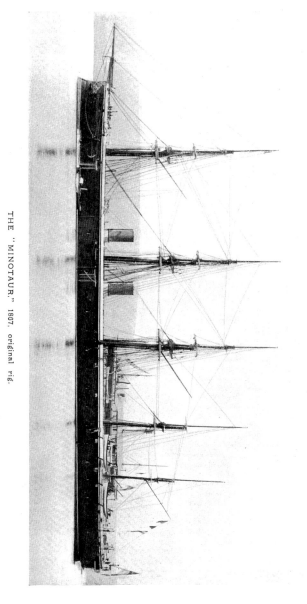

THE "MINOTAUR." 1867, original rig.

From the original negative in the possession of W. A. Bieber, Esq.

SIR E. J. REED.

From a portrait made when he was Chief Constructor of the British Navy.

THE "BELLEROPHON," completed 1866.

From the original negative in the possession of W. A. Bieber, Esq.

THE "ROYAL SOVEREIGN," 1864.

From the original negative in the possession of W. A. Bieber, Esq.

THE "WATERWITCH," completed 1867.

From the original negative in the possession of W. A. Bieber, Esq.

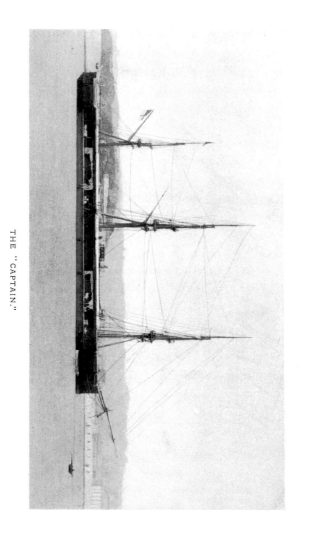

THE "CAPTAIN."

From the original negative in the possession of W. A. Bieber, Esq.

THE "VANGUARD," completed 1874.

From the original negative in the possession of W. A. Bieber, Esq.

THE "HOTSPUR," as originally completed, 1871.

From the original negative in the possession of W. A. Bieber, Esq.

Its birth was necessarily obscure and involved, both sides having the primary idea of attacking the commerce of the enemy and defending their own, rather than of attacking the enemy's fleet. The earlier battles which took place were brought about by the defence of merchant fleets.

None of the battles of 1652 were conclusive, and though marked with extraordinary determination on both sides the damage done was, relatively speaking, small. The general advantage for the year rested slightly with the Dutch, mainly owing to Tromp's victory over Blake, who was found in considerably inferior force in the Downs.

In February of the following year Tromp, with a fleet of seventy warships and a convoy of 250 merchant ships, some of which were armed, met Blake with sixty-six sail in the famous Three Day's Battle.

In the course of this fight the Dutch lost at least eight warships, and a number of merchant-men variously estimated at from twenty-four to forty. The English admitted to the loss of only one ship. At the end of the third day, however, Blake drew off, and the Dutch admiral got what was left of his convoy into harbour.

Oliver Cromwell being now in full power, naval preparations were pressed forward with unexampled vigour, and on June 2nd an English fleet of ninety-five sail under Monk and Deane met Van Tromp and forced him to retreat. Reinforced by Blake with eighteen more ships the English fleet renewed the battle, ultimately driving Van Tromp into harbour with the loss of several ships.

On the 29th July the Dutch ran the blockade and came out. On the 31st a battle began in which Van Tromp was killed, and the Dutch with the loss of many ships, driven into the Texel.

The English fleet, though it lost few ships, appears to have been badly mauled in this final battle, on account of which the Dutch claimed a victory.

D

In the following month the Dutch fleet again came
out, and under De Witt took one convoy to the Sound
and brought another back without interference. Just
afterwards, however, their fleet was so severely injured
by a tremendous three days' gale, that further naval
operations were out of the question. Overtures for
peace were therefore made, and concluded.

The types of English warships in this first Dutch
war are given in Pepy's Miscellany as follows :—

Rate.	Name.	Length of Keel. ft.	Breadth ft. in.		Depth. ft. in.		Burthen Tons.	Highest No. of	
								Men.	Guns.
First	*Sovereign*	127	46	6	19	4	1141	600	100
Second	*Fairfax*	116	34	9	17	4½	745	260	52
Third	*Worcester*	112	32	8	16	4	661	180	46
Fourth	*Ruby*	105½	31	6	15	9	556	150	40
Fifth	*Nightingale*	88	25	4	12	8	300	90	24
Sixth	*Greyhound*	60	20	3	10	0	120	80	18

The principal Dutch vessels were conspicuously
inferior to the best of these English ones, and the war
may be said to have been considerably decided by ship
superiority.   In the peace that followed—which was
really very little better than an armed truce—the Dutch
set themselves to build warships more on English lines.
And, as we shall presently see, they evolved from the
war,* future strategies based on its lessons.

Considering the number of battles and the desperate
nature of them, it is perhaps curious to note the

* Admiral Colomb (*Naval Warfare*) traced the Dutch defeat—or perhaps one
should write, "lack of advantage"—mainly to the fact that the Dutch had a larger
mercantile marine to protect, and merely mentions incidentally the constant
complaints of Van Tromp and others as to the inferiority of Dutch warships
compared to English ones. But since so many of the Dutch merchantmen carried
very fair armaments, and as "tactics" played no part in this war, I prefer to
accept the explanation of the Dutch Admirals, none of whom assigned failures to
the more obvious excuse of being hampered by convoys. Dutch contemporary
accounts of this and following wars appear generally to be nearer the actual
truth than English ones.

relatively small amount of damage done. With the advent of the porthole and the consequent multiplication of guns a hundred and fifty years before, it had seemed that any naval engagement must result in swift mutual destruction. Much the same kind of idea obtained as when at the end of 1910 a squadron of Dreadnoughts almost instantly obliterated a target five miles off. But as in the Armada fights, so in this First Dutch War, an immense amount of fighting was done with comparatively and relatively to what might have been anticipated, small harm on either side.

This result is partly to be attributed to the fact that defence increased with offence. The warship proper was designed to stand hammering, and every increase in size, involving increased gun-carrying capacity, involved also increased strength of construction. Something may also be put down to the very inferior artillery then in use, and the great deal of boarding which took place.

There is some reason to believe that Cromwell, with his complete recognition of the advantages of naval power, with his assiduous energy in the creation of a strong fleet, recognised—as perhaps both Buckingham and Phineas Pett had done before—the advantages of the "big ship." Yet under his rule no appreciable advance in size took place. Nor for that matter did it take place any time within a hundred and fifty years later on.

The reason is interesting. It was purely a matter of trees. The length of a ship was circumscribed by the height of trees; other dimensions by similar hard facts. The beam was dependent on the ship's length; while the draught was governed by the harbours and docking facilities. It is doubtful whether any man ever sought to solve the problem of an invincible navy with more energy than Oliver Cromwell; yet under his rule nothing in the way of improvement was evolved at all comparable with the step taken with the *Royal Sovereign* under the weaker Charles Stuart—Buckingham régime. The limitations of the tree proved the limitations of the ship.

When Cromwell died, his record was left in numbers. The Navy at his death consisted of 157 ships. His architectural improvements were but a new form of bottoms.*

Oliver Cromwell had not been long dead when the Navy—then under Monk—decided to restore the Monarchy. It sailed to Holland, embarked Charles II and James, Duke of York, and established Charles on the Throne without opposition. Monk is popularly regarded as a political time-server. But in his change of sides he made one very important stipulation : that Charles was to pledge himself to the upkeep of the fleet. The fleet accomplished the Restoration. The bulk of evidence is that it did so with little regard for any issue other than the naval one.

THE SECOND DUTCH WAR.

The second Dutch War broke out in 1665. As usual a state of unofficial war had preceded it. Both sides, having thought over the first war, had come to the conclusion that protecting their own merchant ships and attacking those of the enemy at one and the same time was an impossible proposition.

Both officially ordered their merchant ships to keep inside harbour ; but in both nations there were traders who took their own risks at sea and found warships handy to protect them. None the less, this war is of much importance as the first in which the command of the sea, fleet against fleet, received general recognition.

The battles themselves of this war are of little interest. They were marked by that same equality of courage and determination which was an outstanding feature of the First War. Slight early English successes led to little but attacks on merchant shipping ; then the Great Plague paralysed English efforts. The Dutch got to the mouth of the Thames, but a sudden sickness among their crews scared them off after a sixteen days' blockade.

* Charnock, *ex* Fincham.

Following this the French took side with the Dutch; but inconclusive fighting still resulted, till the Dutch, imagining that they had done better than they really had, found themselves engaged in the battle of the North Foreland.

Defeated in this they retired to Ostend, and the English scored on their trade by landing operations and harbour attacks, the result of which Admiral Colomb has estimated as proportionately equivalent to sixty-six million pounds' worth of damage at the present day! But it was conceded on the English side (*vide* Pepys) that it was mainly a matter of luck that this immense blow was struck.

Shortly after this event, the Insular spirit asserted itself with what in these days is known as "Economy and Efficiency." The Duke of York (afterwards James II) opposed it, but it was generally carried that the Dutch were defeated, and that a few economical fortifications would save the country against any further Dutch danger. No one having knowledge of the Dutch agreed. Indeed, the situation was precisely the same as when a few years ago the British Government cut down the Naval Programme. Charles II, peace talk being in the air, cut down expenses probably for his own ends; British Governments of the 1906-1907 era cut down with a view to expending the saving on "social reforms." But the practical results were identical. The Dutch in their era did what the Germans did in our own—met the decrease by an increase. They omitted to consider the ethics involved; they looked merely after their own ends. The result was a great Dutch attack on the Thames, which, though not so serious as the similar previous English attack on them, produced an enormous amount of mischief.

That the Dutch did not bombard London itself was purely a matter of contrary winds and luck. They did destroy numerous new warships on the river, and Sheerness fell entirely into their hands. "Dutch guns were heard in London"—to quote the popular histories. Actually luck favoured the English, and diplomacy secured a peace which the reduced fleet could never have achieved. The pen, for the moment, proved mightier than the sword. England obtained thereby a peace favourable to her, while the Dutch secured a breathing space to enable them to prepare for the Third Dutch War, which, had the Second been carried to its end against them, would never have occurred.

THE THIRD DUTCH WAR.

This War also began in the usual way—irregular attacks on commerce, without any declaration of war, and in March, 1672, an English Squadron wreaked havoc on the Dutch Indiamen. As in the Second War, the Dutch after this prohibited their merchant ships from proceeding to sea. No such prohibition took effect in England, where the merchant navy rapidly increased.

In the Second War the French were the allies of the Dutch. In the Third, they joined in with the English. In both cases their underlying political motive appears to have been to egg Great Britain and the Dutch on to mutual destruction. The assistance actually obtained by the Dutch from the French in the Second War was a minus quantity, and though in the Third, French ships actually joined the English fleet, the advantage therefrom ended there.

The allied fleet, under the command of the Duke of York, consisted of sixty-five English and thirty-six French warships, twenty-two fire ships, and a number of small craft. This fleet lay at Sole Bay (Southwold on the Suffolk coast). Here they were surprised by De Ruyter with ninety-one men of war, forty-four fire ships, and a number of small craft.

The *Royal James*, flagship of the Earl of Sandwich, who commanded one of the two divisions of the English Fleet, was attacked and destroyed by fire-ships, and the Earl was drowned in attempting to escape. The French Squadron under D'Estrées fell back and took little part in the fight. None the less, however, victory rested with the English, and the Dutch retreated to their own coasts, and were blockaded in the Texel. On shore the Dutch were badly pressed by the French armies, their naval energies being restricted accordingly.

With the approach of winter, the Allied fleet was broken up and returned to its harbours. In the early part of the following year, the Dutch conceived the project of blocking the English fleet in the Thames, and prepared eight ships full of stones with that object in view. This appears to have been the first instance of a device similar to that more recently unsuccessfully undertaken by the Americans, at Santiago de Cuba, in the Spanish-American War, and by the Japanese, at Port Arthur, in the Russo-Japanese War. The Dutch attack was never actually made; presumably circumstances did not admit of it. In the view of Admiral Colomb, it was frustrated by the English fleet putting to sea at an earlier date than had been expected.

The Allied fleet formed a junction off Rye, in May. It consisted altogether of eighty-four men-of-war, twenty-six fire-ships and auxiliaries. The English divisions were commanded by Prince Rupert and Spragge. The third division was under D'Estrées as before, but in order to avoid a repetition of what had happened at Sole Bay, the French ships were distributed in all three divisions of the fleet, instead of in a single division as they previously had been.

Having embarked a number of troops, the Allies sailed for Zealand, and found the Dutch fleet concentrating at the mouth of the Scheldt. It consisted of about seventy men-of-war, under De Ruyter, Tromp and Bankert. For some days, owing to fog and bad weather, no fighting was possible ; but on the 28th of May, the Dutch weighed anchor and a battle of the usual sort took place, both sides claiming victory. The loss of life in the Allied fleet, crowded as it was with troops, was very heavy, and no attempt was made to follow up the Dutch, who had retired inside the mouth of the river.

On the 4th of June, the Dutch fleet again came out. The English retired before it. An entirely inconclusive action eventually resulted, after which each fleet returned to harbour.

Having embarked a number of fresh troops at Sheerness, the Allies again put to sea and appeared on the Dutch coast. No landing was, however, attempted; and on the 10th of August the final battle took place. The French fleet on this occasion was allowed to act by itself, and, as before, drew off and left the English to shift for themselves. Spragge, having had two flagships disabled, was drowned in moving to a third, and victory, such as it was, went to the Dutch. No further battles took place, and in 1664 peace was concluded.

The net result of these three wars was in favour of the English, but mainly on the trade issue.

At the beginning of the First, the Dutch had by far the larger merchant shipping. At the end of the Third, the proportion was reversed.

Although tactics, as we understand them, cannot be said to have been employed, certain definite war lessons were undoubtedly learned. It came to be thoroughly believed that the principal use of a fleet was to attack the fleet of the enemy; and on that account these wars are an important feature of English naval history.

Following the conclusion of peace, the English Navy was entirely neglected, and the condition of the ships became so bad that in 1679 a Commission was appointed and thirty new ships were laid down. But the majority of these ships, having been launched, were allowed to decay; Charles II's early interest in the fleet having become a dead letter in his later years.

When James II came to the Throne in 1685, he appointed another Special Commission, and the repair of the Navy was systematically undertaken. The *personnel*, however, was neglected. It remained in a very dissatisfied state, and tacitly agreed to his deposition.

At the abdication of James II, in December, 1688, the Navy consisted of 173 ships, manned by 42,003 men, and carrying 6,930 guns. Of these ships, nine were first-rate, 11 second, 39 third, 41 fourth, 3 fifth, and 6 sixth. There were 26 fire-ships and 39 small craft. The best of the first-rates in those days was the *Britannia*. She was of 1,739 tons, carried 100 guns and a crew of 780 men. Her length was 146 feet, her beam 47 feet 4 inches, and her draught 20 feet. The second-rate ships were 90-gun vessels, third-rate 70 guns, and fourth-rate 54.

During James II's reign, bomb vessels were first introduced and regular establishments of stores were instituted. It is somewhat difficult to assess how far naval progress was actually indebted to this, the first King of England who was a naval officer, and how far to the efforts of a determined few who realised the absolute importance of naval power. Probably of James I, as of all the Stuarts,* it may be said that they realised the principle, but required pressing to act upon it. To thus acting may be traced the unpopularity of at least some of the Stuarts—there are practically no signs that the nation generally understood the importance of a powerful Navy. All the indications are in a contrary direction.

---

* Charles II always had an eye for and interest in improvements in detail, and himself invented new forms of hull, which, however, did not come up to his expectations. Both he and James were devoted to yachting and steered their own boats.

A singular defect of all the Stuarts in naval matters was their inability to appreciate the importance of the human as well as the material element. In the Cromwell régime, all the old abuses in connection with food, clothing and delayed pay, were done away with; to re-appear, however, almost as bad as ever soon after the Restoration.

V.

THE EARLY FRENCH WARS.

THE accession of William of Orange and the French support of James soon brought about a war. Early in 1689 James invaded Ireland with French ships and men. He did sufficiently well there for a considerable English army to be employed against him, and in the summer of 1690, William himself went over to take command, leaving Queen Mary as Regent with little save the militia as military defence and a more or less unprepared fleet.

A Jacobite rising in England was planned. In conjunction with it the French proposed to hold the Channel in superior force to cover the landing of troops in England, and then, by a blockade in the Irish Channel, prevent the return of King William and his army. The attitude of the English fleet was uncertain—a strong Jacobite element being in it—and the scheme was generally a very promising one for the French.

A personal appeal from Queen Mary is said to have secured the allegiance of the English fleet : but in everything else the subsequent French failure was due only to luck and the wisdom of the British Admiral, Lord Torrington.

It was more or less realised that the French would concentrate at Brest. Squadrons were sent out to interfere with this, but convoys and the like bulked largely in their orders. There is not the remotest indication that the Home Government appreciated the danger, which ended in Torrington finding himself opposed by a greatly superior French fleet, which he was ordered to fight at all costs.

Therefrom ensued the battle of Beachy Head, a defeat and a " strategical retirement to the rear" for which Torrington was subsequently court-martialled and acquitted. He alone appears to have realised that his defeat would have meant the success of the French plans, while so long as he could avoid action the threat of his existence must interfere with invasion.

The French movements throughout were somewhat obscure. On the 25th June, according to Torrington, they might have attacked him but did not do so. When the battle took place on the 30th, it was Torrington who attacked. In the subsequent retreat, the French pursued for four days, but did so in line of battle and without much energy. They captured or destroyed five disabled ships, but of real following up of the victory there was none.

The Anglo-Dutch fleet took shelter at the Nore; but the French drew off at Dover, and sailing west attacked Teignmouth and then returned to Brest. Their failure to follow up and destroy Torrington has never been satisfactorily explained.

The panic which they had created in England bore early fruit. Thirty new ships were laid down. Of these seventeen were eighty gun ships of 1000 tons, three were 1050 tons but carried seventy guns only, the remaining ten, sixty gun ships of 900 tons.

In 1692 another Jacobite rising was planned, and a French army collected to assist it. Taught by the experience of Beachy Head the Anglo-Dutch fleet concentrated early. It consisted of no less than ninety-eight ships of the line,* besides frigates and auxiliaries, the whole being under command of Russell. A descent upon St. Malo was the principal objective contemplated.

*	ENGLISH.			DUTCH.	
Ships ...	...	62	Ships ...	...	36
Men ...	...	27,725	Men ...	...	12,950
Guns ...	...	4,500	Guns ...	...	2,494
Frigates, etc....		23	Frigates, etc....		14

Neither side appears to have had much conception of the intentions of the other.   De Tourville, with a fleet of only fifty ships of the line, is supposed to have sailed under the impression that the Dutch had not joined up with the English.

In the fog of early morning on May 19th, he blundered into the entire Anglo-Dutch fleet off Cape La Hogue, and sustained a crushing defeat.   At least twenty-one French ships of the line were lost in the battle itself or destroyed in the harbours they had escaped into.

Following upon this victory came a lull in operations. It would seem to have been the English idea that the French fleet, having been beaten and dispersed, all that remained to do was to get ready to defeat the new fleet that France was preparing, and so the year 1693 passed uneventfully, except that damage was done to trade on either side.

In July, 1694, the Allies made a move, bombarding Dieppe and Havre from a squadron of bombs which had been specially prepared.   In September, Dunkirk received attention from a new war device called '' smoak-boats ''* the invention of one Meerlers, which did not inconvenience anyone very much.   Meerlers also had "machine ships," which likewise did no harm.   These appear to have been an elementary idea on large scale of the modern torpedo—improved fire-ships.

A fleet was generally busy defending trade in the Mediterranean, where for the first time it was permanently stationed.   Nothing in the way of fleet action was attempted by the French, and the next few years were spent in privateering on their part, and bombardments of ports which sheltered privateers on the part of the Allies.

English naval estimates in 1695 amounted to £2,382,172, and the House of Lords, in an address to the King, advocated an increase of the fleet on the grounds that it was essential to the nation that its fleets should always be superior to any possible enemy.   A French

* See Crimean War in a later chapter for a revival of this.

invasion was projected in the winter months ; but abandoned on the appearance of a fleet under Russell.

There is no question that in this war the French did more mischief with their privateers than with their fleets. English trade suffered very heavily; and there were continual complaints about the inability of the fleet to suppress the corsairs, a Parliamentary enquiry, being eventually made into the matter.

The French privateers—"corsairs" is the more correct term—were in substance a species of naval militia, of a quite different status from English privateers sailing under letters of marque. They hailed principally from St. Malo ; trading in peace time and preying on commerce in time of war. There were special regulations under which they were governed. The owner had to deposit a sum of about £600 with the Admiralty as security. He had to pay ten per cent. of the profits to the Admiralty and five per cent. to the Church. Two-thirds of the balance was his profit, the remaining third went to the crew. Often enough the privateer was a royal ship, let out for the purpose, and in the years following the battle of Cape La Hogue, most of the French frigates were on this service, with naval officers and men on board very often.

The privateers carried few guns, their object being to capture prizes, not to sink them. They sailed mostly in small squadrons, so making a considerable number of guns, and were rarely particular about using false colours. It was therefore comparatively easy for them successfully to attack weak convoys: some dealing with the warships and others making prizes ; and the inefficiency laid to the blame of the English fleet in trade protection at that period was, in some measure, at any rate, due to a failure to appreciate the enormous difficulties. Duguay-Trouin himself, records using the English flag to approach an English warship, and firing on her under these colours.

The unhandy warships of those days, faced with light enemies, which they could never overhaul, had a tremendous task set them. That the Navy of William III

era successfully defended anything against men like
Duguay-Trouin and Jean Bart, is of far more moment and
more to be wondered at than any failures. In this particular
war the fast lightly-armed corsair reached its apotheosis
at the hands of veritable experts to a degree impossible
to-day, or for that matter, ever hereafter, unless aircraft
prove able to act as "privateers" of the future—a rôle
which, to date, has been entirely forgotten in all dis-
cussions as to the value of aircraft.

In 1697, the peace of Ryswick was signed. According to Burchett, the net result of the war was the loss of
fifty English warships and fifty-nine French ones. The
historians generally indicate that the French were worn
out with the struggle; but on the whole the English
seem to have been well out of the war also.

It was about this time that Peter the Great appeared
in England, and engaged John Deane, brother of the
famous naval architect, Sir Anthony, to go back to
Russia with him to establish a navy. This is the first
instance of the foundation or reorganisation of a foreign
navy by this country. The experiment was by no means
very successful; the bulk of the English naval officers
taken over by Peter being men who, for various reasons,
had been dismissed from the Royal Navy. Some proved
incompetent, and all of them were quarrelsome.

WAR OF THE SUCCESSION.

The war of the Spanish Succession synchronised
with the accession of Queen Anne, in 1702. In the
interval following the peace of Ryswick the French
fleet had had considerable attention paid to it. The
principal innovation consisted in increasing the size
without (as hitherto) increasing the armament in
ratio. The French three-deckers were now built of
2,000 tons instead of 1,500 as formerly. The superior
sailing qualities, ever a feature of French ships, were still
further enhanced.

In England, though shipbuilding had also been
vigorously pursued, improvements commensurate with

those of France were not made. English ships of the period were, generally speaking, overgunned.

At the outbreak of the war of the Succession, the fleet consisted of seven first-rate, fourteen second-rate, forty-five third, sixty-three fourth, thirty-six fifth, twenty-nine sixth, eight fire ships, thirteen bombs, and ten yachts—a total tonnage of 158,992; an increase of about a third in thirteen years. The first-rates were a new type of ship; the second-rates consisted of the old type first and second-rates—the three deckers of ninety guns and special service eighty-gun two deckers. The third-rates were the staple battle type— two deckers of seventy guns on home service and mounting sixty-two guns when sent abroad. The fourth-rates carried nominally fifty guns and forty-four on foreign service.

One third of the naval power of Europe was English; France and Holland between them made up another third, the balance being represented by the rest of the Powers.* Though the phrase, "Two Power Standard," was then unknown, the fleet, representing as it did the result of agitations in Parliament and else-where for suitable naval power, was clearly based on a similar general idea, and the Two Power Standard theory may be dated from the time of William of Orange.

The general idea of the campaign on the English side was combined naval and military attack on Ferrol— the fleet, consisting of fifty English and Dutch ships of the line and some frigates and transports to the number of 110, being under Sir George Rooke. The military element amounted to 12,000 troops under the Duke of Ormonde. Nothing came of the attempt owing to internal dissentions; and the expedition was on its way back when news was received of Chateau-Renault with a French-Spanish fleet of twenty-one warships at Vigo. A combined attack was delivered and the entire hostile fleet was sunk or captured without much loss, and a valuable convoy captured also.

* Fincham.

In this year there also happened the greatest disgrace that ever befell the Royal Navy. Admiral Benbow, who had risen from the "Lower Deck," was detached with six ships of the line to the West Indies, where he met a French squadron of five, under du-Casse. Two of his captains refused to engage the enemy altogether, and the others, save one, did so but half-heartedly. Benbow was mortally wounded and a French victory gained. On their return to England two of the captains were executed "for cowardice," but timidity had actually nothing whatever to do with the business. It was purely and entirely an act of personal hostility. It is generally put down to Benbow's lowly origin; but officers of the Benbow class were so plentiful, and Benbow had so long been in important positions afloat,* that the "obvious reason" played but a minor part. Benbow's great defect was a lack of that "personality" of which in later years Nelson was the prime exponent. Coupled with this was the state of much of the Navy generally owing to Jacobite intrigues with those who were unable to forget their old allegiance to the Stuarts.

In 1703 very special orders were issued as to cutting down expenditure on non-essentials in ship construction. In this year the ornamental work so conspicuous in ships of the Stuart era was reduced almost to extinction.

The naval events were inconsiderable. A few French prizes were made, and it was found from these that the French theory of increasing dimensions without increasing the armament had reached such a stage that fifty-gun French ships were larger than sixty-gun English ones,† but it was not for some years that practical attention was directed to the point.

In 1704 there took place another of the combined naval and military operations peculiar to this war. This was to Lisbon and in connection with the Austrian Archduke Charles. It is mainly of interest because it led to the

---

* He was Master of the fleet at Beachy Head and also at Cape La Hogue.
† The *Pembroke* (sixty-four) captured by the French in 1710, in this war, had her armament reduced to fifty guns by them.

more or less accidental capture of Gibraltar, and in that it otherwise had much to do with the prevention of a junction of the French Brest and Toulon fleets which was destined to loom so largely in future history that to this day "junctions" remain a principal "idea" for naval manœuvres.

Sir George Rooke, who commanded the main fleet, had with him forty-eight ships of the line and details ; Sir Cloudesley Shovell was in the channel with some twenty-two more.

The Brest fleet sailed for Toulon under the Count de Toulouse. They were chased without effect by Rooke, till near Toulon, when on the evening of May 29th, he gave up the pursuit as too risky, and returned to Lagos, where Shovell joined him on June 16th.

The combined English fleet being now assumed superior to the combined French fleet, attacks on Cadiz and Barcelona were contemplated, but as insufficient troops were available it was decided to attack Gibraltar instead. The motive for doing so does not appear to have been anything greater than that the King of Portugal and the Archduke Charles were worrying the fleet to "do something." Gibraltar was suggested and settled on, apparently, as being as suitable as any other place.

Gibraltar lies at the end of a narrow peninsula. On this peninsula, on July 21st, 1,800 marines from the fleet landed under the Prince of Hesse. As they carried only eighteen rounds per man, the presumption is obvious that either little opposition was expected or else that the attack was merely delivered to satisfy those who had urged that something should be done. The former is generally assumed to be the case, but the latter is by no means improbable. In any case, the marines met with little opposition and demanded the surrender of the fortress, while some of the English ships, under Byng, were warped into bombarding positions under a mild fire from the forts. This occupied a whole day.

Early on the 23rd, fire was opened on both sides, and the inhabitants of the town fled to a chapel on the

E

hill. The bombardment continued till noon, when the "cease fire" was ordered, so that results might be ascertained. It was found that some of the batteries were disabled, and it was then decided to land in the boats and capture them.

On the cessation of fire, the inhabitants, mostly women and priests, who had fled out of the town, began to come back. Sir Cloudesley Shovell (who was on board Byng's flagship) ordered a gun to be fired across these; whereupon they all ran back to the chapel in which they had been sheltered. This gun was taken by the fleet generally to be a signal to re-open the bombardment. Under cover of this firing, the landing party got ashore, and had things much their own way till about a hundred of them were killed or wounded by the blowing up of the Castle.

At this they began to retreat, but reinforcements arriving, they retrieved the position and captured other works without difficulty, establishing themselves between the town and the chapel where the women had taken refuge. Giving this as his reason, the Governor capitulated next day. His entire garrison, according to Torrington's Memoirs, consisted of but eighty men. The Anglo-Dutch force lost three officers and fifty-seven men killed, eight officers and 207 men wounded.

Thus the capture of Gibraltar, " the impregnable." At Toulon, a large French fleet was getting ready for sea—a fleet quite large enough to have done to the English what Teggethoff, in 1866, did to the bombarding Italians at Lissa.

There seems little doubt that Rooke underestimated this fleet. On the other hand, as he had look-outs, and the wind was not in the enemy's favour, the risks he actually ran were trifling compared to those taken by Persano. From which many lessons have been deduced and morals drawn.

In actual fact, however, it is greatly to be doubted whether either commander thought round the matter at all. The " science" of naval warfare is a thing of quite modern origin, and the strategies displayed by most admirals in the past—if studied with an unbiassed mind —are just as likely to be luck as forethought. Analogous to this is Ruskin on the artist Turner. Turner painted wonderful pictures: Ruskin found wonderful meanings in them. These "meanings" were, however, more news to Turner than to any one else!

On August 10th, the French fleet, reported as sixty-six sail, was sighted thirty miles off by a look-out ship. Rooke's fleet at that time was short of five Dutch ships which he had sent away, twelve other ships were watering at Tetuan—miles away from him—and all the marines of the fleet were on shore at Gibraltar as garrison. The light craft were sent into Gibraltar to bring back half the marines as quickly as possible, while the main fleet retreated to pick up the Tetuan division, and later got its marines on board.

The French, meanwhile, either ignorant of the state of affairs, or else from general incompetence, made no attack at the time, and it was not till the 13th that battle was joined by the English bearing down on them. The resulting engagement was indecisive, and the fleets withdrew to repair damages. The French, however, declined to renew action, eventually retreated to Toulon, and never attempted a fleet action again during the war.

Rooke's fleet consisted of fifty-three ships of the line. The French had fifty-two, of which they lost five.

Following the battle of Malaga, the marines were landed again at Gibraltar, together with some gunners and forty-eight guns. The fleet then returned to England, leaving at Lisbon a dozen ships under Sir John Leake— the only ships which, after survey, were considered not to be in urgent need of refit at home. This squadron was subsequently reinforced by eight ships of the line.

The French and Spaniards presently invested Gibraltar by land and sea. In the first attempt the blockading fleet was short of supplies and had to retire to Cadiz. Leake arrived, but finding nothing there returned to the Tagus.

The French then sent a light squadron to assist the siege, and the whole of these were surprised and captured by Leake, on October 29th, 1704. There is reason to believe that this action saved the fortress, as a grand assault was on the *tapis*.

Leake remained at Gibraltar three months, during which time stores and some 2,000 troops were brought in from England ; then, the garrison being now in no straits, the English ships withdrew in January, 1705, to Lisbon to refit, leaving the land investment to proceed. In March, a squadron of fourteen French ships of the line appeared off Gibraltar, but owing to a gale only five got into the ' harbour. Here they were presently surprised and captured by the English. The remaining ships fled to Toulon and the siege was then raised— having lasted five months.

From these operations it is abundantly clear that the English had by now realised that Gibraltar was perfectly safe so long as its sea communications were kept open. De Pointis, the French Admiral, realised the same thing, and in the whole of the naval operations he appears to have been obeying, under protest, orders from the French Government, which at no time appears to have realised the futility of such operations in face of a superior Anglo-Dutch fleet.

Following the abandonment of the siege of Gibraltar, the French became very active with their corsairs, inflicting heavy losses on English trade. On the ultimate inutility of this *guerre de course* much has been written ; but perhaps hardly proper attention has been bestowed on the other side of the question. The French had small stomach for anything of the nature of a fleet action, and there is little or no reason to suppose that had they concentrated on line operations any success would have attended their efforts. Their *personnel* was generally inferior. Their *materiel* on the other hand was superior, and the problem really before them surely was, not which method, " grand battle " or *guerre de course*, was the better, but how best to inflict damage with the means available. And here the *guerre de course* held obvious promise.

In the summer of 1705, a combined land and sea attack was delivered on Barcelona, the Earl of Peterborough being in supreme command of both forces. The town surrendered on October 3rd. The history of Gibraltar was then repeated. The fleet withdrew, leaving Leake with a few ships to watch. The enemy then invested the place, which was relieved just in time by Leake so heavily reinforced that the French squadron made no attempt to fight him. A variety of other towns were then captured by combined attacks, also the Balearic Islands, except Minorca.

In 1706, combined operations on the north of France were arranged for, but ultimately abandoned owing to the weather. Ostend was captured in this year; but a combined attack on Toulon, in 1707, signally failed.

In 1708, the French attempted combined operations on Scotland and reached the Firth of Forth with twenty sail, but an English squadron under Byng arriving they sailed away again at once. The superior mobility of the French was evidenced by the fact that Byng's pursuit resulted in nothing but the capture of an ex-English ship which could not keep up with her French-built consorts. The Anglo-Dutch combined operations of the year resulted in the capture of Minorca. Minor operations took place in the West Indies.

1709 passed mostly in the relief of places which had been acquired and were now besieged. In 1710, the French became more active, capturing one or two English warships and making a combined attempt against Sardinia. This last was frustrated by Sir John Norris. An English attempt on Cette in the same year proved a failure; but conspicuous success attended similar operations in Nova Scotia.

In the following years the principal of such operations as took place were on the American coast. Of these, the chief was an abortive attack on Quebec, mainly remarkable for an extraordinary escape of the entire English fleet one night in the Gulf of St. Lawrence. A military officer, one captain Goddard, insisted that he saw breakers ahead. As no one would credit him he finally dragged the Admiral out of bed and up on deck, by which time the fleet was close on to the breakers. As things were, seven transports were wrecked and nearly a thousand soldiers drowned. The warships very narrowly escaped.*

This disaster led to the abandonment of the expedition. Peace was declared in 1713. The English loss in the war was thirty-eight ships, mounting 1,596 guns; the French lost fifty-two ships, mounting 3,094 guns.† A very large number of English ships became unserviceable during the war, because, despite the fact that many new ships were built and that the bulk of the ships lost by the French entered the English service, the entire navy diminished by twenty-five vessels.

Most of the ships were in poor condition, and in the early years of George I's reign, large sums had to be expended on refits. Foul bilge water was the main cause of internal decay, and in 1715 organised steps were taken for the ventilation of the bilges. A certain increase in size for ships of all classes was also ordered, those of 100 guns being increased by 319 tons, and the eighty-gun ships by sixty-seven tons. This increase, however, by no means brought the tonnage to gun ratio down to the French limits, nor were the improvements in underwater form of much serious moment. The French maintained a superiority in this respect which they held till the present century. To-day, of course, the situation is completely reversed, and for any given horse-power any British ship is appreciably faster than a French one.‡

Some special attention was also devoted to the preparation of timber for immediate use in shipbuilding. This subject was first drawn attention to in 1694, and

---

* This extraordinary story of a soldier saving the fleet is made all the stranger by the fact that Sir Hovenden Walker, the Admiral, was a teetotaller and a vegetarian, an almost unheard of thing in those days.

† Fincham.   ‡ See later references to Sir William White and Sir Philip Watts.

the net result of the enquiries in 1715 did not really go
much further. It was not till eleven years later that the
problem was seriously grappled with.

In 1715, an English fleet under Norris was in the
Baltic, acting against Sweden and allied with the
Russians and Danes, Peter the Great himself being in
chief command. Nothing of moment happened. These
operations extended to 1719, when sides were changed.

In 1718, Spain, which had recently made some considerable efforts towards the creation of naval power,
used her power for an attack on Sicily. Admiral Byng
arriving with a superior English fleet, attacked and
destroyed the greater part of the Spanish squadron in
the Battle of Cape Passaro. No state of war existed.
The Spaniards had attacked an English ally, and this
was Byng's only excuse for action. A few months later
war was formally declared against Spain, and early in
1719, a curious replica of the Armada took place. Forty
Spanish transports, escorted by merely five warships,
sailed from Cadiz for the coast of Scotland; the idea
being that the 5,000 troops which they carried should
co-operate in a Jacobite rising. This "Armada" was
dispersed by a severe gale off Cape Finisterre, and only
a small fraction of it reached the coast of Ross, where a
landing, easily defeated by the military, was made. It
is noteworthy that no fleet met the expedition, and it
was not till a month after its dispersal in a gale that
Norris sailed to look for it!

The remainder of this particular war, which lasted
only three years, was devoted to the re-conquest of
Sicily and the capture of Vigo. Peace was concluded in
1721. In the course of this war the usual combined
attack was made upon Gibraltar in 1720; but the arrival
of an English fleet easily relieved the garrison.

At and about this time the Russian fleet, hitherto
allies, became the enemy, and early in 1720, Admiral
Norris was despatched to assist the Swedes against them.
He appears to have done very little save squabble with
the Swedish admiral as to precedence. In any case the

Russians did much as they listed against the Swedish coast till Sweden had to sue for peace, and Russia became the predominant Baltic naval power. Her position as such was the more extraordinary in that the Russian fleet was technically very incompetent. The situation was mainly brought about by the personal genius of Peter the Great. His ships were generally the speedier, and he issued the strictest orders that no enemy was to be engaged unless at least one-third inferior in power. In the presence of an enemy the Swedes considered nothing,* the English comparatively little. The brain of Peter, was, therefore, an easy match for them, despite the technical inferiority of his *personnel*. This campaign is a most striking illustration of Alexander the Great's maxim "that an army of sheep led by a lion is better than an army of lions led by a sheep."

In 1726, an Anglo-Danish naval demonstration against Russia took place at Kronstadt, but nothing came of the incident, which was repeated equally ineffectually in the following year, when larger preparations were made.

In 1726, the preservation of ships' timbers came once more on the *tapis*, when the results of some experiments commenced six years before, were inspected. Up to about 1720, woods were prepared for use by a system known as " charring." This consisted in building a fire one side of the plank and keeping the other side wet till the required condition was produced. One, Cumberland, invented a system known as " stoving." By this, the wood was put into wet sand and then subjected to heat till the juices were extracted and the wood in suitable condition. A ship was planked with both systems, side by side, and on these being examined in 1726, it was found that while the " stoved " planks were in good condition the " charred " ones were already rotten.

A grateful country vaguely presented Cumberland with one tenth of whatever might be the saving which

---

* Their recklessness was such that Peter had to give orders that no Swedish ship was to be boarded unless the superior officers were killed. Swedish captains, attacked by superior forces, made a regular practice of allowing themselves to be boarded and then blowing up their ships !

his system would produce. Cumberland, however, was equally vague, since he could supply no data as to the amount of heat or time of subjection, and experiments had to be carried out in the Yards in order to ascertain this. The authorities were apparently still ascertaining, when one Boswell, of Deptford Yard, in 1736, hit upon using steam, and his system became at once general—though a few years later it was replaced by boiling the timber.

When George II came to the Throne the country was at peace, but this peace was mainly and entirely secured by the policy of Walpole, who kept the Navy on a war footing. Feeling against Spain ran so high on account of the action of the *Guarda-Costas* in searching English ships in the West Indies, that Walpole's hands were forced in 1739. In the House of Commons, Captain Vernon announced that with six ships he could capture Porto Bello. Promoted to Rear Admiral, he essayed the task, and accomplished it, by coming into close range and landing under cover of a bombardment. His loss was trifling—nineteen killed and wounded, all told. The garrison turned out to have been only 300 strong, of whom forty surrendered. The rest had either been killed or had fled. It is to be observed that no state of war existed at the time.

War with Spain was declared in October, 1739. The English fleet in commission consisted of thirty-eight ships of the line, and there was a reserve of twenty-four ready for immediate service. There were also thirty-six minor vessels in commission and eight in reserve.

An interesting circumstance of this war was the whole-world scale on which naval operations were planned. In substance the scheme was as follows:— Admiral Vernon was to attack the east coast of Darien. Captain Cornwall was to round the Horn, attack the west coast of Darien and then go to the Philippines, where he was to meet Captain Anson, who was to voyage thither via the Cape of Good Hope. The scheme was not carried out in its entirety, as the Cape of Good Hope expedition never sailed, Anson being substituted for Cornwall.

Vernon, having been reinforced with a number of bombs and fire-ships, proceeded, in March, 1740, to attack Cartagena, which he bombarded for four days without much material result. Then he proceeded to Chagres, which, after a two days' bombardment, surrendered to him. A considerable Spanish squadron being reported on its way out, and a French fleet (suspected of hostile designs) also sailing, Vernon withdrew to Jamaica, where he lay till reinforced by twenty ships under Ogle.

Ogle performed his voyage without adventure, except that six of his ships encountered a French squadron and fought it for some little time under the impression that a state of war existed. The error being discovered, the squadrons parted with mutual apologies.*

Ogle arrived in January, 1741. After a short refit the fleet sailed to look for the French and observe them. They presently learned that the French, short of men and provisions, had gone back to Europe. Upon receipt of this news it was decided to attack Cartagena.

Vernon had with him twenty-nine ships of the line, twenty-two lesser craft and a number of transports, carrying 12,000 troops. The seamen and marines of the fleet totalled 15,000. For a time some success was met with, but divided councils, mutual recrimination between Navy and Army, sickness in the troops, all did their share, and eventually the attack was abandoned.†

Attacks on other places led to no happier results, and while efforts were thus being frittered away in the West Indies, the commerce was suffering badly. Petitions from the commercial world to Parliament were of almost daily occurrence. Vernon requested to be recalled, and eventually was superseded, but his successor fared no better than he.

Meanwhile, we must turn aside for a moment to consider the operations of Anson. The following items in connection therewith are summarised from Barrow's *Voyages and Discoveries*, published in 1765.

* Colomb.

† For a very full and detailed account see Chapter XV. of Colomb's *Naval Warfare*.

On arriving at Madeira, Anson, who had left England on the 13th of September, 1740, learned of a Spanish squadron, under Pizarro, lying in wait for him. This squadron, attempting to round the Horn ahead of Anson, encountered a furious gale, and was eventually driven back to Buenos Ayres, with only three ships left, and these reduced to the utmost extremities. A second attempt to round the Horn fared no better, and eventually Pizarro returned to Spain in his own ship, manned chiefly by English prisoners and some pressed Indians. These latter mutinied, but not being joined by the English prisoners, as they had hoped, were eventually defeated.

Anson left Madeira on November 3rd, 1740, and shortly afterwards his crews fell sick, through lack of air, the ships being too deep for the lower ports to be opened. Anson had several ventilating holes cut. Then fever came, carrying off many. Just before Christmas he arrived at St. Catherine's, Brazil, but his hopes of recruiting his men's health were abortive. His own flagship, the *Centurion* lost twenty-eight men dead and had ninety-six others on the sick list.

On January 18th, 1741, Anson sailed for the Horn. A gale scattered his squadron, one ship being separated for a month ; eventually, however, all rejoined. There followed three months' tempests rounding the Horn. Scurvy appeared, the ships got separated again. Finally, on June 9th, the *Centurion* alone reached Juan Fernandez, short of water and only about ten men fit for duty in a watch.

A few days later the *Tryal* appeared at the island, her captain, lieutenant and three men being all who were available for service. A third ship, the *Gloucester*, appeared on June 21st, but so short-handed was she that, though assistance was sent her, it took her an entire fortnight to make harbour ! On August 16th, the victualler ship, *Anna Pink*, arrived, all her crew in good condition, she having put into some harbour en route. Of the other three ships, two, (the *Severn* and *Pearl*)

failed to round the Horn and returned to Brazil, the
third, the *Wager*, was wrecked.

In September, a sail was sighted.   The *Centurion*
put to sea and found her to be a Spanish merchant ship.
From the prisoners it was learned that a Spanish
squadron from Chili had been on the look out for Anson,
that a ship had been lying off Juan Fernandez till just
before his arrival, but that assuming him lost they had
now all gone back to Valparaiso.

Thereafter several prizes were taken, one being fitted
out to replace the *Tryal*, which was abandoned.   The
Anna Pink had also had to be abandoned as useless.

Now began the most extraordinary part of the
enterprise.   Treasure ships were captured, thirty-eight
men landed, held up and captured Payta, a good half of
these attired in feminine costume, which they found in
houses wherein they had sought substitutes for their
rags—only one man drunk in all the sack of the town—
the terror of prisoners, who, when released, refused to
accept liberty till they had thanked Anson for his
courtesy—Anson's insistence on treasure being divided
equally between those who attacked and those who kept
ship, while giving his own share to the attackers—the
night chase of a supposed galleon which turned out to
be but a fire on shore—the fearful sufferings of boats'
crews sent out to look for the treasure ship*—the release
of prisoners, and the Spanish reply thereto by the
despatch of luxuries to the English—the final loss of the
Gloucester, worn out by keeping the sea—the arrival at
Guam of the *Centurion* with only seventy-one men
capable of "standing at a gun" under even any
emergencies—these things belong to special histories.
Here it suffices to give but a general outline, of which
the first event is that having reached Macao and refitted,

---

* The treasure ship was well armed and did not hesitate to engage him.
Anson's success was in some considerable measure attributable to the fact that
not having enough men for the broadside firing of the period, he ordered
independent firing.   It was the Spanish custom to lie down as the enemy fired
a broadside, then jump up and fire back.   Anson's independent firing caused
much unexpected slaughter on them.   This rule of "broadsides" compares
interestingly with the salvo firing of the present day.

Anson went into the Pacific again, and, having given his men considerable training in marksmanship and gun-handling, finally intercepted and captured the Spanish treasure ship that he sought.

On his subsequent return to China with his prize, the experiences of " Mr. Anson " (as he is generally called throughout the history from which I quote) were mainly of a personal nature. Visited by a mandarin who showed a liking for wine, Anson had to plead illness and delegate his duties of glass for glass to the most robust officer he had. He provisioned by weight with ducks (found to be filled with stones to make them heavier) and pigs filled with water. Ultimately he had to go up to Canton with (so far as I can ascertain) the first instance of a crew in regular uniform. To quote from the entertaining contemporary narrative :—

" Towards the end of September, the commodore finding that he was deceived by those who had contracted to supply him with sea provisions ; and that the viceroy had not, according to his promise, invited him to an interview, found it impossible to surmount the difficulty he was under, without going to Canton and visiting the viceroy. He, therefore, prepared for this expedition : the boat's crew were clothed, in a uniform dress, resembling that of the water-men of the Thames. There were in number eighteen, and a coxswain; they had scarlet jackets, and blue silk waistcoats, the whole trimmed with silver buttons, and had also silver badges on their jackets and caps."

Leaving Macao, the *Centurion* reached the Cape of of Good Hope on the 11th of March, 1744. From here, signing on forty Dutchmen, Anson proceeded home.

So ended the most prodigious oversea combined enterprise ever before attempted. Anson was not the first to circumnavigate the world, but few had done so before him, and on that account the real purpose of his expedition has been generally overlooked in the circumnavigation feat.

As ever in British naval history luck was with him ; but something more than "luck" must have been in an enterprise where Pizarro, sent to intercept him, gave up, while Anson fought through the perils of Cape Horn, with his sickly crews and crazy ships.

To resume the general history of the war. In October, 1742, the *Victory* (100) was lost, presumably on the Caskets, though her actual fate was never ascertained. France had now entered into the war; her fleet consisted of forty-five ships of the line; the corresponding English fleet totalling ninety ships of the line.

In 1742, Ogle succeeded Vernon in the West Indies, and a series of small bombardments resulted, usually without success.

Formal hostilities with France (delayed as was the custom of the time) were declared in 1744, and outlying possessions changed hands. Anson, in command of the Channel Fleet in 1747, defeated and captured the Brest fleet, and some minor actions took place, mostly in connection with convoys. The war ended in 1748; its net naval results being as follows :—

	ENGLISH.	SPANISH.	FRENCH.
Warships lost or captured...	49	24	56
Merchant ships captured	3,238	1,249	2,185

The economy order referred to on a previous page was possibly in part responsible for the bad showing made by the English as warships in this war. In any case the standardisation of classes had disappeared, and no two ships were of the same dimensions. Many ships were found so weak at sea that they had to be shored up between decks,* and of all the complaint was continual that they were very "crank" and unable to open their lee ports in weather in which foreign ships could do so. The seamanship, however, was of a high order compared to that of either the French or Spaniards; possibly the very badness of the English ships helped to make the seamanship what it was.

After the war many constructional improvements were suggested and some few of them carried into practice. Among the prizes of the war was a Spanish ship, the *Princessa* of seventy guns, which attracted general admiration. In 1746, a glorified copy of her,, the

* See earlier reference to the same thing in Raleigh's time.

Royal George, was laid down.* At and about this time an era of slow ship-building set in; for example, this *Royal George* was ten years on the stocks. The slow building was part and parcel of the naval policy of the period, and in no way to be connected with what any such tardiness would mean to-day.

A ship on the stocks was more easily preserved from decay than one in the water. With precisely the same idea the authorities at the end of the war disbanded the bulk of the *personnel.* Upon a war appearing likely, the press-gang was always available to supplement any deficiency in the rank and file not filled by allowing jail-birds to volunteer.

Officering the fleet was a less easy matter. The choice lay between retired officers more or less rusty, and the best of the "prime seamen," who had been afloat in such warships as were retained in commission. The Admiralty selected its officers from both indiscriminately. There is this much, but no more, warrant for the idea that in the old days the sailor from forward could rise to the highest ranks, while to-day he cannot do so. The fact is correct enough, but the circumstance had nothing to do with inducements and encouragements. Once on the quarter deck the tarpaulin seaman, if he had it in him, might win his way to high rank and fame, as did Benbow, Sir John Balchen, Captain Cook, and several others. But he obtained his footing on entirely utilitarian grounds which passed away when a more regular system of *personnel* came into custom.

In the year 1753, a Dr. Hales was instrumental in one of the greatest improvements ever effected in the navy. To him was due the adoption of a system of ventilation with wind-mills and air pumps. The immediate result was a very great reduction in the sickness and death-rate on ship-board, the Earl of Halifax placing it on record that for twelve men who died in non-ventilated ships, only one succumbed in the ventilated vessels.

* Is the well-known *Royal George* which capsized at Spithead, in 1782.

Early in 1755, a war with France became probable on account of hostile preparations made in North America.   As a matter of precaution a French squadron on its way out was attacked and two ships captured. Something like three hundred French merchant ships were also taken during the year.   War, however, was not declared on either side!

Early in 1756, news was received of French designs on Minorca, a considerable expedition collecting at Toulon.   After some delay, Byng left England with ten ships of the line, picked up three more at Gibraltar, and sailed to relieve Minorca, where Fort St. Philip was closely invested by 15,000 troops.   Supporting these last was a French squadron of twelve ships of the line, under La Gallisonniére.

On Byng arriving, La Gallisonniére embarked 450 men from the attacking force to reinforce his crews, and on May 20th ensued the battle of Minorca, which resulted in the defeat and retreat of Byng.*   Ten days later the British force in the island surrendered.

Byng was subsequently court-martialled and shot at Portsmouth for having failed to do his utmost to destroy the French fleet.   His ships were indifferently manned and in none too good condition.   He encountered a better man than himself, and there is no reason to suppose that had he resumed action, anything but his total defeat would have resulted.   At the same time, the execution of Byng, *pour encourager les autres*, probably bore utilitarian fruit in the years that were to follow. The execution has since been condemned as little better than a revengeful judicial murder ; but a realisation of the circumstances of the times suggests that other motives than punishment of an individual were paramount.

War was formally declared shortly after the fall of Minorca.   No events of much moment marked the rest of the year 1756, but early in the following year,

---

* Admiral Mahan, *Influence of Sea Power upon History*, p. 286, shows how Byng's dread of anything unconventional in the way of tactics led to the action being indecisive.

Calcutta, which had fallen to the natives, was recaptured by Clive, assisted by a naval force.

In 1758, the Navy consisted of 156 of the line and 164 lesser vessels. The *personnel* was 60,000.

The situation at this time was that in North America the French colonies were being hotly pressed, Louisbourg being invested. The French had a species of double plan—to relieve Louisbourg directly, and also the usual invasion of England.

The relief of Louisbourg came to nought ; a Toulon squadron which came out being driven back by Osborne, while Hawke destroyed the convoys in the Basque Roads. Louisbourg finally fell, four ships of the line that were lying there being burned, and one other captured, together with some smaller craft.

Nearer home, combined naval and military attacks were pressed upon the French coast, Anson wreaking havoc on St. Malo, while Howe destroyed practically everything at Cherbourg.

The invasion of England project remained, however. In 1759, the French had somewhere about twenty ships of the line, under De Conflans, at Brest, twelve at Toulon, under De la Clue, five with a fleet of transports at Quiberon, five frigates at Dunkirk with transports, a division of small craft and flat-bottomed boats at Havre, and a squadron of nine ships of the line with auxiliaries in the West Indies.

These were watched or blockaded by superior British squadrons in every case—the maintenance of blockades being mainly possible owing to the improved ventilation of the ships. Provisions were still bad and scurvy plentiful, but the blockade maintained was better and closer than anything that the French can have antici- pated. This war, indeed, saw the birth of scientific blockade in place of the somewhat haphazard methods which had previously existed. In part, it arose from a better perception of naval warfare, the study of history and the growth of definite objectives. But since side by side with these improvements tactical ideas were

F

nearly non-existent and ships in fighting kept a line of the barrack-ground type regardless of all circumstances,* improvements in naval architecture may claim at least as big a part as the wit of man. Ideas of blockading and watching were as old as the Peloponnesian War, but means to carry them into effect had hitherto been sadly lacking.

To resume, the French fleets being cornered by superior forces, had no option but to wait for lucky opportunity to effect the usual attempted junctions. This opportunity was long in coming, and meanwhile Rodney made an attack on the invading flotilla at Havre, bombarded it for fifty-two hours, and utterly destroyed the flat-bottomed boats which had been collected.

In July, 1759, Boscawen, having run short of water and provisions, had to withdraw from Toulon to Gibraltar, where he began to refit his ships, and De la Clue, learning of this, came out of Toulon in August, slipping through the straits at midnight, with the English in fleet pursuit shortly afterwards.

De la Clue had intended to rendezvous at Cadiz, but having altered his mind, made the almost inevitable failure of getting all his ships to comprehend it.† So it came about that daylight found him near Cape St. Vincent, with only six sail, and eight of Boscawen ships (which he at first took to be his own stragglers) coming up. In the action that followed, three of the French ships were captured, two burned and one escaped. The stragglers of the French fleet got into Cadiz as originally directed, and a few months later escaped back to Toulon.

Thurot, with a small squadron, slipped out from Dunkirk, in October, merely to intern himself in a Swedish harbour.

Hawke continued his blockade of Brest, being now and then driven off by gales, and during one of these

---

* Time after time, hostile ships, having had enough of it, passed away ahead and escaped, because to have pressed them would have "disorganised the line."

† Our own naval manœuvres in recent years have seen more than one disaster from the change of a rendezvous.

absences, Bempart, with his nine West Indian ships, got into Brest. The Brest fleet was apparently very short-handed, or else the West Indian squadron in a very bad way; in any case the crews of the latter were distributed among the former, and De Conflans sailed with only twenty-one ships on November 14th.

The expeditionary force which he proposed to convoy lay at Quiberon, which place owing to weather he did not make till the 20th. There he sighted and gave chase to the blockading English frigates, and in doing so met Hawke's fleet of twenty-three ships of the line.

In the battle of Quiberon which followed, the French lost six ships of the line. Eleven, by throwing their guns overboard, escaped into shallow water, the remainder reached safety at Rochefort. Two English ships ran aground, otherwise little damage was sustained.*

Out of these happenings the French fleet—which, in this year alone, lost thirty-one ships of the line—ceased to have any importance; while to the general naval activity of the English must be attributed the capture of Quebec, by Wolfe.

In 1760, the British ships of the line had sunk to 120 in number, though the *personnel* rose to 73,000. Naval operations were mainly confined to the relief of Quebec and the consequent capture of the whole of Canada, and the suppression of privateering—over a hundred French corsairs being captured in 1760 alone.

The results of privateering have been put at 2,500 English merchant vessels being captured in the four years ending 1760; the French merchant-ship loss being little more than one-third. In 1761, when French naval power had practically ceased to exist, 812 English merchant ships were captured. It must, however, be borne in mind that every year saw great increases in English shipping. Heavy as the numerical losses were, they did not exceed ten per cent., and the bulk of vessels captured were coasters.

* While this battle of Quiberon was in progress, people in England were burning Hawke in effigy for having allowed the French fleet to escape!

French mercantile losses were considerably smaller, but simply for the reason that France had fewer and fewer ships to lose, for her trade was being swept from the sea. English trade on the other hand grew and multiplied exceedingly. It may even be argued that so far from really injuring our trade, the *guerre de course* in this war actually fostered it by the enhanced profits which safe arrival entailed, this attracting the speculative. But for the speculative the loss of larger vessels would have been smaller than it was. These were they, who, on a convoy nearing home waters, sailed on ahead, chancing attack in the hopes of the greatly increased profits to be made by early arrivals. Ships which obeyed the orders of the escorting warships were very rarely captured.

The following years saw the capture of Pondicherry, Dominica, a successful attack on Belle Isle and also a general loss of French colonial possessions. To quote Mahan, "At the end of seven years the Kingdom of Great Britain has become the British Empire."

In 1762, Spain declared war. She had a fleet consisting nominally of eighty-nine sail, but joined in far too late to be of any assistance to France. No naval battle of importance took place.

Peace was signed early in 1763. By it England secured Canada from France, and Spain lost Florida.

During this war the usual complaints about ships' bottoms were made, especially from the West Indian Station; and in October, 1761, the Admiralty ordered a frigate to be sheathed with thin sheets of copper as an experiment. This was at first found extremely successful, but after the lapse of a few years it was noted that chemical action had set up between the copper and the iron bolts at the ships' bottom—most of these bolts being rusted away.

Experiments were, however, continued, since, though the life of a copper bottom was but three to four years, its general advantages were very great. Ultimately iron bolts were abandoned in favour of copper ones. The cost of this came to £2,272 for a ship of the first-rate, and was only relatively satisfactory.

Ever since the Treaty of Paris in 1763, friction had been growing between the Home Country and the North American Colonies. The causes which led to it concern the British Navy only in so far as it was used for the harsh enforcement of the regulations entailed by the Treaty in question—regulations which bore heavily on the Colonists. The rest of the story is merely the tale of political incapacity at home.

The American Colonists, in addition to a few fast sailing frigates which they handled with unexpected aptitude, possessed a so very considerable mercantile fleet, that it was estimated that 18,000 of their seamen had served in the English ships in the late war with France. Consequently, the Colonists were in a position to fit out privateers, and with these, in the first eight years of the war, they captured nearly 1,000 English merchant ships. Their own losses were, however, greater, and it is probable that despite all the military blunders which characterised English conduct of the war, the Colonists would eventually have been worn down but for the active intervention of France in 1778, and Spain a little later.

As regards naval operations against the Americans themselves, these were mainly in the nature of sea transport. Where they were otherwise, they were of an inglorious nature, owing to the total inability of the Home Government to appreciate the position. The naval story of the war is, in the main, the story of frigates attempting difficult channels, and going aground in the attempt. It is of interest mainly because in 1776 one David Bushnell made the first submarine ever actually used in war, and attempted to torpedo the English flag-ship, *Eagle* (64). He reached his quarry unsuspected, but the difficulties of attaching his "infernal machine" were such that he had to rise to the surface for air and abandon the enterprise. His subsequent fate was undramatic—he and his boat were captured at sea on

board a merchant ship, which was carrying him elsewhere for further operations.

France, which had been rendering considerable
secret assistance to the revolted Colonists, had, ever
since the Treaty of Paris, been steadily building up her
Navy, till she had eighty ships of the line and 67,000
men.   The efficiency of the *personnel* had been increased
by the enrolment of a special corps of gunners, who
practiced weekly.   Efforts—which, however, were only
moderately successful—had also been made to break
down the serious class rivalries between those officers
who were of the *noblesse* and those who were tarpaulin
seamen.   But the majority of officers were skilled
tactically, and special orders were issued that to seek
out and attack the enemy was an objective.* Here,
again, another weak point existed: d' Orvilliers, who
commanded the main fleet, also received orders to be
cautious—orders very similar in tenor to those by which
his predecessors in previous wars were hampered.

The fleet of Great Britain, spread over many quarters
of the world, including ships being fitted, consisted of
about 150 ships of the line besides auxiliaries ; but the
actual available force of Home water fleet with which
Keppel sailed just before the opening of the war, was
twenty ships only!

Capturing two French frigates and learning from
them that thirty-two ships were at Brest, Keppel got
reinforcements of ten ships, and on the 27th of July,
1778, met d'Orvilliers, also with thirty ships, off Ushant.
The battle lasted three hours, when the fleets drew
apart without any material result having been achieved.
The tactical ability lay with the French, and but for
the inefficiency of the leader of one French division, the
Duc de Chartres, (the future " Phillipe Egalité") would
have done so still more.   Yet, though Keppel had
obviously done his best, public opinion in England
had expected a great naval victory, and Keppel was

---

* This appears to be the solitary instance in French history in which a use of
the fleet on English lines was ever contemplated.

the subject of a most violent controversy, which soon developed on political lines.

At and about the time of the battle of Ushant, D'Estaing, with twelve ships of the line and five frigates, reached the Delaware. The English fleet under Howe, which consisted of only nine inferior ships of the line, took refuge inside Sandy Hook. D'Estaing came outside and remained ten days in July, but then sailed away.

His failure to operate has been put down to the advice of pilots, but more probably, as pointed out by Captain Mahan, he had secret instructions not to assist the Colonists too actively. The destruction of Hood's fleet would have meant the capture of New York, peace between England and America, and a considerable force released for operations against France. Most of the subsequent movements of the year seem to have been coloured by a similar policy. In 1779, the West Indian islands of St. Vincent and Grenada fell into the hands of the French. Subsequently D'Estaing returned to the North American Coast, but no important operations took place there. Finally he returned with some ships to France, sending the others to the West Indies.

Spain declared war against England in 1780. Her fleet then consisted of nearly sixty ships of the line, which—like the French—were in a more efficient state than in previous wars. Her prime object was the recovery of Gibraltar.

A combined Franco-Spanish fleet of sixty-four ships of the line appeared in the Channel, causing an immense panic in England. The only available English fleet consisted of thirty-seven sail of the line, under Sir Charles Hardy, and this wandered away to the westward, leaving the Channel quite open to the allies, who, however, also wandered about without accomplishing anything. As usual with allies, there were divided councils, and in addition the French fleet, having had to wait long for the unwilling Spaniards, was badly incapacitated from sickness. Thus, and thus only, is their failure to invade

to be explained: they had 40,000 men ready to be transported over, also a naval force ample to defeat any
available English fleet, and able to cover landing
operations as well.

When the war first began, there was in France an
English admiral—that same Rodney, who had destroyed
the invading flotilla at Havre in the previous war—who
by reason of his debts was unable to return to his own
country. In private life he was a merry old soul of
sixty or so, and at a dinner one night boasted that if he
could pay his debts and go back to England, he would
get a command and easily smash the French fleet.
Hearing this, a French nobleman promptly paid his
debts for him, and sarcastically told Rodney to go back
and prove his words.

Rodney, who had the reputation of being an able
officer, but nothing more, got home in 1779. In 1780,
having secured a command for the West Indies, he left
Portsmouth with twenty sail of the line and a convoy
for the relief of Gibraltar. Off Finisterre, he captured
a Spanish convoy carrying provisions to the besiegers.
Off Cape St. Vincent, he fell in with eleven Spanish ships
and attacked them at night, in a gale, blowing up one,
and capturing six. Thence he proceeded to Gibraltar,
relieved it from all immediate danger, Minorca also; and
then sailed for the West Indies. Here, on April 17th,
some three weeks after arrival, he met the French under
Guichen, and made the first attempt at that "breaking
the line" associated with his name. The attempt was
not a success, as his orders were misunderstood by several
of his own captains and his intentions realised and
foiled by his opponents.*

This action was indecisive ; as also were two more
that followed.

In this year (1780), Captain Horatio Nelson, then
only twenty-two years old, made his first appearance

---

* Captain Mahan (*Influences of Sea Power upon History*) has quoted at
length (p. 380) from French authorities to show that only the action of the
captain of the *Destin*, (74) in hurrying to block the gap, prevented Rodney from
getting through the line on this occasion.

in the *Hinchinbrook*, (28) in an attack on San Juan,
Nicaragua. He succeeded, after terrible loss of *personnel*
from disease.

A Spanish squadron then joined the French, but,
an epidemic—that most fruitful of all sources for the
upsetting of naval plans—overtook it. The Spaniards
were incapacitated and the French returned home.
Rodney went to New York, where his operations delayed
the cause of the Colonists; then returning to the West
Indies, operated against the Dutch, who had by now
joined the French and Spaniards.

The general position of Great Britain, in 1781 and
1782, was well nigh desperate. Gibraltar was only held
by a remarkable combination of luck and resolution.
To quote Mahan, "England stood everywhere on the
defensive." She fought with her back to the wall. In
the East Indies, Suffren kept the French flag flying: and
things were generally at a very low ebb, when in 1782
Rodney " broke the line " in the victory of the Battle of
the Saints.

On April 9th, the fleets had come into contact
without much result on either side. On the 12th, De
Grasse, being then in some disorder, with thirty-four
ships, encountered the English with thirty-six in good
order. Rodney and Hood broke the line in two places.
Admiral Mahan has been at pains to show us that this
result was much a matter of luck and change of wind,
and that the victory was by no means followed up as it
might have been. One French ship was sunk and five
were taken, including De Grasse himself, whose losses in
his flagship, the *Ville de Paris*, were greater than those
in the entire English fleet.

To the nation at this juncture, however, anything
savouring of victory was a thing to be made the utmost of,
and Rodney has probably received more than his meed
of merit over what was mainly a matter of luck.

Two features of special interest in connection with
this battle are that, though up to it, British ships had
recently, owing to coppering, proved better sailers than

the French; in the sequel to this fight, the French proved equal to sail away. The rapid deterioration of coppering, already mentioned, may account for some of this, but in this battle there is also reason to believe that the French fleet instituted firing at the rigging. Contemporary statements exist as to the French having made a wonderful number of holes in English hulls without much material result, but these may be dismissed as pardonable temporary bluster. More germane is the fact that the English ships were supplied with carronades*— harmless at long range and deadly at short—for which reason the French tried to keep them at a distance, so that altogether superior efficiency with men and weapons would seem to have played a greater part than any tactical genius on the part of Rodney, in whom a dogged insistence to get at the enemy was ever the main characteristic rather than any "thinking things out." The Mahan estimate of him sorts better with known facts than the estimate of his accomplishment at the time.

As regards Rodney himself, it is interesting to record that Navy and Party were so synonymous at the time, that he, being a strong Tory, had already been superseded by political influence when he won the battle that broke French power in the West Indies. It lies to the credit of the Whigs that both he and Hood, his second in command, received peerages; but the most difficult thing of all to understand to-day, is, that in a life and death struggle such as this war was, the personal political element should have managed to find expression.

In 1782, Gibraltar, which had been twice relieved, was once more in grievous straits. The French had evolved floating batteries for the attack, similar in principle to those which, some seventy years later, were to figure so prominently in the Crimea.

Being merely armoured with heavy wood planks, however, they were easily set on fire with red-hot shot,

---

* I draw this from Mahan (*Influence of Sea Power upon History*) (page 494). Fincham specifically mentions (p. 107) the introduction of carronades *ten* years later.

and the great bombardment failed long before the relieving force, under Howe, arrived. The garrison, however, were in great straits for supplies, and their real relief was Howe's fleet, which the combined Franco-Spanish squadrons did not dare to attack.

The Treaty of Versailles, in 1783, followed soon afterwards. By it the United States of America were recognised, Minorca was given up, but most of the captured West Indian islands restored to Great Britain.

Just before the close of the war, the relative naval strengths were assessed as follows :—*

Description of Vessels.	Great Britain.	France.	Spain.	Holland.
Ships of the Line ...	105	89	53	32
Fifty-gun Ships ...	13	7	3	0
Large Frigates ...	63	49	12	28
Small ditto	69	54	36	
Sloops	217	86	31	13
Cutters	43	22	0	0
Armed Ships	24	0	0	0
Bombs	7	5	14	0
Fire-Ships	9	7	11	6
Yachts	5	0	0	0
TOTAL ...	555	319	160	79

In this list it is interesting to note the British inability to maintain even a Two-Power Standard in ships of the line, whereas in sloops and such like, an enormous preponderance prevailed. For the suppression of privateering on the coastal trade, these small crafts proved very useful. Also worthy of note is the decline of the fire-ship as a naval arm.†

* Fincham *ex* Campbell.
† The fire-ship grew to be less and less of a menace owing to the improved handiness of warships.

The figures as a whole suggest with much clarity that had the Allies been able to act together, Great Britain would never have emerged from the war so well as she did.

The ten years' peace that followed was little more than a breathing space. War was constantly apprehended, and known improvement in French ships were such that they had to be carefully watched. The frigates built in England were made longer than before, with a view to keeping pace with French sailing qualities.

Considerable interest was taken in how far the country was self-supporting in the matter of timber for shipbuilding, a certain reliance on foreign supplies having previously existed. At, and about 1775, the cost of shipbuilding for the East India Company had exactly doubled in a few years. The home supply trouble arose, partly from the increased size of shipping, partly from the tendency of owners to fell trees as early as possible. Out of which special oak plantations were set up in the New Forest or elsewhere, though oak happened to cease to be of value for shipbuilding long before they had grown large enough for the larger timbers.

The question of repairs also came in for consideration, an average of twenty-five years' repair totalling the cost of a new ship. At and about this time also, the building of ships by contract in peace time was first recommended on the grounds that thus the private yards would be better available in case of war.

Regular stores for ships in the dockyards were also instituted, with a view to the speedy equipment of ships in reserve.* It was mainly owing to this last provision, introduced by Lord Barham in 1783, that, though when the war of the French Revolution broke out in 1793 but twelve ships of the line and thirty lesser vessels were in commission, a few months later seventy-one ships of the line and 104 smaller craft were in service. The number of men voted in 1793 was 45,000.

---

* Here again see Raleigh on Elizabethan Customs.

VI.

THE GREAT FRENCH WAR.

THE first incident of the war was connected with Toulon, which was partly Royalist and partly Republican. The story in full is to be found most dramatically rendered in *Ships and Men*, by David Hannay. Here it suffices to say that the Royalists and Moderates having coalesced at the eleventh hour, surrendered the town to Admiral Hood; that the British Government repudiated Hood's arrangements, and that eventually in December, 1793, he was compelled to evacuate the place after doing such damage as he could and bringing away with him a few ships of the French navy.* The incident little concerns our naval history, the Navy being but a pawn in the political game of the moment. Indeed, it is mostly of some naval interest only because two figures, destined to bulk largely in future history, loomed up in it—Captain Horatio Nelson, of the *Agamemnon*, who laughed when the Spanish fleet excused its inaction by saying that it had been six weeks at sea and was disabled accordingly; and Napoleon, who, as much as anyone, served to hurry the English out.

Early in 1794 the British fleet had ninety-five ships of the line in commission, besides 194 lesser vessels. The *personnel* amounted to 85,000.

The centre of interest was the French Brest fleet. Under Villaret-Joyeuse, a captain of the old Navy, made Admiral by the Terrorists, whose cause he had espoused,

* By the burning of the bulk of the ships in Toulon, the French Toulon fleet was rendered non-existent; but the state of affairs with that fleet was such that its fighting value had long been a cypher.

this fleet was by no means inefficient, like the undis-
ciplined Toulon fleet had been.   It carried on board
the flagship Jean Bon St. André, the deputy of the State,
who, whatever his faults, realised the meaning of
" efficiency."   The bulk of the crew were men who had
done well in America.   Howe, on the other hand,
commanded a somewhat raw fleet, hastily brought up to
strength and still by no means " shaken down."

Howe's orders were threefold—to convoy a British
merchant fleet ; to destroy the French fleet ; and to intercept a convoy of French grain coming from America.

From the 5th to the 28th May, Howe was keeping
an eye on Brest and looking for the French convoy, the
interception of which was more important than anything
else, as France was dependent on these grain ships for the
means to live.

On the 28th, the French fleet was sighted a long
way out in the Atlantic.   Villaret-Joyeuse, who was out
to protect the grain convoy at all costs, drew still
further out to sea, Howe following in pursuit.*   Towards
evening, the last French ship *Revolutionnaire* (100), was
come up with and engaged by six British (seventy-four's),
of which one, the *Audacious*, was badly crippled.   The
Revolutionnaire herself was dismasted, but was towed
away by a frigate in the night.

This particular incident   is one of the most
prominent examples of the power of the " monster " ship
as compared with the " moderate dimension " ship† of
the period.   The six did not attack her simultaneously,
and some were never closely engaged.   She was magni-
ficently fought also ; but even when these elements are
subtracted, the fact of the extraordinary resisting power
exhibited remains.   As only the *Audacious*, which
attacked last, did much harm to the Frenchman, the

* In order to bring the enemy to action, Howe formed a detached squadron
of his faster ships. Hannay (*Ships and Men*) extols him because, in this and certain
other movements in the battle, he reverted to the tactics of Monk and other
Commonwealth admirals, and threw aside the conventional practice of his own day.

† For two opposite views of this particular incident, see Admiral Mahan's
Influence of Sea Power on the French Revolution, and Chapter X., of
Brassey, 1894.

explanation in this particular case probably lies in the stouter scantlings required for a ship of 110 guns, compared to smaller ships.

On the following day the action was renewed. Villaret-Joyeuse allowed his tail ships to drop into range of the leading British vessels with a view to crippling them. Howe cut the line, but being somewhat out-manœuvred by the French admiral, obtained no special advantage therefrom. Some of the French ships were, however, disabled, and had to be towed in the general action that was to follow later.

Two days' fog now interrupted operations, but on Sunday, June 1st, battle was joined. The opposing fleets then consisted as follows :—

BRITISH.	FRENCH.
3 of 100 guns.	1 of 120 guns.
4 „ 98 „	2 „ 110 „
2 „ 80 „	4 „ 80 „
16 „ 74 „	19 „ 74 „
25	26

This gives 2,036 British to 2,066 French guns, but as, at least, one Frenchman was considerably disabled, there was probably a slight British superiority.

Howe, more or less, arranged his heavy ships to correspond with the heavy ships of the enemy, and having hove-to half-an-hour for breakfast, flung the old fighting instructions* to the winds and bore right down into the enemy. In the *melée* that ensued, some of the English failed to close, and seven of the French drifted to leeward out of action.

Of the French fleet, two eighty-gun and four seventy-four's were badly mauled and eventually struck, while a seventh French ship, the *Vengeur* (seventy-four) was sunk.† Four were badly disabled, but drifted to leeward out of the fight. On the British side a number of ships were badly damaged.

* The preservation of an orderly line throughout the battle.

† The story of this ship going down firing, her crew crying *Vive la Republique*, is a pure fiction. She surrendered after a very gallant fight, and sank with an English flag flying.

The fleets, having drawn apart, Villaret-Joyeuse
succeeded in getting a portion of his fleet into some sort
of order again, and threatened the disabled English ships.
Howe protected these, but did not renew action ; and
the French, with the disabled ships in tow, made off.

Such was the battle of " the glorious First of June."
Howe has been greatly blamed since then for not having
followed up his victory, but there are not wanting indications that the caution of Curtis, his captain of the fleet, who
pleaded with Howe not to re-engage lest the advantage
gained should be lost, was justified. Villaret-Joyeuse, the
captain, hastily placed in command of a large fleet, was
one of the most, if not the most, capable admirals France
ever had against us. How badly all the French ships had
suffered we now know, but the means of telling it were
absent then. The all-important question of intercepting
the grain convoy was also possibly present in Howe's mind.

Be that as it may, the convoy was not intercepted.
It reached France in safety, and all question of starving
the Revolution into surrender was at an end. On that
account the battle was reckoned as a victory by the
French as well as in England.*

Other naval events of this year (1794) were the capture
of Corsica, by Hood ; and in the West Indies, the capture
of Martinique and St. Lucia. Guadaloupe was also taken,
but quickly re-captured. Among the prizes of the year
was the French forty-gun frigate *Pomone,* which proved
infinitely faster than anything in the English fleet. This led
to much discussion in the House of Commons. A considerable party denied that any such superiority existed; others
alleged that even if so, British ships were better and more
strongly built. Others again attributed the circumstance
to the heavy premiums awarded by the French Government to constructors who produced swift sailing ships.

Nothing of much moment came out of the discussion.
Orders were issued that ships were to be built a little
longer in future, and with the lower deck ports less near

---

* Seeing that, had Howe sunk the grain convoy and then been totally destroyed
himself, the Revolution would still have come to nothing from starvation, this
French view of the matter is intelligible enough and also very reasonable.

the water than heretofore, but the general tendency to over-gun ships in relation to their size still remained.

For the year 1795, the *personnel* of the fleet was increased to 100,000, and provision was made for a very considerable increase of small craft. The Dutch declared war in January, but the year was not marked by any operations of much moment so far as they were concerned.

The principal theatres of naval operations were in the Mediterranean and the Channel. This year is marked by a curious indecisiveness, which had much to do with the formation of Nelson's (who was serving in the Mediterranean as captain of the *Agamemnon*, sixty-four), subsequent character as an admiral.

The British fleet consisted of fifteen ships of the line, under Hotham. The French had got together fifteen sail at Toulon. These made for Corsica, in March, and on the way captured one of Hotham's ships, the *Berwick*. With the remainder, Hotham put to sea, and on the 12th, off Genoa, he was sighted by the French. His fleet was in considerable disorder, and in the view of Professor Laughton, the incapacity of the French alone averted a disaster. In the desultory operations of the next two days, two prizes were taken and two English ships crippled. Nelson, who was mainly responsible for the prizes, urged Hotham to pursue and destroy the enemy, but the admiral refused.*

In July, Nelson, who was on detached service, was met and chased back to Genoa by the whole French fleet, which, however, drew off when Hotham's fleet was sighted. Hotham, with a greatly superior fleet came out, and eventually found the enemy off Hyeres. Chase was ordered and one French ship overhauled and captured; then, on the grounds that the shore was too near, Hotham hauled off.

These operations (or lack of them) on the part of Hotham, are important beyond most. In the view of

---

* It was in connection with this engagement that Nelson wrote, "Had I commanded our fleet on the 14th, either the whole of the French fleet would have graced my triumph, or I should have been in a confounded scrape." Also, commenting on Hotham's "We must be contented, we have done very well "— " Now, had we taken ten sail and allowed the eleventh to escape, when it had been possible to have got at her, I could never have called it well done."

Professor Laughton,* Hotham's indecision was mainly responsible for the rise and grandeur of Napoleon's career. Vigorous action on his part would have written differently the history of the world. As like as not, in addition to no Napoleon, there would also have been no Nelson, to go down as the leading figure in British naval history. The survival of the French fleet rendered possible that invasion of Italy which "made" Napoleon, and those sea battles which made Nelson our most famous admiral.

Villaret-Joyeuse (who had commanded the French fleet in the battle of the First of June) displayed considerable activity in 1795, capturing a frigate and a good many merchant ships. The weather, however, was against him, and he lost five ships of the line wrecked. He, notwithstanding, kept the sea with twelve ships of the line, and with these met Cornwallis with five, off Brest, on June 16th. Cornwallis retired, but was overhauled the next day, and his tail ship the *Mars*, (seventy-four) badly damaged, the French, as usual, firing at the rigging. Cornwallis, in the *Royal Sovereign*, (100) fell back to support the *Mars*, but was well on the way to be defeated when he adopted the clever ruse of sending away a frigate to signal to him that the Channel fleet was coming up. The code used was one known to have been captured by the French, and they, reading the signals, hastily abandoned the pursuit and made off.

Three days later, Villaret-Joyeuse did actually encounter the Channel fleet, under Hood (now Lord Bridport). He made off south, chased by Bridport, who had fourteen ships, mostly three-deckers, of which the French had but one. After a four days' chase, Bridport came up with the tail of the enemy, off Lorient. A partial action ensued, in which three French ships were captured, after which Bridport withdrew. He gave as his reason the nearness to the French shore—exactly the reason that Hotham gave for neglecting a possible victory. In both cases, the reason was rather trivial. The practical assign it to the old age of the admirals

* *Nelson*, by J. K. Laughton.

concerned. To the more imaginative, these two almost incomprehensible failures to take advantage of circumstances gave some colour to Napoleon's theory of "his destiny."

In this year, a number of East Indiamen were purchased for naval use. One of these, the *Glatton*, (fifty-six) was experimentally armed with sixty-eight pounder carronades on her lower deck, and forty-two pounders on the upper. On her way to join her squadron, she was attacked by six French frigates, of which one was a fifty-gun, and two were of thirty-six. She easily defeated the lot—another instance of the "big ship's" advantage in minor combats. Despite this instance of what might be done, the heavy gun idea made no headway, and the *Glatton* remained a unique curiosity, till many years later the Americans adopted it to our great disadvantage.

Towards the end of 1795 (December) Hotham was replaced in the Mediterranean by Sir John Jervis—an admiral of unique personality, who left upon the Navy a mark that easily endures to this day. Somewhat hyperbolically it has been said of him that he was the saviour of the Navy in his own day, and the main element towards its disruption in these times!

Jervis had made his mark in the War of American Independence, as captain of the *Foudroyant*. Discipline was his passion; and by means of it, he had made an easy capture of a French ship. Thereafter, he became a unique blend of martinet and genius.

He was the first openly to re-affirm Sir Walter Raleigh's theory, quoted in an earlier chapter, that fortifications were useless against invasion, and that only on the water could an enemy be met successfully, combatting Pitt himself on this point. When the Great War broke out, his first employment was in the West Indies, where he achieved St. Lucia, Martinique and Guadaloupe. He went to the Mediterranean, at a time when France was numerically superior to us in the Channel, and when Spain was daily expected to declare war.   The fleet to which he went was like all others, tending to a mutinous spirit, and finally he had to go out in the frigate *Lively*.   In those days, for an admiral to take passage in anything less than a ship of the line was considered a most undignified thing.   It rankled so with Jervis that he never forgot it, and years after harped upon it as a grievance.   Of such character was the man who took command in the Mediterranean at the end of 1795.

In 1796, the *personnel* of the Navy was increased to 110,000.   Jervis, in the Mediterranean, did little beyond blockading Toulon, and training his fleet on his own ideas.   Spain declared war in October; but her intentions being known beforehand, Corsica was evacuated, and at the end of the year the Mediterranean was abandoned also, Jervis with his entire fleet lying under the guns of Gibraltar.   Nothing else was possible.

Elsewhere invasion ideas were uppermost in France, and 18,000 troops, convoyed by seventeen ships of the line and thirteen frigates, sailed from Brest for Bantry Bay, at the end of the year.   Only eight ships of the line reached there; a gale dispersed the transports and nothing happened in the way of invasion.   The only other event of the year was the capture of a Dutch squadron at the Cape of Good Hope.   Matters generally were, however, so bad, that attempts were made to secure terms of peace from France.   These attempts failed.

The year 1792 saw 108 ships of the line and 293 lesser vessels in commission.   Something like sixty ships of the line were building or ordered, also 168 lesser craft. The first incident was the Battle of Cape St. Vincent (14th February, 1797).   The Spaniards, having come out of Cartagena, were making for Cadiz, when sighted by Jervis. The rival fleets were :—

BRITISH.	SPANISH.
2 of 100 guns.	1 of 130 guns.
3 ,, 98 ,,	6 ,, 112 ,,
1 ,, 90 ,,	2 ,, 80 ,,
8 ,, 74 ,,	18 ,, 74 . ,,
1 ,, 64 ,,	27 ⌐
15	

The battle is mainly of interest on account of Nelson's part in it. The Spaniards were sailing in no order whatever, the bulk of them being in one irregular mass, the remainder in another. Jervis, in line ahead, proposed to pass between the two divisions, and destroy the larger before the smaller could beat up to assist them. The Spaniards, however inefficient they may have been in other ways, saw through this manœuvre, and their main body was preparing to join up astern of the British, when Nelson, in the *Captain*, flung himself across them and captured two ships by falling foul of them and boarding. Three other ships were captured, the rest escaped. In this battle, as in those of the year before, the same caution about following up the victory was observed, and the age of the admiral concerned has again been produced as the reason. But the thoughtful —taking the previous career of most of those concerned into consideration—may suspect the existence of some special secret orders about taking no risks, as yet unearthed by any historian. The only really workable alternative is Napoleon's " destiny" theory already alluded to. Of the two, the secret order hypothesis is the more practical. Into the whole of these victories not properly followed up, it is also possible, though hardly probable, that the mutinous state of the *personnel* entered.

In the battle of Cape St. Vincent, the Spaniards had an enormous four-decker, the *Santissima Trinidad*, of 130 guns. She was the first ship engaged by Nelson, and was hammered by most of the others closely engaged as well, but her size and power saved her from the fate of the rest of the ships that were with her.

It is difficult even now to assess the exact situation of the mutineers of 1797. The organised self-restraint of the Spithead Mutiny is hard to understand, when we remember the heterogeneous origin of the crews. " Jail or Navy" was an every-day offer to prisoners. Longshoremen, riff-raff, pressed landsmen, thieves, murderers, smugglers, and a few degraded officers, were the raw material whence the crews were composed. They were

stiffened with a proportion of professional seamen, and
it is these that must have leavened the mass, and kept
the jail-bird element in check.

Pay was bad, ship life close akin to prison life,
discipline and punishments alike—brutal, and the food
disgracefully bad. It was this last that brought about
the mutiny. There is an old saying to the effect that
you may ill-treat a sailor as you will, but if you ill-feed
him, trouble may be looked for! One or two isolated
mutinies, like that of the *Hermione*, were due to a
captain's brutality; but mainly and mostly bad food
and mutiny were closely linked.

Commander Robinson* draws attention to the fact
that the pursers themselves were hardly the unscrupulous
rascals they were supposed to be on shore, and that the
system and regulations of victualling were recognised by
the seamen as at the bottom of the mischief.

The same authority quotes a contemporary :—

> "The reason unto you I now will relate :
> We resolved to refuse the purser's short weight ;
> Our humble petition to Lord Howe we sent,
> That he to the Admiralty write to present
> Our provisions and wages that they might augment."

Discontent had, of course, long been brewing, but
the Admiralty seems to have been without any suspicions.
They dismissed the petition as being in no way represen-
tative : later, having received reports to the contrary,
ordered Lord Bridport's fleet at Spithead, to proceed to
sea. On April 15th, when the signal to weigh anchor
was made, the crews of every ship manned the rigging
and cheered. No violence was offered to any officer ;
the men simply refused to work. Each ship supplied a
couple of delegates to explain matters, and after an
enquiry, their demands were granted and a free pardon
given. Delays, however, ensued, and on May 7th, the
fleet again refused to put to sea.

On this occasion, the officers were disarmed, confined
to their cabins, and kept there, till a few days later a

* The British Tar in *Fact and Fiction*.

general pardon was proclaimed, when this mutiny ended. A similar mutiny at Plymouth was equally mild.

Of a very different character was the mutiny at the Nore, which broke out on May 13th, under the leadership of the notorious Richard Parker. Parker was a man of considerable parts, said to have been an ex-officer dismissed the service with disgrace, and to have entered as a seaman. He possessed undoubted ability and considerable ambition. He very clearly aimed at something more than the redress of grievances, since his first act was to put a rope round his own neck by instigating the crew of the *Inflexible* to fire into a sister ship, on board which a court-martial was being held. Subsequently, delegates were sent to the Admiralty with extravagant claims, which—as Parker may have anticipated—were ignored.

Eleven ships of Admiral Duncan's fleet (then blockading the Texel) had joined Parker by the first of June. Duncan was left with but two ships in face of the enemy. By showing himself much and making imaginary signals Duncan managed to conceal the facts from the Dutch : but he had considerable trouble to keep his two ships from joining the mutineers now blockading the Thames.

There is reason to believe that Parker was in touch with the Revolutionists in France and the dissatisfied Irish, but the bulk of the mutineers were altogether uninfluenced by political ideas. The mutiny began to waver. The ships at other home ports were unsympathetic, and Parker and his friends found men cooling off. In order to keep things together it was their custom to row round the fleet* and inspect ships suspected of being "cool,"—the side being piped for them. In one case, however, the boatswain's mate refused to do so, and flung his call at their heads. On coming on board, they sentenced him to thirty-six lashes for "mutinous conduct!" On June 10th, despite this disciplinary system, two of the mutineer ships sailed away under fire

* The title of " delegates " seems quaintly enough to have led Parker and his friends into trouble. The men got hold of the word as " *delicates,*" and interpreted it more or less literally as a claim to superiority.

from the others, and on the 14th, Parker's own ship surrendered and handed him over to the authorities. He was hanged on June 29th.

In the Mediterranean fleet, mutiny broke out in two ships off Cadiz, but Jervis (now Earl St. Vincent), compelled the mutineers to hang their own ringleaders. In connection with this, Nelson, who was now rear admiral commanding the inshore squadron, wrote to St. Vincent :—

"I congratulate you on the finish, as it ought, of the St. George's business, and I (if I may be permitted to say so) very much approve of its being so speedily carried into execution, even although it is Sunday. The particular situation of the service requires extraordinary measures. I hope this will end all the disorders in our fleet : had there been the same determined spirit at home, I do not believe it would have been half so bad."

It is noteworthy that in Nelson's own ship there was no trouble whatever. The ship had had a reputation for insubordination, but shortly after Nelson joined her, a paper intimating that no mutiny need be feared was dropped on the quarter-deck. Nelson brought with him a reputation for taking a personal interest in his men. Then, as now, hard work and a dog's life were not objected to, provided the personal equation were present.

St. Vincent proceeded to stamp out the embers of mutiny in his own fashion. He set himself to invest his rank with every circumstance of pomp, awe and ceremony. Every morning he appeared on the quarter deck in full dress uniform, paraded the Marines, and had "God save the King" played with all hats off. His regulations were catholic enough to embrace lieutenants' shoe-laces. In all the pomp that he created the mutinous spirit was smothered.

To him is due the vast abyss between the quarter-deck and lower-deck which marks the Navy of to-day. Whether this, advantageous as it was a hundred odd years ago, is equally advantageous now, is another matter. It makes a barrier altogether different from that existing between officer and man in the Army—it is something closely akin to the racial differences mark in India ; and this sorts ill with the democratic ideas of to-day, when class distinction is quite a different matter from what it was a hundred years ago.

There are still possible two views of the question. One is embodied in a letter I received some few years ago from a man from the lower-deck. He wrote, "When I was a boy in a training ship, my captain seemed to me something as far away and above me as God himself, and the impression thus created I have carried with me towards all officers ever since. Though in private life I might meet his brother with feeling of perfect equality, I could never be other than ill at ease meeting an officer in the same conditions."

Here, at any rate, is the psychology of what St. Vincent aimed at. To-day, however, one is far more likely to hear about " the side of officers," or that "officers, when cadets, are taught to regard the men with contempt !" The conditions are such, that despite mixed cricket and football teams, mutual sympathy between officers and men is well nigh impossible.

Of "the great God Routine" which St. Vincent set up, it is beyond question that it is to-day an irritating superfluity to both officers and men alike.

To resume. As the Spaniards obstinately refused to come out from Cadiz, St. Vincent sent Nelson in to bombard them with mortar boats; but this attempt to force them out did not succeed. Following upon this, Nelson, with three seventy-four's, one fifty, three frigates and a cutter, was despatched to Santa Cruz. On the night of July 24th, he led a boat attack in person. Most of the boats missed the Mole and were stove in. Such as reached the Mole, were met by a withering fire. Nelson was struck on the right elbow by a grape shot, and taken back to the *Theseus*, where his arm was amputated. Troubridge took command of the 300 odd men who had got ashore, and being surrounded by the Spanish, made terms, whereby the Spaniards found boats for his party to return to their ships. The squadron rejoined St. Vincent, and Nelson sailed for England to recover.

The blockade of the Texel had been vigorously maintained till October, when Duncan returned to Spithead to refit.   He had no sooner done so than the Dutch, under De Winter, came out—presumably with a view to reaching Brest.   Duncan's frigates, however, promptly reported them, and sailing at once he met them off Camperdown, on October 11th.

The rival fleets were:—

BRITISH.	DUTCH.
7 of 74 guns.	4 of 74 guns.
7 „ 64 „	7 „ 64 „
2 „ 50 „	4 „ 50 „
16	15

Duncan's original plan was the old fashioned ship-to-ship system, but in the actual event, the Dutch line was broken.   One of the Dutch fifty-gun ships fell back to avoid the *Lancaster* (sixty-four), five others for some reason or other following her; the remaining nine fought desperately, till further resistance was impossible.

The prizes were:—two seventy-four's, five sixty-four's, two fifties, and a couple of frigates.   Both the captured fifties were lost; the other ships were with great difficulty got to England.   All were found to have been damaged beyond repair, and some of Duncan's ships were in little better condition.   His losses in *personnel* were over 1,000 in killed and wounded.   His crews, it is interesting to note, consisted mostly of Parker's erstwhile mutineers.

During 1797, a few frigates only were lost.   These included the *Hermione*, whose crew mutinied and handed her over to the enemy.   The brutality of her captain, Pigot, whose idea of efficiency was to flog the last two men down from aloft, was the cause of this particular outbreak.*

In 1797, a large ninety-eight gun ship, the *Neptune*, was added to the Navy, also a seventy-four and a sixty-four.   Private yards launched no less than forty-six

* For a very interesting detailed account, see *Ships and Men*, by David Hannay.

frigates and smaller craft, and the total number of war-ships built, building and projected, was 696.*

For the year 1798, the *personnel* voted was 100,000 seamen and 20,000 marines; and the total Naval Estimates amounted to £13,449,388.

In France, Buonaparte was forging to the front, and he threw himself into those schemes for the invasion of England which so appealed to the French mind and so terrified the British public. Ireland was selected as the most suitable spot, and two expeditions were prepared, one at Rochefort, the other at Brest. Of these, one, the Rochefort expedition, materialised in August, reached Killala Bay, in Ireland, and soon afterwards had to surrender to the English Army. The Brest expedition, escorted by a line of battle ship and a number of frigates, was more or less annihilated by Admiral Warren, on October 12th.

As already stated, the Mediterranean had become a species of Franco-Spanish lake. St. Vincent was outside Gibraltar, and he was still there when Nelson, in the *Vanguard*, arrived to join him as rear-admiral, at the end of April.

Nelson, with a small squadron, was at once despatched to discover what the French were doing at Toulon. Rumours of all kinds were current. He found fifteen ships of the line and a great many transports, news of which he sent to the Admiral. On the top of this came a gale, which dismasted the *Vanguard*. She was, however, towed into San Pietro, Sardinia, and hastily re-fitted, and four days later the ships were off Toulon again, only to find that the French had sailed.

Reinforced by ten sail of the line, under Troubridge, Nelson now sailed in search of the French fleet. Reaching Alexandria and finding nothing known there of the French, he worked back to Syracuse, where he re-victualled in cheerful disregard of the neutrality remonstrances of the Governor. Thence he returned eastward, and having received information of where the French had last been

* Fincham.

seen, eventually found them anchored in Aboukir Bay, where he attacked them on the evening of August 1st, 1798.

The rival fleets were:—

BRITISH.	FRENCH.
13 of 74 guns.	1 of 120 guns.
1 ,, 50 ,,	9 ,, 74 ,,
14	10, also 4 Frigates.

The French, under Brueys, were drawn across the Bay in a "defensive position." They were in no way a very efficient force, some of the ships being old and short of guns, all of them rather short-handed, and even so, manned with many new-raised raw men. On the other hand, they were so sure of the safety of their position that their inshore guns were not cleared for action. By all the naval theory of the day this idea of impregnability was justified.

The battle itself was simple enough. Nelson came down with the wind on the French van, approximately putting two of his ships one on either side of each of the Frenchmen, and so on, the rear being unable to beat up to support them. The result was the practical annihilation of the French fleet. Of the thirteen ships of the line, only two escaped in company with two frigates.

So complete a naval victory had never before been known. In all the battles of the previous two or three hundred years, the percentage of losses to the vanquished had been small. The battle of the Nile, therefore, received an attention perhaps beyond its intrinsic worth. As Nelson wrote to Howe:—"By attacking the enemy's van and centre, the wind blowing directly along their line, I was enabled to throw what force I pleased on a few ships." The real point of interest is not the result, which was foregone, but Nelson's ability to see his opportunity and to make the utmost of it. Therein lay his superlative greatness.

Of the prizes, three were found to be new and good ships. One of them, the *Franklin*, was renamed *Canopus*, and as late as 1850 was still on the effective list of the British Navy.

The defeat of the French at the Nile had far reaching effects. Russia, Austria, Turkey, Naples and Portugal formed with England a great anti-French Alliance. A large Russian fleet appeared in the Mediterranean, but accomplished no services there. It was under suspicion of having private designs on Malta rather than of assisting the Alliance.

From 1762 onward, when Catherine the Great came to the Throne of Russia, an enormous number of retired or unemployed English officers took service in the Russian Navy. To one of these, Captain Elphinstone, (who subsequently re-entered the British service) has been traced the origin of the idea upon which Nelson acted in the battle of the Nile. To another, General Bentham, originally a shipwright, who returned to the British service in 1795, was due a revolution in dockyard management. To him was due the introduction of machinery into dockyards : a matter needing much diplomacy and caution, as popular feeling against machinery then ran high. However, by 1798, Bentham had steam engines installed in the dockyards. He also commenced the first caisson known in England, using it for the great basin at Portsmouth Yard. In the face of considerable opposition he also introduced deep docks, basins and jetties at Portsmouth, for the speedy fitting out of ships.

In 1799, the *personnel* was settled at 120,000, and the Naval Estimates were £13,654,000.

In April of this year, the French, under Bruix, with twenty-five ships of the line, came out of Brest, which was being cruised off by Bridport with sixteen sail. Having warned Keith, who was blockading Cadiz, and St. Vincent, who lay at Gibraltar, Bridport fell back on Bantry Bay, where he was reinforced with ten ships.

Bruix ran down south, his orders being to join the Spaniards in Cadiz, but the weather was unfavourable and his crews so illtrained* that he made no attempt to attack

* Troude.

Keith's squadron, but ran on into the Mediterranean. Keith himself joined St. Vincent at Gibraltar.

On May 11th, St. Vincent arrived at Minorca with twenty sail. Nelson, with sixteen ships (of which four were Portuguese) was scattered over the Mediterranean, his base being at Palermo. On the 13th, Bruix reached Toulon, and a week later seventeen Spaniards from Cadiz reached Cartagena.

To prevent these joining up with Bruix, St. Vincent lay between the two bases : but the risk that either fleet might suddenly fall on Nelson was such, that he sent four of his ships to him. He was, however, presently reinforced with five ships, bringing his net total to twenty-one.

St. Vincent's health having now given out, he handed the fleet over to Lord Keith, who learned that Bruix, with twenty-two sail, had left Toulon on the 27th May; but for some reason or other made for that place. Bruix reached the Spaniards at Cartagena, without interference, on June 23rd, and so had thirty-nine ships to oppose to the British twenty-one. These, falling back upon Minorca, were there reinforced by ten ships from home, thus bringing the total up to thirty-one.

Meanwhile, Bruix putting to sea again at once, made for Cadiz, which he reached on July 12th, and leaving again on the 21st, made for Brest; Keith, some two weeks behind him, in pursuit.

The net result of Bruix's cruise was that the French fleet at Brest rose to the enormous total of ninety warships, collected to cover an invasion of England. As, however, Napoleon, who was to command, did not reach France until October, nothing was done in 1799, thus allowing ample time for the concentration of English ships. Had the Brest Armada struck at once, matters for England had been none too rosy, since the only force guarding the Channel was Bridport's fleet of twenty-six sail, at Bantry.

August saw 20,000 Russians landed at the Helder from British transports. These captured the Texel fortifications, inside of which lay what was left of the

Dutch fleet. The Dutch admiral declined to surrender, but his crews refused to fight, and eventually the ships were handed over without firing a shot. The ships were found to be antiquated in design and badly built, and were never of any use to the English Navy.

In the latter part of this year, two Spanish frigates were captured by four English. These ships were bringing home the year's South American treasure. The prize money divided among the four captains amounted to £160,000.

Twenty-one vessels were lost during the year. Only three of them, however, were lost by capture, and of these the largest was a ten-gun brig!

The prizes of the year consisted of eight French frigates, five Spanish frigates and twenty-four Dutch ships. In this year also the very fast French privateer, *Bordelais*, was taken, being chased and overhauled by the *Revolutionnaire*, an ex-French frigate, and the only frigate in the Navy at this time able to catch up with French ones.

The *personnel* granted for the year 1800, was 110,000, with an additional 10,000 for March and April only. The ships in commission were 100 ships of the line, seventeen small two-deckers and 351 frigates and lesser craft.

No naval fighting of much importance took place, but the year was otherwise very momentous. Napoleon, who had made himself First Consul, was busy re-organising the French Navy, and one of his first acts was to offer terms of peace. These, however, were refused by the British Government.

On July 25th, the Danish frigate, *Freya*, out with a convoy, was met by some British ships. She refused to allow "the right of search." Firing followed, and the *Freya* was captured. An embassy, to explain matters to the Danes, went, accompanied by a fleet of nine ships of the line, five frigates and four bombs, under Admiral Dickson.

This action—the intentions of which were obvious—

aroused the resentment of the Russian Emperor Paul. Nelson's suspicion that the Russians wished to capture Malta for themselves, have already been alluded to. These intentions came to light now; for Paul, having got himself declared Grand Master of the Knights of St. John of Malta, seized some 300 British merchant ships in Russian ports, and said that he would not let them go till Malta (which was then besieged and about to fall to the British) was given up to him.

The British Government ignored the Malta claim, and many of the British merchant ships equally ignored the Russian orders about remaining in harbour. Quite a number sailed away; the rest, however, were seized and burned, by Paul's orders. To reinforce himself against very probable reprisals, Paul—presumably influenced by Napoleon—formed the "Armed Neutrality." Russia and Sweden signed on December 16th, and on the 19th, Denmark and Prussia.

Meanwhile Malta, which had been blockaded and besieged by the British ever since the battle of the Nile, was in grievous straits. In February, 1800, the *Genereux*, seventy-four, (one of the two ships of the line which escaped from the Nile) left Toulon, with some frigates, intent on relief. She was, however, intercepted and captured by Nelson.

In March, the *Guillaume Tell*, the other survivor of the Nile, which had been lying at Malta, attempted on the night of the 30th to run the blockade to procure help. In doing so, she encountered the British frigate *Penelope*, which chased her, attacking her rigging. The firing brought up two ships of the line, *Foudroyant* and *Lion*, but the Frenchman made such a defence that both these were disabled before she was reduced to submission, and it was to the *Penelope* frigate that she ultimately struck. This particular fight is generally reckoned as the finest defence ever made by a French ship.

Malta was eventually starved into surrender, and the final capitulation took place on the 5th September, 1800, after a siege of practically two years.

The capture of Malta was perhaps one of the finest exhibitions of "Admiralty" in the whole war. No waste of life in assaults took place : the fortress was systematically starved into surrender by the judicious use of Sea Power to prevent any relief.

In this year (1800), several ships were lost, the principal being the *Queen Charlotte* (100), which was accidentally burned and blown up off Capraja, on the 17th of March. The majority of her crew perished with her. Eighteen other ships were wrecked, while two (a twenty gun and a fourteen) mutinied and joined the enemy. These were the only British ships that actually changed hands. Captures amounted to fourteen ships of from eighty to twenty-eight guns, and a large number of privateers and small craft.

The year 1801 saw the Estimates at £16,577,000. The *personnel* voted was 120,000 for the first quarter of the year, after which it was to rise to 135,000, with a view to dealing with the Armed Neutrality. The number of ships in commission was substantially the same as in the previous year.

The avowed objects of the Armed Neutrality were to resist "the right of search," to secure any property under a neutral flag, that a blockade to be binding must be maintained by an adequate force, and that contraband of war must be clearly defined beforehand. In substance, they amounted to the free importation into France of those naval stores of which she stood most in need. Wisely enough the British Government decided to break up the coalition by diplomacy, if possible, and failing that, by force. Incidentally, it may be noted that the Tsar, who was at the head of the coalition, was more or less a madman, in possession of a very considerable fleet.

In March, 1801, a fleet of twenty ships of the line and a large number of auxiliaries, under Sir Hyde Parker, with Nelson as second in command, sailed for the Baltic. On arrival at Copenhagen, the Danes were found to be moored in a strong position under cover of shore batteries. The attack was confided to Nelson with

H

twelve ships, which fared badly enough for Parker after the battle had lasted three hours to make a signal to withdraw.*   Nelson, however, disregarded this, and continued till the Danish fire began to slacken an hour later.   But as the Danes continually reinforced their disabled ships from the shore, and fired into those which had surrendered, the slaughter promised to go on indefinitely.   Things being thus, Nelson, under a flag of truce, threatened to set fire to the damaged ships and leave their crews to their fate unless firing ceased.   It has been alleged that this was a clever piece of bluff in order to extricate his ships from an awkward position : but all the evidence goes to show that he was fully in a position to carry out his threat, while as he made no attempt to move during the negotiations the bluff story is absurd.   It appears to have been an act of humanity, pure and simple.

Ultimately, the bulk of the Danish fleet was surrendered, and a fourteen weeks' armistice arranged, Nelson explaining that he required this amount of time to destroy the Russian fleet !

Subsequently the Swedish fleet was dealt with, but it took refuge under fortifications.   About the same time news came that the mad Tsar had been assassinated, and that his successor had no wish to continue hostilities.

Nelson (now Commander-in-Chief) appeared off Kronstadt, under the guns of which the Russians had taken shelter in May.   Negotiations followed,† and ultimately Russia was granted the right to trade with belligerents—probably a diplomatic concession in order to detach her sympathy from France.

In the meantime, Napoleon's invasion schemes were shaping.   To this day it is unknown whether he was serious or not at this, or for that matter, any other

---

* He, at the same time, sent a private message to Nelson that if he wished to continue, he was at liberty to do so.   The telescope to his blind eye was merely a little jest on Nelson's part, and in no way disobedience of orders.   Parker's whole object in making the signal to withdraw was to intimate to Nelson that if he deemed himself defeated, he (Parker) would accept responsibility.

† Paul had just been murdered, and Alexander changed his policy.

period. That he intended his preparations to be taken seriously (as they were by all save Nelson) is clear enough. It is further clear from his vast preparations that he would have used his flotilla had the chance occurred; but the mere fact that he never attempted actual invasion is of itself sufficient answer to all the homilies that have been written about Napoleon's inability to understand "Sea Power."

The army at Boulogne, the flat-bottomed boats, all served to keep England in a panic, and that was worth much. He had experience to guide him. Past experience was an English attack on the flotilla like that of Rodney many years before. In August, 1801, such an attack came, Nelson directing it. It was found fully prepared for and defeated with ease.

In the Mediterranean, Ganteaume, who had left Brest with seven ships of the line convoying 5,000 troops, reached Alexandria, but before he could disembark his soldiers, Keith appeared, and he hurried back to Toulon.

Linois left Toulon with a small squadron, and was driven into Algeciras, where he beat off Samaurez and a considerably more powerful squadron. Retreating from this, Samaurez fell in with a Spanish squadron, the ships of which, in the confusion of a night action, attacked each other, with the result that the two best ships were destroyed.

In October, 1801, the preliminaries of the Peace of Amiens were signed and hostilities ceased.

The total losses to the enemy in the war are given as follows by Campbell:—

	FRENCH.	DUTCH.	SPANISH.	TOTAL.
Ships of the line.	45	25	11	81
Fifties	2	1	0	3
Frigates	133	31	20	184
Sloops, etc.	161	32	55	248
			TOTAL ...	516

The corresponding British loss was only twenty-one ships of *all classes*, and of these only two ships of the line were captured. The bulk of British losses was accounted for by wrecks.

VII.

FROM THE PEACE OF AMIENS TO THE FINAL FALL OF NAPOLEON.

WITH the Peace of Amiens the usual reduction of the Navy took place. The 104 ships of the line in commission the year before sank to but thirty-two in 1802. The *personnel* fell to 50,000.

It may here be remarked that of the ships put out of commission a great number were unfit for further service; 111 ships of various classes being in so bad a way that they were sold or broken up. Many others were cut down to serve in inferior rates.

Early in 1803 it became abundantly clear that Napoleon was preparing for a new war, and in May, war was declared on him by the British Government. It is of interest to note that Napoleon, in dismissing the British Ambassador, said to him that he "intended to invade England," adding that he considered it might be "a very risky undertaking." At the time war was declared Napoleon was not quite ready, and never regained the ground thus lost.

Little or nothing happened to show that a great naval struggle was in progress. The French ships lay secure in harbour; the British tossed outside in ceaseless blockade work. But these months of seeming inaction settled the fate of France. The French crews, never very efficient, grew less and less so in harbour, while every day outside, hardened the British and added to their efficiency. Seeing that the British *personnel*, which was but 50,000 at the early part of the year, was suddenly expanded to 100,000 in June, the advantages

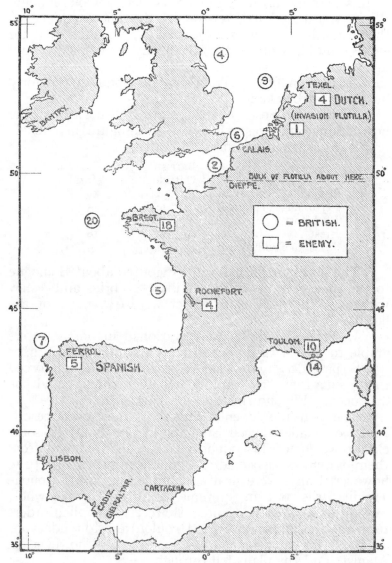

POSITIONS OF THE SHIPS OF THE LINE AT THE OUTBREAK OF WAR
(See next page.)

of this shaking down of raw crews were obvious enough. When eventually battle was joined, the difference between the English and French *personnel* was such that for every round got off by the latter, any British ship could fire *three*! Victory was won long before a single battle shot had been fired. Trafalgar was made a certainty by the great blockades.

When war broke out the general disposition of the hostile squadrons was as follows :—(the figures in brackets representing frigates and small craft)—

	BRITISH. Outside.		FRENCH. Inside.	
Toulon	14	(32)	10	(6)
Ferrol	7	(4)	5	(2)
Rochefort	5	(2)	4	(7)
Brest	20	(11)	18	(7)
Texel to Dunkirk	9	(21)	5	(11)

The invasion flotilla was distributed about Boulogne to the tune of 1,450 of the flotilla, 120 brigs and a few frigates. In the Texel district were 645 more of the flotilla.

Reserve squadrons were stationed in home waters ample to deal with the small craft defending flotillas.

So passed away the year 1803. Both sides reinforced their squadrons as rapidly as new ships could be produced. Beyond this nothing happened.

The year 1804 opened with the same lack of result. Napoleon made himself Emperor in May, and to some extent weakened his squadrons by the removal from them of officers suspected of Republican views. In July, however, things were nearing completion, and Latouche Treville was put in supreme command of the whole expedition against England. He received explicit orders to evade Nelson (who watched Toulon) and to rendezvous at Brest for invasion purposes. He died, however, in August* and the plans fell through.

After some delay, Villeneuve was appointed in his place; but instead of the invasion idea there came plans

* Compare with the similar delay of the Spanish Armada.

of oversea enterprises, possibly designed with a view to drawing all British forces of the moment away from the Channel, thus leaving things clear for an invasion. But again there comes the doubt whether Napoleon ever expected this to succeed, whether he really thought of much else than keeping England perturbed and busy while he matured plans for other parts of Europe, and whether he did not realise that "Sea Power" had its limitations as well as its advantages, and never really sought anything further than to cause Britain to spend so much in naval defence, that she had little left to subsidise his Continental foes with.   Better than most men he was able to estimate Nelson's limitations.   He clearly estimated fully enough that Nelson was no particularly brilliant strategist, and that he was more likely to forecast correctly what Nelson would do, than was Nelson to divine his purpose.   He under-estimated indeed what Nelson really did mean,—the particular genius which made Nelson invincible as a leader of men, how Nelson was a tactician able to gauge exactly the competence of the enemy and to win victory by doing seemingly foolish things accordingly.

At least, it would appear that there Napoleon erred. But there is no judging Napoleon—the strangest mixture of genius and charlatan that the world has ever seen or is ever likely to.   It is even unsafe to say that Napoleon did not foresee Trafalgar; unsafe to believe that in his view, French fleets had no purpose other than to keep the English occupied.   Napoleon is ever the one man in history that no one can ever surely know, whether we take him as the biggest liar who ever lived, or as the greatest genius the world has ever known.

In January, 1804, the British Fleet in commission consisted of seventy-five ships of the line, with forty others in reserve ; 281 lesser craft were in commission and a few in reserve.

The intentions of Spain had long been mistrusted in England.   As a precaution, the Spanish treasure fleet was attacked without warning, and over a million pounds' worth of booty secured. Spain, thereupon, made her intentions clear, and declared war. A few lesser ships changed hands during the year; but even the minor happenings were of small account.

In the year 1805, the number of British ships built, building and ordered, stood at 181 ships of the line, and 532 lesser vessels besides troop-ships, store-ships and harbour vessels. The *personnel* was 120,000 and the Naval Estimates £15,035,630.

Napoleon's "Army of Invasion" now amounted to a nominal 150,000 men* in the Boulogne district alone, men all trained in embarking and disembarking. The famous "Let me be master of the Channel but for six hours" had been uttered.† If ever invasion were seriously contemplated it was so in this year 1805.

There followed those well-known operations—the "drawing away of Nelson," of which so much has been written.

In substance, Napoleon quite understood the situation so far as Nelson was concerned. He understood that Nelson's fleet did not watch Toulon closely. He understood that if Villeneuve came out from Toulon when Nelson was not close by, Nelson would blindly seek him, probably in the wrong direction.

In this, and up to a certain point beyond, Napoleon was entirely correct. But he made one error. He regarded Nelson as a fool. In estimating Nelson to be easily outwitted he was not perhaps far wrong; but beyond that, he failed to understand the man with whom he had to deal.

It was these qualities of Nelson that rendered any invasion hopeless. Nelson had seen enough to know that the fighting value of the enemy was small, and that for him to attack at all costs and all hazards meant no hazard to the result. With one single idea, to find the

---

* Actually never exceeded 93,000.—*Campaign of Trafalgar.*—Corbett.
† Six was sometimes twelve, sometimes longer periods still. The most reasonable explanation is that Napoleon's *real* intentions were to use the army to invade England, if luck and chance threw the opportunity in his way; but otherwise to use it only as a threat.

enemy and destroy him, he was just the one enemy for whom Napoleon's genius had no answering move.

Villeneuve got out of Toulon on January 20th. He cruised about, Nelson cruising elsewhere looking for him. Eventually, Villeneuve, damaged by a gale, returned to Toulon, whence he presently emerged again on March 29th, and sailed for the West Indies. Ten days after he had done so, Nelson learned that the French had passed Gibraltar on April 8th; but delayed by contrary winds and lack of information, the British fleet was a long way behind. As for Villeneuve, he picked up six Spaniards at Cadiz, and went to the West Indies with seventeen ships of the line. Nelson followed far behind with ten. He pressed on so hard, however, that he reached Barbadoes on June 4th, the same day that Villeneuve, not so very far away, left Martinique, where he had been lying.

Therefrom, Nelson sailed south to Trinidad, off which he arrived at the same time as Villeneuve, sailing north, came off Antigua.

On June 11th, Villeneuve (whose crews were already sick) set out to return to Europe. Two days later, Nelson, who had gone north again, followed suit.

These hole and corner movements, impossible to-day, are not of much interest, save in so far as they indicate the certainty of information in these days and the uncertainty in those.

The "decoyed away fleet" idea has nothing in it, because in any such scheme Villeneuve could surely either have doubled back when half-way, or in any case would not have remained in the West Indies.

Nelson sent ahead fast frigates, with information that Villeneuve was returning; consequently arrangements for his reception were made. Off Finisterre, Villeneuve encountered Calder, and an indecisive action resulted. Two Spanish ships were captured. The following day, Villeneuve attempted to attack, but wind and weather prevented. On the third day the wind shifted, but Calder failed to attack. For this he was subsequently court-martialled and severely reprimanded.

Nelson, meanwhile, touched Gibraltar,* then proceeded north to join Cornwallis off Brest, and thence to England in his flagship *Victory*. Villeneuve, having picked up a few more ships at Ferrol, making his total force twenty-nine sail, put into Cadiz,† off which Collingwood maintained a weary blockade of him.

Early in September, news reached England that Villeneuve was at Cadiz, and Nelson left Southsea Beach on September 14th, sailing next day.

Collingwood, off Cadiz, had been reinforced up to twenty-four sail. A martinet officer of the old type, it is likely enough that had Villeneuve come out, he might have done something against the worn-out blockaders. The arrival of Nelson, on September 28th, changed all this. Collingwood's red tape restrictions were countermanded, and the spirit of the entire fleet changed accordingly. As usual, Nelson spared no effort to keep the men fit and healthy.

On the 19th October, Villeneuve came out—driven thereto by threats from Napoleon. As Napoleon had broken up his Boulogne camp on August 26th and by now had the greater part of that army in Germany, his forcing Villeneuve to sea is one of those mysteries which can never be fathomed. He acted in the teeth of naval advice, and there are few more pathetic pictures in history than the disgraced Villeneuve putting to sea to known certain defeat, endeavouring to fire his men with hope.‡

On the 20th October, the Franco-Spanish fleet was at sea with thirty-three ships of the line, the British consisting of twenty-seven. Nelson let the enemy get clear of the land, and then on October 21st, attacked them off Trafalgar.

---

* It was here that he recorded in his diary that he went on shore on July 20th—the first time for close on two years!

† His orders were to go to Brest; but having been frightened by some purely mythical news of a British fleet of twenty-five sail (sent him *via* a neutral ship), he went to Cadiz. As, had he got to Brest, he would have found Cornwallis with thirty-five ships of the line, this piece of precaution (which incidentally led to Trafalgar) saved him for a while.

‡ Rodjestvensky, seeking to inspire the Baltic fleet on its way to Tsushima, is a close modern parallel.

Of this battle so much has been written that any detailed description here is superfluous. To this day, the historians dispute as to what the exact tactics were, and it is doubtful whether anything will ever get beyond Professor Laughton's summary in his *Nelson*. Here the most emphasis is laid on the fact that in his memorandum of October 9th, Nelson expected to handle forty ships against a still larger hostile force. All these matters are, however, but for the academicians. The main facts are that Nelson correctly gauged the inability and gunnery inefficiency of the enemy and sailed down on them in two lines ahead,—they lying in line abreast—a position which, had they been able to shoot well, promised them victory better than any other.

As an exhibition of tactics, Trafalgar was not even original—Rodney in the past had done something very similar. On no principle of "theory" was Nelson right. Simply and solely his genius lay in ability to calculate the human element, to lay his plans accordingly, and to achieve certain victory on that !

Villeneuve did all that was possible ; and several of the French ships fought with remarkable courage. But nothing could avail them against Nelson's understanding that it was quite safe to take this risk of sailing end-on into them and then overwhelming a part of them with superior numbers.

After some four hours' fighting, eighteen of the enemy, including Villeneuve's flagship, the *Bucentaure*, were captured, and the rest drew off.

Nelson himself, within about twenty minutes of falling foul of the enemy was mortally wounded by a musket shot from the tops of the *Redoubtable*.

The losses to the allied Franco-Spanish fleet at Trafalgar in killed and wounded were extraordinarily heavy, averaging something like 300 or more per ship. In one, the casualties amounted to five in every six. This enormous loss was due to the raking broadsides of the English vessels, which wrought terrible destruction.

Nelson's last order had been to anchor. Collingwood,

on whom the command now devolved, saw no object in this; to which is generally attributed the fact that most of the prizes were lost in a gale that followed the battle. Some were wrecked, some re-captured by the enemy off Cadiz, some destroyed to prevent re-capture. All told, only four of the eighteen prizes ever reached Gibraltar. These were the *Swiftsure* (an ex-British ship), and three of the Spaniards, *Bahama*, *San Ildefonso*, and *San Juan Nepomuceno*. All were old and worthless.

From the battle, Dumanoir had escaped with four French ships. With these he made for the Mediterranean, but being intercepted by Sir R. Strachan, was compelled to surrender his damaged ships after a short action. One of the captured ships, the *Duguay Trouin*, was re-named *Implacable*, and till quite recently was a training ship at Devonport.

Although some considerable Franco-Spanish naval force still existed, it was now so scattered in different parts, and so blockaded, that danger from it was no longer to be apprehended. In December, however, two divisions of the Brest fleet, the first consisting of five ships of the line and three other vessels, under Vice-Admiral Leissegues, and the second of six ships of the line and four other vessels, under Rear-Admiral Willaumez, evaded the blockade. They were destined for the West Indies and the Cape respectively. On February 6th, 1806, off San Domingo, Leissegues was met by Sir John Duckworth, and seven ships. Three of the French were captured and two others were run ashore and destroyed. Willaumez eventually reached the West Indies also, but did not accomplish anything of moment, and having lost four ships, finally returned to France.

In 1806, the British *personnel* was 120,000. Estimates £18,864,341. Fleet 551 ships, of which 104 were of the line.

This year was mainly remarkable for the extraordinary inaction displayed by the French, who lay sheltered in creeks and inlets along the coast. However, some of their frigates were captured by boat attack.

For 1807, the *personnel* was 120,000, afterwards increased to 130,000. Estimates £17,400,000. Seven hundred and six ships in service, 104 of them being of the line.

In this year a special system of education for shipwright apprentices and the establishment of a school of naval architecture was recommended. It was not, however, until some years later that anything was actually done in this direction, the old haphazard system of construction being still followed.

In this same year, the " 18-gun brig-sloop " appeared, no less than twenty-five being ordered. These vessels were of about 380 tons, and carried sixteen thirty-two-pounder carronades and two long six-pounders. They were found to be extremely useful vessels. During this year, the Turkish and Italian Navies were suspected of being likely to pass into the hands of France. Sir John Duckworth was, therefore, sent to Turkey with orders to force the Dardanelles and demand the surrender of the Turkish fleet to the British. Failing this he was to capture or destroy it and to bombard Constantinople.

On the 19th of February, the fleet ran through the unprepared Dardanelles without much injury. It was fired on by a small Turkish squadron, most of the ships of which were destroyed. The neighbourhood of Constantinople was reached ; but the Turks refused to agree to what was demanded and busied themselves with strengthening the fortifications of the Dardanelles.

On the 1st of March, Duckworth, having done nothing, save realise his awkward situation, came down through the Dandanelles, running the gauntlet of guns which threw stones weighing nearly half-a-ton, some considerable damage being done to such ships as were hit. These guns were, in some cases, holes bored in the rocks filled with powder and stones ; others were genuine " monster guns."

Operations against Copenhagen, under Admiral Gambier, were opened on a considerably larger scale. He had under him eighteen ships of the line, forty lesser vessels and nearly 400 transports. This fleet arrived early in August, and demanded the surrender of the Danish Navy until such time as peace should come about, when it would be returned to its original owners. This being refused, troops were landed, and on the 1st of September, Copenhagen was bombarded and presently surrended. Fifteen ships of the line and ten other vessels were given up, and one ship, which tried to escape, was captured. Three ships of the line were found building; two of these were taken to pieces and carried away; the third, being more nearly completed, was destroyed. All the naval stores were also brought away from the dock-yard, necessitating the employment of no less than ninety-two of the transports.

Only five of the prizes were considered worthy of taking into the British service. Of these, one was the *Christian VII* (eighty), of 2,131 tons. This ship was so good that four copies of her were built for the British Navy.

In the winter of this year, Sir Sidney Smith, with nine ships of the line, blockaded the Tagus and demanded the surrender of the Portuguese fleet, or else the retirement to South America of the Prince Regent, who naturally enough (and as had been expected) accepted the latter condition and went to South America with the bulk of his fleet. During the year, Curacoa was surprised and captured from the Dutch; St. Thomas and Santa Croix were taken from the Danes. The French being now in possession of Portugal, Madeira was also taken possession of by the British.

Losses to the extent of thirty-nine British ships were sustained during this year, mostly by wreck; one sloop, two brigs and six cutters being the only ships captured by the enemy. At the end of 1807, Russia, which had hitherto been an ally, declared war, owing to the peace of Tilset. England, Austria and Sweden were thus at war with the rest of the continent.

Russia had eleven ships of the line under Senyavin in the Mediterranean. Senyavin made a bolt for the

Baltic with most of them, but having got as far as the Tagus found himself blockaded by Sir Sidney Smith.

A squadron was sent under Samaurez to the Baltic in June to co-operate with the Swedes against the Russians who were in Rogerswick harbour.   An attempt was made to destroy the entire Russian fleet, but owing to a strong boom the operation failed.   The blockade was continued for two months, after which the British fleet retired.

For 1808, the *personnel* was 130,000.   Estimates, £18,087,500.   Ships of the Navy, 842 ; of which 189 were of the line.   Of these, seventy-six were 74-gun ships.

Napoleon had been steadily renovating his Navy ever since Trafalgar, and it now consisted of over sixty ships of the line, besides at least twenty others completing.

A certain increase of naval activity consequently ensued, and early in the year, Admiral Ganteaume, with five ships of the line, escaped from Rochefort in a gale during the absence of the blockading fleet and succeeded in reaching Toulon.   Here he was joined by five more ships of the line and some frigates and transports.   He sailed again and effected the relief of Corfu and thence returned to Toulon.

In August, the Russian Admiral, Senyavin, who all this time had been blockaded in the Tagus, offered to surrender his ships to the British on condition that they should be given back after the war and that he and his men should be free to return to Russia.   These terms were agreed to.

This year saw the launch of the *Caledonia* of 120 guns, the largest ship yet built in England.   She was of 2616 tons.   An interesting item in connection with this ship is that she was designed and ordered to be laid down as long ago as 1794, but steps to build her were not taken until eighteen years later.

For 1809, the *personnel* was 130,000.   Estimates, £19,578,467.   Ships of the Navy, 728 ; of which 113 were of the line.   In this year the maintenance allowance of the British fleet, which had been £3 15s. od. per man per month, was increased to £4 16s. od.

In February, owing to a gale, the British fleet blockading Brest had to withdraw ; and Willaumez came out with the object of collecting a few ships at Rochefort and Lorient, and then sailing to relieve Martinique. He was, however, found and blockaded in the Basque roads, and attack on him by fireships was suggested.

In April, Lord Cochrane was sent out with a squadron to attack by fire-ships. Three of these were the special invention of Cochrane. The hold of each was filled with powder casks and sand, covered in with big booms and topped with hand grenades and rockets.

On the 11th, Cochrane, leading the expedition with one of his "explosion" vessels, went in to attack; to discover that the enemy had anticipated things and built a boom. This, however, was struck by Cochrane's vessel, which was then blown up, shattering the boom to pieces. The rest of the fire-ships came down through the gap, but were badly handled in the majority of cases, and no French ships were fallen on board of. The " explosion vessel " had, however, created such a panic that the French ships cut their cables and drifted ashore, except one ship, which was grappled with, but succeeded in disengaging.

When day broke, the French ships were seen to be mostly ashore, and Cochrane urged immediate attack. Gambier, however, displayed considerable lack of energy, consequent on which many of the French got off. Three ships were, however, captured and destroyed, and two others were destroyed by the French themselves.

Cochrane thought that it should have been possible to destroy the whole fleet, and made use of his being a Member of Parliament publicly to oppose the vote of thanks to Lord Gambier. Gambier then demanded a courtmartial, which was undoubtedly "packed." He was acquitted ; and Cochrane, one of the most brilliant officers of the Navy of that day, was compelled to leave

Submarines in the Channel
W. W. Wyllie

SUBMARINES IN THE CHANNEL.

WARSHIP OF THE TIME OF KING ALFRED.

RICHARD 1st IN ACTION WITH THE SARACEN SHIP.

BATTLE OF SLUYS—1340.

PORTSMOUTH HARBOUR—1912.

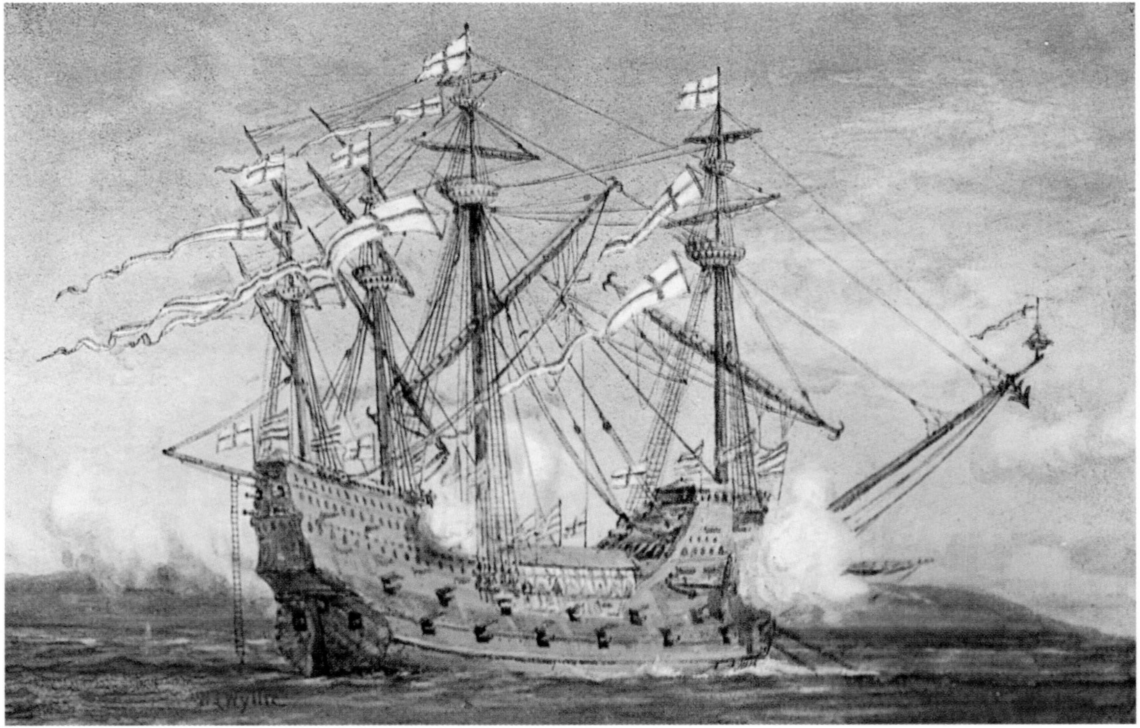

THE "GRACE DE DIEU"—1515.

THE SPANISH ARMADA—1588.

W. L. Wyllie

THE END OF A "GENTLEMAN-ADVENTURER."—THE "REVENGE."—CAPTURED BY SPANIARDS, 1591.

the Service.   Until his re-instatement, many years afterwards, he spent his career in the service of the revolting
Spanish colonies in South America.

Napoleon had long been fortifying and improving
the Scheldt, and in 1809 the decision to destroy it was
come to.   The expedition, which left England on the
28th July, consisted of thirty-seven ships of the line,
thirty-nine frigates or intermediates, fifty-four sloops or
brigs, together with 400 transports, carrying 39,000
troops, under the Earl of Chatham.   The fleet was
commanded by Rear-Admiral Sir Richard Strachan.

The object of the expedition was to destroy all ships
there and demolish the dockyard and fortifications.
But, owing to delays, the French had ample warning of
the impending attack, and put all their ships up the river
out of reach.   It was also found impracticable to attack
the dockyard or Antwerp.   Flushing was therefore
blockaded, and surrendered on the 15th August.   One
thirty-eight gun frigate was captured, and a frigate and
a brig building in the dockyard were burned, while the
timbers of a seventy-four gun ship that was building
were carried away to Woolwich, and a ship, afterwards
named the *Chatham*, built from them.

Walcheren was also captured.   Twelve thousand
troops were left garrisoning Walcheren.   Of these, nearly
half died of disease in the swamps, after which the place
was evacuated.

In October, a French squadron with transports
slipped out of Toulon during the absence of Collingwood,
who was blockading the port with fifteen ships of the line
and a number of smaller vessels.   On the evening of
October 24th, three French ships of the line and a frigate
were sighted and chased.   On the following morning two
of the ships of the line were driven ashore, where their
crew set fire to them and abandoned them; the other
ship of the line and the frigate managed to get into
Cette, whence they subsequently got safely back to Toulon.
Of the convoy, the transports and the smaller vessels,
which had made up the rest of the French squadron, some

J

were captured, the others ran into Spanish harbours and took shelter under the fortifications.   Eleven of these had taken shelter at Rosas, and were cut out by boat attack.

The remaining naval operations of the year were the capture of Senegal, Cayenne, and French Guiana.

In the Baltic, the Russian fleet was blockaded.   One or two boat actions were the only incidents of the year.

For the year 1810, the *personnel* rose to 145,000, and the total estimates amounted to £18,975,120.   The number of ships in commission were 108 ships of the line and 556 lesser vessels.

In the Mediterranean, Collingwood resigned his command on account of ill-health, and died on his way back to England.   He was succeeded by Sir Charles Cotton.   There were no incidents of moment, for though the French had been busily building ships inside Toulon, the only use made of these was one or two small sorties when the blockading force happened to be weak.

In the Channel, French frigates and large privateers were very active.   Of the privateers, several were captured or destroyed, but the frigates held their own.

Abroad, Guadalope was captured by a combined naval and military attack in a series of operations in the Antilles.

In July, the Isle of Bourbon was captured, and following this an attack was then made on Mauritius, which was the head-quarters of a considerable French privateer fleet.   The first attack was delivered by Captain Pym on Grand Port.   He had with him four frigates.   Two French frigates and two smaller vessels lay inside.

On August 22nd, the first attempt was made, but owing to Captain Pym's ship, the *Sirius*, getting aground, it was delayed until next day.   In the next day's attempt, both the *Sirius* and *Magicienne* ran aground, almost out of range.   The other two ships, *Iphigenia* and *Néréide*, got in and drove the French ships ashore. Firing from them, however, still continued, and ultimately the *Néréide* had to surrender.   The two British ships which had run ashore, were blown up by orders of Captain Pym. The *Iphigenia* succeeded in getting out of the harbour with the crews of these two ships, but while warping out was surprised and also captured by another French squadron. The entire attack proved a failure. The incident is mainly of interest as being the only instance in the war in which a British squadron sustained defeat.

Following upon this, a more serious attack was made on Mauritius; 10,000 troops were embarked, accompanied by one ship of the line and twelve frigates. A landing was effected at the end of November, and the island subsequently surrendered.

In the Baltic, Sweden, which had hitherto been a British ally, joined the French side. The Russian fleet was still blockaded by Admiral Samaurez, but as the Tsar was known to be wavering in his allegiance to Napoleon, no actual hostilities took place against him, and during the greater part of the year British merchant ships freely traded with Russian ports.

When peace was declared between England and Russia, the ships of Senyavin which had been captured in the Tagus were restored, but they contributed nothing to naval history. During the year, five frigates were captured from the French and two British frigates were captured by the enemy. British losses of the year included one ship of the line and seven frigates wrecked or blown up to prevent capture, as well as some smaller vessels.

For the year 1811, the *personnel* remained at 145,000. The Estimates were £19,822,000, and the number of ships in commission were 107 of the line, and 513 of inferior rates.

A considerable blockading squadron was still maintained off Toulon, but the French ships there, though they occasionally came out into the Road, were extremely careful to avoid any engagement.

On March 13th, a small battle, which took place off Lissa between six French frigates, accompanied by five smaller vessels, under Dubourdieu, and a British squadron, consisting of three frigates and a twenty-two gun ship, commanded by Captain William Hoste, indicates very clearly the inferiority to which the French fleet had fallen. One French ship was driven ashore and two others surrendered.

This sort of thing was in no way unique, and a single ship action of the same year is an even more startling example. The British sloop *Atlanta* (eighteen) met and engaged the *Entrepennant* (thirty-two). After an engagement lasting two-and-a-half hours the French frigate struck, having lost thirty men killed and wounded, the total loss to the British ship being only five men wounded.

In this year the island of Java was captured from the Dutch, and there were a number of small actions in the Channel, mostly the attacks of praames on small British ships. The total loss to the enemy consisted of three French frigates captured, two French frigates destroyed and one wrecked. Two Venetian frigates were also captured. The losses to the British Navy during the same period were much more heavy: three ships of the line, five frigates and an eighteen-gun brig-sloop were wrecked. Three small ships were captured and various other small vessels became unserviceable, the total loss in these amounting to fifty-one.

In January, 1811, the report of the Commission of 1806 was first brought into operation by the introduction of apprentices to be trained at the Royal Naval College, at Portsmouth. This was known as the School of Naval Architecture, and was the first genuine attempt at introducing science into naval construction. Students were given three days technical work a week and three days theoretical in mathematics and theory, under Dr. Inman. From the School of Naval Architecture the students were sent to the Navy Office, and also to the various dockyards for the study of routine. Unfortunately, however, the experiment was received with disfavour by many of the old-type of dockyard officer, with the result that most of the students were either not proficient or else became disgusted and found employment elsewhere.

For the year 1812, the *personnel* still remained at 145,000. The Estimates were £19,305,759. Ships in commission amounted to 102 ships of the line and 482 lesser vessels, with a certain number of ships in reserve. At and about this period various experimental ships were built, of which the most interesting was the floating battery *Spanker*. She was of somewhat amateur construction ; intended to carry guns of the largest size and mortars for bombardment and harbour defence. The main deck had an over-hang fitted with scuttles, down through which guns could be fired. The idea of this was, that supposing she were attacked by boats, these would go under the over-hang and very easily be destroyed. In practice, however, there was so much miscalculation that the over-hang was only a few inches above the water-line. The ship was also found to be so unmanageable that she was very shortly relegated to harbour service.

The blockades of Toulon and the Scheldt were continued, but nothing of much naval interest took place. A small French squadron broke out of Lorient, but after cruising about for three weeks and making a few prizes, returned to Brest and was blockaded there.

In the Baltic, peace was made with Sweden, and war definitely broke out between France and Russia, this being the war which culminated in Napoleon's disastrous invasion of Russia.

In the Channel and in the Mediterranean a number of single ship actions took place, and one ship, the *Rivoli* (seventy-four), built at Venice for the French Navy, was captured. This particular ship held out for 4½ hours, and at the time of her surrender had only two guns left available and fifty per cent. of her crew were out of action. She was captured by the *Victorious* (seventy-four).

The most important naval event of the year was the American declaration of war against England. The war had been prepared for some time, and the American Navy, such as there was of it, was in a very efficient and up-to-date state. It contained no ships of the line, but a number of very heavily-armed frigates, manned by

well-trained crews.   In the single ship actions that
ensued the Americans were almost invariably victorious.

For the year 1813, the *personnel* was 140,000 ; the
Estimates £20,096,709. Ships in commission, 102 of the
line and 468 inferior vessels.   The problem of meeting
the American frigates was very seriously considered
and a certain number of large ships were razeed with
a view to meeting the American frigates on more even
terms.

The most famous event of the year was the fight
between the *Shannon* (British) and the *Chesapeake*
(American).   The former was rated at thirty-eight, but
actually carried fifty-two guns.   The latter was rated at
thirty-six, but carried fifty.   She had done well, but at
the time of the fight had just been re-commissioned with
a new crew, of whom a number were British deserters
and some forty were Portuguese.   The *Shannon*, on the
other hand, had been in commission for some years ;
and Captain Broke had assiduously trained his men in
gunnery, having anticipated the " dotter " of to-day.

Being in this state of efficiency he came off Boston
and sent in a challenge to the captain of the *Chesapeake*.
Whether the challenge was actually received or not, the
Chesapeake came out accompanied by yachts crowded
with sightseers and a cargo of handcuffs for the
anticipated British prisoners.

Firing was not opened until the two frigates were
only fifty yards apart.   It lasted only about ten minutes,
when the *Chesapeake* being almost blown to pieces, the
Shannon fell aboard her and carried her by boarding in
another five.

The rest of the war with America, which lasted well
on into 1815, is of no great naval interest except for the
side issues involved.   In a series of actions, the American
big gun theory was triumphantly demonstrated, and
more than once small British squadrons were wiped out.
No material result, however, followed in consequence.
On the other hand, Washington was attacked in 1814,
and the public buildings burned, again without much

material result.   The real interest of the war lies in side issues.

The submarine appeared in this war, but the American authorities refused to give it any official sanction, and attempts made against British ships were by private individuals who had ignored the express orders of the American authorities.   None of the experimenters were successful, but this was mainly a matter of luck.

A matter of greater interest was the construction of an American war vessel, the *Fulton*.   The *Fulton*—which was driven by a steam paddle in the centre of the vessel, and was armoured with wood so thick that none of the shot of the period could get through it, was armed with two 100-pounder guns on pivot mountings and carried a ram shaped bow—can undeniably lay claim to being the precursor of the *Monitor* or *Merrimac*, and also to being the first steam warship.   She took too long to complete, however, to take any part in the war; but had the war continued, few British ships could have survived her attacks, presuming her to have been seaworthy.

To resume : 1813 as regards the French was not productive of much in the way of naval operations. The French had by now built so many new ships at Toulon, that they were actually superior to the blockading British squadron.   But they made no attempt to use this superiority, and nothing resulted except a few small skirmishes.   A few insignificant captures were made on the British side.

At the beginning of the year 1814, there were ninety-nine ships of the line in commission and 495 lesser vessels.   The *personnel* amounted to 140,000, and the estimates £19,312,000.

A number of single ship actions took place between frigates, and in most of these a considerable improvement in French efficiency was noted.   Nothing, however, was done with the larger ships, and the war ultimately ended with the deportation of Napoleon to Elba.

No sooner was peace declared than the fleet was

greatly reduced and a large number of ships sold or broken up. Nineteen ships of the line and ninety-three other vessels were thus disposed of. The *personnel* for the year 1815 was reduced to 70,000 for the first three months and 90,000 for the remainder of the year. The estimates stood at £17,032,700, of which £2,000,000 was for the payment of debts.

The re-appearance of Napoleon and the events which culminated in the battle of Waterloo did not lead to any naval operations, and with the final deportation of Napoleon to St. Helena, a further reduction of the fleet took place. The estimates sank to £10,114,345, and considerable reductions of officers and men were made.

VIII.

GENERAL MATTERS IN THE PERIOD OF THE FRENCH WARS.

N AVAL uniform, as we understand it, first came into use for officers in the days of George II.,* who so admired a blue and white costume of the Duchess of Bedford that he decided then and there to dress his naval officers in similar fashion. No very precise regulations were, however, followed, and for many years uniform was more or less optional or at fancy of the captain.

The first uniform consisted of a blue coat, with white cuffs and gold buttons. The waistcoat, breeches, and stockings were white. The hat was the ordinary three-cornered black hat of the period with some gold lace about it and a cockade. Other officers wore uniforms which were slight variants upon this : while as special distinguishing marks only the captain (if over three years' seniority) wore epaulettes upon both shoulders. A lieutenant wore one only.

From time to time the uniform was altered slightly, mostly as regards the cuffs and lapels ; but enormous latitude was allowed, and some officers even dressed as seamen.

There was no general uniform whatever for the men ; though circumstances led to the bulk of the men in any one ship being dressed more or less alike.

This was the result of the " slop chest." This was introduced about the year 1650, and amounted to nothing more than a species of ready-made tailor ship at which

* *The British Tar in Fact and Fiction*, Commander Robinson, R.N.

men at their own expense could obtain articles of clothing. Later on it became compulsory for newly-joined men, whose clothes were defective, to purchase clothing on joining, to the tune of two months' pay.

These articles being supplied to a ship wholesale, were naturally all alike, and so the men of one ship would all be more or less uniformly attired. Men of another ship might be dressed quite differently, though also more or less like each other. But any idea of uniform as "uniform," right up to Trafalgar, was entirely confined to one or two dandy captains, and they mainly only considered their own boat's crews.* Some fearful and wonderful costumes of this kind are recorded.

Uniform wearing of the "slop chest" variety was, however, always regarded as the badge of the pressed man and jail bird. The " prime seaman " who joined decently clad was allowed to wear his own clothes, and these were decided by fashion. There were dudes in the Navy in those days, and contemporary art records a good deal of variety. In our own day, when exactitude is at a premium, it has erred badly enough to depict bluejackets with moustachios.† In the old days it was probably even more careless still. Consequently everything as to the costume of men in the Nelson era required to be accepted with caution. It is, however, clear from the more reliable literary and descriptive sources that the dandy sailor existed very freely. The prime seaman loved to hall-mark himself by his costume.

On board ship in dirty weather he wore anything and his best when coming up for punishment.‡ In a general way fashion always worked from the officers' uniform, with fancy additions. A natty blue jacket was the essential feature, with as many brass buttons as the owner

---

* *Vide* Anson's boat's crew in his trip up to Canton. Some captains spent a good deal of money in providing white shirts for their boat's crews. Others indulged in purely fanciful attires.

† A year or two ago a famous Royal Academy picture showed a fleet of Dreadnoughts cruising at sea with the steam trial water tanks on board !

‡ To wear the smartest possible clothes on coming up for punishment was invariable routine. It was hoped that a smart appearance would mitigate the captain's wrath.—*Vide, Sea Life in Nelson's Time,* John Masefield.

could afford. A red or yellow waistcoat seems to have been *à la mode*. Trousers, preferably of white duck, but sometimes of blue, were also " the fancy." Sometimes these were striped. In all cases they were ample, free, and flowing, as they are at the present day. Convenience of tucking up on wet decks is the usual explanation ; but there is good reason to believe that idle fashion of the Nelson days had just as much or more to do with the modern bluejacket's trousers.

The quaint little top hat of the midshipman was generally worn by the Lower Deck dandy. A pig tail was also a *sine quâ non* during the period of the Second Great War.

The origin of the pigtail is wrapped in some mystery. It has been variously ascribed to copying the French Navy* and to imitating the Marines, who wore wonderfully greased pigtails at this period.

To complete the rig the seamen used to decorate themselves with coloured ribbons let into their clothes. They lived a hard life, and much has been written upon the subject. But the evidence generally tends to prove that the " prime seaman " as a rule had a far better time of it than those who (failing to recognise that conditions have altered to-day) appear to realise.† The lack of liberty, entailed by the presence of so many men who would assuredly desert on half a chance, was so general and so long-standing that it is doubtful whether it was felt to any really great extent. Custom covers most things.

To our modern ideas the punishments afloat were horribly brutal ; but here again it is necessary to remember the difference in era. Floggings and kindred punishments were plentiful enough ashore ; and there is a good deal of evidence to indicate that they were taken as " all in the day's work afloat." The victim was usually " doped " by his messmates, who saved up part of their rum tots for the purpose, and the horrors of the cat have

* To this day the British bluejacket calls himself a " matlo "—a corruption of the French matelot ; so this pigtail introduction theory may be correct enough.

† See Food, a page or so further on.

undoubtedly been somewhat exaggerated. It was undeniably brutal and cruel ; but, to select a homely simile, so were dental methods a few years ago. Our fathers submitted to things in this direction which none of us would, or, for that matter, could stand nowadays. The bulk of contemporary evidence is that the (to our eyes) brutal punishments of the Navy of a hundred odd years ago were never regarded as serious grievances by those who stood to undergo them.

The actual grievances revolved entirely around the administration of undeserved punishments. A certain number of captains misused their powers and perogatives, but only a small percentage did so. At no time does the average captain appear to have been a brutal bully. This is, however, to be qualified by the midshipmen, of whom a certain number deliberately bullied men into doing things for which they got brutally punished afterwards. But outside this the conditions were by no means so horrible as generally depicted. The real sufferers were the pressed landsmen, who certainly learned to be seamen in a very hard school.

It is necessary, however, even here to remember the times and the conditions. This view is borne out by the Great Mutiny. The mutineers, even at the Nore, never demanded the abolition of the cat. When trouble was connected with it in any way, it was over its unreasonable use, as, for instance, in the insensate flogging of the last two men off the rigging, which led to the Mutiny in the *Hermoine*. This—which entailed punishing the smartest men since these had furthest to go—goaded the prime seamen to desperation and sympathy with the landsmen element afloat, which was ever in a semi-mutinous condition. It is impossible to hold that Captain Pigot of the *Hermoine* did not deserve his fate. But Pigots were comparatively rare, and captains like Nelson by no means scarce. Nelson had no hesitation in flogging men, but he flogged justly, and no troubles ever occurred in any ship commanded by him. For that matter it was characteristic of the time that a captain might be a Tartar, and yet be quite popular with his crew so long as he was just. The " prime seamen " who formed the nucleus of the ship's company realised the necessity of severe measures and strict discipline in order to tame the human ullage which made up the rest of the crew.

In this connection it is interesting to note that towards the end of the period there began to creep in the commencement of a later classification of ratings not liable to corporal punishment.

Had life afloat in the days of the Great War been quite as terrible as it is often depicted as having been, the volunteer element of trained seamen could hardly have existed, nor could the glamour of the sea have brought so many raw volunteers as it did. When a ship was commissioned, the first step was advertising for men. The advertisements were specious and alluring enough ; but the captain's character generally had most influence on the response ; and all the essential seamen element, unless they had spent all their money, were pretty wary as to who they shipped with.

To be sure it did not take the seaman long to lose his money. On a ship paying off he received a considerable accumulated sum, and every kind of shark and harpy was on the lookout to relieve him of it. He got gloriously drunk and so remained while the money lasted, and in this condition the press-gang often got him.

The press-gang was a legalised form of naval conscription. In theory any seafaring man who could be laid hands on might be taken ; in practice all was fish that came to the press-gang's net.

The press-gang, armed with cudgels and cutlasses, used to operate at night, generally in the naval towns,* but at times also further afield. It laid hands upon all and sundry, hitting them over the head if they resisted.

A cargo secured, the men were taken on board and kept between decks under an armed guard pending

* The curious, who wander into the by-lanes off Queen Street, Portsea, will still find heavy iron gates in places. Inside these gates those anxious to escape the press-gangs used to take refuge.

examination by the captain and surgeon. Certain people, such as apprentices or some merchant seamen, were exempt and had to be liberated. Badly diseased men were also let loose again. Verminous and dirty folk were scrubbed with a brutality which created subsequent cleanly habits. Their clothes were either fumigated or else thrown away altogether, and fresh clothing supplied from the " slop chest " at so much off their pay.

If within a fortnight the pressed man cared to call himself a volunteer he received a bounty ; but, whether he volunteered* or not, once aboard the ship there he remained till death or the paying off of the ship years later. It was this confinement to the ship which led to so much agitation, and was made one of the principal grievances of the mutineers at Spithead.

On the side of the authorities it has to be remembered that had any man been allowed ashore he would certainly never have been seen again, at any rate, so long as he had any money. In most fleets also, an attempt at a substitute was made by allowing ship to ship visiting. Such visits invariably resulted in drunken bouts and subsequent floggings. Nelson went further—he instituted theatricals on shipboard. It is generally clear that—very crudely, of course—the authorities were not blind to the desirability of relieving the tedium of imprisonment on board ship.

The feeding of the men in the days of the Great War is generally considered to have been villainous. It was one of the causes of the Mutiny ; but there is some reason to believe that it was not invariably bad. Rodney's fleet is said to have been excellently provisioned, and much of what has been written about " thieving pursers " in the past is now known to be mythical. It was a classical legend that the purser stole and swindled with bad food. He might do so, and many did. But all did not, either from honesty or because they did not get the chance. Under Nelson or Rodney an unscrupulous

---

* The " bounty " offered, however, was a decided inducement. Cases of bounties as high as £70 can be found.

purser stood to have a very bad time indeed, and there were others very keenly alive to the fact that good feeding and efficiency went hand in hand. The bad food at the time of the mutinies seem to have been a feature of that particular time, and even so due rather to mismanagement than much else. For the rest, the real culprits were economists on shore, who had no connection whatever with the Fleet, and were merely interested in husbanding the financial resources of the country.

The provisions as made were almost uniformly good, and the stories of unscrupulous contractors who, in league with the pursers, foisted inferior food on the Fleet, may mostly be dismissed. Such cases occurred now and again, but comparatively rarely. " Rogues in authority " were mainly mythical. There are yarns by the score. There are corresponding yarns to-day, quite as plentiful, which the careless historian of the future will no doubt swallow. For example, at the present day it is an article of faith with every bluejacket that the first lieutenant pockets odd sixpences out of the canteen, and nothing ever can or ever will remove the impression.

It is absolutely absurd ; but within the last ten years I have had it chapter and verse all about the peculation of 1s. 4d. by a first lieutenant whose private income ran well into five figures ! It is a sea-legend so hoary that bluejackets honour it, no matter how ridiculously improbable. The purser of the days of the Great War was not perhaps entirely clean handed, but as Commander Robinson has pointed out,* even at the Spithead Mutiny, when the provision question was very much to the fore, the mutineers did not complain of the purser, but of the system and regulations. It was people on shore, not the man afloat, who, when it came to the point, mixed up the instrument with the handlers thereof.

The Spithead trouble, which was purely naval (the Nore Mutiny was more or less political) arose entirely, so far as food was concerned, out of the economists already

* *The British Tar in Fact and Fiction.*

referred to. Vast stores of provisions had been accumulated, and many were going bad. Pursers received very strict orders to use up the old " likely to decay soon " before touching the new. The result was the issue of decayed pork, stinking cheese, and mildewed biscuits to an unprecedented degree. A badness that had hitherto been more or less occasional chanced just about the Mutiny period to be general.

The men were by no means starved or badly fed, presuming the food to be good. The usual scale was somewhat as follows :—A daily issue of a pound of biscuit and a gallon of beer or else a pint of wine ; and when these were exhausted, one gill of Navy rum diluted with three of water twice a day. On Tuesdays and Saturdays an issue of 2lbs. of beef was made ; on Sundays and Thursdays 1lb. of pork. Over the week the issue of other articles was 2lbs. pease, 1½lbs. oatmeal, 6ozs. of butter, an equal amount of sugar, and 12ozs. of cheese and half-a-pint of vinegar nominally per man ; but actually every four men took the provisions of six. Nine pounds of meat a week could hardly be called starvation fare even to-day, and in those times it was an extraordinarily liberal diet for men who at home would not have had anything like it.* Except in cases with admirals like Collingwood (who in the matter of understanding the ratio of health to efficiency was about the most incompetent admiral the British Navy ever had), it was generally seen to that, whenever possible, fresh provisions could be purchased from traders who regularly visited blockading fleets.

Furthermore rations were normally varied so far as circumstances would permit, and when possible fresh beef and mutton were substituted for the salt meat allowance. Nelson went to almost extravagant lengths in these directions ; but the majority of other officers were not far behind. Whatever hell the Lower Deck of the Fleet entailed, the blame in hardly any case lay with the

* There are West Country villages to-day in which, to my own knowledge, one pound of meat a week is an outside estimate of what is eaten per head.

officers, executive or otherwise, but entirely with civilian officials and Members of Parliament with ideas of their own about economy. All the reliable evidence is to the effect that the responsible authorities desired their fighting men to live (relatively speaking) like fighting cocks, that the difference between the ideal and the real was due to civilian influence, and that even so it was only really thoroughly bad just before the Great Mutiny. Had it been a regular thing the Mutinies would probably never have happened, the men would have been too used to the conditions to find in them a special cause of complaint.

The whole trouble in messing in the old days arose out of quality, not quantity. The beef and pork were almost invariably bad, owing to the system of using up the old provisions first, with a view to economy. Every ship carried tons of good provisions going bad, while those already bad and decayed were being consumed. Consequently the men starved in the midst of relative plenty.

It remains to add that the officers fared little better.* On the whole, taking their general shore food into consideration, it may be argued that they fared worse. As a rule, they had to eat what the men ate, a fact too often forgotten by those who believe that the officers of those days generally peculated on provisions for the men.

Both aft and forward there was one consolation. Liquor was plentiful enough for anyone who wanted to be half seas over by eventime. So was the hard life lived, with an occasional battle to break the monotony.

To both officers and men battle seems to have been the "beano" of to-day. Conditions on board were not rosy enough to make life worth clinging to, while battle

---

* There were those who accepted weevils in ship's biscuits as mites in Gorgonzola cheese are accepted to-day ! Unpalatable as ship's biscuit is, there is a certain acquired taste about it. In the later nineties I have frequently seen it handed round as a species of dessert in the wardroom, every senior officer taking some and enjoying it. In the 1890 manœuvres the wardroom officers of "C fleet" did three weeks on "ships" only, in quite a casual way, though the quality even then left something to be desired.

meant a good time afterwards to those who got through unscathed. There was only one terror—being wounded. The horrors of the cockpit are beyond exaggeration. The surgeons did their best. They were poorly paid men* and expected to find their own instruments: only if they could not did they borrow tools from the carpenter.†

They heated their instruments before use so as to lessen the shock of amputation ; they doped their patients with wine or spirit so far as might be. They took all as they came in turn, whether officer or man. If anyone seemed too badly wounded to be worth attention they had him taken above and thrown overboard. If, at a hasty glance, taking off an arm or a leg, or both, seemed likely to promise a cure, they gave the wounded man a tot of rum and a bit of leather to chew, and set to work ! The wounded who survived were treated with a humanity which makes the " more humanity to the wounded " of the Spithead mutineers a little difficult to understand at first sight. They were fed on delicacies ; and anything out of the ordinary on the wardroom table was always sent to them. They also got all the officers' wine.

On the other hand, time in the sick bay was deducted from their pay,‡ and they were liable to all kinds of infectious diseases caught from the last patient.

To satisfy the demands of the economists, lint was forbidden and sponges restricted, so that a single sponge might have to serve for a dozen wounded men. Blood-poisoning was thus indiscriminately spread, and a wounded man thus infected with the worst form of it, was mulcted in his pay for medicines required. When the Spithead mutineers demanded " more humanity to the wounded " those were the things that probably they had in mind. It has further to be remembered that

* They began at 4s. a day, working up to 11s. a day after six years, and 18s. a day at twenty years' service, which few ever reached.

† For extremely detailed accounts of surgery in action see *Sea Life in Nelson's Time*, John Masefield.

‡ A form of this rule exists to-day. A man wounded in action is not now mulcted ; but a man who tumbles down a hatchway and breaks his leg has to suffer " hospital stoppages," and " pay for his own cure," to a certain extent.

a man wounded too badly to be of any further use afloat was flung ashore without pension or mercy. The surgeons were fully as humane as their brethren ashore, possibly much more so, from the mere fact that any community of men flung together to sink or swim together compels common sympathies. To the men the purser was classically a thief, the surgeon a callous brute, the officers generally brutes of another kind. This cheap view of the situation has been perpetuated *ad lib.* But all the best evidence is to the effect that, as a rule, and save in exceptional cases, most of those on board a warship pulled together, and that all strove to make the best of things. The things to be made the best of were few, no doubt, and the grumblers and growlers are the folk who have left most records. Allowing for the different era, similar growls can be found to-day. To-day the contented man says nothing ; the discontented says a little, and outside sympathisers say a great deal. The truth probably lies with the actually discontented's version somewhat discounted. In the days of the Great War, the same fact probably obtained. Unquestionably the seaman proper loved the sea and his duty, despite all hardships and drawbacks. To this fact is to be attributed the easy victories of the Great Wars, and, relatively to corresponding shore life, sea life afloat can hardly have been quite so black as most people delight to paint it.*

The pay of the Navy of the period remains to be mentioned. It ran as follows :—

Captain—6s. to 25s. a day, according to the ship, plus a variety of allowances.
Midshipmen—£2 to £2 15s. 6d. a month.
Surgeons—11s. to 18s. a day, with half-pay when unemployed.
Assistant-Surgeons—4s. and 5s., with half-pay when unemployed.

* Commander Robinson, R.N., in *The British Tar in Fact and Fiction,* seems to have got nearer the true picture than those who have painted things in darker and more lurid colours. He is practically the only writer upon the subject who has realised that many old yarns are capable of being discounted.

Chaplains—About 8s. 6d. a day, with allowances.

Schoolmasters—£2 to £2 8s. a month, with bounties.

Boatswains—£3 to £4 16s. a month.

Boatswain's Mate—£2 5s. 6d. a month.

Gunner—£1 16s. to £2 2s. a month.

Carpenter—£3 to £5 16s. a month, according to the ship.

Quartermaster—£2 5s. 6d. a month.

Sailmaker—£2 5s. 6d. a month.

Sailmaker's Assistant—£1 18s. 6d. a month.

Master-at-Arms—£2 0s. 6d. to £2 15s. 6d. a month.

Ship's Corporals—£2 2s. 6d. a month.

Cook—11s. 8d. a month and pickings.

Able Seaman—11s. a month (33s. a month after 1797).

Ordinary Seaman—9s. a month (25s. 6d. a month after 1797).

Landsman—7s. 6d. a month (23s. a month after 1797).

Ship's Boy—13s. to 13s. 6d. a month.

As a rule the men received their pay in a lump when the ship paid off. Hence those extraordinary scenes of dissipation with which the story books have made us sufficiently familiar. Jews* and women soon fleeced the Tar, who was generally too drunk to know what he was doing, there being dozens of willing hands ready to see to it that he was well plied with liquor.

FLAGS.

In the year 1800 the Union flag was altered to its present form by the incorporation of the red cross of St. Patrick. This flag, the Union Jack, was used for flying on the bowsprit,† and at the main masthead by an Admiral of the Fleet. To hoist it correctly, *i.e.*, right side up, was a special point of importance in the Fleet of Nelson's day, and many a foreigner seeking to use British colours got bowled out from hoisting the flag

---

* It is only fair to the Hebrew race to say that " Jew " was a generic term for a special type of person who grew rich on advancing money to sailors and selling them shoddy articles at ridiculously enhanced prices. Quite a large number of them were not of the Jewish race.

† To-day this is flown at the bow only when a ship is at anchor.

incorrectly, *i.e.*, without the greater width of white being uppermost in the inner canton nearest the staff.   To this day many people on shore do the same.

The ensign was coloured according as to whether the Admiral was " of the white," " blue," or " red."   It was flown, as till quite recently, from the mizzen peak.

For battle purposes this variety ensign died out after Trafalgar, where, in order to avoid confusion, Nelson ordered all ships to fly the white ensign—he himself being a Vice-Admiral of the white, while Collingwood was Vice-Admiral of the blue.   Trafalgar was thus the first battle to be fought deliberately under the white ensign.

IX.

THE BIRTH OF MODERN WARSHIP IDEAS.

IN 1816 took place the bombardment of Algiers, whereby 1,200 Europeans who were in slavery were released. None of these, however, proved to be British subjects. A noticeable feature of the bombardment was the heavy damage done by the large ships engaged.

For the year 1817 the *personnel* stood at 21,000 only. Ships in commission were fourteen of the line and 100 lesser craft. Two hundred and sixty-three (of which eighty-four were of the line) were laid up "in ordinary" and the remaining ships were condemned.

In this year a new rating of ships was introduced. Up till now the carronades had not been included in the armament of ships. Under the new rating they were included, and so the thirty-eight gun ship actually carrying fifty-two guns appeared for the first time with her proper armament.

Although the Navy was so reduced, considerable attention was paid to shipbuilding and improvement of construction. Trussed frames were introduced, and a variety of other inventions which had long been in use in France. Much attention was paid to the strong construction of the bow, with a view to resisting raking fire.* Sterns were also made circular to enable more guns to bear aft. A curious objection to this was made on the grounds that in time of war it was the enemy

* At Trafalgar, the *Victory*, as she bore down, suffered heavily from the shot that penetrated her thin forward bulkhead.

who would be in retreat and most in need of stern fire, and that by the introduction of this into the British Navy the enemy would copy and so have the advantage of being better able to defend himself than heretofore ! It was, however, pointed out that perhaps war vessels propelled by steam might be met with in blockades, and that it would be extremely important to sail away from these and be able to destroy them while so doing !

The years 1818 and 1819 passed uneventfully. The *personnel* was 20,000, and the estimates averaged between six and seven million pounds. They remained at about this figure for several years, and beyond some slight operations in Burmah, in 1824, the British Navy performed no war services till the year 1827. In the Burmese operations, the *Diana*, a small steam paddle vessel, took part. It is also of some interest to record that Captain Marryat, the naval novelist, commanded the *Lorne* (twenty) in these operations.

In 1827, the combined fleets of England, France and Russia, met those of the Turks and Egyptians at Navarino, in connection with the war between Turkey and Greece. The allied fleet consisted as follows :—

BRITISH
{ Three ships of the line.
Four frigates.
Several other vessels.

FRENCH
{ Three ships of the line.
Two lesser vessels.
Two schooners.

RUSSIAN
{ Four ships of the line.
Four frigates.

The combined Turko-Egyptian fleet consisted of three ships of the line, fifteen large frigates, eighteen corvettes, and a number of gun-boats, etc.

The Turkish fleet was anchored in the harbour. The combined fleet sailed into the harbour and anchored to leeward of the Turks. These fired upon some English boats and a general action ensued, in which the greater part of the Turko-Egyptian fleet was destroyed with the loss of somewhere about 4,000 men. The Allies lost 650, and the principal English ships were so damaged that they had to be sent home for repairs.

At and about this time, and right on for some years, an enormous number of experiments were carried out between ship and ship with a view to improving the sailing qualities, and side by side with this, the question of propulsion other than by sail was first seriously considered. A certain number of small steam tugs had been added to the Navy, there being no less than twenty-two such built in the reign of George IV. Of these the largest was built in 1835. Very little reliance was placed on steam at first for any possibilities outside towing and harbour-work, and a great deal of energy was expended in devices to enable ships to be moved by manual labour. In place of the "sweeps" of ancient history, paddles were fitted, and in 1829 the *Galatea* (forty-two) frigate was thus moved at a speed of three knots in a dead calm.

The *Galatea* was commanded by Captain, afterwards Admiral Sir Charles, Napier, who so long ago as 1819 had been concerned in financing an unsuccessful attempt to run iron steamers on the Seine. The first ship in which hand paddles were tried was the *Active*, frigate. No success was met with, but Napier evolved a different system for the *Galatea*. Those of the *Active* were worked by the capstan; Napier installed a series of winches along each side of the main deck. It took about two-thirds of the ship's company to work them.

The earliest known use of steam was as long ago as in the year 1543. The account of it was in the original records which had been preserved in the Royal Archives of Simancas, among the State Papers of the city of Catalonia, and those of the Naval Secretary of War, in the year 1543, and was extracted on the 27th August, 1825, by the keeper, who signed his name "Tomas Gonzalez."

The inventor, a naval officer named Garay, never revealed the secret of his invention, but mention is made of a "cauldron of boiling water" and "wheels of complicated movement on each side of the vessel." He succeeded in obtaining a speed of "two leagues in three hours," also "at least a league an hour" with his device, fitted to a 200-ton vessel named *Trinidad*.* Honours were bestowed on Garay, but the monarch who had patronised him, being busy with other matters, did not follow up the invention. Otherwise much naval history might have been different from what it is.

In 1736, Jonathan Hulls took out a patent in England for a stern wheel. It should be remembered that at this time the question of means of propulsion other than by sail was eagerly considered, and that paddles came to be tried in the place of oars, with a view to more continuity of action. Steam ideas somewhat trended to the idea of sucking water in forward and ejecting it aft. The screw propeller also was known certainly at as early a date as the paddle.

In 1789, a sixty-feet boat was driven for nearly seven miles an hour with a twelve horse-power engine, but for a very long time nothing was expected except canal work and towing. Even as steam progressed, it did so in the merchant service first.

By the year 1818, however, the Americans had built a sea-going steamer, *Savannah*, which crossed the Atlantic to Russia. On her return voyage the United States was reached twenty-five days after leaving Norway.

In England, in the year 1821, a steam mail service, between Holyhead and Dublin, was established, and in 1823 a steam mail service between England and India was seriously asked for, and in 1829 the subject again came upon the *tapis*.

In 1839, the steam liner *Great Britain*, was laid down. She was 322 feet long overall and a beam of fifty-one feet, and a displacement of 2,984 tons, with 1,000 horse-power. It was originally intended to make her a paddle-vessel. Instead of that, however, she was made a screw-steamer, and made her first trip in December, 1844, when she succeeded in exceeding her anticipated speed.

This serious attention to steam in the mercantile marine naturally attracted considerable interest in

* *Ex* Fincham, where the report is given in full.

the Navy, the more so as two naval officers, Captains Chappel and Claxton, were the principal promoters of the mercantile enterprises. It was, however, generally pointed out that useful as steam might be for such purposes, it was unsuitable for warships proper, on account of the liability of the machinery to damage, and the practical impossibility of combining paddles with sailing. It was laid down that the first essential of a warship was to be able to sail, that if steam power could be usefully applied as an auxiliary it might be " desirable."

After considerable experiments and investigations, it was found possible to place the machinery under the water-line, but the paddle-wheels were still exposed, and the armament space available was so slight, that steam did not gain much favour.

The first steam vessel actually brought into the British service was the *Monkey*, built about the year 1821. She was bought into the service and used as a tug.

In the following year, the *Comet* was specially built for the packet service,* but none of these were steam warships.

In 1843, the success of the *Great Britain* influenced the Admiralty, and the *Penelope* (forty-six) was cut apart and lengthened by sixty-five feet, and had engines of 650 horse-power fitted to her.

In 1844, the Earl of Dundonald (Cochrane) submitted plans to the Admiralty for a steamer of 760 tons, called the *Janus*. This vessel was built with an engine of his own design, but as this was a failure, ordinary engines were fitted.

In all these steamers the gun-fire was chiefly end-on, but in 1845 the *Odin* and the *Sidon*, especially designed for broadside fire, were put in hand.

So long ago as the year 1825, the paddle was recognised as a source of danger for warships, and in that year a two-blade propeller, designed by Commander Samuel Brown, was accepted.

* The mail packet service was under the Admiralty in those days.

In 1836, Ericsson (subsequently to be of *Monitor* fame) patented some propellers in England, but as he met with very little sympathy from the authorities, he retired to America.   The main objections to the propeller appears not to have been due to any lack of appreciation so much as opposition from those who had invested heavily in paddle-propulsion plant.

In 1842, however, the Admiralty seriously took the question up.   The *Rattler*, of 777 tons, and 200-horse-power, was lashed stern-to-stern with the paddle-yacht *Electro* of the same displacement and horse-power.   Both ships were driven away from each other at full speed, and the *Rattler* succeeded in towing the *Electro* after her. After this, in 1844, a screw frigate, the *Dauntless*, was ordered to be constructed ; but as late as the year 1850, steam was merely regarded as an auxiliary, and received little or no consideration outside that.

The use of iron instead of oak as a material for shipbuilding was first seriously considered about the year 1800.   In 1821, an iron steamer was in existence, and in 1839 the *Dover* was ordered to be built for Government service as a steam packet.   In 1841, the *Mohawk* was ordered by the Admiralty for service on Lake Huron, but the first iron warship for the Royal Navy proper was the *Trident*, of 1850 tons and 300 horse-power, built at Blackwall, by Admiralty orders, in 1843.

Iron, as a material for warship construction, was looked on with considerable suspicion, both in England and in France.   Experiments were conducted at Woolwich with some plates rivetted together like the sides of an iron ship, these plates being lined inside with cork and india-rubber, (the first idea of a cofferdam).   It was expected that this preparation, which was known as " kamptulicon," would close up after shot had passed through and prevent ingress of water.   This was found to be quite correct, but the egress of shot on the other side had quite the opposite result.   The plates were sometimes packed with wood and sometimes cased with it, but the general result of the experiments was held prejudicial to the use of iron, which was supposed to splinter unduly compared to wood.

The importance of deciding whether warships should be built of iron or wood was accentuated by the necessity of replacing those heavy warships which had been converted to auxiliary steam vessels. All such proved to be cramped in stowage and bad sea boats.

So long ago as 1822, shell-guns had been adopted. Consequently, in the experiments as regards iron, shell-fire had to be taken into consideration.

In 1842, experiments were made with iron plates three-eighths of an inch thick, rivetted together to make a total thickness of six inches. It was, however, reported that at 400 yards these were not proof against eight-inch guns or heavy thirty-two pounders. These matters were taken into consideration by Captain Chads, whose official report was as follows:—

"The shot going through the exposed or near side generally makes a clean smooth hole of its own size, which might be readily stopped; and even where it strikes a rib it has much the same effect; but on the opposite side all the mischief occurs; the shot meets with so little resistance that it must inevitably go through the vessel, and should it strike on a rib on the opposite side the effect is terrific, tearing off the iron sheets to a very considerable extent; and even those shot that go clean through the fracture being on the off side, the rough edges are outside the vessel, precluding the possibility almost of stopping them.

"As it is most probable that steam vessels will engage directly end-on I have thought it desirable to try today what the effect of shot would be on this vessel* so placed, and it has been such as might be expected, each shot cutting aways the ribs, and tearing the iron plates away sufficient to sink the vessel in an instant."

In 1849 an official report stated that:—

"Shot of every description in passing through iron make such large holes that the material is improper for the bottom of ships.

"Iron and oak of equal weight offering equal resistance to shot, iron for the topsides affords better protection for the men than oak, as the splinters from it are not so destructive.

"Iron offering no lodgment for shells in passing through the side, if made with single plates it will be free from the destructive effects that would occur by a shell exploding in a side of timber."

* The seventy-three ton iron steamboat *Ruby*.

Certain modifications were then introduced and tried in the year 1850, and Captain Chad's report was that :—

" With high charges the splinters from the shot were as numerous and as severe as before, with the addition in this, and in the former case, of the evils that other vessels are subject to, that of the splinters from the timber.

"From these circumstances I am confirmed in the opinion that iron cannot be beneficially employed as a material for the construction of vessels of war."

As a result of this report, seventeen iron ships which were building, the largest being the *Simoon*, of nearly 2,000 tons, were condemned; and it was definitely decided that ships must be built of wood, and that iron in any form was disadvantageous.

The advantages of the shell were fully understood, and at least half of the guns of the ships of the line of the period were sixty-five cwt. shell guns. Experiments had fully taught what shell-fire might be expected to accomplish. General Paixham, the inventor of the shell gun, had long ago stated that armour was the only antidote to shell, and the fact that armour up to six inches had been experimented with indicates that this also was understood. Between the appreciation of the fact and acting upon it, there was, however, a decided gulf. In the British Navy, as in others also, the natural conservatism of the sea held its usual sway.

Matters were at about this stage when, in the year 1853, the Russian Admiral Nachimoff, with a fleet consisting of six ships of the line, entered the harbour of Sinope, on the 30th November, 1853, and absolutely annihilated, by shell fire, a Turkish squadron of seven frigates which were lying there. The damage wrought by this shell-fire was terrific. "For God's sake keep out the shells" is generally believed to have been the cry of most naval officers about that period, though there is some lack of evidence as to whether this demand was ever actually made, except by the Press. The terrible effect of shell-fire was, however, obvious enough; but as stated above it was really well-known before the war test that so impressed the world.

When the Crimean War broke out in 1854, the British *personnel* stood at 45,500, and the Estimates were £7,197,804.   On the 28th March, war was formally declared.   Naval operations in the Crimean war were almost entirely of secondary note.   Some frigates bombarded Odessa, in April, and a certain amount of damage was done along the Caucasian coast.

In September, the British fleet, consisting of ten ships of the line, two frigates and thirteen armed steamers, convoyed an enormous fleet of Turkish and French war-ships crammed with troops for an attack on Sebastopol. The Russian fleet lay inside that harbour and made no attempt whatever to destoy the invading flotilla, though it might easily have done considerable mischief, if not more. Instead of that, the ships were sunk at the entrance of the harbour, and the siege of Sebastopol presently commenced. On October 17th, the Allied fleet attempted to bombard Fort Constantine, but the ships were soon defeated by the shore defences and many of them badly injured.

The French, who had formed somewhat more favour-able opinions of iron armour than we had, had, after Sinope, already commenced the construction of five floating batteries which were to carry armour.   They were wooden ships of 1,400 tons displacement, with four-inch armour over their hulls.   They carried eighteen fifty-pounder guns and a crew of 320.   As originally designed they were intended to sail, although they were fitted with slight auxiliary steam power.   When completed they were found unable to sail, so pole masts were fitted to them.   Artificial ventilation was also supplied and their funnels were made telescopic.   The designs of these vessels were sent to the British Admiralty, who, after considerable delay, built four copies, the *Glatton*, *Meteor*, *Thunder*, and *Trusty*.   These, however, were not completed in time to take any part in the war.

So soon as the French armoured batteries were ready they were sent out to the Crimea, where they joined a large fleet which had been prepared to attack Kinburn, which was bombarded in October, 1855. In a very short while the forts were totally destroyed, and with very small loss to the armoured batteries. The effect created by this was so great that four more armoured batteries were ordered in England, the *Etna*, *Erebus*, *Terror*, and *Thunderbolt*.

In the Baltic, to which a British fleet, under Admiral Napier, had been sent, the Russians kept behind the fortifications at Kronstadt, and nothing was accomplished beyond the bombardment of Sveaborg, and the destruction of the town and dockyard. Some small bombardments also took place in the White Sea and on the Siberian coast, where Petropavlovsk was attacked and the attack was defeated, and such other actions as took place were generally unsuccessful. It had become abundantly clear that against fortifications wooden ships had very small chance of success.

Incidental items of naval interest are that in this particular war, Captain Cowper Coles mounted a sixty-eight-pounder gun upon a raft named the *Lady Nancy*. This attracted so much attention from the small target, light draft and steady platform, that Coles was sent home to develop his ideas. In this war also, mines appeared, the Russians dropping a good many off Kronstadt. Those used by the Russians were filled with seventy pounds of powder, and exploded on contact by the familiar means of a glass tube of sulphuric acid being broken and the acid falling into chlorate of potash.

No material damage was done to ships by this means, but a considerable number of those who had picked them up and investigated them were injured.

The ingenuity and new means of offence were, however, by no means confined to the Russians, for a Mr. Macintosh, after the failure of the first bombardment of Sebastopol, evolved a system of attacking fortifications with a long hose supported by floats, through which naptha was to be pumped. Being set alight with some potassium, the fort attacked would be immediately smoked out.

Experiments at Portsmouth having proved that this system was "simple, certain and cheap," Mr. Macintosh proceeded to the Crimea with his invention at his own expense.   He was eventually given £1000 towards his expenses, but no attempt was made to employ the system. It is by no means clear how the necessary potassium was to be got into the water at the requisite spot.

The same war also produced the fire-shell of the British Captain Norton.   This appears to have been a resurrection of the old idea of Greek fire.   It could be used from a rifle or from a shell-gun, and like the previous invention "rendered war impossible," and again like the previous invention does not appear to have ever materialised into practice.

On the practical side more results were achieved. The Lancaster gun which fired an oval shot was actually used with success in the war.   From it the rifled gun presently emerged.   There also emerged the then amateur invention of one Warry, who invented a new type of gun capable of firing sixteen to eighteen rounds per minute.   The idea of wire wound guns was also apparent, and Mr. Armstrong* (as he then was), suggested the idea of percussion shell.   It is interesting to note that these last were received with extreme dissatisfaction in the Navy on the grounds that they might go off at the wrong time.

Of the Crimean War, however, it may be said that though it was not noted for naval actions, it was probably the most important war in its indirect results on the Navy that ever took place.   It brought in the armoured ship, the rifled gun, and what was ultimately to develop into the torpedo.   It saw the crude birth of " blockade mines " and rapid fire guns ; everyone of them inventions that, judging by the slow progress of steam, would— failing war to necessitate swift development—have been still in the experimental stage even to-day.   To-day, war being a nearer possibility than in the 1850 era, progress is more rapid, and no invention of practical

* The Lord Armstrong, founder of Elswick, etc.

value fails to secure full tests. Yet there are not wanting those who prophesy that theDreadnoughts of to-day merely reproduce in another form the 120 screw ships of the line of sixty years ago ; and that the next great naval war may well bring about changes every whit as drastic as any that the Crimean War caused to come into being.

The torpedo to-day is fully as great a menace to the modern ship of the line as the shell gun was to those of 1853. The submarine is an infinitely greater menace to it than the crude Russian mines of the Crimean War ever were. Endless potentialities reside in aircraft.

Wherefrom it may well be argued that out of the next great naval war (despite whatever lesser wars in between may have taught), the battleship is likely to be profoundly modified.

That it will be swept out of existence is improbable. The whole lesson of history is that the "capital ship" will ever adjust itself to the needs of the hour. It has always been the essential rallying point of lesser craft— the mobile base to meet the mobile base of the enemy.

Meanwhile, it is beyond question that at the time of the Crimean War the British Navy from one cause and another was little better than a paper force.

It is plain enough that at the time of the Crimean War very little remained of the fleet of the Nelson Era. The fleet "worried through," but very clearly it had reached the end of its tether.

The reason why will be found in the next chapter.

L

X.

THE COMING OF THE IRONCLAD.

THE period immediately following the Crimean War saw a gradual change in the relations between England and France. In 1858 a panic similar to those with which later years have familiarised us began to arise, and in December, 1858, and January, 1859, a committee sat under the Administration of Lord Derby " to consider the very serious increase which had taken place of late years in the Navy Estimates, while it represented that the naval force of the country was far inferior to what it ought to be with reference to that of other Powers, and especially France, and that increased efforts and increased expenditure were imperatively called for to place it on a proper footing."

This committee found that whereas in 1850 there were eighty-six British ships of the line to forty-five French ones, this ratio had altogether ceased to exist ; and that both Powers had now twenty-nine screw ships of the Line. Any other large ships had ceased to count.

In 1859 there also appeared in the famous " Leipsic Article," commenting on the decline of the British Fleet and the rise of the French. Certain extracts from this, though dealing with the past for the most part, are here given *en bloc*, for they indicate very clearly the circumstances in which, under pressure from German influences, the modern British Navy came to be founded. It is, to say the least of it, questionable whether but for this Teutonic agitation public opinion in England would ever have been aroused from its lethargy in time. This epoch-making article appeared in the *Conversations Lexicon*, of Leipsic.

After some prelude the article referred to the appearance of the French Fleet in the Crimean War :—

"The late war in the East (Crimean) first opened the eyes of Englishmen to the true position of affairs, and it was not without some sensation of alarm that they gazed at this vision of the unveiled reality. Here and there, indeed, an allusion, having some foundation in fact, had been heard, during the Presidency of Louis Napoleon, and had drawn attention to the menaced possibility of an invasion of the British Isles ; but such notions were soon overwhelmed by the derision with which they were jeeringly greeted by the national pride.

" Those expressions of contempt were, however, not doomed to be silenced in their turn by the sudden apparition in the autumn of 1854 of thirty-eight French ships of the line and sixty-six frigates and corvettes, fully manned and ready for immediate action. During the three preceding years Louis Napoleon had built twenty-four line-of-battle ships, and in the course of the year 1854 alone thirteen men-of-war were launched, nine of which were ships of the line. In addition to these, the keels of fifty-two more, comprising three ships of the line and six frigates, were immediately laid down. The English had thus the mortification to be obliged not only to cede to their allies the principal position in the camp, but also reluctantly to acknowledge their equality on that element whereon they had hoped to reign supreme."   . . .

* * * *

" If we carried our investigation no further than this we should naturally conclude that, with such a numerical superiority, sufficient in itself to form a very respectable armament for a second-rate power, England has very little to fear from the marine of France. We must not forget, however, that quality as well as numbers must be considered in estimating the strength of a Fleet. When we take this element into our calculations, we shall find the balance very soon turned in favour of France. We perceive, then, that while the English list comprises every individual sail the country possess, whether fit for commission or altogether antiquated and past service (and some, like the *Victory*, built towards the close of the last or the beginning of this century), the French Navy, as we have observed, scarcely contains a single ship built prior to the year 1840 ; so that nearly all are less than twenty years old. This is a fact of the greatest importance, and indicates an immense preponderance in favour of France. Though many of England's oldest craft figure in the ' Navy List ' as seaworthy and fit for active service, we have no less an authority than that of Sir Charles Napier (in his Letter to the First Lord of the Admiralty in 1849) that some are mere lumber, and many others cannot be reckoned upon to add any appreciable strength to a Fleet in case of need. Independently, too,

of the introduction of the screw, such fundamental changes have
been introduced, within the last fifty years, both into the principles
of naval architecture and of gunnery, that a modern 120-gun ship,
built with due regard to recent improvements, and carrying guns of
the calibre now in ordinary use, would in a very short space of time
put *ten* ships like the *Victory hors de combat*, with, at the same time,
little chance of injury to herself.

" It is time, however, to turn our attention to another important
part of the *material*, namely, artillery.   Under this head we purpose
designating, not only to the number of guns and their calibre, but
also the mode in which they are served, for in actual warfare this, of
course, is a primary consideration.   If we take the received history
of naval warfare for the basis of our investigation, we cannot fail to
remark one notable circumstance in favour of the English, which
can only be ascribed to their superiority in the use of this arm.   That
circumstance is the important and uniform advantage they have had
in the fewer number of casualties they have sustained as compared
with other nations with whom they may have chanced to have been
engaged.   To prove that our assertions are not made at random,
we subjoin some statistics in support of this position.   In April,
1798, then, the English ship *Mars* took the French *L'Hercule* ; the
former had ninety killed and wounded, the latter 290.   In the preceding February there had been an engagement between the English
Sybil and French *La Forte*, in which the killed and wounded of the
former numbered twenty-one, and those of the latter 143.   In
March, 1806, the English ship *London* took the French *Marengo* ;
the English with a loss of thirty-two, the latter of 145 men.   On the
4th November, 1805, two English ships of the line engaged four
French vessels, and the respective losses were, again, 135 and 730.
On the 14th February, 1797, in an action between the Fleets of England and Spain, the English lost 300 and the Spaniards 800.   On
the 11th of October of the same year, in the engagement off Camperdown, between the English and Dutch, the respective losses were
825 and 1,160.   On the 5th July, 1808, the English frigate *Seahorse*
took the Turkish frigate *Badere Zuffer*, and of the Turks there fell 370
against fifteen English.   Finally, in the same year the Russian ship
of the line *Wsewolod* was taken by two English ships of the line, with
a loss to the latter of 303, and to the former of only sixty-two.

" This contrast, so favourable to England, has been constantly
maintained, and can only be attributable to her superior artillery.
Her seamen not only aimed with greater precision, and fired more
steadily than those of the French and of other nations, but they had
the reputation of loading with far greater rapidity.   It was remarked,
in 1805, that the English could fire a round with ball every minute,
whereas it took the French gunners three minutes to perform the
same operation.   Then, again, the English tactics were superior.

It was the universal practice of the French to seek to dismast an adversary ; they consequently aimed high, while the English invariably concentrated their fire upon the hulls of their adversaries ; and clearly the broadside of a vessel presents a much better mark to aim at than the mere masts and rigging.   British guns were also usually of higher calibre, for though they bore the same denomination, they were in reality much heavier.   Thus, the English *Lavinia*, though nominally a frigate of forty tons, actually carried fifty ;   and thirty-six and 38-gun frigates nearly always carried forty-four and forty-six.   The English ship *Belleisle*, at Trafalgar, though said to be a seventy-four, carried ninety pieces of ordnance, while the Spanish ship she engaged, though called eighty-four, had in fact, only seventy-eight guns.   From this disparity in the number and calibre of their guns, as well as in the mode in which they were served, it resulted that France and her allies lost eighty-five ships of the line and 180 frigates, while her antagonist only suffered to the extent of thirteen ships of the line and eighty-three frigates.

   " It was not until the close of the war that France became fully aware to what an extent her inferiority in the above respects had contributed to her reverses ;   otherwise the unfortunate Admiral Villeneuve would not invariably have ascribed his mishaps to the inexperience of his officers and men, and to the incomplete and inferior equipment of his vessels.   The truth was, that not only was the artillery, as we have shown, inferior, but the whole system in vogue at that period on board French ships was antiquated, having continued without reform or improvement for two hundred years ; it was deficient, too, in enforcing subordination, that most essential condition of the power and efficiency of a ship of war."

The French *inscription maritime* is then dealt with at great length, after which occur the following passages, even more interesting perhaps to-day than when they were written :—

   " In considering, then, what perfect seamanship really is, we must first adopt a correct standard by which to estimate it.   The English sailor has been so long assumed as the perfect type of the *genus* seaman, that the world has nearly acquiesced in that veiw, and *even we in Germany have been accustomed to rank our crews below the English, though it is an unfair estimate.**   There are no better sailors in the world than the German seamen, and there is no foreign nation that would assert the contrary.   On the other hand, it has also been the fashion universally to abuse French seamanship, and to speak of her sailors as below criticism.   None proclaimed this opinion more loudly than the English ;   but in so doing they recurred to the men they had beaten under the Revolution and Bonaparte.   The Crimean

* The italics are mine.—F.T.J.

War, however, opened their eyes, and taught them that the French
sailors of to-day were no longer the men of 1806, and that, to say the
least, they are in no respect inferior to the British.   England had for
years been compelled to keep up a large effective force always ready
for action, in consequence of the nature of her dependencies, which,
as they consist of remote colonies across distant seas, required such
a provision for their protection.   This gave her an immeasurable
superiority in days gone by.   But since France in 1840 discovered her
deficiency, it has been supplied by the maintenance of a permanent
experimental Fleet, which, under the command of such Admirals as
Lalande de Joinville, Ducas, Hamelin, and Bruat, has been the nur-
sery of the present most effective body of officers and men ; which,
since 1853, have not ceased to humble the boasted superiority of
England, besides causing her many anxious misgivings.

Anyone who had the opportunity of viewing the two Fleets
together in the Black Sea or the Baltic, and was in a position to draw
a comparison, could not fail to be convinced that everything connected with manœuvring, evolutions, and gunnery was, beyond
comparison, more smartly, quickly, and exactly executed by the
French than by the English, and must have observed the brilliant
prestige which had so long surrounded England's tars pale sensibly
beside the rising glories of her rival."

That this was not merely captious criticism is borne
out by the following extracts from " The Life and
Correspondence of Admiral Sir Charles Napier, K.C.B.":—

" We have great reason to be afraid of France, because she
possesses a large disposable army, and our arsenals are comparatively
undefended—London entirely so—and we have no sufficient naval
force at home.   Of ships (with the exception of steamers) we have
enough ; but what is the use of them without men ?   They are only
barracks, and are of no more use for defence than if we were to build
batteries all over the country, without soldiers to put into them."

*   *   *   *

" Such were our inadequate resources for defence, had the
Russians been able to get out of the Baltic, and make an attempt on
our unprotected shores."   .   .   .

*   *   *   *

" The great difficulty consisted in manning of such a fleet.
Impressment was no longer to be thought of ; but, strange to say,
the Bill which had passed through Parliament, empowering, in case
of war, the grant of an ample bounty to seamen, was not acted upon,
and consequently most of the ships were very inefficiently manned—
some of them chiefly with the landsmen of the lowest class.   Nothing

had been done towards the training of the men, and no provision was even made to clothe them in a manner required by the climate to which they were about to be sent."   . . .

* * * *

" Our Ambassador likewise warned the British Government that the Navy of Russia could not with safety be under-estimated, and, moreover, the Russian gunners were all well trained, while those of the British Squadron were *most deficient in this respect.* The object of the Russians, in wishing to get their best ships to Sveaborg, was the impression that Cronstadt would be first attacked ; in which case, calculating on the strength of the forts to repel an assault, they would have fresh ships wherewith to assail our disabled and weakened fleet, should they be obliged to retreat. Sir Hamilton Seymour warned our Government of the great number of gunboats the Russians could bring out, eighty of which were to be manned by Finns, fifty men to each boat."   . . .

* * * *

" Such," says the author of the biography, " were the reasons, no doubt powerful enough, for hurrying off, even without pilots, the ill-appointed and under-manned squadron placed under Sir Charles Napier's command, at this inclement season of the year, when the periodical gales of the vernal equinox might be daily expected. The squadron, on leaving Spithead, consisted of four sail-of-the-line, four blockships, four frigates, and four steamers (not a single gunboat) ; and with this force, hastily got together, for the most part manned with the refuse of London and other towns, destitute of even clothing, their best seamen consisting of dockyard riggers and a few coastguard men—and without the latter, it has been alleged, the squadron could not have put to sea—with this inefficient force did Sir Charles Napier leave our shores, to offer battle to the Russian Fleet, consisting of seven-and-twenty well-trained and well-appointed ships of the line, eight or ten frigates, seven corvettes and brigs, and nine steamers, besides small craft and flotillas of gunboats, supposed in the aggregate to number one hundred and eighty."   . . .

* * * *

" It is, probably, an unprecedented event in the annals of war, or, at least, in those of our history, that a fleet should be sent out, on a most momentous service so ill-manned that the Commander was directed to endeavour to ' pick up,' if possible, foreign seamen in foreign ports, and so ill-provided with munitions of war, that he was restricted in the use of what he most required, in order to render his inexperienced crews as efficient as possible. It is equally worthy of record that the Board of Admiralty, throughout the whole campaign, never supplied the Fleet with a single Congreve rocket, although it was no secret that great numbers had been made in London for the Russians, to whom they were of far less use than to the British Fleet, which could not well undertake any bombardment without them.   The Board of Admiralty must have been perfectly aware of the condition, in these respects, of that Fleet on whose efficiency so much depended, and from which so much was expected, for, in a letter to Sir Charles Napier, from a member of that Board, I find it recorded as his opinion, that the Emperor of Russia ought either to burn his Fleet, or try his strength with the British Squadron whilst he mustered double their numbers, and whilst our crews were ' so miserably raw ! '   Yet this inefficiency was fully and frankly admitted by Sir James Graham, from whom infrequent instructions arrived to supply the deficiency of good men by picking up foreign sailors in the Baltic.   The anxiety of the First Lord upon this point was excessive.   He was continually inquiring whether the Admiral had been able to ' *pick up any Swedes or Norwegians,* who were good sailors and quite trustworthy.'   He was told to ' enter them quietly.'   If he could not get Swedes and Norwegians, ' even Danes would strengthen him, for they were hardy seamen and brave.   There was, it is true, a difficulty with their Governments, but if the men enlisted freely, and came over to the Fleet, the First Lord did not see why the Admiral should be over-nice, and refuse good seamen without much inquiry as to the place from whence they came.'

" Admiral Berkeley, moreover, instructed the Admiral to the same effect.   ' Have any of your ships tried for men in a Norwegian port ?   *It is said that you might have any number of good seamen from that country.'*   On the 18th of March the Admiral had been apprised that the *James Watt,* the *Prince Regent* and *Majestic* would now join him ; ' *but men are wanting,* and it is impossible to say how long it will be before they are completed.'   On the 4th of April Admiral Berkeley stated :   ' Notwithstanding   the   number   of   landsmen entered, we are come nearly to a dead standstill as to seamen ; and after the *James Watt* and *Prince Regent* reach you, I do not know when we shall be able to send you a further reinforcement, *for want of men* !   *Something must be done, and done speedily, or there will be a breakdown in our present rickety system.'* "

The   German   article   produced   a   great   stir   in England.   This was followed up by the publication in 1859 of *The Navies of the World,* by Hans Busk, M.A., of Trinity College, Cambridge, who, while nominally casting cold water on the " Leipsic Article," added fuel to the fire.   This writer was one of the first to concentrate attention upon the fact that the French were building " iron-plated ships."

From this scarce and remarkably interesting work I quote the following :—

" The determination of the French Government to build a number of iron or steel-cased ships imperatively obliges us to follow their example. The original idea of plating ships in this way, so as to render them shot-proof, is due, not, as is generally supposed in this country, to the present Emperor, but to a Captain in the French Navy, who, about a quarter of a century since, suggested that all wooden vessels should be sheathed with composite slabs of iron of fourteen or fifteen centimetres in thickness ; that is to say, with stout plates of wrought-iron having blocks of cast metal between. A similar suggestion was made among others by General Paixhans ; but one of the first to reduce it to practice was Mr. Stevens, of New York, the well-known steamship builder, who about ten years ago communicated to Mr. Scott Russell the results of a long series of experiments, instituted by the American Government for the purpose of testing the power of plates of iron and steel to resist cannon-shot. Mr. Lloyd, of the Admiralty, proposed the adoption of plates 4ins. in thickness, instead of a number of thinner sheets, as recommended by the Emperor. The English and French floating batteries were as is well known, protected upon Mr. Lloyd's plan. From trials recently made, however, it has been pretty well ascertained that this iron planking, on whatever principle applied, will only repel hollow shot or shells ; heavy solid projectiles of wrought iron, or those faced with steel having been found, on repeated trials, to perforate the thickest covering which has ever been adopted, and that, too, even at considerable ranges.

" Mr. Reed, already alluded to, proposes to protect only the midship portion of the ship, and to separate it from the parts fore and aft by strong water-tight compartments, so that, however much the extremities might suffer, the ship would still be safe and the crew below protected ; but, as he himself admits, there would obviously be no defence against raking shot.

" The French vessels last alluded to, follow the lines and dimensions of the *Napoleon* (one of the best, if not the finest ship in their Navy) ; but they will only carry thirty or thirty-six guns, and the metal sheathing will be from ten to eleven centimetres (about 4¼ins.) in thickness. Two similar ships are to be commenced here forthwith ; and as the First Lord of the Admiralty has prophetically warned us that they will be the most expensive ships ever constructed in this country, it is earnestly to be hoped that they may be found proportionately valuable, should their powers ever come to be tested ; they will each cost from £126,000 to £130,000 or £4,200 per gun ; the ordinary expense of a sailing man-of-war being about £1,000, and of a steamer from £1,800 to £2,000 per gun."

After this follow various statistics of the French
Fleet of no particular interest here except for the
following passage :—

" Irrespective of the above are the four *fregates blindées*, or iron-
plated frigates, two of which are now in an advanced state at Toulon.
    " These ships are to be substituted for line-of-battle ships ;
their timbers are of the scantling of three-deckers ; they will be
provided with thirty-six heavy guns, twenty-four of them rifled,
and 50-pounders, calculated to throw an eighty pound percussion
shell. Such is the opinion of French naval officers respecting the
tremendous power of these ships, that they fully anticipate the
complete abolition, within ten or a dozen years, of all line-of-battle
ships."

Here it is desirable to leave ships for a moment
and deal with the corresponding stage of gunnery, which
began to take on its modern form contemporaneously
with the ironclad ship. In 1858-9 began that contest
between the gun and armour, which can hardly be said
to be ended even in our own day (1912), for improved
kinds of armour are still being sought and experimented
with. To quote the work of Hans Busk and its contemporary summary :—

" A number of guns, cast at Woolwich, were sent to Mr. Whitworth's works at Manchester to be bored and rifled. In April, 1856,
trial was made with a brass 24-pounder of the construction above
described. The projectiles employed on that occasion varied from
two to six diameters in length, and a very rapid rotary motion was
communicated to them. The gun itself weighed 13cwt. ; the bore,
instead of being of a calibre fitted to receive a spherical 24-pound
shot, was only of sufficient capacity to admit one of 9 pounds.
The hexagonal bore measured 4ins. in diameter, and was rather
more than 54ins. long. It was entirely finished by machinery, and
the projectiles were fitted with mathematical precision, the spiral in
both cases being formed with absolute accuracy. The gun, externally,
had only the dimensions of a 24-pound howitzer, but it projected
missiles of 24 pounds, 32 pounds, and 48 pounds each, the additional
weight having been obtained by increased length. Upon this new
system, then, it will be seen that guns capable, under the old plan,
of supporting the strain of a 24-pound ball, may be made with ease
to throw a 48-pound shot ; the reduction of the calibre allowing of
a sufficient thickness of metal being left to ensure safety. The
32-pound and 48-pound projectiles used in the above experiments

were respectively 11¾ins. and 16½ins. in length. They were pointed at the foremost extremity, being shaped and rounded somewhat like the smaller end of an egg. At the base they were flat, and slightly hollowed towards the centre. The gun was mounted for the occasion upon an ordinary artillery carriage, which shows no symptoms of having been strained, nor of being in any way injured by the concussions to which it had been subjected."

* * * *

" Subsequently, some further experiments were made with the same gun with reduced elevation, when the projectiles, striking the ground at comparatively short distances, rebounded again and again till their momentum was expended. The first shot thus fired weighed 32 pounds, the charge of powder being only 3 ounces, and the gun having an elevation of 2 degrees. The projectile made its first graze at a distance of 92 yards, furrowing the ground for about 7ft., and leaving distinct indications of its rotary axial motion. It rose again to an elevation of about 6ft., grazing, after a further flight of 64yds. The third graze (owing probably to the hard nature of the soil at the point last struck) was at a distance of 70yds. further ; after which it traversed some ploughed land, grazing several times, coming finally to rest after having accomplished altogether a distance of 492yds.

" The second shot also weighed 32 pounds ; the charge, as before, consisted of 3 ounces of powder ; but this time the elevation given to the gun was 3 degrees. The projectile first grazed the ground at a point 108yds. from the muzzle ; the second graze was 126yds. further ; but happening to touch the lower bar of an iron fence— a circumstance which appeared to affect its flight—it dropped finally after having accomplished 490yds. Some further experiments were then made with shot weighing 48 pounds each.

" These very reduced charges rendered it necessary to make use of wooden wads to fill the cavities in the base of the projectiles. This had a tendency to reduce very much the power of the gun.

" A further trial with the hexagonal gun was made at Liverpool on the 7th of May. Several shots, varying from 24 to 48 pounds in weight, were fired. The first, weighing 24 pounds, with a charge of 11 pounds of powder, attained a distance of 2,800 yards, the elevation given having been 8 degrees. These experiments could hardly be said to have exhibited the *maximum* capacity of the gun, having been interrupted by the rapid rising of the tide. The average range of several 48-pound shots was 3,000 yards, but there is little doubt but that a much greater distance will be achieved when Mr. Whitworth has perfected some guns he is now constructing.

" A good deal of attention having previously been drawn to the subject of Armstrong's gun, respecting which few particulars had been allowed to transpire, on the 4th of March last the Secretary-

at-War made an official statement to the House, and gave some
details as to its alleged capabilities. Without describing its construction, he stated that one piece, throwing a projectile of 18
pounds, weighed but one-third as much as the ordinary gun of
that calibre. With a charge of 5 pounds of powder, a 32-pounder
attained a range of 5¼ miles ; at 3,000 yards its accuracy, as compared with that of a common gun, was stated to be in the proportion
of 7 to 1. At 1,000 yards it had struck the target 57 times succes-
sively, and after 13,000 rounds the gun showed symptoms of
deterioration.   In conclusion, it was said that the destructive
effects occasioned by this new ordnance exceeded anything that
had been previously witnessed, and that in all probability it was
destined to effect a complete revolution in warfare.

Armstrong's own statement was :—

" Schemers whose invention merely figure upon paper, have
little idea of the difficulties that are encountered by those who carry
inventions into practice. For my part, I had my full share of such
difficulties, and it took me nearly three years of continual application
to surmount them. . . . .   Early last year a committee was
appointed to investigate the whole subject of rifled cannon.   They
consisted of officers of great experience in gunnery ; and after having
given much time for a period of five months to the guns, projectiles,
and fuses which I submitted to them, they returned a unanimous
verdict in favour of my system.   With respect to the precision and
range which have been attained with these guns, I may observe that
at a distance of 600 yards an object no larger than the muzzle of an
enemy's gun may be struck at almost every shot.   At 3,000 yards a
target of 9ft. square, which at that distance looks like a mere speck,
has on a calm day been struck five times in ten shots.   A ship would
afford a target large enough to be hit at much longer distances, and
shells may be thrown into a town or fortress at a range of more than
five miles.   But to do justice to the weapon when used at long distances, it will be necessary that gunners should undergo a more
scientific training than at present ; and I believe that both the
naval and military departments of Government will take the necessary measures to afford proper instruction, both to officers and men.
It is an interesting question to consider what would be the effect of
the general introduction of these weapons upon the various conditions of warfare.   In the case of ships opposed to ships in the open
sea, it appears to me that they would simply destroy each other, if
both were made of timber.   The day has gone by for putting men in
armour.   Fortunately, however, no nation can play at that game
like England ; for we have boundless resources, both in the production
and application of iron, which must be the material for the armour.
In the case of a battery against a ship, the advantage would be greatly

in favour of the battery, because it would have a steady platform for its guns, and would be made of a less vulnerable material, supposing the ship to be made of timber. But, on the other hand, in bombarding fortresses, arsenals, or dockyards, when the object to be struck is very extended, ships would be enabled to operate from a great distance, where they could bid defiance to land defences."

After some observations, the author continued :—

" Notwithstanding the high estimation in which Sir William Armstrong's guns are held, and deservedly so from their great intrinsic merit, they have certainly in Mr. Warry's great invention a rival that may eventually be found to eclipse them.

" The Armstrong gun cannot be fired oftener than three times a minute, and the bore, it is said, has to be constantly sluiced with water ; whereas Warry's admits, as has been affirmed, of being discharged 16 or 18 times a minute, or 1,000 an hour, without difficulty, though of course not without heating, as some reporters have misrepresented. Guns of the former description are expensive, and must be made expressly by means of special machinery. Mr. Warry, on the other hand, asserts that he can convert every existing gun into a breech-loader upon his principle, and at a moderate outlay : an advantage of the greatest moment at the present time.

" This gun is fired by means of a lock. On one side of the breech there is a lever, so contrived that by one motion of the hand it is made to cock the hammer and to open the chamber. A second movement closes the charger again, pierces or cuts the cartridge, places a cap on the nipple, and fires the gun almost simultaneously.

" With a due supply of ammunition, therefore, a destructive torrent of shot and shell may be maintained *ad libitum.* It is not difficult to form a conception of the havoc even one such gun would occasion if brought to bear upon the head of an advancing column.

" The inventor has, besides, made application for a patent for a new coating he has devised for all kinds of projectiles, in lieu of any leaden or metallic covering, which has been found very objectionable in actual practice. The new coating, it is said, reduces the ' fouling ' to a minimum.

" But we cannot turn even from this very brief consideration of the improvements in modern cannon without offering a few observations relative to an invention of a different kind, but one that may possibly prove of greater moment than either of the guns that have been described. This is the composition known as ' Norton's liquid fire.' In the terrific character of its effect it rivals all that has been recorded of the old Greek fire, at the same time that it is perfectly manageable, and may be projected from an Enfield rifle, from a field-piece, or from heavier ordnance. The composition Captain Norton uses consists of a chemical combination of sulphur, carbon, and phosphorus. He merely encloses this in a metal or even in a wooden shell, and its effect upon striking the side or sails of a ship, a wooden building, or indeed any object at all combustible, is to cause its instant ignition. This ' liquid fire ' has apparently the property of penetrating or of saturating any substance against which it may be projected, and such is its affinity for oxygen that it even decomposes water and combines with its component oxygen. Water, consequently, has no power to quench it, and if burning canvas, set on fire in this way, be trodden under foot and apparently extinguished it soon bursts again into flames."

It is not uninteresting to reflect that although Norton's liquid fire came to nothing, yet the present century has already seen three variations on the idea.

The first instance is the type of big shell used by the Japanese at Tsushima. Little is known as to their exact composition, but they were undoubtedly extremely inflamable.

Captain Semenoff in " The Battle of Tsushima " thus describes them :—

" The Japanese had apparently succeeded in realising what the Americans had endeavoured to attain in inventing their ' Vesuvium.'

" In addition to this there was the unusual high temperature and liquid flame of the explosion, which seemed to spread over everything. I actually watched a steel plate catch fire from a burst. Of course, the steel did not burn, but the paint on it did. Such almost non-combustible materials as hammocks, and rows of boxes, drenched with water, flared up in a moment. At times it was impossible to see anything with glasses, owing to everything being so distorted with the quivering, heated air."

* * * *

" According to thoroughly trustworthy reports, the Japanese in the battle of Tsushima were the first to employ a new kind of explosive in their shells, the secret of which they bought during the war from the inventor, a colonel in one of the South American Republics. It was said that these shells could only be used in guns of large calibre in the armoured squadrons, and that is how those of our ships engaged with Admiral Kataoka's squadron did not suffer the same amount of damage, or have so many fires, as the ships engaged with the battleships and armoured cruisers."

The second instance is the Krupp fire shell designed for use against dirigible balloons. The third is the " Thermite shell," which, early in 1912, was proposed

for adoption in France. It was calculated that one
12-inch A.P. shell exploding would melt half a ton of
steel.

The following passage from Hearns Busk is of
interest :—

" In 1855 Mr. Longridge, C.E., proposed to construct cannon
of tubes covered with wire wound round them so tightly as almost
entirely to relieve the inside from strain. On the 25th of June of
the same year Mr. Mallet read a paper advocating the construction
of cannon of successive layers of cylinders, so put together that all
should be equally strained when the gun is fired ; thus the inside
would not be subject to fracture, while the outside would be useless
as in a cast mass. His method of effecting this was, as is well known,
to have each cylinder slightly too small to go over the one under it,
till expanded by heat, so that when cool it compresses the interior
and is slightly strained itself. Thirty-six-inch mortars have been
made on the principle, and if they have failed with 40lbs. of powder,
cast-iron must have failed still less. In 1856 Professor Daniel Tread-
well, Vice-President of the American Academy, read a paper to
that body recommending the same principle of construction ; and
Captain Blakely has himself for some years been endeavouring to
urge its adoption by argument and direct experiments. In December,
1857, some trials were made with guns constructed by that officer ;
and the result of a comparative trial of a 9-pounder with a cast-iron
service gun of similar size and weight gave results proving the sound-
ness of his views ; for Captain Blakely's gun bore about double the
amount of firing the service gun did, and being then uninjured, was
loaded to the muzzle, and was thus fired 158 times before it burst."

From these contemporary extracts it will be seen
that by 1859 the germ of nearly every modern idea in
connection with gunnery existed, and has since developed
somewhat on " trial and error " lines for at any rate the
greater part of the intervening period.

The contemporary situation as regards defence is
also best summed up from the authority from whom the
above gunnery extracts are taken :—

" The result of numerous trials appeared to convince those best
competent to judge of such matters, that iron plates, or, rather, slabs,
eleven centimetres (about 4½ins.) in thickness, would offer adequate
protection to a ship from the effects of hollow shot. Acting upon this
impression, four floating batteries, resembling in most respects those
constructed here, were ordered to be built, and notwithstanding the

enormous difficulties connected with such an undertaking, these four
vessels were turned out, complete in all respects, in ten months—an
astonishing instance of the resources of French dockyards and the
ability of French engineers.

" From this event may be dated the commencement of a new
epoch in naval tactics.   The next problem was to determine whether
a form better adapted for progression than that of these batteries
could not be given to vessels sheathed in a similar manner.   Hence
originated the iron-plated frigates (*frégates blindées*).   The intention
of their designer is, that they should have a speed and an armament
at least equal to that of the swiftest existing frigates, but their
colossal weight, and consequently their great draught of water, must
almost preclude the fulfilment of this expectation. Should they prove
successful, a number of larger ships of the same kind are to be commenced forthwith.   It is difficult to understand how, in the case of
these ships being found to answer, it will be possible for us to avert
a real " reconstruction " of our Navy, or, how any other nation,
aiming to rank as a maritime Power, can avoid the adoption of a
similar course.   In fact, the necessity has been appreciated, and we
are already at work.   But a good deal has to be accomplished ere the
use of such vessels become universal.   If these iron-plated vessels
do resist shell, it seems certain, as has been already stated, that solid
shot will either perforate at short ranges any thickness of metal that
has yet been tried, or will so indent the sheathing at longer distances
that the internal lining and rib-work of oak will be riven, shattered
loosened, or crushed to an extent that would almost as speedily put
the ship *hors de combat* as if she had but been built after the old
fashion, much, as in days gone by, upon the introduction of gunpowder into warfare, the use of armour was found rather to aggra-
vate, than to ward off, the injuries inflicted by gunshot.   It was the
result of the operations against Kinburn that more particularly gave
rise to the high opinion at present entertained in favour of these
vaisseaux blindées.   Unwieldly and cumbersome as they appeared,
they were certainly a great improvement upon the floating batteries
used by the French and Spanish against Gibraltar in 1782.   Those
were merely enormous hulks, destitute of masts, sails, or rigging ;
their sides were composed of solid carpentry, 6ft. 6ins. in thickness,
and they carried from nine to twenty-four guns.   When in action,
streams of water were made to flow constantly over their decks and
sides, but notwithstanding every precaution, such an overwhelming
storm of shell and red-hot shot was poured upon them by the English
garrison, that they were all speedily burnt.   Not so the *Devastation*,
La Lave, and *La Tonnante* before the Russian fortress above mentioned, on the memorable 14th October, 1855.   At 9 p.m. they
opened fire, and in an hour and twenty-five minutes the enemy was
silenced, nearly all the gunners being killed, their pieces dismounted,
and all the ramparts themselves being for the most part demolished.

To accomplish this destruction in so short a space of time, the three batteries, each carrying eighteen fifty pounders (supported, of course, by the fire of the English vessels), advanced in very shallow water within 800 yards of the walls, receiving themselves very little damage in comparison with the immense havoc they occasioned."

From the above extract it is clear that the " impenetrable coat of mail " idea, popularly supposed to have led to the introduction of ironclads, never existed to any appreciable extent. Indeed, when the Committee, alluded to on an earlier page, concluded its labours in 1859, it merely recommended the conversion of nineteen more sailing ships into steamers. It was Sir John Pakington who decided to lay down a couple of " armoured steam frigates," and to build them of iron instead of wood.

The French *fregates blindées* were wooden ships, armoured. John Scott Russell is said to have been Pakington's chief adviser in this matter of building iron armoured ships and disregarding all the laborious conclusions of Captain Chads against iron hulls.

As regards the general recommendations of the Committee already referred to, these had resulted in 1861 in there being no less than sixty-seven wooden unarmoured ships of the Line building or converting into " screw ships."

The two iron-plated steam frigates were decided on without any popular enthusiasm concerning them. Now and again retired Admirals paid surreptitious visits to the French " *blindées* " and returned with alarming reports ; but, with the possible exception of flying machines, no epoch-making thing ever came in quite so quietly as the ironclad. The wildest dreamer saw nothing in it beyond a variation on existing types. The ironclad was something which, by carrying a great deal of weight, could keep out shell, beyond that no one seems to have had any particular ideals whatever, except perhaps Sir Edward Reed.

Early in 1859 designs for a type of ship to " answer " the French *fregates blindées* were called for, and fourteen

M

private firms submitted designs. All, however, were discarded.

Details of the designs submitted were as follows :—*

Designer.	Length.	Breadth	Dis-pl'm't. Tons.	Speed. Knots.	Wt.of Armour Displ.	Wt. of Hull Displ.	I.H.P. of Eng.
Laird	400.0	60.0	9779	13½	.11	.51	3250
Thames Co...	430.0	60.0	11180		.10	.58	4000
Mare	380.0	57.0	7341		.13	.46	3000
Scott Russell	385.0	58.0	7256		.18	.38	3000
Napier	365.0	56.0	8000	13½			4120
Westwood & Baillie	360.0	55.0	7600	13½	.16	.36	4000
Samuda.....	382.0	55.0	8084	13½	.16	.57	2500
Palmer	340.0	58.0	7690	13½			4500
Abethell	336.0	57.0	7668				2500
Henwood ...	372.0	52.0	6507		.18	.40	2500
Peake	354.9	56.0	7000		.14	.46	3000
Chatfield ...	343.6	59.6	7791		.14		
Lang	400.0	55.0	8511	15	.14	.53	2500
Cradock	360.0	57.6	7724		.20	.42	2500
Admiralty Office	380.0	58.0	8625	14			

The Abethell and Peake designs were wooden hulled, all the others iron ships.

The two ships, *Warrior* and *Black Prince*, as actually laid down, differed from the Admiralty design in certain details. The beam was increased slightly, and the displacement rose from 8625 to 9210.

The *Warrior* was laid down on the 25th May, 1859, at the Thames Ironworks, Blackwall ; the *Black Prince* a little later at Glasgow.

In substances they were ordinary wooden frigates, built of iron instead of wood, with armour to protect most (but not all) of the guns. This was done by a patch of armour amidships, covering about 60% of the side. It was deemed advisable to protect the engines ; otherwise as like as not the armour would have been over the battery only. Waterline protection was entirely un-realised, the steering gear of the *Warrior* being at the mercy of the first lucky shot.

* From *Naval Development of the Century*, by Sir N. Barnaby, K.C.B.

This, as Sir N. Barnaby has pointed out, was due
to accepting existing conditions :—

" The tiller was necessarily above the water-line and was outside
of the cover of the armour. The wooden line-of-battle ships, with
which the designers of these first iron-cased ships were familiar, had
required no special water-line protection, and when wheel ropes or
tiller were shot away the ship did not cease to be able to fight. The
line-of-battle ships, which they knew so well, had a lower, or gun
deck about four feet above the water-line, and an orlop deck about
three feet below the water-line. Between these two decks the ship's
sides were stouter than in any other part, and shot did not easily
perforate them. When a shot did enter there, between wind and
water, as it was called, ample provision was made to prevent the
serious admission of water.

" In this between-deck space the sides of the ship were kept free
from all erections or obstructions. The " wing passages " on the
orlop were clear, from end to end of the ship, and they were patrolled
by the carpenter's crew, who were provided with shot plugs of wood
and oakum and sail cloth with which to close any shot holes. As
against disabled steering gear there were spare tillers and tiller ropes,
and only injury to the rudder head itself was serious."

It is easy to-day to indicate where the old-time
designers erred ; and later on they realised and repaired
their error with commendable promptitude. The really
interesting point is that British designers evolved the
ideal thing for the day, while the French evolved
the idea of the ideal thing for the to-morrow. Un-
happily for the latter, their evolution was unable to survive its birth till the day of its utility. *La Gloire,* the
first French ironclad, was broken up more years ago
than any can remember ; the *Warrior* and the *Black
Prince,* though long ago reduced to hulk service,* still
float as sound as when in 1861 the *Warrior* first took the
water. To the French belongs the honour of realising
what armour protection might mean ; but to England
goes the credit of reducing the idea to practical
application.

The *Warrior* was designed by Messrs. Scott Russell
and Isaac Watts, the Chief Constructor. Her length
between perpendiculars was 380 feet. She carried

* The *Warrior,* now (1912) forms part of the *Vernon* Establishment at Portsmouth.

originally a uniform armament of forty-eight 68-pounders smooth bores, weighing 95cwt. each. These fired shell and cast-iron spherical shot. The guns were carried as follows :—Main deck, thirty-eight, of which twelve were not protected by armour. On the upper-deck, ten, also unprotected.

This armament was subsequently changed to two 110-pounder rifled Armstrongs on pivot mountings, and four 40-pounders on the upper-deck ; while the main-deck battery was reduced to thirty-four guns. At a later date it was again altered to four 8-inch 9-ton M.L.R., and twenty-eight 7-inch 6½-ton M.L.R.

In addition to her armour the *Warrior* was divided into 92 water-tight compartments, fore and aft. She had a double bottom amidships, considerably sub-divided (fifty-seven of the compartments), but no double bottom in the modern sense.

The *Warrior's* engines, by Penn, were horizontal single expansion. On trial they developed 5,267 I.H.P., and the then excellent speed of 14·079 knots.* Her six hours' sea speed trial resulted in a mean 5,092 H.P. and 13·936 knots.

Save for her unprotected steering gear, the *Warrior* may be described as a brilliant success for her era. She was launched on December 29th, 1860, and completed in the following year. The *Black Prince* was completed in 1862.

The *Warrior* and *Black Prince,* under a system which long endured in the British Navy, were followed by a certain number of diminutives, of which the first were the *Defence* and *Resistance,* of 6,150 tons, with speeds of just under 12 knots, and an armament of 16 guns. The armour was the same, but the battery protection was extended fore and aft, so that all guns were inside it. These ships were completed in 1862.

Three more ships were projected, of which the *Hector* and *Valiant,* completed in 1864 and 1865, were of

---

* *Our Ironclad Ships,* by (Sir) E. J. Reed. Sir N. Barnaby in *Naval Development of the Century* gives 5,470=14.36 knots.

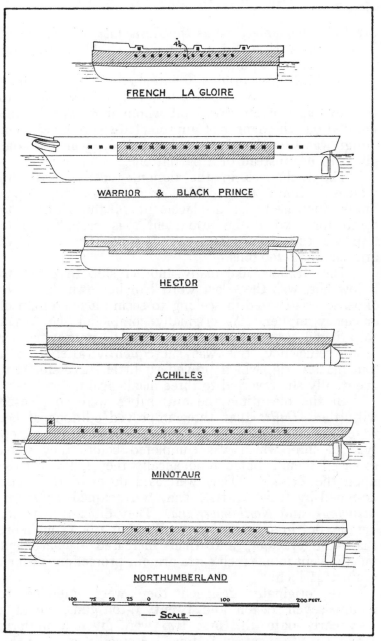

FRENCH LA GLOIRE

WARRIOR & BLACK PRINCE

HECTOR

ACHILLES

MINOTAUR

NORTHUMBERLAND

100   75   50   25   0   100   200 FEET.

— SCALE. —

EARLY BRITISH BROADSIDE IRONCLADS.

precisely the same type as the *Resistance*, but displaced 6,710 tons, with about a knot more speed, and carried a couple of extra guns.

A third ship, originally intended to have been of the same class, was the *Achilles*, but, mainly owing to the influence of Mr. Reed (of whom more anon), who pointed out the danger of unprotected steering gear, her design was altered and a complete belt of 4½-inch armour given to her instead of a partial one.

These changes in the design, together with an increased horse-power which produced on trial 14.32 knots, increased the displacement of the *Achilles* to 9,820 tons, while the armament was brought up to fourteen 12-ton guns and two 6½-ton. The weight of armour was 1,200 tons.

The *Achilles*, like many another ship that was to follow her, was the " last word " of her own day. No expense was spared in seeking to secure a maximum of efficiency in her. As originally completed she was a ship-rigged vessel, but with a view to improving her sailing efficiency, this was subsequently altered to a four-masted rig, which proved so little successful that eventually she reverted to three masts again.

In the meantime the authorities were so pleased with the *Achilles* that three improved editions of her were designed. They were not completed until a new type of ship, which was completed before they were, replaced them ; but chronologically they followed close upon the *Achilles*. They were laid down in 1861, and designed by Isaac Watts. They were named *Agincourt*, *Minotaur*, and *Northumberland*. They differed in minor details, but in substance were all about 1,000 tons more than the *Achilles*, and their increased displacement mostly went in one inch extra armour protection (5½-inch against 4½-inch).

As originally designed they were intended to mount seven 12-ton and twenty 9-ton guns, but at a very early date the first two were given a uniform armament of seventeen 12-ton. A small portion of this armament of the upper deck was provided with armoured protection for right-ahead fire.

In appearance they were magnificent ships, fitted with five masts. Being 400 feet between perpendiculars they were the largest ships of their time, and at sea always proved very steady under both sail and steam.

These ships were the subject of violent disputes between the Controller of the Navy and their constructor. The Controller insisted that they were extravagantly large ships, as compared to French ships. The constructor insisted that it was essential that for any given power and protection a British ship must be larger than a foreign one, because of her more extended probable duties, and the consequent necessity of a larger coal supply.*

At and about this period there were a number of wooden ships-of-the-line building, which had been laid down from the year 1859 onwards. Following the French fashion, they were converted into ironclads. These ships, displacing from 6,100 to 6,830 tons, were the *Repulse, Royal Alfred, Zealous* (laid down 1859), *Caledonia, Ocean, Prince Consort, Royal Oak* (1860).†

The upper-decks of these ships were removed, and they were fitted with side armour, which was 4½ inches in the earliest to be treated, and 5½ inches in the latest. All of them carried sixteen 9-ton guns and four 6½-ton, with provision for ahead fire.

The experiment, though useful as a temporary expedient, was very expensive, and several of the ships had to be lengthened before anything could be done to them. None of them were very successful, and most of them disappeared from the Navy List at an early date.

This ends the period of " broadside ironclads " ; of the best of which it may be said that they were nothing but efforts to adapt new ideals to old methods.

---

* Apparently the first instance of the putting forward of a principle which later on profounly affected construction.

† In 1863, three ironclads, the *Lord Clyde* and *Lord Warden*, of 7,840 tons, and a small ship, the *Pallas*, 3,660 tons, were constructed with wooden hulls, in order to use up the stores of timber which had been accumulated.—See p. 70, *Our Ironclad Ships*, by Sir E. J. Reed.

XI.

THE REED ERA.

I N 1862 Mr. (afterwards Sir) E. J. Reed, was appointed Chief Constructor, and proceeded at once to produce the type of ship chiefly associated with his name. His ideals ran in the direction of short, handy ships of medium size, as heavily armed as possible, and with a good turn of speed. His arguments in favour of these ideals he afterwards described as follows :—*

" The merits of iron-clad ships do not consist in carrying a large proportion of weights to engine-power, or having a high speed in proportion to that power ; but rather in possessing great powers of offence and defence, being comparatively short, cheap, and handy, and steaming at a high speed, not in the most economical way possible, but by means of a moderate increase of power on account of the moderate proportions adopted in order to decrease the weight and cost, and to increase the handiness."

Generally speaking, his views were very revolutionary. The greatness of Sir E. J. Reed lay in the fact that he was the first man to conceive of the ironclad as a separate and distinct entity. Previously to him the ironclad was merely an ordinary steamer with some armour plating on her.

His first ship was the *Bellerophon*, of 7,550 tons displacement. She embodied distinct novelties in the construction of her hull, described by her designer in the following passages :—*

" The *Warrior* and the earlier ironclads are constructed with deep frames, or girders, running in a longitudinal direction through

---

* *Our Ironclad Ships*, by Sir E. J. Reed.

the greater part of the length of the ship, combined with numerous strong transverse frames, formed of plates and angle-irons, crossing them at right angles. In fact, up to the height of the armour the ship's framing very closely resembles in its character that of the platform or roadway of a common girder bridge, in which the principal or longitudinal strength is contributed by the continuous girders that stretch from pier to pier, and the transverse framing consists of short girders fitted between and fastened to the continuous girders. If we conceive such a platform to be curved transversely to a ship-shape form, and the under side to be covered with iron plating, we have a very fair idea of the construction of the lower part of the *Warrior*. If, instead of this arrangement, we conceive the continuous longitudinal girders to be considerably deepened, and the transverse girders to be replaced by so-called 'bracket-frames,' and then, after curving this to a ship-form, add iron-plating on both the upper and the under sides, we have a correspondingly good idea of the construction of the lower part of the *Bellerophon*. The *Bellerophon's* construction is, therefore, identical in character with the cellular system carried out in the Menai and other tubular bridges, which system has been proved by the most elaborate and careful experiments to be that which best combines lightness and strength in wrought-iron structures of tubular cross-section. The *Warrior's* system, wanting, as it does, an inner skin of iron—except in a few places, such as under the engines and boilers—is not in accordance with the cellular system, and is inferior to it in strength. As regards safety, also, no comparison can be made between the system of the *Warrior* and that of the *Bellerophon*. If the bottom plating is penetrated, in most places the water must enter the *Warrior's* hold, and she must depend for safety entirely on the efficiency of her watertight bulkheads. If the *Bellerophon's* bottom is broken through, no danger of this kind is run. The water cannot enter the hold until the inner bottom is broken through, and this inner bottom is not likely to be damaged by an ordinary accident, seeing that it is two or three feet distant from the outer bottom. Should some exceptional accident occur by which the inner bottom is penetrated, the *Bellerophon* would still have her watertight bulkheads to depend on, being, in fact, under these circumstances in a position similar to that occupied by the *Warrior* whenever her bottom plating is broken through ; while an accident which would prove fatal to the *Warrior* might leave the *Bellerophon* free from danger so long as the inner bottom remained intact."

As to be related later, the *Vanguard* disaster tended to contravert this optimism—but of that further on. The point of present interest is the recognition and establishment of a principle which, however common-place to-day, was in those days a complete novelty and a special feature of the iron ship as a peculiar war entity.

Equally of interest, in some ways more so, are the following anticipations of torpedo possibilities. The torpedo is such a familiar thing to-day that it is hard to throw ourselves back into the point of view necessary to appreciate the prophetic instincts of the man who created the first vessels which can really be called " battleships."

" It may be proper in this connection to draw attention to the fact that the probable employment of torpedoes in a future naval war has not been lost sight of in carrying out these structural improvements. Up to the present time torpedoes have been used almost solely for coast and harbour defence, and have, under those circumstances, proved most destructive, as a glance through the reports of the operations of the Federal Fleet at Charleston and other Confederate ports will show. It is still doubtful, however, whether these formidable engines of war can be supplied with anything like the same efficiency at sea under the vastly different conditions which they will there have to encounter. The Americans have, it is true, proposed to fit torpedo-booms to their unarmoured ocean-cruisers, such as the *Wampanoag*, and a naval war would doubtless at once bring similar schemes into prominence. Nothing less than actual warfare can be expected to set the question at rest ; but whatever the result of such a test may be, it is obviously a proper policy of construction to provide as much as possible against the dangers of torpedoes ; and it must be freely admitted that the strongest ironclad yet designed, although practically impenetrable by the heaviest guns yet constructed, would be very liable to damage from the explosion of a submerged torpedo. No ship's bottom can, in fact, be made strong enough to resist the shock of such an explosion ; and the question consequently arises : How best can the structure be made to give safety against a mode of attack which cannot fail to cause a more or less extensive fracture of the ship's bottom, even if it does no more serious damage ? In our recent ships, as I have said, attempts have been made to give a practical answer to this question. Seeing that the bottom must inevitably be broken through by the explosion of a torpedo which exerts its full force upon the ship, it obviously becomes necessary to provide, as far as possible, against the danger resulting from a great in-flow of water. This is the leading idea which has been kept in view in arranging the structural details of our ships to meet this danger, and the reader cannot fail to perceive that the double bottom and watertight subdivisions described above are as available against injury from torpedoes as they are against the injuries resulting from striking the ground."

Details of the *Bellerophon* were as follows :—

Displacement—7,550 tons.
Length—300ft. between perpendiculars.
Beam—56ft. 1in.
H.P.—6,520.
Mean Draught—26ft. 7ins.
Guns—Ten 12-ton M.L.R., five 6½-ton M.L.R. (changed in 1890 to ten 8-in. 14-ton B.L.R., four 6-in., six 4-in. ditto).
Armour (iron)—Belt 6in., Battery 6in., Bulkhead 5in., Conning tower 8in.
Speed—14.17 knots.
Coal—650 tons.
Launched—1865 ; completed, 1866.
Cost—Hull and machinery—£322,701.

The 12-ton guns were on the main deck, the 6½-ton on the upper deck, two of them being in an armoured bow battery. The *Bellerophon*, completed in 1866, was ship rigged, and carries the then novel feature of an armoured conning tower, abaft the mainmast.* She proved extremely handy, her turning circle being 559yds. as against 939yds. for the *Minotaur* and 1,050yds. for the *Warrior*. A balanced rudder, introduced in her for the first time, helped this result to some extent ; but the well thought-out design of this, the first real " battleship," was the main cause.

The *Bellerophon* was followed by a series of " improved *Bellerophons*," which will be dealt with later. First, however, it is necessary to revert to the coming of the turret-ship.

So long ago as the Crimean War Captain Cowper-Coles had introduced the *Lady Nancy*, " gun-raft," previously mentioned in connection with that war. In

---

* The American monitors all had conning towers ; but British masted battleships were without them.

the year 1860 his plans had matured sufficiently for him to make public the designs of a proposed turret ship, with no less than nine turrets in the centre line, each carrying two guns which were to recoil up a slope and return automatically to position.

There has been much discussion in the past as to whether Coles, or Ericsson, the designer of the *Monitor*, first hit upon the turret-ship idea.   As a matter of fact neither of them invented it, as the idea was first propounded in the 16th century, and " pivot guns " had long existed.   In so far as adapting the idea to modern uses is concerned, Ericsson was first in the field, but his turret revolved on a spindle.   The merit of the Cowper-Coles design was that he evolved the idea of mounting the turret on a series of rollers, thus making it of real practical utility.

Coles' ideal turret ship was not received officially with any great show of enthusiasm ; as a matter of fact it was an impracticable sort of ship.   The famous fight between the *Monitor* and the *Merrimac*, early in 1862, in the American Civil War, was, however, followed by a perfect " turret craze."   Turret ships were popularly acclaimed as essential to the preservation of British naval power.   The idea of a sea-going ship without sail power was unthinkable ; but the turret ships for coast defence purposes were demanded with such insistence that in 1862 Captain Coles, now more or less a popular hero, was put to supervise the reconstruction of the old steam wooden line-of-battleship *Royal Sovereign* into a turret ironclad.

This ship was originally a three-decker.   Coles cut her down to the lower deck, leaving a freeboard of ten feet.   The sides were covered with $4\frac{1}{2}$-inch iron armour. Four turrets were mounted on Coles's roller system, the forward turret carrying two and the other three one $12\frac{1}{2}$-ton guns.   These turrets were generally five inches thick, but at the portholes were increased up to ten inches. They were rotated by hand power.   There was one funnel, in front of which a thinly armoured conning tower was placed. Three pole masts were fitted. This ship was completed in 1864, and was fairly successful on trials. The cost of conversion was very heavy, and being wooden-hulled her weight-carrying ratio was small, 1837 tons to 3,243 tons, weight of hull.

Coles was at no time satisfied with this old three-decker as a proper test of his ideas, and his agitation was so far successful that the *Prince Albert* was presently built to his design. She was an iron turret-ship, generally resembling the *Royal Sovereign*, though carrying only one gun in each turret.

Particulars of her are :—

    Displacement—3,880 tons.
    Length—240ft. p.p.
    Beam—48ft. 1in.
    H.P.—2,130.
    Mean Draught—20ft. 4ins.
    Speed—11.65 knots.
    Coal—230 tons.
    Guns—Four 9-in. 12-ton M.L.R.

To the same era belong three armoured gunboats—*Viper*, *Vixen*, and *Waterwitch*—of about 1,230 tons each, armed with a couple of 6½-ton M.L.R. guns, armour 4½ins. The *Waterwitch*, which was slightly the heavier, was fitted with a species of turbine, sucking water in ahead and ejecting it astern (a very old idea revived). This was moderately successful, as the trial speeds of the three were :—

    Viper—8.89 knots.
    Vixen—9.59 knots.
    Waterwitch—9.24 knots.

In the *Vixen* twin screws were for the first time tried.

The *Prince Albert* was completed in 1866, the same year as the *Bellerophon*. Long before she was completed, Coles was agitating for the application of his principles to a sea-going masted ship.

Sir E. J. Reed has left it on record that his attitude in the matter was that of an interested observer. He was at no time blind to the advantages that the turret system conferred ; but, unlike the Coles' party, he was equally observant of its disadvantages. At a very early date he threw cold water on the masted turret-ship idea, and insisted that for a sea-going turret-ship to become practicable she must be mastless. He further pointed out that for a given weight eight guns could be mounted broadside fashion for four carried in turrets.

He developed his own ideas in the *Hercules*, laid down in 1866. The *Hercules*, except that recessed ports were introduced to supply something like end-on fire to the battery, was an amplified *Bellerophon*. Particulars of the *Hercules* (which was always a very successful ship) are :—

Displacement—8,680 tons.
Length—325ft.
Beam—59ft. $\frac{1}{2}$ins.
Mean Draught—26ft. 6ins.
H.P.—6,750.
Guns—Eight 18-ton M.L.R., two 12$\frac{1}{2}$-ton M.L.R., four 6$\frac{1}{2}$-ton M.L.R.
Armour (iron)—9in. 6in. Belt and Battery.
Speed—14.00 kts. (14.69 on the measured mile trials).
Coal—610 tons.
Cost—Hull and machinery, £361,134.

The *Hercules* was completed in 1868, contemporaneously with the completion of the *Agincourt* and *Northumberland*, which were very slowly finished.

At and about the same time the *Penelope* was built. She was designed for light draught and river service, her maximum draught being kept down to 17$\frac{1}{2}$ft. She carried eight 9-ton guns and had a 6-inch belt. Sir E. J. Reed being absent from office, his chief assistant, afterwards Sir N. Barnaby, was mainly responsible for this ship. She was given twin screws.

Captain Coles meanwhile continued to demand

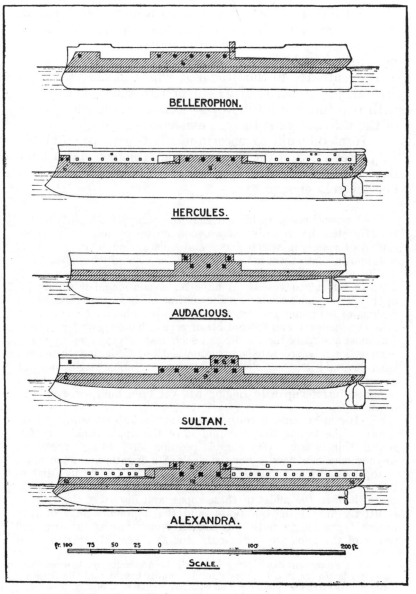

BELLEROPHON.

HERCULES.

AUDACIOUS.

SULTAN.

ALEXANDRA.

ft. 100   75   50   25   0   100'   200 ft.

SCALE.

BROADSIDE AND CENTRAL BATTERY SHIPS OF THE REED ERA.

turret-ships, and in 1865 submitted a design for a sea-going turret-ship, which was referred to a Committee of Naval Officers. They declined to approve the design, but expressed much interest in the principle involved, and recommended that an Admiralty design on similar principles should be worked out, and a ship built to it. This eventuated in the *Monarch*, which in substance was an ordinary ironclad of less freeboard than usual (14ft.) with two turrets on the upper deck, carrying each a pair of the heaviest guns then in existence (25 tons).

It is difficult to ascertain what part (if any) Sir E. J. Reed had in the design of the *Monarch*. At a later date in the work already referred to (1869) he criticised her severely enough.*

" I have already intimated that the enlarged adoption of the turret system has usually been associated in my mind with those classes of vessels in which masts and sails are not required. It is well known that others have taken a wider view of its applicability, and have contended that it is, and has all along been, perfectly well adapted for rigged vessels. I have never considered it wholly in-applicable to such vessels : on the contrary, I have myself projected designs of sea-going and rigged turret-ships, which I believe to be safe, commodious, and susceptible of perfect handling under canvas. But most assuredly the building of such vessels was urged by many persons long before satisfactory methods of designing them had been devised ; and my clear and strong conviction at the moment of writing these lines (March 31, 1869) is that no satisfactorily designed turret-ship with rigging has yet been built, or even laid down.

" The most cursory consideration of the subject will, I think, result in the feeling that the middle of the upper deck of a full-rigged ship is not a very eligible position for fighting large guns. Anyone who has stood upon the deck of a frigate, amid the maze of ropes of all kinds and sizes that surrounds him, must feel that to bring even guns of moderate size away from the port holes, to place them in the midst of these ropes, and discharge them there, is utterly out of the question ; and the impracticability of that mode of proceeding must increase in proportion as the size and power of the guns are increased. But as a central position, or a

---

* At a subsequent date, after he had left the Admiralty, he designed the *Independencia* for Brazil. This ship, afterwards bought into the British Navy as the *Neptune*, was simply an enlarged *Monarch*. Probably, however, the general features of the ship were specified by the Brazilians.

nearly central position, is requisite for the turret, this difficulty has had to be met by many devices, some of them tending to reduce the number of the ropes, and others to get them stopped short above the guns. In the former category come tripod masts; in the latter flying, decks over the turrets; the former have proved successful in getting rid of shrouds, but they interfere seriously with the fire of the turret guns, and are exposed to the danger of being shot away by them in the smoke of action; the latter are under trial, but however successful they may prove in some respects, they will be very inferior in point of comfort and convenience to the upper decks of broadside frigates. In the case of the *Monarch*, which has a lofty upper deck, neither the tripod system nor a flying deck for working the ropes upon has been adopted. A light flying deck to receive a portion of the boats, and to afford a passage for the officers above the turrets, has been fitted; but the ropes will be worked upon the upper deck over which the turrets have to fire, and consequently a thousand contrivances have had to be made for keeping both the standing and running rigging tolerably clear of the guns. It seems to me out of the question to suppose that such an arrangement can ever become general in the British Navy, especially when one contrasts the *Monarch* with the *Hercules* as a rigged man-of-war. Nor is the matter at all improved, in my opinion, in the case of the *Captain* and other rigged turret-ships in which the ropes have to be worked upon bridges or flying decks poised in the air above the turrets. Such bridges or decks, even if they withstand for long the repeated fire of the ship's own guns, must of necessity be mounted upon a few supports only; and I am apprehensive that in action an enemy's fire would bring down parts, at least, of these cumbrous structures, with their bitts, blocks, ropes, and the thousand and one other fittings with which a rigged ship's deck is encumbered, with what result I need not predict.

* * * *

" It is well known that both in the *Captain* and in the *Monarch* the turrets have been deprived of their primary and supreme advantage, that of providing an all-round fire for the guns, and more especially a head fire. This deprivation is consequent upon the adoption of forecastles, which are intended to keep the ships dry in steaming against a head sea, and to enable the head-sails to be worked. When it first became known that the *Monarch* was designed with a forecastle (by order of the then Board of Admiralty) there were not wanting persons who considered the plan extremely objectionable, and who took it for granted that as a turret-ship the new vessel would be fatally defective. The design of the *Captain* shortly afterwards, under the direction of Captain Coles, with a similar but much larger forecastle, was an admission, however, that

N

the Board of Admiralty did not stand alone in the belief that this
feature was a necessity, however objectionable. Both these ships,
therefore, are without a right-ahead fire from the turrets, the
Monarch having this deficiency partly compensated by two forecastle (6½-ton) guns protected with armour, while the *Captain* has
no protected head-fire at all, but merely one gun (6½-ton) standing
exposed on the top of the forecastle."

Time has shown that he was quite correct in his
views ; but in 1866 and the years that followed he was
regarded as unduly conservative and non-progressive.

Captain Coles objected to the *Monarch* altogether.
He insisted with vehemence that she did not in the least
express his ideas. She had a high forecastle, also a
poop; these features depriving her of end-on fire, except
in so far as a couple of 6½-ton guns in an armoured forecastle supplied the deficiency. The Admiralty replied
that a forecastle was essential for sea-worthiness ; but
Coles was so insistent that eventually he was allowed to
design a sea-going turret-ship on his own ideas, in conjunction with Messrs. Laird, of Birkenhead, who had
already had considerable experience in producing masted
turret-ships.* Coles was given a free hand. As a naval
officer his form of turret displays the practical mind ;
as a ship designer he was simply the raw amateur. The
Captain, which he produced, accentuated every fault
of the *Monarch*, except in the purely technical matter of
rigging being in the way of the guns. Coles got over this
by fitting tripod masts (which Laird's had evolved before
him†) ; but for the light flying bridges of the *Monarch*
he substituted a very considerable superstructure erec-
tion. For the *Monarch's* armoured two-gun forecastle,
which he had so violently condemned, he substituted a
much larger unarmoured, one-gun structure. Owing to
an error in design, his intended 8-ft. freeboard was
actually only 6ft., and his ideal ship resulted in nothing

* The *Scorpion* and *Wivern*, built for the Confederate States and bought
in 1865. The Peruvian *Huascar* also ante-dated the *Captain* in design. All of
these were low freeboard ships. Coles had something to do with the
designs of all.

† All the above ships had one or more tripod masts.

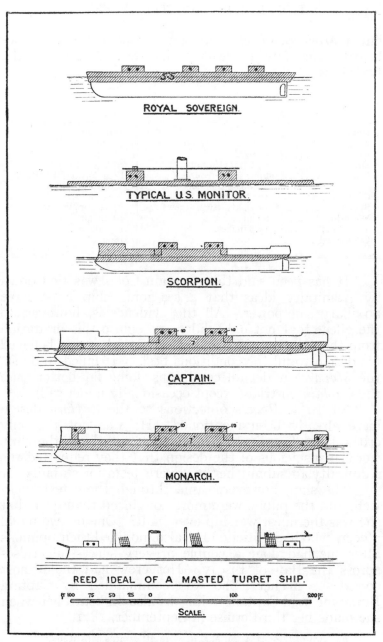

ROYAL SOVEREIGN.

TYPICAL U.S. MONITOR.

SCORPION.

CAPTAIN.

MONARCH.

REED IDEAL OF A MASTED TURRET SHIP.

SCALE.

TURRET-SHIPS OF THE REED ERA

but a *Monarch* of less gun power, and of 8ft. less free-board. Her fate is dealt with later. Details of the two ships are :—

	Captain.	*Monarch.*
Displacement ...	6900 tons.	8320 tons.
Length (*p.p.*)	320 feet.	330 feet.
Beam...........	53 feet.	57½ feet.
Draught	25ft. 9½in. (*mean*)	26ft. 7in. (*max.*)
Guns	Four 25 ton M.L.R., two 6½ ton, do.	Four 25 ton M.L.R., three 6½ ton, do.*
Coal	500 tons.†	630 tons.
Speed	14.25 kts. (twin screws).	14.94 (single screw).
Waterline Belt ..	8-6 inches.	7-6 inches.
Turrets	13-8 inches.	10-8 inches.
Completed	1869.	1869.

It has been said that Captain Coles was tied down by Admiralty ideas that a sea-going ship must have auxiliary sail power. All the evidence is, however, to the effect that not only did he recognise this limitation from the first, but that he concurred with it and believed his design to fill the conditions best. It failed to do so, the *Monarch* under all conditions doing far better than the *Captain* on trial (except occasionally under sail).

Sir E. J. Reed's objections to the *Captain* design have already been mentioned. He was not the only critic, since Laird's, of Birkenhead, who built the ship, were so suspicious of the design that they requested the Admiralty to submit her to severe tests for stability.

The ship, however, came through these tests very well, and the public were more convinced than ever that she was the finest warship ever built. One or two naval officers who had criticised her also modified their opinions after she had done a couple of very successful cruises across the Bay of Biscay. Her crew had the utmost confidence in her. She was commanded by Captain Burgoyne, and Captain Coles was also on board her when she made her third cruise in September, 1871.

* For two of these, 12½ ton M.L.R. were afterwards substituted.
† Coles had projected 1,000 tons; but 500 was all that she could take.

On the 6th September she was off Cape Finisterre in company with the Channel Fleet, consisting of the *Lord Warden, Minotaur, Agincourt, Northumberland, Monarch, Hercules, Bellerophon,* and the unarmoured ships *Inconstant* and *Bristol.* Admiral Milne came on board her from the *Lord Warden,* and drew attention to the fact that she was rolling a great deal,* but nobody on board the *Captain* agreed with him that this was dangerous. During the night a heavy gale suddenly arose, and in the morning the *Captain* was missing. Eighteen survivors reached the land with the story of what had happened.

From this it appears that about midnight the ship was under her topsails, double reefed. She had steam up, but was not using her screw. The ship gave a heavy lurch, righted herself, and the captain gave the order " Let go the topsail halyards," and immediately afterwards, "Let go fore and main topsail sheets." The ship, however, continued to heel, and " 18 degrees " was called out. This increased until 28 degrees was arrived at. With the ship lying over on her side some of the crew succeeded in walking over her bottom, and these were practically the only survivors. Immediately afterwards the ship went down stern first. There were at this time sc .e five and twenty survivors, including Captain Burgoyne and Mr. May, the gunner. Some of these were in the launch, others clinging to the pinnace, which was floating bottom upwards. Captain Burgoyne was amongst those who were clinging to the pinnace, and that was the last seen of him. A few of the men in the pinnace succeeded in jumping into the launch and so escaped. The rest were never seen again.

The subsequent court-martial placed it on record that " The *Captain* was built in deference to public opinion and in opposition to the views and opinions of the Controller of the Navy and his Department." The instability of the ship and the incompetence of Captain Coles to design her were emphasised.

* She was then rolling from 12½ to 14 degrees.

After the loss of the *Captain* considerable panic on the subject of turret-ships arose. The *Monarch* was submitted to a number of tests which, however, generally proved satisfactory, and there was never anything to be said against her except that the forecastle and the poop necessitated by her being a rigged ship, negatived one of the principal advantages of the turret system.

To the loss of the *Captain* is to be traced some of the extraordinary opposition which the *Devastation* idea subsequently encountered.

The various writings of Sir E. J. Reed make it abundantly clear that just as in the *Bellerophon* he had realised that an ironclad battleship must be something more than an old-type vessel with some armour on her, so he realised from the first that the ordinary sea-going warship with turrets on deck, instead of guns in the battery, was no true solution of the turret problem. There is ample evidence that he studied the monitors of the American Civil War with a balanced intelligence far ahead of his day, taking into consideration every *pro* and *con* with absolute impartiality, and applying the knowledge thus gained to the different conditions required for the British Fleet. It is no exaggeration to say that he was the only man who really kept his head while the turret-ship controversy reigned ; the one man who thought while others argued.

He swiftly recognised the tremendous limitations of the American low-freeboard monitors, and at an early date evolved his own idea of the " breastwork monitor," which began with the Australian *Cerberus*, and ended with the predecessor of the present *Dreadnought*. The ships of this type varied considerably from each other in detail ; but the general principle of all was identical. All, whether coast-defence or sea-going, were " mastless " ; all, while of low freeboard fore and aft, carried their turrets fairly high up on a heavily armed redoubt amidships. Side by side with them he developed the central battery ironclads of this particular era. He ceased to be Chief Constructor before either type reached its apotheosis ; but all may be deemed lineal descendants of his original creations.

First, however, it is desirable to revert to the Reed broadside and central-battery ships.

The *Audacious* class, which followed closely upon the *Hercules*, and were contemporary in the matter of design, were avowedly " second-class ships," intended for service in distant seas. The ships of this class, of which the first was completed in 1869 and the last in 1873, were the *Audacious, Invincible, Iron Duke, Vanguard, Swiftsure,* and *Triumph.* As the sketch plan illustrations indicate, the main deck battery in them was more centralised than in the *Hercules,* while instead of the bow battery they carried on their upper decks four $6\frac{1}{2}$-ton guns capable of firing directly ahead or astern.

Excluding the converted ships, the *Audacious* was the eleventh British ironclad to be designed in point of date of laying down, but in the matter of design she followed directly on the eighth ship—*Hercules.*

Her weights, as compared with the *Bellerophon,* were :—

Name.	Weight of hull.	Weight carried.
Bellerophon	3652 tons.	3798 tons.
Audacious	2675 tons.	3234 tons.

In some of these ships the principle of wood-copper sheathing was re-introduced ; the iron ships having been found to foul their hulls more quickly than wooden hulled ships. The *Swiftsure* and *Triumph* (the two latest) were the ones so treated. Sir E. J. Reed was not responsible for the experiment, which was entirely an Admiralty one.   It proved successful enough, the loss of speed being trifling.

Details of the *Audacious* class :—*

Displacement—6,010.
Length—280ft.

* The *Audacious* herself was "modernised" in the later eighties. Her sailing rig was removed and a " military rig " substituted. Some minor changes in her lesser guns were also made.

Beam—54ft.
H.P.—4,830.
Mean Draught—23ft. 8ins.
Guns—Ten 12-ton M.L.R.
Coal—500 tons.
Belt Armour—8ins. to 6ins.

	Audacious	Iron Duke	Invincible	Van-guard	Swiftsure	Triumph
Speed	13.2	13.64	14.09	13.64	13.75	13.75
Builder of Ship ...	Glasgow	Pembroke	Glasgow		Jarrow	Jarrow
Builder of Machin'y	Ravenhill	Ravenhill	Napier		Maudslay	Maudslay
Launched .	1869	1870	1869	1869	1870	1870
Completed	1869	1871	1870	1871	1872	1873
Cost-Hull & Machin'y	£246,482	£196,479	£239,441		£257,081	£258,322

The sheathing increased the displacement of the two latest ships by about 900 tons in the *Swiftsure*, and some 600 tons in the *Triumph*. These two were single-screw ships only, whereas all the others were twin-screw.

In September, 1875, the *Vanguard* was rammed and sunk by the *Iron Duke*.

The finding of the Court Martial was as follows :—

" The court having heard the evidence which had been adduced in this inquiry and trial, is of opinion that the loss of Her Majesty's ship *Vanguard* was occasioned by Her Majesty's ship *Iron Duke* coming into collision with her off the Kisbank, the Irish Channel, at about 12-50 on the 1st September, from the effects of which she foundered ; that such collision was caused—First, by the high rate of speed at which the squadron, of which these vessels formed a part, was proceeding whilst in a fog ; secondly, by Captain Dawkins, when leader of his division, leaving the deck of the ship before the evolution which was being performed was completed, as there were indications of foggy weather at the time ; thirdly, by the unnecessary reduction of speed of H.M.S. *Vanguard* without a signal from the vice-admiral in command of the squadron, and without H.M.S. *Vanguard* making the proper signals to the *Iron Duke* ; fourthly, by the increase of speed of H.M.S. *Iron Duke* during a dense fog, the speed being already high ; fifthly, by H.M.S. *Iron Duke* improperly shearing out of the line ; sixthly, for want of any fog signals on the part of H.M.S. *Iron Duke*.

" The court is further of opinion that the cause of the loss of H.M.S. *Vanguard* by foundering was a breach being made in her side by the prow of H.M.S. *Iron Duke* in the neighbourhood of the most important transverse bulkhead—namely, that between the engine and boiler rooms, causing a great rush of water into the engine room, shaft-alley, and stoke-hole, extinguishing the fires in a few minutes, the water eventually finding its way into the provision room flat, and provision rooms through imperfectly fastened watertight doors, and owing to leakage of 99 bulkhead. The court is of opinion that the foundering of H.M.S. *Vanguard* might have been delayed, if not averted, by Captain Dawkins giving instructions for immediate action being taken to get all available pumps worked, instead of employing his crew in hoisting out boats, and if Captain Dawkins, Commander Tandy, Navigating-Lieutenant Thomas, and Mr. David Tiddy, carpenter, had shown more resource and energy in endeavouring to stop the breach from the outside by means at their command, such as hammocks and sails—and the court is of opinion that Captain Dawkins should have ordered Captain Hickley, of H.M.S. *Iron Duke*, to tow H.M.S. *Vanguard* into shallow water. The court is of opinion that blame is imputable to Captain Dawkins for exhibiting want of judgment and for neglect of duty in handling his ship, and that he showed a want of resource, promptitude, and decision in the means he adopted for saving H.M.S. *Vanguard* after the collision. The court is further of opinion that blame is imputable to Navigating-Lieutenant Thomas for neglect of duty in not pointing out to his captain that there was shallower water within a short distance, and in not having offered any suggestion as to the stopping of the leak on the outside. The court is further of opinion that Commander Tandy showed great want of energy as second in command under the circumstances. The court is further of opinion that Mr. Brown, the chief engineer, showed want of promptitude in not applying the means at his command to relieve the ship of water. The court is further of opinion that blame is imputable to Mr. David Tiddy, of H.M.S. *Vanguard*, for not offering any suggestions to his captain as to the most efficient mode of stopping the leak, and for not taking immediate steps for sounding the compartments and reporting from time to time the progress of the water. The court adjudges Captain Richard Dawkins to be severely reprimanded and dismissed from H.M.S. *Vanguard,* and he is hereby severely reprimanded and so sentenced accordingly. The court adjudges Commander Lashwood Goldie Tandy and Navigating-Lieutenant James Cambridge Thomas to be severely reprimanded, and they hereby are severely reprimanded accordingly. The court imputes no blame to the other officers and ship's company of H.M.S. *Vanguard* in reference to the loss of the ship, and they are hereby acquitted accordingly."

This disaster drew attention to the ram, the more so when it became known that the *Iron Duke* was uninjured. Ram tactics had, of course, been heard of before, and had been discussed at great length by Sir Edward Reed in 1868. At that date, although one or two special ram-ships had been built, Sir E. J. Reed had expressed a certain amount of scepticism as to whether the ram could be successfully used in connection with a ship in motion, and pointed out that in the historical instance of the *Re d'Italia* at the battle of Lissa, the ship was stationary. He further had written :—*

" Even if the side were thus broken through, any one of our iron-built ships would most probably remain afloat, although her efficiency would be considerably impaired, the water which would enter being confined to the watertight compartment of the hold, enclosed by bulkheads crossing the ship at a moderate distance before and abaft the part broken through. In fact, under these circumstances the ship struck would be in exactly the same condition as an ordinary iron ship which by any accident has had the bottom plating broken, and one of the hold-compartments filled with water, so that we have good reason to believe that her safety need not be despaired of, unless, by the blow being delivered at, or very near, a bulkhead, more than one compartment should be injured and filled. All iron ships can thus be protected to some extent against being sunk by a single blow of a ram, and our own vessels have the further and important protection of the watertight wings just described ; but wood ships are not similarly safe. One hole in the side of the *Re d'Italia* sufficed to sink her ; but this would scarcely have been possible in an iron ship with properly arranged watertight compartments. The French, in their latest ironclads, have become alive to this danger, and have fitted transverse iron bulkheads in the holds of wood-built ships in order to add to their safety. No doubt this is an improvement, but our experience with wood ships leads us to have grave doubts whether these bulkheads can be made efficient watertight divisions in the hold, on account of the working that is sure to take place in a wood hull. This fact adds another to the arguments previously advanced in favour of iron hulls for armoured ships ; for it appears that an iron-built ship, constructed on the system of our recent ironclads, is comparatively safe against destruction by a ram, unless she is repeatedly attacked when in a disabled state, while a wood-built ship may, and most likely will, be totally lost in consequence of one well-delivered heavy blow."

* *Our Ironclad Ships*, by Sir E. J. Reed.

This is in strange contrast to the fate of the *Vanguard*, but the finding of the Court Martial indicates that the precautions taken were hardly such as were contemplated by the ship's designer ! Furthermore, she appears to have been struck immediately on one of the water-tight bulkheads, and so, instead of being left with seven of her eight compartments unfilled, she had only six unfilled. The shock, also, was such that most of the other bulkheads started leaking ; and in addition to this the double bottom is said to have been filled with bricks and cement,* and so less operative than it might otherwise have been, since any shock on the outer bottom would thus be immediately communicated to the inner one.

The actual successor of the *Hercules*, in the matter of first-class ships, was the *Sultan*. She differed from the *Hercules* merely in a somewhat increased draught and displacement, and increased provision for end-on bow fire—four $12\frac{1}{2}$-ton guns able to fire ahead being substituted for the one smaller gun in the *Hercules*.

This end-on fire was given because ram-tactics were then coming greatly into favour. Particulars of the *Sultan*,† which was the last of the central battery ironclads to be designed and built by Sir E. J. Reed, are as follows :—

Displacement—9,290 tons.
Length—325ft.
Beam—59ft. $\frac{1}{2}$in.
H.P.—7,720.
Mean Draught—26ft. 5ins.
Guns—Eight 18-ton M.L.R., four $12\frac{1}{2}$-ton M.L.R.
Coal—810 tons.
Armour (iron)—9ins., 8ins., and 6ins.
Speed—14.13 knots (single screw).

* *Ironclads in Action*, by H. W. Wilson.
† The *Sultan* was built as a ship-rigged ship. In 1894-96 she was " reconstructed," two military masts being substituted for her original rig. She was also re-engined and re-boilered by Messrs. Thompson, of Clydebank. Beyond going out for the naval manœuvres one year she did not, however, perform any service in her altered condition, and is now used as a hulk.

Builder of Ship—Chatham.
Builder of Machinery—Penn.
Cost—Hull and machinery, £357,415.
Launched—1870 ; completed for sea in 1871.

Sir E. J. Reed's " breastwork monitors " have already been referred to. They were received with little enthusiasm by the Admiralty, and the first of them were merely Colonial coast defence vessels. These were :—

Name.	Displ'm't. Tons.	Speed. Knots.	Armour. Inches.	Turret Armour.	Completed.
Cerberus	3480	9.75	8	10	1870
Abyssinia	2900	9.59	7	10	1870
Magdala	3340	10.67	8	10	1870

In general design all were identical, a redoubt amidships carrying two centre line turrets and a small oval superstructure between. Twin screws were employed.

The belief in the ram already alluded to had by now attained such proportions that a ship specially designed for ramming was called for, and the *Hotspur* was the result. Nothing written by Sir E. J. Reed (and he wrote a great deal) indicates that he was in sympathy with her design, though nominally responsible. The *Hotspur* was not even a turret-ship. She carried a fixed armoured structure of considerable size,* inside of which a single 25-ton gun revolved, firing through the most convenient of several ports. She was fitted with two masts with fore and aft sails. Particulars of her were :—

Displacement—4,010 tons.
Length—235ft.
Beam—50ft.
H.P.—3,060.
Mean Draught—21ft. 10ins.
Guns—One 25-ton M.L.R., two 6½-ton.
Belt Armour—11in. to 8in. ; complete belt.
Turret Armour—10in.

* Later on this was removed and an ordinary revolving turret, carrying *two* 25 ton guns, substituted.

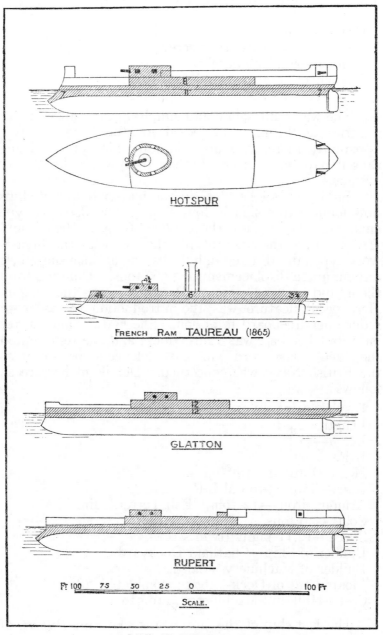

HOTSPUR

French Ram TAUREAU (1865)

GLATTON

RUPERT

Ft 100   75   50   25   0   100 Ft

SCALE.

RAMS OF THE REED ERA.

Coal—300 tons.
Speed—12.8 knots (twin-screw).
Builder—Napier, Glasgow.
Launched—1870 ; completed, 1871.
Cost—Hull and Machinery, £171,528.

She was built solely and simply as an " answer " to a series of " rams " projected for the French Navy, apparently more with an Admiralty idea of not being caught napping " in case," than from any belief in her efficacy.

Sir E. J. Reed's ideas in the matter of turret-ships now found expression in four ships of the *Cerberus* type enlarged. These were the *Cyclops, Gorgon, Hecate,* and *Hydra.* Like their prototype, they were of the breast-work type, and differed only in having an inch more belt armour and a displacement of 3,560 tons. Differing from them, and perhaps more on Reed lines, was the *Glatton.* Her special feature was the introduction of water to reduce her freeboard in action. She had a single turret only, but her belt was 12ins. thick, and she represented the, then, " last word " in coast defence ships, so far as the British Navy was concerned. Details of her are as follows :—

Displacement—4,910 tons.
Length—245ft.
Beam—54ft.
H.P.—2,870.
Mean Draught—19ft. 5ins.
Guns—Two 25-ton M.L.R.
Armour (iron)—12-10in. Belt Turret, 14in.
Coal—540 tons.
Speed—12.11 knots (twin screw).
Builder of Ship—Chatham Dockyard.
Builder of Machinery—Laird.
Floated out of Dock—1871 ; completed, 1871.
Cost—Hull and Machinery, £219,529.

The last ship of this group was the ram *Rupert,* of 5,440 tons, laid down at Chatham, in 1870. She was, in

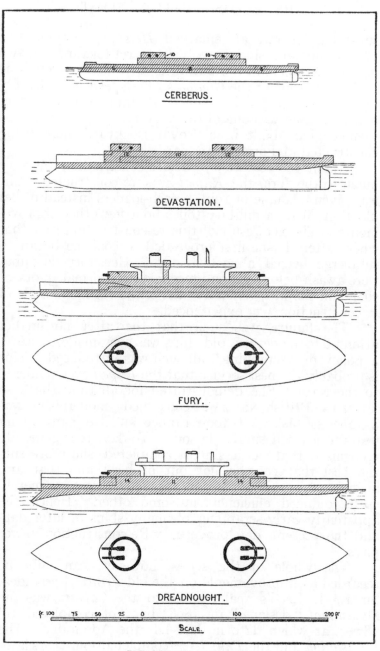

CERBERUS.

DEVASTATION.

FURY.

DREADNOUGHT.

SCALE.

BREASTWORK MONITORS.

substance, merely an enlarged *Hotspur*, carrying two 18-ton guns in a single revolving turret forward and two 64-pounders behind the bulwarks aft. Her armour was slightly inferior to the *Glatton's* : her speed considerably higher—14 knots being aimed at, though it was never reached. She was one of the very few ships which had their engines built in a Royal Dockyard, hers being constructed at Portsmouth Yard.

About the year 1890, when re-construction was very much to the fore, the *Rupert* was re-constructed. She was given a couple of 10in. breech-loaders instead of her old 10in. M.L., a military-top, and a few other improvements. The net result of this re-construction was that when, after it, she first proceeded to coal she began to submerge herself almost at once. Her torpedo tubes were awash before she had received her normal quota of coal, and she was, generally, the most futile example of re-construction ever experienced.

The failure was such that thereafter no further attempt to modernise old ships was ever made, instead, a policy of " scrapping" all such was introduced. This is probably the best service that the *Rupert* ever rendered to the Navy. She demonstrated for all time that—so far as the British Navy was concerned—modernising was a hopeless task. It took France and Germany many years to learn a similar lesson. To-day, it is generally recognised that, as a ship is completed, she represents the best that can be got out of her ; and that any attempt to improve her in any one direction merely spells reduced efficiency in some other. Hence the apparently early scrapping of many ships of later date and the present day proverb, " Re-construction never pays."

The whole of the series, however, can only be regarded as improvements on the old *Prince Albert* idea. Sir E. J. Reed's real answer to the *Captain* was the *Devastation*, designed in 1868, but not completed till 1873 ; at which date he had left the Admiralty. The *Devastation* and the *Thunderer* (completed four years later

THE "DEVASTATION," as completed, 1873.

From the original negative in the possession of W. A. Bieber, Esq.

THE "INFLEXIBLE," as originally completed, 1881.

Photo by]

THE "BENBOW"—A SHIP OF THE "ADMIRAL" CLASS.

[Symonds & Co.

SIR N. BARNABY
(A recent photograph).

SIR WILLIAM WHITE.

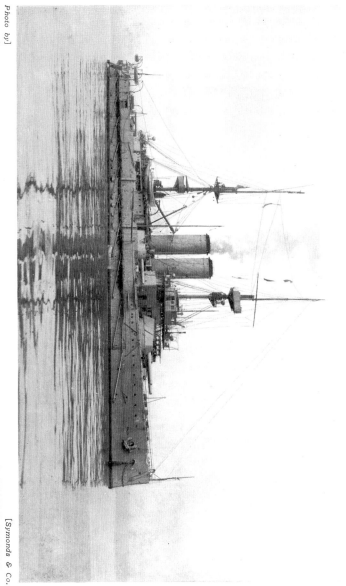

Photo by]
[Symonds & Co.

THE "KING EDWARD VII" AS SHE WAS IN HER FIRST COMMISSION AS LORD CHARLES BERESFORD'S FLAGSHIP.

SIR PHILIP WATTS.

GENERAL CUNIBERTI.

Photo by]

THE "LION," as finally completed in 1912.

[Abrahams & Sons, Devonport.

than her sister) cost Sir E. J. Reed his position. In them he introduced all his ideas as to what the sea-going turret-ship should be. He carried the Admiralty with him ; but before ever the *Devastation* was set afloat, it was " proved " to the satisfaction of the general public that she was an " egregious failure." The date of her design is about 1868, though, as mentioned above, she was not completed till 1873. The *Dreadnought* of more or less these times was nothing in the way of novelty compared to the *Devastation* of the later sixties.

Details of the *Devastation* (laid down Nov., 1869), were :—

> Displacement—9,330 tons.
> Length—385ft.
> Beam—62ft. 3ins.
> Mean Draught—25ft. 6ins.
> H.P.—6,650.
> Guns—Four 35-ton M.L.R.*
> Belt Armour—12in. and 10in. (iron).
> Turret Armour—14in. (iron).
> Coal—1,800 tons.
> Speed—13.84 knots (twin-screw).
> Where Built—Portsmouth Dockyard.
> Builder of Machinery—Humphreys.
> Launched—1871 ; completed, 1873.
> Cost—Hull and Machinery, £353,848.

On her trials the *Devastation* proved completely successful. An interesting and little known item in connection with her is that as designed she was to carry two signal masts,† one forward of the turrets, one aft. For these, on completion, a single mast on the superstructure was substituted.

How the *Devastation*, even after successful completion, was received by the public can be gleaned

---

* About the year 1890-2 *Devastation* and *Thunderer* were re-boilered and re-armed with 10-inch B.L.R.

† c.f. Frontispiece to *Our Ironclad Ships*, E. J. Reed.

from the following extracts from the contemporary press :—*

"It is a weakness with the officers and men of any of Her Majesty's ships to ' crack up ' the vessels to which they belong, and it is rarely that a bluejacket growls openly against his ship. The warm confidence expressed in the ill-fated *Captain* by her unfortunate crew is well remembered, and is sufficient to prove that even the first of this necessarily uncomfortable class of monitors was not met by the seamen of the Fleet in any complaining spirit, but that they submitted to the discomforts imposed upon them with characteristic cheerfulness.   When, therefore, an unmistakable feeling of dissatisfaction prevails throughout a ship, and no hesitation is shown in expressing it, we may be certain that there is some valid reason for so unusual an occurrence. We hesitated to give currency to reports which reached us during the cruise of the *Devastation* round the coast with the Channel Squadron, as we had good reason to believe that it was the intention of the Admiralty to pay her off, and berth her in Portsmouth harbour as a tender to the *Excellent*, the advantage of so doing being that a very large number of men passing thiough the School of Gunnery would thus be enabled to become acquainted with the latest improvements in the turret system. . . .   But since the arrival at the Admiralty of Rear-Admiral Hornby, late in command of the Channel Squadron, who certainly should be able to form a correct estimate of the *Devastation's* fitness in every respect for sea service, it has been determined that she shall be ordered to Gibraltar, there probably to remain during the coming winter as a kind of ' guardo.' A cruise across the bay in the month of November is not looked forward to by the present crew, who have had a little experience both of being stifled by being battened down and of being nearly blown out of their hammocks when efforts at ventilation are made by opening every hatch. Her qualities as a sea-boat have been fairly tested, and the present notion of filling her up with stores for six months' further service, and then stowing her away at Gibraltar, leads to the conclusion that on this point at least the value of the counsel of the First Lord's new Naval adviser is not altogether apparent."
 . . . . "It is needless to comment on the facts. They speak for themselves. The condensers will be repaired, no doubt, and strengthened and modified ; but no engineer can guarantee that they will not fail again, or, if they turn out a permanent job, that the cylinders will not split, or some other of the mishaps to which marine engines in the Navy are subject may not happen. If the failure takes place in the day of battle it will constitute little short of a national calamity. Even as it is, it must be looked on as a most

* *Naval and Military Gazette.*

fortunate circumstance that the sea was perfectly smooth and the vessel near a port. Had the breakdown occurred during the six hours' run of the ship—which was to have been made on Wednesday —and in a stiff breeze blowing on a lee shore, the ship might have been lost before an effort could have been made to save her. Very important improvements in marine engines of large size must be made before we can reconcile ourselves to the adoption of mastless sea-going monitors."

With such labour and travail was the modern British battleship born ! Public opinion decidedly modified naval construction—leading, as it did, to a considerable delay with the *Thunderer*,* the re-designing of the *Fury*, and the building of some old-type ships which else had probably never been constructed.

As already mentioned, Sir E. J. Reed left the Admiralty before the *Devastation* was completed. None the less the ships which immediately followed were in all essential particulars " Reed Ships," and so are included in this chapter.

The *Devastation*, owing to the Committee on Designs, received certain minor modifications before completion. These mainly concerned the hatches. Her sister ship, the *Thunderer*, built at Pembroke and engined by Humphrys, was held back, pending the *Devastation*'s trials, and not completed till 1877.

Save that in one turret she carried a couple of 38 ton (12.5-inch) instead of 35 ton (12-inch) guns, she was a replica of the *Devastation*.

A third ship of the same type, named the *Fury*, was in hand, but criticisms of the *Devastation* caused her to be re-designed, and she was eventually completed as the *Dreadnought*. In her the very low freeboard forward and aft of the *Devastation* type was done away with, and freeboard maintained at a uniform medium height.

The *Devastation* and *Thunderer* had their armour-plates amidships pierced with square port-holes. These with some reason were attacked as likely to weaken the armour very considerably, and the *Dreadnought* was

* She was about nine years from laying down to completion !

built entirely wall-sided and so depended on artificial ventilation, known in the Navy in those days as " potted air," even more than her predecessors.

Particulars of the *Dreadnought* :—
Displacement—10,820 tons.
Length—320ft.
Beam—63ft. 10in.
Draught—26ft. 9in.
Armament—Four 38-ton M.L.R., two 14in. torpedo tubes.
Armour (iron)—Belt 14-11in., Bulkheads 13in., Turrets 14in.
H.P.—8,210 = 12.40 knots.

In the original design of the *Fury* provision was made for a conning tower with a heavily-armoured communication tube. She proved a very successful ship. No sisters were ordered, probably because the Admiralty wished to see how she did before committing themselves to the type. Ere she was finished a different fashion in warships had set in. The cost of the *Dreadnought* was about £600,000.

The *Alexandra* was designed long after Reed had left the Admiralty. That famous constructor had nothing whatever to do with her. None the less she was the apotheosis of his box-battery ironclad ideas and for that reason is included in his era. She was simply an " improved *Sultan*."

Particulars of her :—

Displacement—9,490 tons.
Length (between perpendiculars)—325ft.
Beam—63⅔ft.
Draught—26½ft.
Armament—Four 25-ton M.L., ten 18-ton M.L., four above-water torpedo dischargers (14in.)
Armour (iron)—12-6in. belt, flat deck on top of it. Bulkheads 8-5in. Battery 12-6in.
Horse-power—9,810 = 15 knots.
Coal—680 tons = 2,700 knots at 10 knots (nominal).

She was built at Chatham Dockyard ; engined by Humphrys ; completed for sea, 1877.

Four of the 18-ton guns were carried in an upper deck battery, and had end-on training.   The other guns were carried in the main-deck battery, which was some 10ft. high.   The 25-ton guns had a right-ahead training.

After completion she served as Mediterranean flagship, though at the bombardment of Alexandria the flag was transferred to the *Invincible,* which, being of lighter draught, was able to enter the inner harbour. At a later date (about 1890) she was " partially reconstructed." For her original barque rig a three-masted military rig was substituted, and six 4-inch Q.F. were mounted on top of her upper deck battery.   She has been described as the apotheosis of Reed broadside ideas, and a very apotheosis she was.   No broadside or central battery ironclad of the British or any other Navy ever equalled her, and she dropped out of the first rank only because the big gun rendered broadside ships entirely obsolete.

GUNS IN THE ERA.

The principal guns (all M.L.R.) in the Reed Era were as follows :—

Weight in tons.	Bore in inches.	Length in Calibres.	Weight of Projectile. lbs.	Muzzle Velocity. f.s.	Muzzle Energy. f.t.	Penet'n Iron at	
						yds. 2000	yds. 1000
38	12.5	16	810	1575	13,930	16	18
35	12	13½	707	1390	9470	13	15
25	12	12	609	1288	7006	11	12
25	11	12	544	1314	6560	13	14
18	10	14½	406	1379	5360	10	12
12½	9	14	253	1440	3695	9	10
9	8	15	174	1384	2391	7	8
6½	7	16	112	1325	1400	6	7

In the early part of the period Armstrong breech-loaders up to 120 pounders had been in use, but the elementary breech blocks were so unsatisfactory that the Navy quickly discarded them, and adhered to muzzle-loaders long after all other Powers had given them up.

The big muzzle loaders tabulated above were of a very elementary type also. They were made by shrinking red hot wrought-iron collars over a steel tube ; and it was never quite certain how far the interior would be affected. The projectiles never fitted accurately, with the result that there was considerable leakage of gas and very erratic firing. The rifling consisted of five or six grooves into which studs in the projectile fitted.

In 1872 some experiments were carried out, the *Hotspur* firing at the *Glatton's* turret at a range of 200 yards. The first shot missed altogether, the other two struck the turret, but not at the point aimed at. The turret was not appreciably damaged, though theoretically it should have been completely penetrated. This eventually led to the invention of an improved gas check—reference to which will be found at the end of the Barnaby Era further on.

UNARMOURED SHIPS OF THE ERA.

Contemporaneously with the *Hercules* the *Inconstant* was designed. She was inspired by the United States *Wampanoag*, a type of large, fast, unprotected, heavily-gunned frigate, to which the Americans had always been partial. The *Wampanoag*, as a matter of fact, never reached expectations, whereas the *Inconstant* was a decided success so far as she went. She marked, so far as the British Navy was concerned, the first appearance of the theory that speed and gun power—in other words, " the offensive "—might be developed advantageously at the cost of defensive arrangements, a theory which still survives in the " battle-cruisers " of to-day, though of course in a very modified form. None the less, the *Inconstant* represents the germ idea of our present battle-cruisers, and is supremely important on that account.

Particulars of the *Inconstant* were :—

Displacement—5,780 tons.
Length (between perpendiculars)—337⅓ft.
Beam—50¼ft.
Draught (mean)—25½ft.
Guns—Ten 12½ ton M.L.R., six 6½ ton M.L.R.
H.P.—7,360 = 16 knots (trial 16.2).
Speed—Sixteen knots (trial 16.2).
Built at Pembroke Dockyard. Completed for
    sea 1868 at a cost of £213,324. She had an
    iron hull, wood-sheathed and coppered. A
    coal supply of 750 tons gave a nominal radius
    of 2780 miles. She was ship-rigged and sailed
    well.

She was followed by a couple of variants on her, the *Raleigh* and *Shah*, the former 5,200 tons and the latter 6,250 tons.

The *Shah* was originally named the *Blonde*, but rechristened out of compliment to the Shah of Persia, who was visiting England at the time of her launch.

At a later stage in her career (1877) the *Shah*, then flagship on the S.W. Coast of America, fought a much-criticised action with the Peruvian turret-ship *Huascar*, a Laird-built monitor, carrying a couple of 12½ ton guns, launched in 1865, and generally of the same type (though smaller) as the British *Hotspur* and *Rupert*.

The *Huascar* had been seized by the Revolutionists and practically turned into a pirate ship. In attacking her the British Admiral de Horsey gave hostages to fortune, seeing that it was an axiom of those days that an unarmoured ship was helpless against an ironclad monitor. He had, however, no alternative.

As things turned out, the *Huascar* never succeeded in hitting either the *Shah*, or the *Amethyst* which accompanied her, while the British flagship, having a speed advantage, the efforts of the *Huascar* to ram her were futile. The *Huascar* was hit about thirty times, and one man was killed on board her, but the damage done to the turret-ship was practically nil. The engagement is of further special interest as for the first time a torpedo was used from a big ship in action. The range, however, was too great and no hit was secured.

During the night following the action an attempt was made to torpedo the *Huascar* from the *Shah's* steam pinnace, but the enemy could not be found. Yet it is probable that the knowledge of the *Shah's* torpedoes was the reason why Pierola surrendered the *Huascar* next morning to the Peruvian fleet.

It must have been abundantly clear to him that he had next to nothing to fear from the British gunfire, while a single water-line hit from him would probably have put the *Shah* entirely at his mercy, save in so far as her torpedoes might make attempts to ram fatal to him.

XII.

THE BARNABY ERA.

THE characteristic *motif* of the Barnaby designs has been described as a "maximum of offensive power and the minimum of defence." This is not altogether correct ; though as a generalization it is no very great exaggeration. In every Barnaby design proper, offence was the first thing sought for, but defence as then understood was by no means overlooked as to-day it appears to have been.

The bed rock " Reed idea " was to produce a ship which could attack and destroy the enemy without much risk of being damaged in doing so. The " Barnaby idea " was that " the best defensive is a strong offensive " ; and a strict subordination of defence to what might best serve the attack on the same displacement.

The first big armoured ship to be laid down at all on Barnaby principles, the *Inflexible*, was built under somewhat peculiar circumstances. In the years 1871 a Committee was appointed. One of its findings was as follows :—

" As powerful armament, thick armour, speed, and light draught cannot be combined in one ship, although all are needed for the defence of the country ; there is no alternative but to give the preponderance to each in its turn amongst different classes of ships which shall mutually supplement one another."*

Amongst the Committee's suggestions had been the abolition of the complete belt, and its concentration amidships. This recommendation was mainly intended to

---

* Most of the criticism past and present of the Barnaby era is rendered worthless by an ignoring of this report.

refer to cruising ships rather than to ships definitely intended for the line of battle ; but the idea soon spread.

These suggestions had already been embodied in a modified form in the *Shannon*, of which particulars will be found later on.   The *Shannon*, however, was frankly a " belted cruiser," and no idea had then been entertained of adapting a similar system for heavy armoured ships.

In the year 1874, however, it transpired that the Italians were evolving an entirely new type of battleship, the *Duilio* and *Dandolo*, and adopting a central box system.   By this means they were able to protect the citadel with 22-inch armour and mount four 100-ton guns in two turrets *en echelon*, so that all four could bear ahead and astern as well as on either broadside.   The seriousness of the situation was increased by the fact that in most of the tactical ideas of the day, end-on approach figured largely.*

Compared with these Italian designs, the most powerful British ironclad of those days, the *Dreadnought*, with a belt of only 14-inch to 11-inch armour, and bearing but two of her four 38-ton guns end-on, cut a sorry figure.

It was deemed essential to build a " reply."   The largest gun actually available at the time was, however, the 81-ton M.L. ; so this was adopted for the new ship. The *Inflexible* being frankly an adoption of Italian ideas, she can hardly be described as the design of any one man ; Sir N. Barnaby having been tied down to an extent with which (from his subsequent writings) he did not, it would appear, altogether agree.   A smaller central citadel than that of the Italian ships was adopted, but the thickness was carried to 24-inch, the thickest armour ever introduced into an ironclad either before or since.   The bulkheads were 20-in.   The freeboard of the central redoubt was 10ft.   Round about it, fore and aft, on an armoured raft-body were built a bow and stern, with superstructures curtailed to the centre line sufficiently to allow of

---

* This is instanced by the increasing ahead fire given to the broadside ironclads.

unimpeded end-on fire from the big guns, which, like those of the Italians, were placed in échelonned turrets.

With a view to satisfying the " masted turret-ship " ideal, an absurd brig rig was fitted to the *Inflexible*. With this it was possible for the ship to drift before the wind, haystack-fashion, but the rig was so much of the " placebo " order that it was designed to be taken down and thrown overboard in case of action! At a later date it was removed altogether and a military rig substituted.

The *Inflexible* was crammed with novelties. Like the *Devastation* she was the " *Dreadnought* " of her time. Chief among her innovations were the adoption of submerged torpedo tubes (of which she had two), the mounting of Nordenfeldts as a definite anti-torpedo-boat armament, and an ingenious anti-rolling arrangement, whereby water was admitted amidships to counteract the roll. This was very partially successful ; but in 1910 the idea reappeared in a slightly altered form and is now used in certain big Atlantic liners.

An ingenious feature of the *Inflexible* concerned the big guns. In the *Devastation* and *Dreadnought* types these could be run in and loaded inside the turret. With the much larger guns of the *Inflexible* this was impossible, without a very considerable increase of the size of the turrets. Outside loading without protection was recognised as unsuitable and practically impossible. A special glacis was, therefore, designed, which admitted of outside loading under cover, and at the same time ensured that, in the event of premature discharge, the projectile would emerge above the waterline and not below it.

This device is of special interest as the " last word " of those muzzle-loading guns to which the British Navy adhered so long as it possibly could. Had it been thought of earlier, the British Navy might perhaps have adhered to muzzle-loaders even longer than it did. As things were, the *Inflexible* device came too late to stay the tide which had already begun to set strongly in the breechloader direction.

Details of the *Inflexible* were :—

Displacement—11,880 tons.
Length (between perpendiculars)—320ft.
Beam—75ft.
Maximum Draught—26½ft.
Armour—Belt amidships 24-16-inch, beyond that
    a protective deck only; 22-14-inch bulkhead, all
    iron ; and 17-inch compound armour turrets.
Armaments—Four 81-ton guns (to which eight
    4-inch breechloaders were added later on).
    Two submerged tubes and two above-water
    launching appliances for torpedoes.
Horse-power—8,010 (I.H.P.).
Speed—13.8 knots.
Coal—1,300 tons = nominal 10-knot radius of
    5,200 miles.
Built at Portsmouth Dockyard. Engined by
    Elder. Completed 1881.

On completion she was sent to the Mediterranean,
with Captain Fisher (afterwards Admiral of the Fleet, Lord
Fisher) in command of her. He was the chief gunnery
officer of those days and the founder of the torpedo
school. At the time it was put on record that, asked
by a Press interviewer what he would do if the fortunes
of war brought it about that he had to encounter a
similar " last word " in naval construction, he replied
that he would keep away from her till nightfall, and then
send in the, then, novel second-class torpedo-boats which
the *Inflexible* carried, to settle the foe. Over which statement the historian of fifty years hence may yet place Lord
Fisher among the prophets. To-day (1912) thirty years
later, similar ideas obtain, but have got no further. Fifty
years hence——?

In 1882 the *Inflexible* was the central figure at the
bombardment of Alexandria. The damage she did was
infinitesimal compared to the ideas which the public had
formed of her. Far more actual mischief was done by
Lord Charles Beresford in a trivial gunboat, the *Condor*,

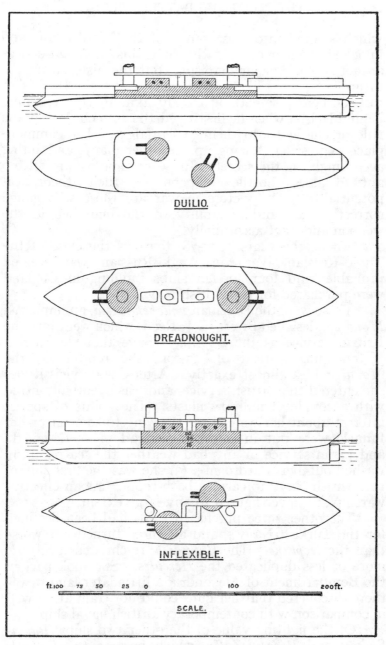

DUILIO.

DREADNOUGHT.

INFLEXIBLE.

ft.100   75   50   25   0   100   200ft.

SCALE.

EARLY TURRET-SHIPS OF THE BARNABY ERA.

which steered into close range of the hostile guns and
knocked them over.   At the time this was regarded as
an act of spectacular heroism ; but the historian of the
future is far more likely to discover in it (as in the Fisher
torpedo-boats) something closely akin to the reasoning
behind Nelson when he destroyed the French fleet at the
Nile or charged into them at Trafalgar.   The common-
place expression, " sizing up the other man," and acting
accordingly, is the secret.   In peace time we are all too
apt to assess hostile weapons at their theoretical
potentiality.   The victors in war are those who gauge
correctly the handling ability of the man behind the
weapon and—act accordingly.

About the years 1877-78, towards the close of the
Turco-Russian War, an Anglo-Russian war seemed
probable, and four foreign ships building in England
were purchased for the British Navy.

These were the Brazilian *Independencia*, an improved
Monarch, designed by Sir E. J. Reed, which went into the
British service as the *Neptune*.   Save that she carried
38-ton guns instead of 25-ton, she reproduced the
Monarch idea almost exactly.   After certain vicissitudes
she entered the British service, and was eventually fitted
with a couple of military masts.   The points of special
interest about her were that (1) owing to some error her
funnels were put in sideways instead of as designed ;
and (2) in service in any bad weather the sea regularly
washed out her wardroom ; (3) she was the first ship of
the British Navy to carry a bath-room.   As an effective
warship she never figured to any large extent.

The other three purchased ships had been destined
for the Turkish Navy ; and all three turned out worse
than the *Neptune*.   The *Hamidieh*, re-christened *Superb*,
more or less duplicated the *Hercules*.   She took part in
the Bombardment of Alexandria a little later, and it was
there discovered that her guns could not train at all well
in comparison with contemporary British naval ships.

Of the fighting value of the other two ships, *Pakyi-
Shereef* and *Boordyi-Zaffir*, which became the *Belleisle*

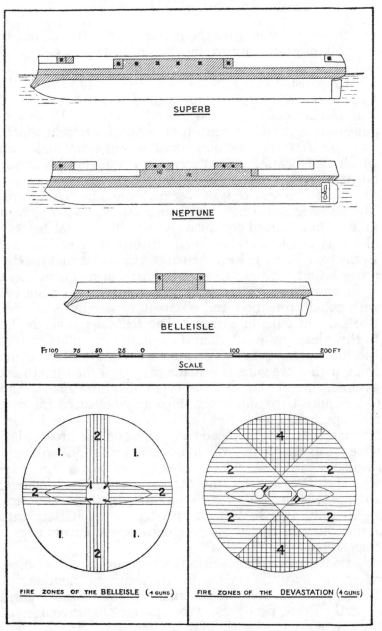

SUPERB

NEPTUNE

BELLEISLE

Fт 100   75   50   25   0   100   200 Fт

SCALE

FIRE ZONES OF THE BELLEISLE (4 GUNS)

FIRE ZONES OF THE DEVASTATION (4 GUNS)

FOREIGN SHIPS PURCHASED FOR THE NAVY IN 1877-78.

and *Orion*, the least said the better. They turned out to be nothing but improvements on a type of " coast defender," already obsolete, diminutives of the original Reed broadside idea applied to a *Hotspur* type hull. In place of the single 25-ton gun of the *Hotspur*, they carried four similar guns—the old 12-inch 25-ton M.L. These guns were carried in a central raised battery, from which, as in the *Hotspur*, one gun could always bear, and from which two bearing on an exact and unlikely broadside might be looked for.

No useful service was ever performed by these ships. The *Belleisle* ended her service as a target, the *Orion* as a hulk. They proved conclusively that the central battery idea was obsolete and so far probably did good service. In the past Sir E. J. Reed had argued, and for that matter proved, that for a given weight of armour and armament eight guns, four on either broadside, could be mounted with equal protection and economy of weight as against two pairs of guns in turrets.* The *Belleisles* gave the lie to this idea, however, when it came to be applied to half the number of guns. The step from that to the same thing with more guns was made easy, and the turret idea assured, out of the *Belleisle* type. To the *Belleisle* and *Orion* more than any other ships may be traced the first real appreciation of " angles in between "—the demonstration that " right ahead " or " right on the broadside " were ideal positions which no enemy would willingly assume.

The *Devastation* and her sisters had, of course, anticipated this idea ; but to the *Belleisle*, at most fighting angles only able to bring a quarter of her battery into action, may be traced most modern developments in gun disposition.

Contemporaneous with the special Barnaby ships, reference may be made to the entirely nondescript *Téméraire*. She may be described as an absolute hybrid —partly Reed, partly Barnaby, partly gun inventors of the era, and partly nothing in particular.

* *Our Ironclad Ships.*

Details of this ship are :—

Displacement—8,540 tons.
Length (between perpendiculars)—285ft.
Beam—62ft.
Draught—27¼ft.
Armament—Four 25-ton 11-inch M.L. (two in barbettes), four 18-ton M.L.—two above water torpedo tubes.
Armour (iron)—Complete 11-8in. belt. Bulkheads 8-5in. Barbettes 10-8in. Battery 10-8in.
Horse-power—7,520 = 14.5 knots.
Coal—620 tons = 2,680 miles at economical speed (nominal).

The *Téméraire* was unique in the world's navies in that two of her 25 ton guns were carried—one forward, one aft—on special Moncrieff mountings, an adaption for naval purposes of the " disappearing gun," invented for forts of that era. The gun, loaded under cover, was raised to fire by hydraulic mechanism, and then recoiled to the loading position. The ship was otherwise essentially of the Reed box-battery type ; the other two 25-ton guns being in a central main-deck battery, and capable of a good deal of ahead fire. The other big guns (18 tons) were cut off from the 25-ton by an armoured bulkhead, and merely had the ordinary broadside training.

Like the *Inflexible*, the *Téméraire* had a heavy brig rig. Towards the end of her active service career this was replaced by a military rig ; but all her active work was done as a brig. She was built at Chatham Dockyard, engined by Humphrys, and completed for sea in 1877.

In 1882 she was at the bombardment of Alexandria, and there did more execution than any other ship. Her subsequent career was uneventful, and in her own way she was a " monstrosity " as much as the *Polyphemus* was. She is generally understood to have been a " naval officers' ideal " ship, rather than the regular production of the Chief Constructor. Whether this be true is, at least,

P

doubtful.   Certainly she may equally well be regarded as
the forlorn hope of those who looked to see the general
principles of the central battery ironclad adapted to suit
the new ideas as to ironclads.   French ideas* also had
probably something to do with her peculiar design.

The idea embodied in the *Inflexible* was so pleasing
to the authorities at that period that she was duplicated
in two smaller vessels of the same type, the *Ajax* and
Agamemnon, though the precise purpose for which these
vessels were built is difficult to fathom.   They were in
every way inferior to the *Inflexible*, and mainly of interest
as indicating the definite abandonment of the idea of the
masted battleship, and they were also the last ships to
mount muzzle-loading guns :—

Particulars of these ships were :—

Displacement—8,660 tons.
Length (between perpendiculars)—280ft.
Beam—66ft.
Draught (mean)—24ft.
Guns—Four 38-ton M.L., two 6-inch 81-cwt. B.L.
Horse-power—5,440.
Speed—13.25 knots.

These were followed by the *Colossus* and *Edinburgh*,
which were laid down in 1879.   In these ships the 12-
inch breechloader was adopted, and an attempt at what
was then a very considerable speed was made.   An
auxiliary armament made its first really definite appearance, five 6-inch guns being mounted on the superstructure.

Particulars of these ships were :—

Displacement—9,420 tons.
Length (between perpendiculars)—325ft.
Beam—68ft.
Draught (mean)—26ft. 3ins.
Guns—Four 45-ton B.L.R., five 6-inch, 89-cwt. do.
Horse-power—7,500.
Speed—15.50 knots.

* In this connection see *Imperieuse* and *Warspite* later on

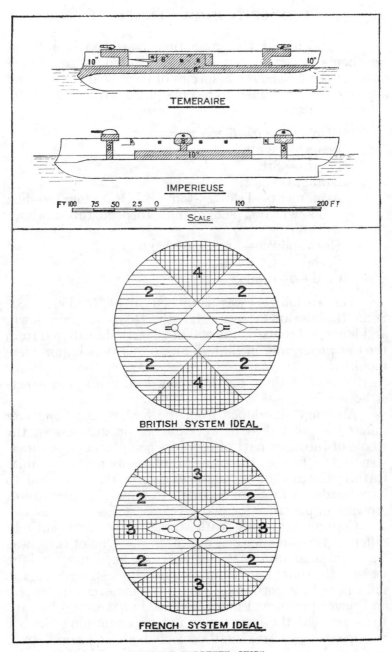

TEMERAIRE

IMPERIEUSE

FT 100   75   50   25   0   100   200 FT
SCALE

BRITISH SYSTEM IDEAL

FRENCH SYSTEM IDEAL

BARNABY BARBETTE SHIPS.

At and about the same time considerable interest was being taken in rams. This resulted in the laying down of the *Conqueror*, a species of improved *Rupert*, and a type of ship destined to be enlarged upon in the future.

Particulars of the *Conqueror* were :—

> Displacement—6,200 tons.
> Length—270ft.
> Beam—58ft.
> Draught—24ft.
> Armament—Two 45-ton B.L.R., four 6-inch 89-cwt. do., six 14-inch torpedo tubes (above water).
> Horse-power—(maximum) 6,000.
> Speed—15.5 knots.
> Coal—650 tons.

The *Conqueror* was launched in September, 1881. Some three years later a sister, the *Hero*, was laid down, and launched towards the end of 1885. She differed from the *Conqueror* only in that all four of her 6-inch guns were mounted on the superstructure, whereas the *Conqueror* carried two of them on the main deck inside the superstructure.

Although developed from the *Rupert*, the *Conqueror* differed a good deal in appearance, on account of the whole of the after part of the ship being one huge superstructure. In her, the superstructure, as a very definite feature instead of a mere accessory, may be said to have made its first appearance, to remain as a factor of growing importance for many years.

Contemporaneous with these ships two entirely different types made their appearance. One of these was the " torpedo ram " *Polyphemus*, an absolutely unique vessel, the outcome (though not so designed) of the influence of the torpedo. The ship was never duplicated, and never performed much service, but it would be rash to assert that the future may not see something like her re-appear. She was first projected as a " ram " pure and simple, so long ago as 1873, and designed by Barnaby to suit the specifications of certain naval officers as embodying their ideals of the warship of the future. This is the generally accepted theory, though Sir N. Barnaby* has made public a somewhat different view of the matter, and according to him, Admiral Sir George Sartorius, the naval officer principally concerned, lost his interest in the *Polyphemus* when it was decided to give her an armament of torpedo tubes and some quick-firers against torpedo attack. So far as can be gauged, the torpedo tubes were likewise a naval innovation with which Sir N. Barnaby was also not much in sympathy. At any rate, he has put on record the view* that :—

"The introduction of torpedoes made the ship far more costly than she need have been, and it is possible that the type would have been continued and improved had the simplicity of the ram been adhered to."

The *Polyphemus* performed little useful service ; her life on the Navy List was short ; and she is always spoken of as a " failure." Officers who served in her were, however, invariably enthusiastic about her, and had war occurred during the time that she was in existence there is no telling what she might have accomplished or how profoundly she might have affected naval construction.

In essence the *Polyphemus* was a semi-submerged craft, those parts of her which were above water being merely a light superstructure for the accommodation of her crew in peace time.

She was of 2,640 tons displacement, length 240ft. between perpendiculars, beam 40ft., and a normal mean draught of 20ft. In form she was cigar-shaped, plated with 3-inch armour on the upper part of her curved sides. With 5,520 I.H.P. she had the then very high speed of 17.8 knots. She carried 300 tons of coal, sufficient for a nominal radius of 3,400 miles at economical speed.

Her principal feature, however, was the fitting of five submerged tubes, one in the bow the others on the broadside. For repelling a torpedo attack she carried six 6-pounders and a couple of machine guns.

* *Naval Developments of the Century*, by Sir N. Barnaby, pp. 163-164.

It is here of interest to relate that some years later the U.S. Navy created a species of *Polyphemus* imitation in the "ram" *Katahdin*. To a certain extent they had anticipated her likewise in the *Alarm*, 720 tons, launched in 1873, which carried a 15-inch smooth-bore gun *under water* in her ram, and the *Intrepid* (launched 1873), of 1,123 tons, of which no details ever transpired, and it may be said that she was "strangled at birth." But the *Polyphemus's* ancestry is undoubtedly American. The *Katahdin* (first produced as the "ram" *Ammen*) was not launched till 1893. She was of 2,050 tons and seventeen knots and having no torpedo tubes, being a "ram" pure and simple, exactly reproduced the Sartorious-Barnaby idea. She soon disappeared from the U.S. Navy List, and she never did anything. She doubled the armour of the *Polyphemus*, whilst lacking her torpedo armament. Since then, the idea has found expression in three small U.S. "semi-submerged" boats, with the torpedo as their main armament ; but these three boats never got beyond the "designed" stage. No other nation ever exhibited the least interest in the *Polyphemus* idea.

Reference has already been made to the *Shannon*, which was the first armoured cruiser of the British Navy. She was launched towards the end of 1875 and completed two years later. In substance she was a development of the idea which first found expression in the *Inconstant*, heavy armament being preferred to the protection of the guns. A narrow belt of armour with a maximum thickness of 9-ins. protected three-quarters of the water-line. This belt commenced at the stern and ended in a bulkhead some 70ft. from the bow. Forward of this bulkhead was an under-water protective deck, and a certain amount of armour was concentrated on the ram under water. The bulkhead, which was from 9in. to 8in. thick, rose to the upper deck, and afforded protection to a couple of 18-ton muzzle-loaders, capable of right-ahead fire. The remainder of her armament consisted of seven 12½-ton guns, and was entirely unprotected.

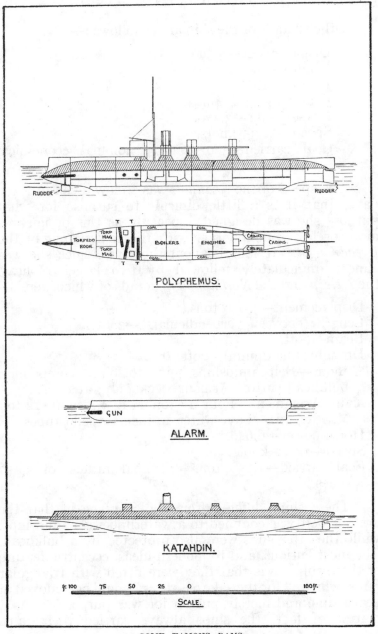

POLYPHEMUS.

ALARM.

KATAHDIN.

ft. 100   75   50   25   0   100 ft.

SCALE.

SOME FAMOUS RAMS.

Other details of the ship are as follows :—

 Displacement—5,390 tons.
 Length—260ft.
 Beam—54ft.
 Draught—23ft. 4in.
 Horse-power—3,370.
 Speed—12.35 knots.
 Coal carried—580 tons = nominal economical radius of 2,260 miles.

The speed of the *Shannon* was so low, even in those days, that it is a little difficult to surmise for what purpose she was designed, especially as this design was more or less contemporary with the re-designing of the *Dreadnought*.* It found favour, however, since she was almost immediately followed by two larger replicas, the *Nelson* and the *Northampton,* details of which were :—

 Displacement—7,630 tons.
 Length (between perpendiculars)—280ft.
 Beam—60ft.
 Draught (maximum)—26ft. 6in.
 Armour—Belt amidships, 9in. to 6in., compound : bulkhead ditto. Armour deck only, at ends.
 Main Armament—Four 18-ton M.L.R., eight 12-ton M.L.R., two above-water 14-inch torpedo tubes.
 Horse-power—6,640.
 Speed—14.41 knots.
 Coal carried—1,150 tons = nominal radius of 3,850 miles.

These ships differed from the *Shannon* in that the armour belt was confined to a waterline strip amidships, while the after guns were also protected by a bulkhead. The most curious, and to modern ideas, eccentric feature of these ships, was that they were fitted with triangular rams, which, " for the sake of safety," could be removed in peace time and merely put on for war purposes ! As a matter of fact, the ships always carried their rams

---

 * Re-designed to give extra protection.

without rendering themselves dangerous to anybody. On the other hand, shortly after construction, the *Northampton* was run into by a small trading schooner, which cut her down to the water's edge. The ships, therefore, started with an unfavourable reputation, which the *Northampton* followed up by a total inability to make even her moderate designed speed. The *Nelson*, on the other hand, proved herself a comparatively good steamer, so much so that at a later date she was to a certain extent modernised. Both ships were originally heavily masted, the idea being to perform most of their peace service when convenient under sail. The *Nelson* sailed moderately well, but the *Northampton* very badly. It was possibly with some view to remedying this that some years later, when it was decided that the *Imperieuse*, originally built as a brig, should be given a military rig, her lofty iron fore and mainmast were taken out of her and substituted for the two equivalent masts in the *Northampton*. The change, however, was not satisfactory, as thereafter she sailed if anything worse than ever.

At and about this year protected cruisers made their first appearance in the *Comus* class. Of these altogether eleven were built, the best known of these being the *Calliope*, which in the early nineties became famous through steaming out of Samoa Roads in the teeth of a hurricane, which utterly destroyed every foreign vessel anchored there at the same time. The *Comus* class consisted of the *Calliope, Calypso, Canada, Carysfort, Champion, Cleopatra, Comus, Conquest, Constance, Cordelia,* and *Curacoa.* They averaged 2,380 tons displacement, though the first mentioned, which were the last to be built, were slightly larger. The original armament consisted of two 6-ton muzzle-loaders and twelve 64-pounders. This was afterwards varied by the substitution of breechloaders. The ships generally had a speed of about thirteen knots, and were completed between the year 1877, for the earliest, and 1884 for the latest. They had a 1½-inch protective deck for the engines amidships.

These ships, which were generally officially known as the "C" class cruiser, were undoubtedly diminutives of the *Shannon*, or, at any rate, inspired by a similar idea.

Besides growing downwards the idea also grew upwards, and resulted in the building of six ships of the "Admiral" class, of which the first was the *Collingwood*. These, which were the apotheosis of the Barnaby idea, represented an absolute revolution in naval construction, so far as big ships were concerned.

The "Admirals" were not all identical, as they formed four different groups in the matter of displacement and three in armament. In all, however, the integral idea was the same. Amidships was a narrow belt, 150ft. long by 7½ft. wide, which sufficed to protect engines, boilers, and communication tubes of the barbettes. This belt varied in thickness from 18ins. to 8ins. of compound armour. The ends of the belt were closed up by 16-inch bulkheads. Forward and aft was merely a curved protective deck ; there was also a flat protective deck on top of the armour belt. The ships were of low freeboard, forward and aft, but had a large superstructure built up amidships. At either end of the superstructure, with their bases unprotected by armour except for the communication tubes already referred to, were many-sided barbettes with plates set at an angle of about forty-five degrees. These barbettes were about 11½ins. thick, and carried each a couple of the heaviest guns then available. These were 12-inch breechloaders in the *Collingwood*, and 13.5-inch in the other ships, except the *Benbow*, which mounted one 16.5 inch 110-ton in each barbette instead. An auxiliary armament was mounted inside the superstructure. The speed of these ships was about seventeen knots, and was considerably in excess of the average for the period.

As compared with the *Colossus* and *Edinburgh* class of the same date and era of design, the "Admirals" were somewhat inferior in armour protection, but because of that secured a far better speed and a greatly superior big gun command.

Name.	Collingwood.	Rodney, Howe.	Anson, Camperdown.	Benbow.
Displacement, tons	9,500	10,300	10,600	10,600
Length (*p.p.*) ft.	325	325	330	330
Beam, ft.	68	68	68½	68½
Draught (*mean*) ft.	26¾	27¼	26¾	27¼
H.P.	9,500	11,500	11,500	11,500
Nominal Speed, knots	16.5	16.7	17.2	17.5
Armament	4-12in., 6-6in.	4-13.5, 6-6in.	4-13.5, 6-6in.	2-16.25, 10-6in.
Built at	Pembroke Yard	Rodney, Chatham Yd. Howe, Pembroke Yd.	Anson, Pembroke Yd. Camperdown, Por'th	Thames, I.W.
Engines by	Humphrys	Rodney, Humphrys Howe, Humphrys	Anson, Humphrys Camperdown, Maud'y	Maudslay
Armour belt	18in.-8in.	18in.-8in.	18in.-8in.	18in.-8in.
barbettes	14in.-12in.	11½in.-10in.	16in.-6in.	12in.-4in.
bulkheads	16in.-6in.	16in.-6in.	14in.-12in.	18in.-6in.*
Armament	4-12in., 6-6in., and smaller, 2 sub. and 4 above water tubes	4-13.5, 6-6in., and smaller as Collingwood	4-13.5, 6-6in., and smaller, as Collingwood	2-16.25, 10-6in., and smaller, as Collingwood

In all the " Admiral " class the armour weighed about 2,500 tons—say, 20 per cent. of the displacement. This proportion has never been very greatly varied from either before or since, and the popular idea that Barnaby designs sacrificed armour weight for other features is entirely incorrect. The real Barnaby ideal is better described (the conditions of his own time being kept in mind) as an attempt to put into practice " everything or nothing," so far as protection was concerned. To-day, a compromise is in fashion, and Barnaby is very much out of date. It may well be but a phase in the cycle of naval design. Properly to appreciate the " Admiral " class ideal, we have to translate it into the ideal which obtains to-day. Thus put, the " Admirals " would be somewhat swifter than our existing battle-cruisers, their vitals would be invulnerable and their armaments superior to that of any potential enemy. They would not, in fact, very greatly differ from Admiral Bacon's conception (some two years old at the time of writing) of the battleship of the future, in which he predicted the disappearance of much of the side armour of to-day.

The coming of the medium calibre quick-firer soon rendered the " Admirals " obsolete and even ridiculous. The medium calibre quick-firer profoundly modified design until the developments of the big gun enabled it to act well beyond the effective range of the medium gun, and incidentally enabled it to fire nearly as fast as the elementary quick-firers were built to do. Thus we have come back to something very akin to the condition under which the Barnaby ships were designed.

These ships could not, perhaps, be described as an absolutely original idea, save in so far as the British Navy was concerned, since the Italian *Italia* was launched in the same year that the *Collingwood*, the first of the "Admirals" was laid down. The *Italia*, equally abnormally fast (or faster) for the period, carried four 100-ton guns échelonned in one large heavily armoured barbette amidships, but had no water-line belt whatever, and relied entirely upon an armour-deck to protect the motive power.   In the "Admirals" the motive power was thoroughly protected by the vertical belt amidships, while flotation otherwise depended upon internal sub-divisions.

The "Admiral" class idea was re-developed into armoured cruisers in a somewhat curious fashion.   At that time the French Navy was second in the world, and French ideas of construction commanded a great deal of respect.   French notions at that era ran largely to single gun positions, four guns being separately disposed in four barbettes placed one ahead, one astern, and one on either side.   The particular point of this arrangement was that while British designs accepted two or four big guns bearing, the French system allowed for a definite mean of three.   More practically put, this may be translated into a conception that an enemy would use every effort to avoid positions in which four big guns could be brought to bear on him, and seek those in which he was exposed to two only. A gun-arrangement which gave three big guns bearing in *any* position seemed therefore far more practicable.

It stands to the credit of Sir N. Barnaby (or else to the credit of the Admiralty of the era) that they recognised the impossibility of any such manœuvres in fleet actions, but that at the same time they realised how heavily it might tell in cruiser duels, out of which the *Imperieuse* and *Warspite* were born.

Details of these ships :—

Displacement—8,400 tons.
Length (between perpendiculars)—315ft.
Beam—62ft.
Draught (maximum)—27⅓ft.
Armament—Four 9.2 24-ton B.L., six 6-inch, 89cwt., six torpedo tubes.
Horse-power—10,000 = 16.75 knots.
Coal—1,130 tons = nominal radius of ten knots of 7,000 miles.
Armour—Belt amidships of 10in. compound, with 9-inch bulkheads, 8-inch barbettes.   No armour to lesser guns.   3-inch protective deck fore and aft, and on top of belt.

The *Imperieuse* was built at Portsmouth Dockyard and engined by Maudslay. The *Warspite*, built at Chatham, was engined by Penn. Both were completed in 1886 at a total cost of about £630,000 each. They were copper sheathed, and (like the *Inflexible*) originally were to carry a heavy brig-rig. This was removed at an early stage, and a single military mast between the funnels substituted. The *Imperieuse's* masts were subsequently put in the *Northampton* (*which see*). Both proved faster than anticipated ; but the coming of the quick-firer placed them in the semi-obsolete category almost as soon as they were completed. The type was never repeated. To-day (1912) the *Imperieuse* still exists as a depot ship for destroyers ; the *Warspite* has long since gone to the scrap heap. Years after their conception a modernised version of them was to some extent reproduced in the *Black Prince* class. In their own day, however, they appeared and that was all.

The " battleship of the future " ideal of those days had to some extent been foreshadowed in the *Benbow*, with her couple of 110-ton guns. The monster gun was " the vogue " and no way of carrying it on existing displacements allowed of more than two such pieces being mounted.

The idea of the moment became the mounting of guns capable of delivering deadly blows, and (corollary therewith) protection to ensure that that deadly blow could be delivered with relative impunity. Since the secondary gun had now come in, auxiliary guns and a secondary battery were a *sine quâ non*; but the ideal ship was to be one incapable of vital injury from such weapons. On lines such as these the *Victoria* class was designed.

The call was for an improved *Benbow*. The armament was to be no less and, if possible, more ; while better protection was an essential feature.

Details of the *Victoria* type, of which only two were built, are as follows :—

Displacement—10,470 tons (approximately that of the *Benbow*).

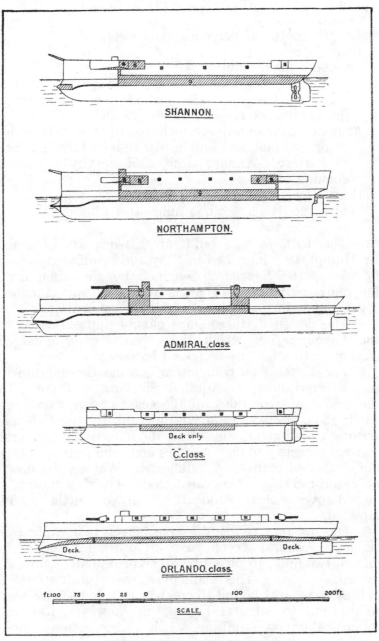

SHANNON.

NORTHAMPTON.

ADMIRAL. class.

Deck only.

C. class.

Deck. Deck.

ORLANDO. class.

ft.100 75 50 25 0 100 200ft.

SCALE.

CHARACTERISTIC BARNABY SHIPS.

Length (between perpendiculars)—340ft.

Beam—70ft.

Draught (maximum)—27¼ft.

Armament—Two 110-ton guns (in a single turret), one
9.2 (aft), twelve 6-inch ; twenty-one anti-torpedo
guns, and six torpedo tubes (14-inch).

Armour (compound)—18-inch to 16-inch belt amidships, redoubt and bulkheads, 18-inch turret, 2-inch
in battery. Armour deck, and heavily armoured
conning tower.

Horse-power—14,000 = 16.75 knots.

Coal—1,200 tons = 7,000 miles at 10 knots.

The *Victoria* was built at Elswick and engined
by Humphrys ; launched in 1887 and completed for sea
in 1889. The *Sanspareil*, engined by the same firm,
but built at Blackwall (Thames Ironworks) was launched
a year later, but completed about the same time.

The design of these ships closely approximated to
the *Conqueror*, of which they were merely enlarged
editions with a heavily increased battery.

The *Victoria* on completion became the flagship in
the Mediterranean of Admiral Sir George Tryon. In
the course of evolutions off the coast of Syria on June
22nd, 1893, she was rammed and sunk by the *Camperdown*. The disaster, which cost the lives of the Admiral
and 321 officers and men, teaches no useful lesson, saving
the danger of transverse bulkheads. Water-tight doors
were shut too late. The sea entered. The ship gradually
turned over, then suddenly " turned turtle " and
capsized.

The mystery of her loss has never been fully explained. Admiral Tryon gave an order for the fleet,
then in two lines, to turn inboard sixteen points, while at
six cables apart. This manœuvre, with turning circles
as they were, was bound to create a collision. This was
pointed out to Admiral Tryon, who, however, took no
notice of the representations. It has since been assumed
that he went suddenly mad. A more reasonable explana-

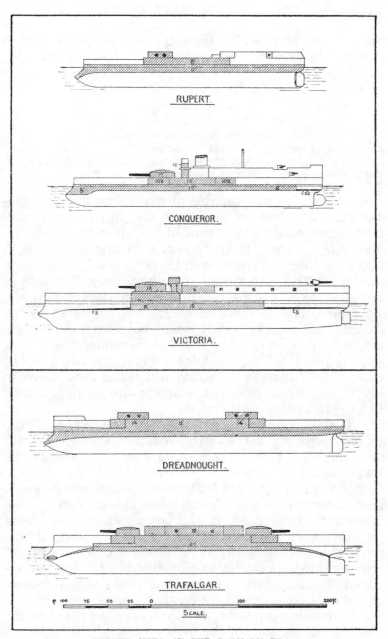

RUPERT.

CONQUEROR.

VICTORIA.

DREADNOUGHT.

TRAFALGAR.

SCALE.

TURRET SHIPS OF THE BARNABY ERA.

Q

tion is that he intended the ships to " jockey with their
screws " (a manœuvre which he never employed as a rule),
and forgot to mention the fact, though details of evidence
in the court-martial hardly bear this out.

The exact signal as made was :—

" Second division alter course in succession sixteen points to
starboard, preserving the order of the Fleet."

" First division alter course in succession sixteen points to
port, preserving the order of the Fleet."

This signal was capable of more than one interpretation. Along one of them each ship in the two squadrons might easily have rammed the other in succession,
according to some interpretations. Using screws, both
divisions might have closed in very closely but quite
safely. Acting other than simultaneously they might
anyway have effected the manœuvre without disaster.
At eight cables (a distance which was suggested to the
Admiral an hour before) it might have been done quite
safely. There have been other explanations also.

In the Fleet at the time everything was believed
except the " blunder " theory, which has gone down to
history. To this day that is accepted with reservation.
But the rest is mystery.

The *Camperdown*, in turning, crashed into the
Victoria, striking her forward, curiously enough directly
on a bulkhead, just as the *Vanguard* was struck when she
was rammed.

It was not expected that the *Victoria* would be sunk.
Had the water-tight doors been closed during the
manœuvre, instead of at the last moment, she would
probably have remained afloat. As things were, it was
impossible to close many at the time the order was given,
but her low-freeboard also played a part. The sea invaded the door on the starboard side of the superstructure
and thence got everywhere on that side of the ship. It
was that which threw her over and capsized her, but the
chance circumstance of the blow on the lateral bulkhead
should not be forgotten. The *Victoria* was struck just

on one of the points where all the odds were against her being struck.

The *Sanspareil* had an uneventful career, and was eventually sold out of the Service somewhat suddenly under the "scrap-heap" policy of Admiral Fisher in 1904.

Following upon the *Imperieuse* type, an entirely new class of armoured cruisers, the *Orlandos*, were designed.   Just as the *Victorias* were improved and enlarged *Conquerors*, so the *Orlandos* were "improved *Merseys*."   Particulars of these ships, of which seven were built altogether, are as follows :—

Displacement—5,600 tons.
Length (between perpendiculars)—300ft.
Beam—56ft.
Draught (maximum)—22½ft. (actually more).
Armament—Two 9.2in. B.L. ; ten 6in. ; and six torpedo tubes.
Armour (compound)—Belt amidships 10in., with 16in. bulkheads.   Protective deck at ends.   All guns protected by shields only.
Horse-power—8,500 = 18 knots.
Coal (maximum)—900 tons = nominal radius of 8,000 miles.

They were built as follows :—

NAME.	BUILDER.	ENGINED BY
Orlando	Palmer	Palmer.
Australia	Glasgow	Napier.
Aurora	Pembroke	Thompson.
Galatea	Glasgow	Napier.
Immortalité	Chatham	Earle.
Narcissus	Hull	Earle.
Undaunted	Palmer	Palmer.

They were laid down in 1885 and 1886.   The *Orlando* was completed in 1888, all the others in 1889. They were launched in 1886 and 1887, and some of them, fitted with wooden guns ("Quakers"), served to swell the Fleet at the great Jubilee Review of 1887. All made over their designed speeds on trial, but they did their trials "light." In service all proved fairly useful, and the *Undaunted,* with Lord Charles Beresford as her captain in the Mediterranean, "made history" to the extent of first creating an Anglo-American *entente,* beginning with the U.S.S. *Chicago,* captained then by the now universally known naval author, Admiral Mahan. Beresford first achieved fame in the *Condor* at Alexandra, in 1882; but it was in the *Undaunted* that he first "made history" by ending the previously existing hostility between the British and U.S. Navies; and establishing the naval brotherhood of those who speak the same language.

The *Orlandos* were the last of the essentially Barnaby ships. Barnaby was associated with the Navy thereafter; but the *Nile* and *Trafalgar,* though produced under his régime, were not "Barnaby ships," and differences of opinion with the Admiralty about them eventuated in his resignation.

The tide of naval opinion was then setting back in the old *Dreadnought* direction. More complete protection was being demanded. The quick-firer was just coming in and its potentialities seemed enormous. The secondary battery had to be protected. Destruction of communications on board began to take on a fresh and more serious aspect. In a word, the Admiralty reverted to Reed ideas, and in reverting exaggerated those ideas. In such circumstances the general idea of the *Trafalgars* was born.

Sir N. Barnaby totally dissented from the Admiralty line of thought. In his view the size of a ship could not legitimately be increased unless her offensive powers increased in proportion; in the *Trafalgar* idea both speed and armament were reduced as compared to the *Admiral* class, and over a thousand odd tons added entirely to carry extra defensive armour. Over which dispute he resigned his position.

Details of the *Nile* and *Trafalgar* as built are :—

Displacement—11,940 tons.

Length (between perpendiculars)—345ft.

Beam—73ft.

Draught (mean)—27½ft.

Armament—Four 13.5-inch, six 4.7 Q.F., also smaller guns, and four 14-inch torpedo tubes, of which two were submerged.

Armour (compound)—Belt, 230ft. long (*i.e.*, 8oft. longer than in the *Admirals* and *Victorias*), 20-16in., with 16-14-inch bulkheads, protective deck at ends and over main belt.

Over this a redoubt 141ft. long, 18in. thick. Above the redoubt a battery, 4in. thick. Turrets, 18in.

Horse-power—12,000 = 17 knots.

Coal—(normal) 900 tons; (maximum), 1,200 tons = 6,500 miles at 10 knots.

The *Nile* was built at Pembroke and engined by Maudslay. She was laid down in April, 1886, launched in March, 1888, and completed some two years later. The *Trafalgar* was laid down at Portsmouth in January, 1886, and launched in September, 1887. Her machinery was supplied by Humphrys. The armour of these ships weighed no less than 4,230 tons, *i.e.*, some 35 per cent. of the displacement instead of the more usual 25 per cent. or so. The then first Lord of the Admiralty took the occasion of the launch to remark that the days of such armoured ships were over, and that probably these were the last ironclads that would ever be built—the future would lie with fast deck-protected vessels ! As, for three years, no more armoured ships were laid down, he at least enunciated a definite policy when these heavily armoured editions of the *Admiral* class were put afloat. They differed from the *Admirals* in that turrets were reverted to instead of barbettes, and, as already mentioned, they were really nothing but modernised versions of the old *Dreadnought*.

At a later date 6-inch Q.F. were substituted for the
4.7's; but no other schemes of modernising the ships
ever came to a head.

Four ships of the *Amphion* Class—*Amphion, Arethusa, Leander,* and *Phæton,* of which the first (*Arethusa*)
was laid down in 1880—represented the first Barnaby idea
of the protected cruiser.   They were of 4,300 tons displacement, and 16.5 knots nominal speed.   They carried
ten 6-inch guns, and a $1\frac{1}{2}$-inch deck amidships.   According to the ideas of those days they were heavily over-
gunned.   They always steamed well ; but it is doubtful
whether Barnaby, left to himself, would ever have
produced them.   Incidentally, they were always bad
sea-boats.

In 1883, completed about the same time as the
Victoria, the *Mersey* class—*Mersey, Thames, Severn,* and
Forth—of 4,050 tons displacement, and carrying two
8-inch and ten 6-inch, were commenced : practically
early essays at the *Orlando* class idea which followed.
The *Orlandos,* on only a thousand or so tons more displacement, carried 9.2's instead of 8-inch, had armour-
belts as well as protective decks, and were a good knot
faster.   Both the *Amphions* and *Merseys* may be described as representing strictly naval Admiralty ideas—
the *Orlando,* Barnaby ones.   Each type was quickly
rendered obsolete by the coming of the quick-firer ; but
the Barnaby type of cruiser, for 20 per cent. extra displacement certainly offered better chances than any rival
proposition, if only we consider matters in the light of
what existed in those days and what promised best at
that time.

So ends the Barnaby era.   Barnaby's constructional
ideas were blown to mincemeat by the advent of the
quick-firer.   Even to-day (1912) they seem somewhat
obsolete.   Yet a few years hence (if big ships survive)
they stand every chance of being reverted to, because
to-day the big gun has more or less come back to

where it was in 1875-1885. Barnaby, though he worked into its era, never realised the preponderance or possible preponderance of the " secondary gun." In his era it fired too slowly to count for very much ; in our own (1912) range neutralises whatever it may have accomplished in the rapidity of fire direction.

Likely enough, the reversion to Barnaby ideals, which is reasonably probable for the immediate future, will be merely a phase ; and casual historians will ever put him down as the naval constructor who was least able to anticipate the years ahead of his creations. But a hundred years hence Barnaby may come into his own in a way little suspected to-day. A hundred years hence, when all the most modern ideas are ancient history, Barnaby may stand with Phineas Pett, and the Navy which he created stand for something infinitely more than the scrap heap to which a later age swiftly relegated it. Only the historian of the distant future can estimate him at his real face value. His own generation never placed much faith in his ships ; the generation that followed generally regarded them with scorn. It was probably wrong, but only the future can prove it to have been so.

GUNS IN THE ERA.

The guns which especially belong to the Barnaby era were as follows :—

Cal. ins.	Weight in tons.	Length in cals.	Weight projectile lbs.	Muzzle velocity f.s.	Muzzle energy ft.	Penetration 2000 yds.	
						iron.	comp.
M.L. 16	81	18	1684	1590	29,530	22	15
B.L. 16.25	110	30	1800	2148	57,580	29	19
13.5	67	30	1250	2025	35,560	26	17
12	45	25	714	2000	18,060	19	12½
9.2	22	25	380	1809	8622	15	10
8	14	30	210	2200	7060	14	9
6	5	26	100	1960	2665	8	5

In the early part of the period, guns of the Reed era, down to the 10-inch 18-ton M.L., were also made use of ; but, generally speaking, the Barnaby designs coincide with early breechloading types.   It is interesting to note that the 81-ton gun figured in one ship only (the *In-flexible*), and that after this the 38-ton 12.5 M.L. was reverted to, to be replaced in later designs by the 45-ton 12-inch B.L.

The M.L. guns available for early Barnaby designs were considerably superior to earlier examples of their type ; as after the fiasco of the *Glatton* trials*, copper gas checks were introduced.   These were affixed to the base of the projectile and expanded on firing.   They led to a certain increased power and accuracy ; but, even so, only of a relative nature compared with the better results obtained from breechloaders.   The *Thunderer* gun disaster, which after many experiments was found to have been caused by doubly loading the gun, added another argument to the anti-muzzle-loader cause.

The 12-inch, which was the first large B.L. to be introduced, compared as follows with the 12-inch M.L. :—

Gun.	Length in cals.	Weight tons.	Muzzle energy. ft.	Weight of projectile lbs.	Penetration of iron at		
					Muzzle. in.	1000 yds. in.	2000 yds. in.
12in. M.L	13½	35	9470	706	16	15	13
12in. B.L	25	45	18,060	1250	30½	28	26

The enormous difference in efficiency was of course traceable to other causes than the adoption of the breech-loader instead of the old M.L. ; but this was, equally naturally, overlooked ; which, perhaps, was just as well—otherwise the muzzle-loader might have per-sisted to quite recent times.   Though the *Thunderer* disaster showed that a M.L. could be loaded twice over by accident; this was an obviously unlikely thing to occur again.   The impression was made by the fact that the 12-inch B.L. was far more powerful than the old

* *See* Reed Era.

16-inch M.L. It was possibly this which directly led to the " monster-gun craze " of the Barnaby era, the way to which had already been shewn by the 16-inch M.L. Incidentally it is interesting to note that the present (1912) monster gun era is the third in which, after a period of adhesion to a 12-inch gun, greatly increased calibres have suddenly and more or less generally been resorted to.

THE COMING OF THE TORPEDO.

Reference has been made in the past chapter to Sir E. J. Reed's recognition of the possibilities of the torpedo ; and floating mines were, of course, well known. It was not, however, till 1874 that either mine or torpedo came to be regarded at all seriously.

The earliest Whitehead " fish torpedo " was produced in 1868 ; though it was then little more than a curiosity. It was a crude weapon, although it embodied, with two notable exceptions, most of the features that it possesses to-day. Its motive power was compressed air ; it carried an explosive head with a sensitive pistol.

The secret was bought by the British Government at an early stage. It was made strictly confidential ; indeed, to the present day, the internal mechanism of a torpedo is more or less sacred. Most other nations purchased the secret also, and guarded it with like care !

It is but fair to add that this ridiculous situation was brought about by the inventor, who particularly specified that the balance chamber must not be revealed even to admirals commanding fleets, but only to specially selected officers.

The main difficulty about it was how to discharge it. For some while only two methods existed : the first, a mechanism of catapult type which hurled the torpedo into the water ; the other, by a crude application of dropping gear, suitable, of course, for launches only. In either case, especially the former, there was a strong element of uncertainty as to the direction the torpedo would take; for one to describe a circle and return to the firer was not unknown.*

The charge was inconsiderable, and range and speed very small.

An instrument called the Harvey torpedo was more or less contemporaneous with the Whitehead. It was a very primitive idea, consisting as it did merely in attempting to tow explosives across the course of an enemy. It was too obviously cumbersome to cause disquietude, and with the invention of torpedo tubes passed into oblivion.

The advantages of the torpedo tube were quickly recognised; and though the range was still little over a hundred yards or so—at any rate, so far as any probability of hitting was concerned—the torpedo quickly became a part of the armament of all important ships. So much was this the case that the submerged tube was developed with sufficient celerity to be adopted into the equipment of the *Inflexible*, of 1874 design.

None the less, however, the possible results of torpedo attack remained uninvestigated till 1874, and even then only came to be inquired into after the *Oberon* experiments, which were primarily if not entirely brought about by the advent of the observation mine as a practical thing.

The mine's arrival counted for little; the automobile torpedo being at the moment much in the public eye, the point that the *Oberon* experiments were primarily designed to test the effect of mines got somewhat lost sight of. The essential fact is that by 1874 the fact of other enemies to the ship than the gun was established. For a long time it affected ship design no further than the gradual introduction of an anti-torpedo-boat armament; but this was mainly due to Sir E. J. Reed having in the *Bellerophon* design endeavoured to anticipate torpedo effect. In 1874, and onward therefrom for some time, the double bottom, combined with water-tight

* In the Chili-Peruvian War—as late as 1879-81—a torpedo fired from the *Huascar* did this.

bulkheads, was considered a suitable " reply " to the " new arm," and it was not for many years that torpedo nets were in any degree appreciated.

In the later eighties some torpedo experiments were conducted against the old ironclad *Resistance,* in which the Bullivant net defence system proved altogether superior to the cumbersome old wooden booms which were in use: but, despite this, nothing was done for many a year, and the old pattern was adhered to.

ESTIMATES IN THE ERA.

Financial Year.	Amount.	Personnel.
1869	9,996,641	63,000
1870	9,370,530	61,000
1871	9,789,956	61,000
1872	9,532,149	61,000
1873	9,899,725	60,000
1874	10,440,105	60,000
1875	10,825,194	60,000
1876	11,288,872	60,000
1877	10,971,829	60,000
1878	12,129,901	60,000
1879	10,586,894	58,800
1880	10,566,935	58,800
1881	10,945,919	58,100
1882	10,483,901	57,500
1883	10,899,500	57,250
1884	11,185,770	56,950
1885	12,694,900	58,334

XIII.

THE WHITE ERA.

THE appointment of Sir William White as Chief Constructor more or less synchronised with a considerable revolution in naval construction and ideas.

The institution of naval manœuvres drew great attention to the sea-going quality of various types of ships. The manœuvres of 1887 mostly centred around the *Polyphemus*, and her charging a boom at Berehaven. Little was here proved except that boom defences were easily to be annihilated. In 1888, however, the manœuvres were of a much more extensive nature, and a Committee was appointed to consider and report upon them, especially with regard to the following points :—

"The feasibility or otherwise of maintaining an effective blockade in war of an enemy's squadron or fast cruisers in strongly fortified ports, including the advantages and disadvantages of—

(a) Keeping the main body of the blockading Fleets off the ports to be blockaded with an inshore squadron.

(b) Keeping the main body of the blockading Fleets at a base, with a squadron of fast cruisers and scouts off the blockaded ports, having means of rapid communication with the Fleet.

(c) In both cases the approximate relative number of battleships and cruisers that should be employed by the blockading Fleet, as compared with those of the blockaded Fleet.

"The value of torpedo-gunboats and first-class torpedo boats both with the blockading and blockaded Fleets, and the most efficient manner of utilising them.

"As to the arrangements made by B squadron for the attack of commerce in the Channel, and by A squadron for its protection.

" As to the feasibility and expediency of cruisers making raids on an enemy's coasts and unprotected towns for the purpose of levying contribution.

" As to the claims and counterclaims made by the Admirals in command of both squadrons with regard to captures made during the operation.

" As to any defects of importance which were developed in any of the vessels employed, and their cause.

As Supplementary Instructions there were :—

(1) As to the behaviour and sea-going qualities of, or the defects in, the new and most recently commissioned vessels, as obtained from the reports of the Admirals in command of the respective squadrons.

(2) The general conclusion to be drawn from the recent operations."

A summary of the findings* is as follows :—

" That to maintain an effective blockade of a Fleet in a strongly fortified port a proportion of at least five to three would be essential and possibly an even larger proportion, unless a good anchorage could be found near the blockaded port which could be used as a base, in which case a proportion of four to three might suffice, supposing the blockading squadron to be very amply supplied with look-out ships and colliers."

Torpedo boats were condemned as being of little value to blockaders, though useful to the blockaded. For blockade purposes the torpedo-gunboats of the *Rattlesnake* class were highly commended.

Attention was drawn to the large number of deck hands employed down below on account of the insufficient engine-room complements, and the excess of untrained stokers. The case of the *Warspite* was specifically mentioned. In order to break the blockade at sixteen knots she sent thirty-six deck hands down below at a time when every available deck hand would have been required above had the operations been real war.

A special supplementary report was called for as to the sea-going qualities of the ships. Considerable

* The full report is to be found in Part IV of *Brassey's Naval Annual*, 1888-9.

historical interest attaches to this particular report, and the following extracts are especially interesting :—

Admiral class.

" So far as could be judged, these vessels are good sea-boats, and their speed is not affected when steaming against a moderate wind and sea ; but we are of opinion that their low freeboard renders them unsuitable as sea-going armour-clads for general service with the Fleet, as their speed must be rapidly reduced when it is necessary to force them against a head sea or swell.

" On the only occasion on which the *Collingwood* experienced any considerable beam swell she is reported to have rolled 20 degrees each way ; this does not make it appear as if the *Admiral* class will be very steady gun-platforms in bad weather.

" They are said to be ' handy ' at 6 knots and over.

" In the *Benbow* much difficulty was experienced in stowing the bower anchors. This is the case in all low freeboard vessels, more or less, but the evil appears to have been intensified in this instance by defective fittings, and by the fact of her being supplied with the old-fashioned iron-stocked anchors instead of improved Martins.

" Serious complaints are made from these ships that the fore-castles leak badly, and that the mess-deck is made uninhabitable whenever the sea breaks over the forecastle at all ; it would seem that this defect might be remedied."

This opinion was not shared by Admiral Sir Arthur Hood, who commented as follows :—

" I cannot concur in this opinion, my view being that the objects of primary importance to be fulfilled in a first-class battleship are : (1) That, on a given displacement, the combined powers of offence and defence shall be as great as can be given ; (2) that she shall be handy and possess good speed in ordinary weather, combined with sea-worthiness ; (3) that she shall have large coal-carrying capacity. I certainly do not consider that the *Admiral* class, which, on account of their comparatively low freeboard forward, must have their speed reduced when steaming against a heavy head sea or swell to a greater extent than is the case with the long, high freeboard, older armour-clads, as the *Minotaur, Northumberland, Black Prince,* are for this reason rendered unsuitable as sea-going armour-clads for general service with a Fleet. The power of being able to force a first-class battleship at full speed against a head sea is not, in my opinion, a point of the first importance, although in the case of a fast cruiser it certainly is. Admiral Tryon draws an unfavourable comparison between the speed of the new battleships and that of the long ships of the old type, when steaming against a head sea. I admit at once that vessels like the *Minotaur* class would maintain their speed and make better weather of it when being forced against a head sea than would the *Admirals* ; but this advantage, under these exceptional conditions, cannot for a moment be compared with the enormous increase in the power of offence and defence possessed by the *Admirals*."

The *Conqueror* and *Hero* were reported to roll a great deal. Being short they felt a head sea quickly, and on account of their low freeboard it was found impossible to drive them against a heavy sea at anything approaching full speed. Incidentally these ships were known as "half-boots."

Here, again, Admiral Sir Arthur Hood dissented. In connection with these points, Admiral Tryon submitted a report in which he emphasised as he had done with the *Admirals*, that however fast these short ships might be in smooth water, their speeds fell off rapidly in a seaway.

The *Mersey* class were described as being handy, steady gun platforms and able to fight their guns longer than most ships.* The captain of the *Severn*, however, reported a view that the 8-inch guns should be removed and lighter pieces substituted. Admiral Baird agreed with this. Sir Arthur Hood, in his comments, stated that he was " decidedly opposed " to any reduction of armament, both in this case and that of the other cruisers.

The *Arethusa* type were reported to roll so heavily when the sea was abeam or abaft, that " accurate shooting would be impossible and machine guns in the tops would be useless."

The Committee concurred with Admiral Baird that the armament of these should be reduced.

For the *Archer* class it was unanimously suggested that lighter guns should be fitted forward. Sir Arthur Hood agreed with this view, which, however, was never carried into effect.

---

* It is worthy of note that these ships were abnormally " over-gunned " according to the ideas which were then in official favour, and which, later on, came more into favour still. The same applies to the *Arethusa* class.

Particular interest attaches to the *Rattlesnake** class of torpedo-gunboats—these vessels being really proto-types of the destroyers of the present day. They were reported as " safe, provided they were handled with care." Their handiness was unfavourably reported on. It was strongly urged that the 4-inch gun mounted forward should be removed. This, however, was never done.

With reference to any new vessels of this type, the Committee reported as deserving immediate considera-tion :—

> (1) Generally strengthen the hull in this type of vessel.
> (2) Raise the freeboard forward.
> *or* (3) " Turtle-back " the forecastle.

In the gunboats that followed the freeboard forward was considerably raised ; but when destroyers came to be built several years later, it is interesting to observe that the turtle-back forecastle was adopted, and it was not till after over a hundred had been built that the high fore-castle, recommended so long before, appeared in the *River* class.

The report concluded :—

" The proportion of untrained (2nd class) stokers which were drafted to several of the ships appears to have been too large ; in point of physique they are reported as unequal to their work, and in many instances the experience of these men in stokehold (or any other work on board ship) was nil.

" As a means of affording opportunities for training newly-raised stokers we recommend that at least one year should be served by them as supernumerary in a sea-going ship before they are considered fit to be draughted as part complement to any vessel ; we further are of opinion that a Committee should be appointed to inquire into the sufficiency or otherwise of the complements allowed in the steam department of each class of ship, the propor-tion of 2nd class stokers which should be borne, and the amount of

---

* It is interesting to note that the Laird firm, who built the *Rattlesnake*, which was easily the fastest of her class, made her engines considerably heavier than Admiralty specifications. For this they were fined £1,000, which sum however, was remitted after the brilliant success of the ship in the manœuvres above referred to.

training which they should be required to undergo before they can usefully be borne as part complement in a fighting ship."

An agitation as to the state of the Navy, which was commenced in the year 1887, mainly by the initiative of the *Pall Mall Gazette,** finally resulted in the passing of the Naval Defence Act of 1889. This provided for the construction of a total of seventy vessels, consisting of ten armoured ships, nine first-class cruisers, twenty-nine second-class cruisers, four third-class and eighteen torpedo gunboats, to be built as quickly as possible at the estimated cost of £21,500,000.

The substantial part of the programme of 1886 had consisted of two big turret ships, the *Nile* and *Trafalgar,* and two armoured cruisers, *Immortalité* and *Aurora* of the *Orlando* class. In 1887 nothing larger than second-class cruisers was laid down ; and in 1888 the most important vessels on the programme were only the protected cruisers, *Blake* and *Blenheim.* There was, therefore, ample material for panic.

Details of the *Blake* class :—

Length (*p.p.*)—375ft.
Beam—65ft.
Guns—Two 9.2in., 22-ton B.L.R., ten 6-in. Q.F., eighteen 3-pdr.
H.P.—20,000.
Designed speed—22.0 knots.
Coal—1500 tons.
Builder of Ship—*Blake,* Chatham ; *Blenheim,* Thames Ironworks.
Builder of machinery—*Blake,* Maudslay; *Blenheim,* Thames Ironworks.
Launched—*Blake,* 1889 ; *Blenheim,* 1890.

Special features of these ships were a combination of

* Mr. W. T. Stead, who edited the *Pall Mall Gazette* at that time, intimated some twenty years later that Lord Fisher was behind him in commencing the agitation. Lord Charles Beresford, then in political life, brought the Bill forward.

R

the armament of the *Orlando* class with greatly increased speed secured by the development of deck armour in place of the belts of the *Orlando* class. In so far as a special type of ship may be said to be the development of some predecessor, the *Blake* and *Blenheim* may be described as enlarged *Merseys*. They were, however, unique on account of their relatively great length and great increase of displacement as compared with preceeding vessels. In them the armoured casemate, a leading characteristic of nearly all Sir William White's ships, made its first appearance. It was employed in the *Blake* and *Blenheim* for four main deck guns, the upper deck guns being behind the usual shields.

The coming of the casemate, curiously enough, attracted little attention, compared to its importance. It may be said to have rendered possible the return to main deck guns in unarmoured ships. In the *Orlando* class, ten 6-inch guns were all bunched together on the upper deck amidships. Since these ships were designed the 6-inch quickfirer had made its first appearance, and the largest possible distribution of armament was therefore desirable. The adoption of the two-deck system of the *Blake* and *Blenheim* secured this much larger distribution, rendering it impossible for a single shell to put more than one of the five broadside 6-inch out of action, whereas in the *Orlando* class at least three guns were at the mercy of a single shell.

Another novelty of the type was the introduction of a special armoured glacis around the engine hatches. This system had, of course, been used before in the Italian monster ships *Italia* and *Lepanto*, but it was first introduced in the British Navy in the *Blakes*.*

The ships were very successful steamers, for all that neither made her expected twenty-two knots on trial.

* In 1899 the *Blake* was re-boilered. The ships remained upon the effective list till 1906, when they were converted into seagoing depot ships for destroyers, most of their guns being removed. They now carry each 670 tons of coal of their own, and 470 tons stowed in one cwt. bags for use by destroyers.

Trial results :—

> *Blake*: Eight hours natural draught, mean I.H.P.—
> 14,525 = 19.4 knots.
> *Blenheim* : Eight hours' natural draught, mean
> I.H.P.—14,925 = 20.4 knots.
> *Blake* : Four hours' force draught, mean I.H.P.—
> 19,579 = 21.5 knots.
> *Blenheim* : Four hours' forced draught, mean
> I.H.P.—21,411 = 21.8 knots.

The principal item of the Naval Defence Act was eight first-class and two second-class battleships. All these ships were designed by Sir William White, and may be described as battleship editions of the *Blake* and *Blenheim*, so far as the disposition of their armament was concerned. For the rest they may be described as attempts to combine in one ship the best features of the Read and Barnaby ideals. In place of the low freeboard of the *Admiral* class, seven of the *Royal Sovereigns* were given high freeboard fore and aft, with the big guns about twenty-three feet above water. The eighth ship, the *Hood*, was modified to suit the ideals of Admiral Hood, and was to some extent an improved *Trafalgar*, her big guns being in turrets some seventeen feet above the water, in turrets instead of *en barbette* with guns exposed as in the rest of the class.

In them, among other special features, 18-inch torpedo tubes were first introduced instead of 14-inch, and a stern torpedo tube appeared.

The original idea of end-on torpedo tubes was torpedo attack from the bow in place of the ram. The *Polyphemus* was the first ship in which an end-on tube appeared (submerged). In cruisers of a later date the bow tube was found to injure speed, and there was always the danger of a ship over-running her own torpedo. On this account the bow-tube never secured in the British Navy that vogue which it obtained, and still has, in Germany.

The stern-tube appears to owe its origin to an idea that a defeated or overpowered ship, running from an enemy, might save herself by it : dim ideas of " runaway tactics " had also begun to appear.

Sir William White never claimed for himself that he had anticipated the future in any way in his torpedo armament, even when defending himself against criticisms, to the effect that he gave " too little for the displacement." Yet his torpedo innovations, besides discounting the future, all helped to swell the total weight ; as also did many internal strengthenings of the kind which do not show on paper. Possibly he did not realise his own greatness as the designer of a class of ship which was so much better than any contemporary vessel, that even in these days of " Super-Dreadnoughts " the *Royal Sovereigns* are still looked back upon with respect, and invariably regarded as marking the beginning of an entirely new phase in ship construction.

In April, 1889, their designer read a paper about them at the Institution of Naval Architects, in which the principal points which he claimed were that much superior command of guns was given, and that the auxiliary armament was nearly three times the weight of that of the *Trafalgars*. The following points were also mentioned by him :—

" (a) 'That (it was officially decided that) it was preferable to have two separate strongly protected stations for the four heavy guns, rather than to have a single citadel.'

" (b) 'That on the whole the 4-inch armour amidships, from the belt deck to the main deck, associated as it would be with the internal coal bunkers, sub-divided into numerous compartments, might be considered satisfactory ; but that if armour weight became available, it could be profitably utilised in thickening the 4-inch steel above the middle portion of the belt.'

" I would draw particular attention to the first of these conclusions, since it expresses a most important distinction between the two systems of protection.

" With separate redoubts, placed far apart, the two stations are isolated, and there is practically no risk of simultaneous disablement by the explosion of shells, or perforation of projectiles from the heaviest guns. Each redoubt offers a small target to the fire of an enemy, and its weakest part—the thick steel protective plating on the top—is of so small extent that the chance of its being struck is extremely remote. Serious damage to the unarmoured turret bases therefore involves the perforation of the thick vertical armour on the redoubts.

" With a single citadel, extending the full breadth of a ship, the case is widely different.

" Over a comparatively large area of the protective deck-plating in the neighbourhood of each turret, perforation of the deck, or its disruption by shell explosions at any point, involves very serious risk of damage to the turret bases and the loading apparatus. In fact, such damage may be effected and the heavy guns put out of action while the thick vertical armour on the citadel is uninjured. Moreover, as the turrets stand at the ends of a single citadel, there is a possibility of their simultaneous disablement by the explosion of heavy shell within the citadel.

" This last risk may be minimised (as in the *Nile* and *Trafalgar*) by constructing armoured ' traverses' within the citadel ; but it cannot be wholly overcome, so long as both turrets stand in one armoured enclosure.

" It may be thought that the risk of damage to a 3-inch steel deck situated 11 ft. above water is remote ; but I think the facts are as stated, when actions at sea are taken into account.

" For example, if a ship of 70 to 75 ft. beam is rolling only to 10 degrees from the vertical, which is by no means a heavy roll, she presents a target having a vertical (projected) height of 13 to 14 ft. to an enemy's fire, and even if she is a steady, slow-moving ship, she will do this four or five times in each minute.

" Now, at this angle of inclination, assuming the flight of projectiles to be practically horizontal, even the thickest protective steel decks yet fitted in battleships are liable to serious damage from the fire of guns of moderate calibre, and this danger is increased by the employment of high explosives. Of course, I do not mean to say that this damage is to follow from fire intentionally aimed at the protective deck ; but with a great and sustained volume of fire, such as is possible with a powerful auxiliary armament, and especially with quick-firing guns, it is obvious that there is a very real danger of chance shots injuring seriously the wide expanse of the protective deck at the top of a long citadel.

" Again, it must be noted that the chances of damage to a deck placed 10 or 11 ft. above water, and with large exposed surfaces in the neighbourhood of the turrets when a ship is inclined or rolling, are greater far than those of a deck 7 or 8 ft. lower, and with 5-inch armour on the sides protecting the deck from the direct impact of shells containing heavy bursters. It is for the naval gunner to estimate these chances of injury ; but, unless I am greatly mistaken, their verdict will be that a far greater number of shots are likely to strike at a height of 8 to 10 ft. above water than at a height of 4 to 5 ft.

"These considerations, I submit, amply justify the selection of the separate redoubt system, in association with the thin side armour above the belt, and the lowering of the protective deck to the top of the belt in the new designs.

"It may be urged that, if the redoubt system be adopted, it should be associated with side armour and screen bulkheads of greater thickness than 5-inch steel, and more strongly backed. This is perfectly practicable, but necessarily costly, involving an additional load of armour, and a corresponding increase in the size of the ship."

The designs were vigorously criticised by Sir Edward Reed, whose chief objections centred on the fact that the lower-deck protection was thin armour only. Sir William White combatted this idea, and proved very conclusively that, according to the needs of the moment, his views were correct. It is, however, worthy of record that at a later date with the *Majestic* class (see a few pages further on), he effected modifications which brought his ships more into line with what Sir Edward Reed had advocated. It should, however, be mentioned that this was not done until improvements in armour construction rendered possible things that were certainly impossible in the days of the *Royal Sovereigns*.

In connection with the later career of the *Royal Sovereign* class these items may be added. On completion they were found to be singularly simple in all their internal arrangements, and extraordinarily strong. When they went to the scrap-heap in 1911-12, they were, constructionally, practically as good as when built. They proved to be good sea boats, but at first rolled very badly, which resulted in their getting an unenviable notoriety in this respect. This was, however, completely cured by the fitting of bilge keels, after which the ships were everything that could be desired in the way of being steady gun platforms.

The ever increasing vogue of the quickfirer tended to render them rather quickly obsolescent over things which to-day would count much less than they did in the past. The defects of the *Sovereigns*, as realised not very long after completion, were :—

> (1) That the big guns' crews were practically unprotected, and easily to be annihilated by the newly-introduced high explosive shells of the secondary armament of an enemy.
>
> (2) Only four of the ten 6-inch were armour protected; which also was considered a fatal drawback.

In the first case nothing was ever done ; but in the second, about the year 1900, casemates were fitted for the upper-deck guns of all ships except the *Hood**, which on survey was found unsuitable for such reconstruction.

The only thing that remains to add is that, although in the course of years, the ships lost the speeds for which they were designed, up to the very end they proved capable of doing about thirteen knots indefinitely.

In addition to the *Sovereigns* two " second-class battleships " were built, the *Centurion* and *Barfleur*, of which details are :—

> Displacement—10,500 tons. Complement, 620.
> Length—(Waterline) 360ft.
> Beam—70ft.
> Draught—(Maximum) 27ft.
> Armament—Four 10-inch, ten 4.7-inch, eight 6-pounders, twelve 3-pounders, two Maxims, two 9-pounder boat guns. Torpedo tubes (18-inch)—two submerged and one above water in the stern.

The *Barfleur* was laid down at Chatham in November, 1890, launched in August, 1892, and completed two years later. The *Centurion*, laid down at Portsmouth in March, 1891, was launched a year later, but completed before her sister.

---

* This ship very greatly exceeded her nominal displacement of 14,200 tons. She was actually 15,400 tons. The essentially White ships were, on the other hand, of about their nominal displacement. Of the *Hood* it may further be added that she was greatly inferior to the others as a sea-boat—a serious set-off against her superior big gun protection.

The ships were armoured generally on the *Royal Sovereign* plan, with 12-inch belts which, however, were only 200ft. long, instead of 250ft.　The bulkheads were six inches only, and the upper belt (nickel steel) an inch less than in the big ships.　The barbettes were reduced to nine inches only, but on the other hand were made circular instead of pear-shaped, and 6-inch shields were provided for the big guns—probably as the result of criticisms of the unprotected big guns of the *Sovereigns*. With a few early exceptions as to the shape of the base, and with certain variation in form, this kind of " turret " has been adhered to ever since in the British Navy and copied into every other.

Both ships were engined by the Greenock Foundry Company, and designed for 13,000 H.P., with forced draught, giving a speed of 18.5 knots, which speed both exceeded on trial.　This high speed and their coal endurance—they carried a maximum of 1,125 tons, sufficient for a nominal 9750 mile radius—makes them something more than the " second-class battleships " which they nominally were.

Compared to the *Sovereigns* they were :—

	Barfleurs.	*Sovereigns.*
Minus Points :		
Displacement (tons)	10.500	14,100
Principal guns..........	4-10 in., 10-4.7	4-13.5, 10-6in.
Armour belt	12 inches.	18 inches.
Plus Points :		
Horse Power	13,000	13,000
Speed	18.5	17
Nominal endurance (kts).	9,750	7,900

From which the existence of an elementary conception of the " battle-cruiser " of to-day seems fairly apparent.　To-day the battle-cruiser, instead of having guns of reduced calibre, carries a reduced number, but the general principle of " moderate sacrifices for increased speed " obtains.

The *Barfleur* and *Centurion* proved excellent steamers and good sea-boats.　Their defect was their weak armament, and in 1903 it was decided to remedy this.　In

that year they were "reconstructed." Their 4.7's were
taken out and 6-inch guns substituted, and the six on
the upper deck were put into casemates. As a species
of make-weight the foremast was taken out of both
ships ; but this made little difference. The "improvements" were a total failure ; the ships were immersed far
below what they had been designed for, and they never
thereafter realised much more than about sixteen knots.
Within seven years they were removed from the Navy
List altogether, and such service as they performed after
modernising was entirely of a subsidiary order.

For the first-class cruisers of the Naval Defence Act
reduced examples of the *Blenheim* were decided on.
These vessels were the *Edgar, Endymion, Grafton, Hawke,
St. George, Gibraltar, Crescent,* and *Royal Arthur* (formerly designated as the *Centaur*). They were launched
between 1891 and 1892, averaging 7,350 tons (unsheathed) and 7,700 tons (sheathed and coppered, in the
case of the last four mentioned). Except the two last,
all had the *Blenheim* armament of two 9.2 and ten
6-inch. The two latter had a couple of extra 6-inch on
a raised forecastle substituted for the forward 9.2.

No attempt was made to obtain the high speed of
the *Blenheims*—19.5 knots being the utmost aimed at.
Not only, however, did the *Edgar* class exceed expectations on trial, but they proved most remarkably good
steamers in service. No engine-room defects of moment
were even encountered in any of them, and twenty years
after launch most were still able to steam at little short
of the designed speed. Like the battleships, they were
given 18-inch torpedoes in place of the 14-inch of the
Blenheims.

In the course of their service careers, the *St. George*
(or rather her crew) earned distinction in the Benin
Expedition. The *Crescent* was served in by King
George V., and the *Hawke* achieved notoriety by ramming
the *Olympic* in the Solent in 1911.

The lesser cruisers of the Naval Defence Act numbered altogether 28. Of these twenty belonged to the

Apollo class of 3,400 tons (unsheathed) and 3,600 tons (sheathed). They were *Apollo, Andromache, Latona, Melampus, Naiad, Sappho, Scylla, Terpsichore, Thetis, Tribune* (unsheathed), and *Aeolus, Brilliant, Indefatigable* (named *Melpomene* in 1911), *Intrepid, Iphegnia, Pique, Rainbow, Retribution, Sirius,* and *Spartan* (sheathed).

In all, the armament was two 6-inch and six 4.7, with lesser guns, and, above-water, 14-inch torpedo tubes. The speed was twenty knots in the unsheathed, and a quarter of a knot less in the sheathed ones.

When built all proved able to steam very well, but after some years service certain of them fell off very badly in speed. Others, however, remained as fast as when they were built—the *Terpsichore,* in 1908, averaging 20.1 knots, and the *Aeolus,* in 1909, nearly nineteen knots.

During their service, the *Melampus* was commanded by King George as Prince George, while the *Scylla,* under Captain Percy Scott, gave birth to the " dotter," and the " gunnery boom " which followed. In 1904 and onwards seven of them, scrapped from regular service— the *Latona, Thetis, Apollo, Andromache, Iphegnia, Intrepid,* and *Thetis*—were totally or partially disarmed and converted into mine layers.

The remaining eight cruisers of the Act—*Astræa, Bonaventure, Cambrian, Charybdis, Flora, Forte, Fox,* and *Hermione*—were increased in size up to 4,360 tons, and given a couple of extra 4.7, and 18-inch in place of 14-inch tubes. Instead of their 4.7's being mounted in the well amidships, they were placed on the upper deck level, a much better position in a sea-way, but they never proved themselves quite such good ships for their size as did the earlier type. They served to illustrate the general rule that slight improvements on a design are rarely satisfactory, and that while every staple design has its defects, it is extremely difficult to remove one drawback without creating another. Moreover, such improvements invariably cause increased cost, and an essential with the small cruiser is that it shall be cheap enough to be numerically strong. Four *Astræas* cost as much as five *Apollos*. They were rather more sea-worthy, but no faster—if as fast. The total broadsides obtained were only *one* 4.7 more and *two* 6-inch *less*.* A considerably greater possible bunker capacity was obtained ; but the normal supply (400 tons) was the same for both.

In the British Navy, in 1908-11, a precisely similar thing obtained. It is probably inevitable. In the German Navy, between 1897 and 1907, displacement for small cruisers rose from 2,645 to 4,350 tons, with prac-tically the same armament. But here the horse-power rose from about 8,500 or less to 20,000, and designed speeds in proportion, from a twenty-one knots (not made) to a 25.5, which, on trial, turned out to be 27,000 I.H.P. and over twenty-seven knots.

Here, however, there was a definite aim—increased speed, with only trivial improvements in any other direction. With similar British cruisers the defect has invariably been " general improvements " on what the original design *might have been* if plotted a year or two later than it actually was. There is no question—or very little—but that Germany in its ultra-conservative policy has gauged the situation better than any British Admiralty ever did.

Minor cruisers must be cheap to construct. Any improvement in them must have a definite intrinsic value. Lacking that, it is worth very little. The *Astræas*, as cited, indicated how a supposed advantage may even be a real deficit from another point of view.

The value of increased speed cannot be put into £ s. d., but armament easily can be. Like reconstruction, minor " improvements " on a design rarely pay. With the original conception the naval architect is given certain data for which he arranges accordingly. Ordered to improve upon it in any direction he can only add displacement and upset the balance of everything.

The Naval Defence Act also included a certain

* 4 *Astræas* = 8—6in., 16—4.7.   5 *Apollos* = 10—6in., 15—4.7.

number of third-class cruisers—*Pallas, Pearl, Philomel,* and *Phœbe*—for the ordinary service, and five similar ships for the Australian station, originally named *Pandora, Pelorus, Persian, Phœnix,* and *Psyche.* These were later altered to Australian names, *Katoomba, Mildura, Wallaroo, Tauranga,* and *Ringarooma.* They were of 2,575 tons, with 2½ decks, armaments of eight 4.7-inch and four above-water 14-inch tubes. The designed speed was 19 knots.

Thirteen torpedo gunboats, improved *Rattlesnakes,* were laid down under the Act, corresponding to nine others of the normal Programme, of which two were for Australia. The Naval Defence boats were *Alarm, Antelope, Circe, Gleaner, Gossamer, Hebe, Renard, Speedy*— all laid down in 1889, as also were the *Whiting* (afterwards *Boomerang*) and *Wizard* (renamed *Karahatta*) for Australia. Those laid down normally in the previous year were the *Salamander, Seagull, Sheldrake, Skipjack, Spanker, Speedwell,* for the British Navy. Two others, *Assaye* and *Plassy,* were built for the Indian Marine at and about this time. All carried a couple of 4.7-inch guns, were of about 750-850 tons displacement, and were first known as " catchers." They were all intended to steam at 19 knots or over, with locomotive boilers ; but in service none ever did. At a later date, reboilered with water-tubes, many reached or exceeded the designed speed, and the majority in 1912 were still in service for auxiliary purposes—many being specially fitted as mine sweepers, and the rest used as tenders for various services.

They are of considerable interest on account of the fact that the destroyers of 1909-12 are practically the same displacement and general shape, with a not very dissimilar armament—two 4-inch instead of two 4.7. The modern destroyers, however, are approximately ten knots faster—an interesting commentary on engineering improvements in the course of twenty years ! More interesting still, however, is the fact that Sir William White should have evolved twenty years ago almost exactly what—except in the matter of modern speed possibilities—is to-day the recognised ideal for destroyers.

In the British Navy the torpedo gun-boats never got beyond the " catcher " stage—they never had the opportunity ; but it is worthy of note that the first two ships to be torpedoes under anything like modern war conditions—the Chilian *Blanco Encalada* and the Brazilian *Aquidaban*—were both sunk by vessels of almost exactly the same type as the " catchers," and not by torpedo boats.

So far as the British Navy was concerned, the " catchers " tested in the " secret manœuvres " of 1891 did uncommonly well. They hung about off the torpedo bases, and though only about one to four, accounted for at least 90 per cent. of the hostile torpedo boats. To this very success, perhaps, was due the fact that in their own day they were not thought of as an offensive arm against big ships—destruction of the torpedo boat was then the principal aim in view. This they fulfilled. The South American Republics discovered their " other uses," and so really led the way to the evolution of the destroyer of a later era.

Perhaps the only nation which really read the lesson involved was Germany. So long ago as 1895 she had launched the 2,000-ton " small cruiser " *Hela* ; in 1898 the *Gazelle* of 2,645 tons was set afloat. For years Germany added to the *Gazelle* class, at a time when all the rest of the world had decreed that " third-class cruisers " were useless. Not for many a year did the British Admiralty discover that Germany had seen the matter of the *Lynch* and the *Sampaio** better than any other Power.

Neither of these ships in attacking got hit. They got home without. But they might have been hit. Germany evolved something that even if hit badly would still float long enough to get off her torpedoes.

---

* The *Lynch* and *Condell* (launched 1890) sank the Chilian *Blanco Encalada* in 1891 ; the *G. Sampaio* (1893) the Brazilian *Aquidaban* in 1894.

Till the Chilian " catchers " in 1891 proved their offensive abilities, no one had ever considered that side of the question. To this day Germany has never really received her meed of credit for perceiving that a small third-class cruiser has potentialities with torpedoes against a battleship at night.

So late as 1912 there has been much comment about German small cruisers being inadequately gunned, a clear indication that just as in the past there was a difficulty in conceiving of the torpedo-gunboat for other than her nominal use, so to-day the possibilities of the small cruiser in the rôle of destroyer are still apt to be generally overlooked.

In February, 1893, there was laid down the *Renown*, the only armoured ship of the 1892-93 Estimates, an improved *Centurion*, with thinner belt armour. Harvey armour—three inches of which had the resisting value of four inches of compound or six inches of iron—was adopted in this ship for the first time. Influences other than taking advantage of the reduced weight required for a given protective value were, however, at work, as in the *Renown*, sacrifices were made at the waterline in order to secure better protection to the lower deck side.

Details of the *Renown* :—

> Displacement—12,350 tons.
> Length (between perpendiculars)—380ft.
> Beam—72⅜ft.
> Draught—(maximum) 27ft.
> Armament—Four 10-inch, ten 6-inch 40 cal., twelve 12-pounders, four submerged 18-inch tubes, and one above water-line in stern.
> Armour—8-6in. belt, 200ft. long amidships, 6in. side above. Bulkheads 10-6in., barbettes 10in., casemates, main deck ones 6in., upper deck ones, 4in.
> Horse-power—12,000 = 18 knots.
> Coal—(normal), 800 tons; (maximum), 1,760 tons = nominal 7,200 miles at ten knots.

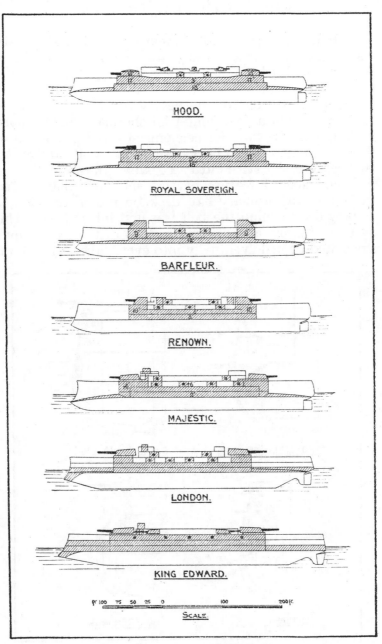

HOOD.

ROYAL SOVEREIGN.

BARFLEUR.

RENOWN.

MAJESTIC.

LONDON.

KING EDWARD.

SCALE.

BATTLESHIPS OF THE WHITE ERA.

Built at Pembroke ; engined by Maudslay ; she
was launched in May, 1895, and completed for sea in
April, 1897, having taken no less than 4¼ years to build.
Cost, £746,247.

She proved one of the best steamers ever built for
the Navy.   On a four-hour trial she made 18.75 knots,
with 12,901 I.H.P.   Her economical speed proved to be
fifteen knots.   She always steamed well, and after
thirteen years' service did 17.4 knots with ease.

The special feature of this ship was that in her,
instead of the ordinary flat deck on top of the belt, a
sloping deck behind the belt was first introduced.   This
system—rigidly adhered to in the British Navy ever
since, and copied eventually into every other Navy—was

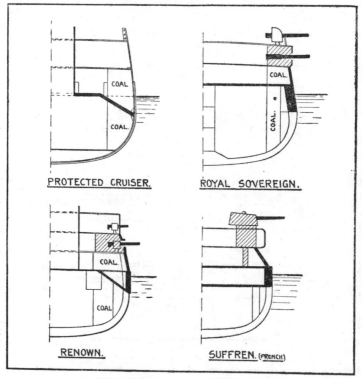

SYSTEMS OF WATERLINE PROTECTION.

based upon the idea of re-inforcing the deck-protected cruiser with side armour. The principle involved was that at whatever angle the belt might be hit and penetrated : the incoming projectile would then meet a further obstruction at a 45° angle, calculated to present a maximum of deflecting resistance. Professor Hovgaard and others have since indicated that, weight for weight, three inches of inclined deck armour, having to be spread more, represent as much or more tons as six inches of vertical armour (the nominal equivalent), and protective decks behind armour are to-day much thinner than of yore and little better than " splinter decks." The principle, however, remains, as originated by Sir William White, and is, perhaps, the most characteristic feature of his era : seeing how universally the idea was copied.

The French were the last to adopt it. Instead, they used the flat deck below the belt in addition to the one on top of it. This was made use of so late as the *République* and *Liberté* class. While ideally better for resisting projectiles which might penetrate the belt, it was impossible of really practical application amidships, on account of the difficulty of keeping the engines entirely below it.

The *Renown* was the first ship to carry all her secondary guns in casemates. She was fitted as a flagship, and first served on the North American Station. When Admiral Fisher went from there to the Mediterranean he took the *Renown* with him as flagship, presumably with the idea that speed was better than power in a flagship. The *Renown's* fighting power was small even then, but she was well fitted for the social side of flagship work—so nicely, indeed, that the flash-plates of the big guns had been taken up so as not to interfere with ladies' shoes in dances !

After leaving the Mediterranean the *Renown* was still further converted into a " battleship yacht," the six-inch guns being removed. She was painted white, and used to convey the then Prince of Wales to India.

S

Thereafter she practically disappeared from the effective list and eventually became a training ship for stokers.

The *Renown* was followed by the ships of the Spencer programme, nine battleships of the *Majestic* class, which were spread over the 1893-94 Estimates, and those of the next year. The *Majestics* were in substance amplified *Renowns*, their special and particular feature being that in place of the two amidships belt of varying thickness a single belt of 16ft. wide of a uniform 9in. thickness was substituted.

In the *Majestics*, the 13.5, which had been for so long the standard gun for first-class battleships, disappeared in favour of a new type of 12-inch, a Mark VIII. of 35 calibres. The two types compare as follows :—

Bore. Inch.	Length. Cals.	Weight. Tons.	Projectile. lbs.	Maximum Penetration against K.C. (capped projectiles).	
				at 5000 yds. in.	at 3000 yds. in.
13.5	30	67	1250	9	12
12	35	46	850	$11\frac{1}{2}$	$14\frac{1}{2}$

The new gun was, therefore, superior in everything except weight of projectile, and that was not considered much in those days. To-day, of course, it has quite a special meaning.

In the *Majestics*, except in the first two, all-round loading positions for the big guns were introduced in place of the cumbersome old system whereby, after firing, the guns had to return to an end-on position, tilt up, and at a fixed angle take their charges at what was little but an adaption for breechloaders of the loading system evolved twenty years before for the old *Inflexible*.

Details of these ships :—

Displacement—14,900 tons.
Length—(between perpendiculars) 390ft., (over-all) 413ft.
Beam—75ft.

Draught—(mean), 27½ft., (maximum) about 30ft.

Armament—Four 12-inch 35 cal., twelve 6-inch 40 cal., sixteen 12-pounders, twelve 3-pounders. Torpedo tubes (18-inch), four submerged and one above water in stern.

Armour (Harvey)—Belt, (220ft. by 16ft.) 9in. Bulkheads, 14in. Barbettes, 14in. with 10in. turrets. Casemates, 6in.

Horse-power—12,000 = 17.5 knots.

Coal—(normal)1,200 tons; (maximum) 2,200 tons = nominal radius of 7,600 miles at 10 knots and 4,000 at 15 knots.

The ships were built, etc., as follows :—

Name.	Laid down.	Builder.	Engined by
Magnificent...............	Dec. '93	Chatham	Penn
Majestic	Feb. '94	Portsmouth	Vickers
Hannibal.................	April, '94	Pembroke	Harland & Wolff
Victorious	May, '94	Chatham	Hawthorn, Leslie
Mars	June, '94	Laird	Laird
Prince George	Sept. '94	Portsmouth	Humphrys
Jupiter	Oct. '94	Clydebank	Clydebank
Cæsar	March, '95	Portsmouth	Maudslay
Illustrious	March, '95	Chatham	Penn

Mostly they were completed inside two years, the only ones which took appreciably longer being the *Hannibal* and the *Illustrious*. In these and the *Cæsar* an innovation introduced in the others—the placing of the chart house round the base of the foremast with the conning tower well clear ahead—was done away with, and the old system of the bridge over the conning tower reverted to. In the *Cæsar* and *Illustrious*, laid down later than the others, an improvement was effected by the introduction of circular instead of pear-shaped barbettes. The *Majestic, Magnificent,* and *Cæsar* were built in dry dock instead of on slips—the first instance of this since the days of early coast-defence monitors.

The total cost was approximately a million per ship.

On trials most of them exceeded the designed speed, but all were light on trials. They proved very handy ships, with circles of 450 yards at fifteen knots. Coal consumption was always high.

Compared to the *Sovereigns*, the following figures are of interest :—

Name.	Displace- ment (tons).	Weight of Armour (tons).	Weight of Armament & Ammunition (tons).	H.P.	Normal Coal (tons).
Majestics......	14,900	4260	1500	12,000	1200
Sovereigns	14,100	4600	1410	13,000	900

The total dead weight carried in armament, armour, and coal thus works out at practically the same figure, despite the rise of 800 tons in displacement. On these grounds certain attacks were made upon the ships, mainly by those who argued against the unarmoured ends. The criticisms were, however, mainly of the captious order— the ships were certainly the finest specimens of naval architecture of their day.

At a later date electric hoists were fitted to the 6-inch guns, and 400 tons of oil fuel was added to the fuel capacity (the maximum bunker capacity being reduced by 200 tons). The first ship to be so fitted was the *Mars*. Another innovation was shifting the torpedo nets, first in the *Mars*, then in all the others, from the upper deck to the main deck level ; the idea being to keep the nets clear of the 6-inch guns.

The *Majestic* and *Magnificent* served for a long time as flagships in the Channel Fleet. Admiral Sir F. Stephenson and Sir A. K. Wilson flew their flags in the *Majestic*, of which ship Prince Louis of Battenberg was at one time captain.

It was during the early service of the *Majestics* in the Channel Fleet that " invisible " colours for warships first came into consideration, all ships up to that date being painted with black hulls, white upper works, and yellow masts and funnels. For these experiments the *Magnificent* was painted black all over, the *Majestic* and *Hannibal* were given grey and light green upper works respectively. The latter was really the more " invisible " of the two, but both ships were left with black hulls. Ultimately a grey, a little darker than that which the Germans had long used, was adopted as the regulation, though for some time it varied greatly between ship and ship, following the old system under which a good deal of latitude in painting was allowed.*

To this era, 1894-95, belong two groups of protected cruisers, the *Powerfuls* and the *Talbots*. The latter, nine in all, were merely enlarged (5,600 tons) editions of the later cruisers of the Naval Defence Act, and call for no comment. The former group were the *Powerful* and *Terrible*, " replies " to the Russian *Rurik* and *Rossiya*. They displaced nearly as much as the battleships— 14,200 tons—and ran to the then unheard of length of 500ft. between perpendiculars. They carried no belt armour whatever, but were given stout protective decks, no less than 6in. on the slopes amidships. The two big guns (40 calibre, 9.2) were given 6in. Harvey barbettes, the twelve other guns† (6-inch) being in 6-inch casemates. Sixteen 12-pounders were disposed about the upper works. Designed horse-power 25,000 = 22 knots. Total bunker capacity of 3,000 tons, equal to a nominal 7,000 miles at fourteen knots. Both ships were laid down in 1894, the *Powerful* by Vickers and the *Terrible* at Clyde-bank. They were launched in the following year.

In service the *Powerfuls* proved capable of keeping up a speed of twenty knots almost indefinitely. For the rest, they were unhandy ships with large turning circles. At the time of the South African War, both of them were at the Cape, and did service with landed naval brigades. Of these, one from the *Powerful*, with some 4.7's on

* In 1894 the *Thunderer* had her upper works painted in black and white chequers, like the old three-deckers of the Nelson era. Ships with the top of their upper works yellow were also not uncommon.

† About 1902-3 four additional casemates for 6-inch guns were added on top of the four amidship casemates.

special Percy Scott gun-carriages, materially assisted in the defence of Ladysmith.

During the year 1911 the decision was come to that it was not worth while preserving either ship, on account of the large crews required and their comparatively small fighting value under modern conditions.

Two considerable novelties were embodied in these ships. The first of these was the adoption of electrical gear for the big guns. The other and more far-reaching was the adoption of Belleville boilers.

THE BATTLE OF THE BOILERS.

Owing to favourable reports of their use in the French Navy, Belleville boilers were in 1895 experimentally fitted to the *Sharpshooter*, torpedo gunboat; but the decision to adopt them in large ships was taken from French rather than any British experience. Trouble and failure were freely predicted. With the result frequently attending lugubrious predictions, very little trouble has ever been experienced with either ship, and then only in the very early stage when the water-tube boiler was an almost unknown curiosity to the engine-room staff.

The chief advantages claimed for Belleville boilers were the higher working pressures, economy in maintenance and fuel consumption, saving of weight, rapid steam raising, and great facility for repairs.

The Belleville was the first water-tube boiler to come into prominence; other types, however, soon appeared. In the period 1895-98, torpedo gunboats were experimentally fitted as follows :—*Sharpshooter*, Belleville ; *Sheldrake*, Babcock ; *Seagull*, Niclausse ; *Spanker*, Du Temple ; *Salamander*, Mumford ; *Speedy*, Thornycroft—these three last being of the small tube type. Other existing types were the Yarrow, White-Foster, Normand, Reed, Blechynden, all these being of the small tube type also, and regarded as suitable for small craft only.*

* The large tube Yarrow now so general, did not appear till at a later date.

In the matter of big ships, so far as the British Navy was concerned, "water-tube boiler" for some years meant Bellevilles only, whence it came that in the insensate "Battle of the Boilers," which presently broke out, Bellevilles were the main object of attack in Parliament and elsewhere. Actually, of course, the whole principle was in the melting pot. All the elements opposed to change in any form rallied to the attack, led on and influenced in some cases by those whose interests were bound up with the old style cylindrical boilers. It was all over again the old story of the fight for the retention of the paddle against the screw propeller, with an equal disregard for facts.

Unfortunately the party of progress played somewhat into the hands of the reactionaries. In fitting the Belleville type only, they had not much alternative, other types being then in a less forward state. The error made was that in the wholesale adoption of a new type of steam generator, requiring twice the skill and intelligence necessary for the old type, it was practically impossible to train quickly enough a sufficiency of engineers and stokers. Hence troubles soon arose. An even greater error was that the boilers were mostly built in England to the French specifications, without, in many cases, sufficient experienced supervision ; and minor " improvements," such as fusible plugs and restricting regulations, were introduced by more or less amateur Admiralty authorities—which also produced trouble.

For example, French practice had taught that adding lime to the feed water was desirable ; but in many British ships this rule was ignored. Again, one Belleville essential was to throw on coal in very small quantities at a time, in contradistinction to the old cylindrical practice in which shovelling on enormous quantities of coal was the recipe for increased speed. This feature was often disregarded.

The Belleville, ever a complicated and delicate mechanism, if its full efficiency is to be secured, was a worse boiler for the experiments than many of the simpler types of to-day would have been. But no water-tube boiler of any type would have stood any chance of success against the opposition. There were some terrible times in the boiler rooms in those days. One or two ships whose chief engineers had been specially trained in France secured marvellous results, usually by ignoring Admiralty improvements and regulations.* But for one success there were many early failures.

The agitation triumphed to the extent of a Committee of Inquiry being appointed. An interim report of this Committee made a scape-goat of the Belleville, to the extent of recommending that no more should be fitted. But the victory of the retrogrades ended there. A species of compromise with public opinion inflamed against the water-tube system was temporarily adopted, and absurd mixed installations of cylindrical and water-tube boilers were fitted to some ships. Four large tube types were selected as substitutes for Bellevilles, the Niclausse, Dürr (a German variant of the Niclausse), the Babcock and Wilcox, and the Yarrow large tube.

It may approximately be said that every water-tube boiler is a species of compromise between facility for rapid repair on board ship and complication, and the need of great care in using and working. It is usual to put the Belleville at one end of this scale and the Yarrow (large tube) at the other, this last boiler now requiring little, if any, more care than the old type of cylindrical.

In the course of comparatively short experiments, both the Niclausse and the Dürr were found to possess most of the alleged deficiencies of the Belleville without its advantages ; and it was decided to fit all future types of large ships with the Babcock and Yarrow types only. The absurd mixture of cylindrical and water-tube boilers

* Comparatively recently a ship—best left unnamed—made wonderful speed. With a new Engineer Commander she suddenly lost 25 per cent. of her horse-power. The newcomer was rather inexperienced in the type, and closely followed Admiralty regulations. Presently the ship recovered her power—he had given up following the book ! It is only fair to say that the restrictive regulations of the Admiralty were mostly forced upon them by people ashore, who probably had not even a nodding acquaintance with the engine-room of a warship, or warship requirements.

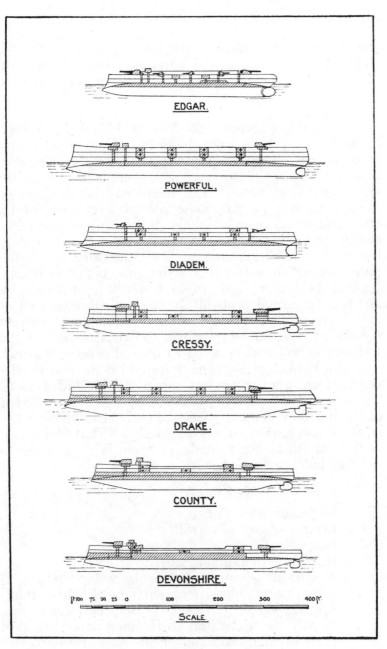

EDGAR.

POWERFUL.

DIADEM.

CRESSY.

DRAKE.

COUNTY.

DEVONSHIRE.

SCALE.

PRINCIPAL CRUISERS OF THE WHITE ERA.

was wisely done away with. Curiously enough, the Belleville boiler, once the agitation had ceased, also ceased to be troublesome. This was no doubt due to the increased experience which had been gained in the interim.

Both the Babcock and Yarrow boilers have been immensely improved since the days when they were first brought out. Something of the same sort is, of course, true of all the standard types, and there is to-day hardly any question as to which of them may be the best or worst. Each type has some special advantage of its own, and in no case, probably, is that advantage sufficiently pronounced to render any one type absolutely the best. When adopted by the Admiralty the Belleville was certainly the best water-tube boiler available. Had it been persisted in and not "improved" by amateurs it would probably have done quite as well as any type adopted to-day. The real issue was mainly not one of type, but of principle. That principle was the water-tube boiler as opposed to the old type cylindrical.

The Estimates for 1896-97 provided for five battleships which were somewhat sarcastically alluded to as "improved" *Majestics*. These ships were the *Canopus* class, and they mark a species of early striving after the ideal of the battle-cruisers of to-day. That is to say, certain sacrifices were made in them with a view to securing increased speed.

Particulars of these ships :—

> Displacement—12,950 tons.
> Length—(over all) 418ft.
> Beam—74ft.
> Draught—(maximum) 26½ft.
> Armament—Four 12in., 35 cal., twelve 6in. 40 cal.,
>   ten 12-pounders, four submerged tubes (18in.)
> Armour—Harvey-Nickel.   Belt amidships 6in.
>   with 2in. extension to the bow and 1½in. skin
>   aft on the waterline.   Bulkheads and barbettes
>   12in.   Turrets 8in.

Horse-power—31,500 = 18.25 knots.
Coal—(normal) 1,000 tons; (maximum) 2,300 tons
= nominal radius of 8,000 miles at 10 knots.

The adoption of Harvey-Nickel armour, which was of superior resisting power to Harvey armour in the ratio of about 5 to 4, partly, but not entirely accounted for the thinning of the armour of this class.   Theoretically, the 9in. armour belt of the *Majestic* was equal to 18in. of iron, while the belt of the *Canopus* class was equal to about 15in. of iron.   In place of the 4in. deck of the *Majestics*, the *Canopus* class had only a 2½in. deck.   The thin bow (2in.) plating was introduced as a sop to a public agitation against soft-ended ships.   Such a belt is, of course, perfectly useless against any heavy projectile, or, for that matter, against 6in., except at very long range indeed.   Sir William White never made any secret of his cynical disbelief in these bow belts.   They are and always have been what doctors call a " placebo."

In the following year the sixth ship of this class was built—the *Vengeance*.   She differed from the others in the form of her turrets, which were flat sided for the first time.   In her also a mounting was first introduced, whereby, in addition to being loaded in any position, big guns could also be loaded at any elevation.

Some other details of the *Canopus* class are :—

Name.	Built by	Engines by	Laid down.	Completed.
Canopus	Portsmouth	Greenock	Jan. '97	1900
Goliath......	Chatham	Penn	Jan. '97	1900
Albion	Thames I.W.	Maudslay	Dec. '96	1902
Ocean.......	Devonport	Hawthorn Leslie	Feb. '97	1900
Glory	Laird	Laird	Dec. '96	1901
Vengeance ..	Vickers	Vickers	Aug. '97	1901

The cruisers of the following year were eight cruisers of the much discussed *Diadem* class, small editions of the *Powerful* (11,000 tons), and carrying a pair of 6-inch guns in place of the 9.2's of the *Powerfuls*.   For the first four (the *Diadem*, *Andromeda*, *Europa*, and *Niobe*) a speed of 20.5 knots only was provided, but in the late four (the *Argonaut, Ariadne, Amphitrite,* and *Spartiate*) the horse-power was increased to 18,000, in order to provide twenty-one knots. At the present time (1912) these ships have for all practical purposes already passed from the effective list, all the weak points of the *Powerfuls* being exaggerated in them.

In the Estimates for the years 1895 to 1898, provision was made also for eleven small third-class cruisers of the " P " class of 2135 tons and twenty knot speed. The armament consisted of eight 4-inch guns. On trials most of them did well, but in a very short time their speeds fell off, and at the present time, such of them as remain on the active list are slower than the far older cruisers of the *Apollo* class.

In the Estimates for 1897-98, in addition to the *Vengeance,* already mentioned, three improved copies of the *Majestic* were provided.   These ships were :—

Name.	Laid down.	Built at.	Engines by.
Formidable	March, '98	Portsmouth	Earle
Irresistible.........	April, '98	Chatham	Maudslay
Implacable	July, '98	Devonport	Laird

The only difference between them and the *Majestics* lies in advantage being taken of improvements in gunnery and armour to increase the offensive and defensive items. The absurd 2-inch bow belt of the *Canopus* was repeated in them, but raised within 2½ft. of the main deck.   A 40-calibre 12-inch was mounted, also a 45-calibre 6-inch.

These were the first ships of the British Navy in which Krupp cemented armour was used.   This armour, generally known as " K.C.," has approximately a resisting power three times that of iron armour.   That is to say, the 9in. belts of the *Formidables* were approximately 33 per cent. more effective than the similar belts of the *Majestics.*   These ships proved faster and more handy, easily exceeding their designed eighteen knots.   Their superior handiness was brought about by a superior form of hull—the deadwood aft being cut away for the first time in them.

In this year's Estimates armoured cruisers definitely re-appeared, six ships of the *Cressy* type being laid down.

Particulars of these :—

> Displacement—12,000 tons.
> Length—454ft.
> Beam—69½ft.
> Draught—(maximum) 28ft.
> Armament—Two 9.2, 40 cal., twelve 6-inch, 45 cal., twelve 12-pounders, two 18in. submerged tubes.
> Armour—6in. Krupp belt amidships, 250ft. long by 11½ft. wide, 2in. continuation to the bow. Barbettes 6in. Casemates 5in.
> Horse-power—21,000 = 21 knots.
> Coal—(normal) 800 tons; (maximum) 1,600 tons.

Name.	Laid down.	Built at.	Engined by.
Sutlej	Aug. '98	Clydebank	Clydebank
Cressy	Oct. '98	Fairfield	Fairfield
Aboukir	Nov. '98	Fairfield	Fairfield
Hogue	July, '98	Vickers	Vickers
Bacchante	Dec. '99	Clydebank	Clydebank
Euryalus	July, '99	Vickers	Vickers

In substance these ships were armoured editions of the *Powerful*. They steamed very well in their time, but have now fallen off considerably and are no longer of much importance. Total weight of armour 2,100 tons. An innovation introduced in these ships was the fitting of non-flammable wood, which at a later date was objected to on the grounds that it deteriorated the gold lace of the uniforms stored in drawers made of it. The *Cressy* was completed in 1901 ; the others, excepting the *Euryalus*, in 1902. This latter ship was greatly delayed from various causes, and not completed until 1903.

The 1898-99 Estimates consisted of three battle-ships and four armoured cruisers. The battleships were practically sisters of the *Formidable*, but differed from her in that the main belt, instead of being a patch amidships, had a total length of 300ft. from the bow.   At the bow it is 2in., quickly increasing to 4in., 5in., 6in., and finally to 9in., and this provided a measure of protection that the 2in. belts of preceding ships could never afford.   The flat-sided turrets, first introduced in the *Vengeance*, were also fitted in these ships, the *Formidables* having the old pattern turrets.

The advantages of flat-sided turrets lie in the fact that K.C. can be used for them instead of the relatively softer non-cemented.   K.C. is not applicable to curved surfaces, for which reason barbettes, casemates, and batteries with curved portholes in them and rounded turrets cannot be constructed of it.   Flat-sided turrets consist of a number of flat plates placed to meet each other at predetermined angles, thus forming one homogeneous whole.

These battleships were :—

Name.	Laid down.	Built at.	Engines by.
London	Dec. '98	Portsmouth	Earle
Bulwark	March, '99	Devonport	Hawthorn
Venerable	Nov. '99	Chatham	Maudslay

All were completed in 1902.

The cruisers of the same year, the *Drake* class, are " improved " *Cressies*, with increased displacement, power and speed.   The increased displacement allowed of four extra 6-inch guns being mounted, these being placed in casemates on top of the amidships casemates.

Particulars of the *Drake* class :—

Displacement—14,000 tons.
Length—(over all) 529½ft.
Beam—71ft.
Draught—(maximum) 28ft.
Armament—Two 9.2, 45 cal. (instead of 40 cal., as in the *Cressies*), sixteen 6-inch, 45 cal., and fourteen 12-pounders, two submerged tubes (18in.).

Armour—2,700 tons, as in *Cressy*, except that the casemates are 6in. thick.

Horse-power—30,000 = 23 knots. Boilers, 43 Belleville.

Coal—(normal) 1,250 tons; (maximum) 2,500.

These ships were altogether superior to the *Cressy* class. On trial they all easily made their contract speeds and subsequently greatly exceeded them. It was discovered that increased speed was to be obtained by additional weight aft, and this was so much brought to a fine art that weights were adjusted accordingly, and in one of them, seeking to make a speed record, the entire crew were once mustered aft in order to vary the trim !

Building details are as follows :—

Name.	Laid down.	Completed	Built at.	Engines by.
Good Hope	Sept. '99	1902	Fairfield	Fairfield
Drake	April, '99	1902	Pembroke	Humphrys & T.
Leviathan	Nov. '99	1903	Clydebank	Clydebank
King Alfred ..	Aug. '99	1903	Vickers	Vickers

For some years these were the fastest ships in the world. In 1905, in a race by the Second Cruiser Squadron across the Atlantic, with ships of nominally equal speed, the *Drake* came in first. In December, 1906, at four-fifths power for thirty hours, she averaged 22.5 knots. In 1907, the *King Alfred* averaged 25.1 knots for one hour, and made an eight hours' mean of 24.8. They proved very economical steamers, being able to do nineteen knots at an expenditure of eleven tons of coal an hour, and though they are now getting old, as warships go, they have never yet been beaten on the results achieved by horse-power per ton of displacement.

The Estimates of 1898-99 included a supplementary programme of four armoured ships which, like the *Canopus* class, again foreshadowed the battle cruisers of to-day. These were the famous *Duncan* class, and may be described as slightly smaller editions of the *London*, with armour thickness sacrificed for superior speed. The belt amidships was reduced from 9in. to 7in., but against this the belt at the extreme bow was made an inch thicker, and 25ft. away from the ram became 5in. thick. The displacement sank by 1,000 tons, the horse-power was increased by 3,000, and the speed by one knot.

The total weight of armour is about 3,500 against 4,300 tons in the *Londons*. The *Duncans* may be regarded as a species of recrudescence of Barnaby ideas, plus a later notion that a well-extended partial protection was better than a more concentrated protection of less area. Generally speaking, they were improved duplicates of the *Canopus* class, in the same way that the *Formidable* and the ships that followed her were duplicates of the *Majestic*. Two ideas were obviously at work. In other forms these two ideas have (with variations) existed to the present day. Then it was purely a question between ratios devoted to speed and protection. To-day (1912) matters have been so far modified that increased displacements are given to secure speed advantages, but protection remains proportionately as it was. Reduced armament has always been accepted.

Construction details of the *Duncans*, of which two more figured in the estimates for 1899-1900 :—

Name.	Laid down	Built at.	Engines by.
Duncan	July, '99	Thames, I.W.	Thames, I.W.
Russell	March, '99	Palmer	Palmer
Cornwallis...........	July, '99	Thames, I.W.	Thames, I.W.
Exmouth	Aug. '99	Laird	Laird
Albemarle	Jan. '00	Chatham	Thames, I.W.
Montagu	Nov. '99	Devonport	Laird

The *Montagu* was wrecked on Lundy Island in 1906.

Contemporaneous with the *Drakes*, and extending over four ships in the Estimates of 1898-99 to two in the following and four in the year later, ten armoured cruisers were provided for, which in essence were little but an attempt to provide a normal second-class protected cruiser of the *Talbot* class, with armour protection. These ships—the *County* class—are of 9,800 tons displacement, and may also be regarded as diminutives of the

Drake and *Cressy* classes, with a touch of the *Diadems* thrown in. In place of the fore and aft 9.2's of the *Drake* and *Cressy*, they were supplied with a couple of pairs of 6-inch guns mounted in turrets fore and aft. The belt amidships was reduced to 4in. (a thickness in K.C. which has no virtues over armour of earlier type) with the usual extension of 2in. to the bow. The twin turrets, in which, like those of the *Powerful*, electrical control was once more introduced, have never given satisfaction, being very cramped for working purposes, and probably no more efficient than single gun turrets would have been, certainly less than the single gun 7-5in. turrets, originally proposed as an alternative, would have been. Had the ships been regarded frankly as modern variants of the second-class protected cruisers, they probably would have been esteemed more than they were. Unfortunately they have always been regarded as " armoured ships " and discounted on account of their obvious inferiority to the *Drakes*. In the matter of steaming all of them have invariably done well (except in the case of the *Essex*, over which a mistake in design was made). The anticipated twenty-three knots was made quite easily, once certain early propeller difficulties were overcome. The Boiler Commission, already referred to, affected these ships, in so far that, instead of the hitherto inevitable Bellevilles, the *Berwick* and *Suffolk* were given Niclausse boilers and the *Cornwall* Babcocks. The total weight of armour is 1,800 tons.

Details of the construction of this class are :—

Name.	Laid down.	Built at.	Engines by.
Essex	Jan. '00	Pembroke	Clydebank
Kent	Feb. '00	Portsmouth	Hawthorn
Bedford	Feb. '00	Fairfield	Fairfield
Monmouth	Aug. '99	L. & Glasgow	L. & Glasgow
Lancaster	Mar. '01	Elswick	Hawthorn L.
Berwick	April,'01	Beardmore	Humphrys
Donegal	Feb. '01	Fairfield	Fairfield
Cornwall	Mar. '01	Pembroke	Hawthorn
Cumberland	Feb. '01	L. & Glasgow	L. & Glasgow
Suffolk	Mar. '02	Portsmouth	Humphrys & T.

All were completed during 1903 and 1904.

T

For the year 1900-01 only two battleships were provided: the *Queen*, built at Devonport and engined by Harland and Wolff, and the *Prince of Wales*, built at Chatham and engined by the Greenock Foundry Co. These were laid down in 1901 and completed in 1904. They were copies of the *Londons* in every detail, saving that, instead of being enclosed, their upper deck batteries were left open as in the *Duncans*. The *Queen* was given Babcock boilers instead of Bellevilles.

The 1901-02 Estimates provided three battleships and six armoured cruisers of the *County* class. These were the last ships designed by Sir William White. The battleships, of which eight were built altogether—three for 1901-02, two for the next year—were of a different type from any which had preceded them, and to some extent may be said to mark the birth of the *Dreadnought* era. That is to say, in them the old idea of the two calibres, 12in. and 6in., died out, and heavier auxiliary guns began to appear.

Particulars of these ships, the *King Edward VII.* class, are as follows :—

Displacement—16,350 tons.
Length—(over-all) 453¾ft.
Beam—78ft.
Draught—(maximum) 26¾ft.
Armament—Four 12-inch, 40 cal., four 9.2, 45 cal., ten 6-inch, 45 cal., twelve 12-pounders, fourteen 3-pounders, five 18-inch submerged tubes (of which one is in the stern).
Armour—As in the *London* (but a 6in. battery instead of casemates).
Horse-power—18,000 = 18.9 knots.
Coal—(normal) 950 tons; (maximum) 2,150 tons, also 400 tons of oil, except in the *New Zealand*.

Name.	Laid down.	Built at.	Engines by.
Commonwealth	June, '01	Fairfield	Fairfield
King Edward	Mar. '02	Devonport	Harland & W.
Dominion	May, '02	Vickers	Vickers
Hindustan..............	Oct. '02	Clydebank	Clydebank
New Zealand (now Zelandia)	Feb. '03	Portsmouth	Humphrys & T.
Africa	Jan. '04	Chatham	Clydebank
Britannia	Feb. '04	Portsmouth	Humphrys & T.
Hibernia	Jan. '04	Devonport	Harland & W.

Except the last three, all were completed in 1905. The others were completed very shortly afterwards.

The boilers fitted to these ships varied considerably. The *King Edward, Hindustan,* and *Britannia* were given a mixed installation of Babcocks and cylindricals; the *New Zealand* Niclausse boilers; the other ships Babcock only. In the *Britannia,* super-heaters were also fitted to six of her boilers. The point differentiating these ships from their predecessors was the mounting of four 9.2 guns in single turrets at the angles of the superstructure. Equally novel was the placing of 6-inch guns in a battery behind the armour on the main deck.* Fighting tops, a feature of all previous ships, disappeared, and in place of them fire-control platforms were substituted.

When produced, these ships were considered as something like the " last word " ; but in service later on it was very soon found that the two calibres of big guns rendered fire-control extremely difficult, and they have been a somewhat costly lesson in that respect. They cost about £1,500,000 each, and were found to be all that could be desired tactically, their turning circles with engines being only about 340yds. at fifteen knots. All of them did not make their speeds on trials, and some have never quite come up to expectations in that respect, but they have all proved remarkably reliable steamers.

Six armoured cruisers provided for in the 1901-02 Estimates were the *Devonshires.* These were originally intended to have been enlarged *Counties,* carrying a single

---

* This idea was borrowed from the Continent. Germany had long adopted batteries, and nearly every other nation had followed suit.

7.5 fore and aft, in place of the twin 6-inch turrets of the prototype ships. The design was, however, modified to the extent of substituting a single 7.5 for each of the forward pairs of 6-inch casemates.

Details of these ships are :—

> Displacement—10,850 tons.
> Length (between perpendiculars)—450ft.
> Beam—68½ft.
> Draught—(maximum) 25½ft.
> Armament—Four 7.5, six 6-inch, 45 cal.; two 12-pounders, twenty-two 3-pounders, two 18in. torpedo tubes submerged.
> Armour—Belt, (length 325ft. from the bow, width 10½ft.), 6in. amidships, thinning to 2in. right forward. Barbettes 6in. Turrets 5in. Casemates 6in.
> Horse-power—21,000 = 22.5 knots.
> Coal—(normal) 800 ; (maximum) 1,800 tons.

Other details are :—

Name.	Laid down.	Built at.	Engined by.
Devonshire	Mar. '02	Chatham	Thames I.W.
Antrim	Aug. '02	Clydebank	Clydebank
Argyll	Sept. '02	Greenock Foundry	Greenock F.C.
Carnarvon	Oct. '02	Beardmore	Beardmore
Hampshire	Sept. '02	Elswick	Elswick
Roxburgh...........	June, '02	L. & Glasgow	L. & Glasgow

Like the *King Edwards*, various boilers were given to them. All of them have one-fifth cylindrical boilers. The *Devonshire* and *Carnarvon* were otherwise given Niclausse ; *Antrim* and *Hampshire*, Yarrow ; *Argyll*, Babcock ; and *Roxburgh*, Dürr. The designed speed was exceeded by all on trials, but none have proved successful steamers ever since. They were completed between 1904 and 1905.

These were the last ships to be designed by Sir William White. He resigned his position from ill-health ; but, like his predecessors, left under a cloud—at any rate, with his services not really appreciated. He had created a magnificent fleet ; but its very magnificence made many of his designs look poor on paper against any foreign construction of less displacement, but—*on paper* —of equal or superior qualities. It is the fate of the naval architect in peace-time to be judged on paper with small regard to issues such as nautical qualities, constructional strength, and a score of other details which are not to be expressed by any statistical formulæ, but yet make all the difference between efficiency and the absence of it.

Sir William White's period of office was marked by an almost complete naval revolution. It began with the quick-firer and the disappearance of the low freeboard battleships. It ended with the coming of submarines, fire-control, and wireless. In between, it included the coming of the destroyer, the re-birth of the armoured cruiser ; the arrival of the water-tube boiler, new forms of hull, unprecedented advances in both guns and armour—in fact, almost every conceivable change. Through these troubled waters with a steady hand and cool brain Sir William White guided the destiny of the Fleet and the millions and millions of pounds expended in shipbuilding. Naval construction never stands still. Already his era is " the pre-*Dreadnought* " one, and to present-day ideas the term " pre-*Dreadnought* " is already very nearly akin to " pre-historic." His creations preserved the peace, for which very reason they failed to secure glory. Already some have gone to the scrap-heap, and others are well on their way thither to join the Reed and Barnaby ships in that oblivion to which modern *Dreadnoughts* will just as surely go in their season. More might be said : but *cui bono*? Such public epitaph as Sir William White received when he retired was of the " about time, too ! " order. The creator of the finest fleet that the world has ever seen left office with less honour and no more public interest than did half-a-dozen mediocre admirals who had chanced to fly their flags in some of his creations. It is not given for the stage manager to stand in the lime-light reserved for the principal actors. But the historian of a hundred years hence, placing great Englishmen in perspective, will assuredly place Sir William White far ahead of many who loom greater in the public eye to-day.

GUNS IN THE ERA.

The guns which especially belong to the White era are as follows:—

Designation.	Weight. Tons.	Projectile. lbs.	Velocity. f.s.	Maximum Penetration with capped shot against K.C. at	
				5000 yds.	3000 yds.
13.5, 30 cal.	67	1250	2016	9	12
12in., 35 cal.	46	850	2367	$11\frac{1}{2}$	$14\frac{1}{2}$
12in., 40 cal.	50	850	2750	16	20
10in., 32 cal.	29	500	2040	$5\frac{1}{2}$	$7\frac{1}{2}$
9.2, 30 cal.	24	380	2065	4	6
9.2, 40 cal.	25	380	2347	$6\frac{3}{4}$	$9\frac{1}{4}$
9.2, 45 cal.	27	380	2640	$8\frac{3}{4}$	$11\frac{1}{4}$
7.5, 45 cal.	14	200	2600	$5\frac{3}{4}$	$7\frac{1}{2}$
6in., 40 cal.	$7\frac{1}{2}$	100	2200	—	—
6in., 45 cal.	7	100	2535	—	$4\frac{1}{2}$

PURCHASED SHIPS.

In the year 1902 two ships, the *Constitucion* and *Libertad,* were laid down at Elswick and Vickers-Maxim's respectively for the Chilian Government. They were designed by Sir Edward Reed, and compare interestingly with the *King Edwards* in being much longer and narrower. It will be remembered that in the past Reed ideals had always centred round a " short handy ship." They had also always embodied the maximum of protection, while these ships carried medium armour only. His ships had, further, always been characterised by extremely strong construction, while these verged on the flimsy, the scantlings being far lighter than in British naval practice.

Out of all which it has been held that they represented the Reed ideal of armoured cruisers interlaced with whatever limitations the Chilian authorities may have specified.

Particulars of these ships, which in 1903 were purchased for the British Navy and renamed *Swiftsure* (ex *Constitucion*) and *Triumph* (ex *Libertad*) :—

Displacement—11,800. Complement, 700.
Length—(over all) 470ft.
Beam—71ft.
Draught—(Maximum) 24ft. 8in.
Armament—Four 10-inch, 45 cal. ; fourteen 7.5-inch, 50 cal. ; fourteen 14-pounders, four 6-pounders, four Maxims ; two 18-inch submerged tubes.
Armour—Practically complete belt 8ft. wide, 7-inch thick amidships, reduced to 3-inch at ends. 10-inch bulkheads at ends of thick portion of belt. Redoubt above, (250ft. long), 7-inch on sides, 6-inch bulkheads to it. Deck 1½-inch on slopes amidships, 3-inch on slopes at ends. Barbettes 10-inch, with 8 to 6-inch turrets. Battery and upper deck casemates, 7-inch.
Horse Power—14,000 = 20 knots. Yarrow boilers.
Coal—(Normal) 800 tons. (Maximum) 2,000 tons.

These ships compare interestingly with the *King Edwards* and *Devonshires*, between which they struck a mean, as follows :—

	King Edward.	Swiftsure.	Devonshire.
Displacement	16,350	11,800	10,850
Principal Guns ..	4—12in.	4—10in.	4—7.5
	4—9.2	14—7.5	6—6in.
	16—6in.		
	5—18in. tubes	2—18in. tubes	2—18in. tubes
Armour belt	9—2in.	7—3in.	6—2in.
Speed	18.9 knots	20 knots	22.25 knots
Coal (Normal) ...	950	800	800
Coal (Maximum) .	2,150 — 400 (oil	2,000	1,800

Other items of interest are that the armament of the *Swiftsures* (10-inch and 7.5's) had somewhere about that time been laid down by Admiral Fisher as the ideal armament of the future, on the principle that the best possible was " the smallest effective big gun, and the largest possible secondary gun."

In service these ships never proved brilliantly successful. They rarely managed to make their speeds successfully, and there was a great deal of vibration with them. They were shored up internally in places with a view to strengthening them. On the other hand, it should be mentioned that some of these alleged defects have been put down to conservatism in nautical ideas, and that the shoring up was not really required. Their great drawback was that so far as the British Navy was concerned they were neither one thing nor the other, being too light in heavy guns to be satisfactory with the battleships, and too slow to act with the cruisers. Had there been six or so of them they would, possibly enough, have formed an ideal squadron. Being two ships only, they of necessity became round pegs in square holes.

NAVAL ESTIMATES IN THE ERA.

Financial Year.	Amount.	Personnel.	Ships.		
			Battleships	Armoured Cruisers.	Protected Cruisers.
1887-88	12,476,800	62,500	—	—	3
1888-89*	13,082,800	62,500	—	—	2
1889-90	13,685,400	62,400	—	—	—
1890-91	13,786,600	65,400	8	—	42
1891-92	14,557,856	68,800	2	—	—
1892-93	14,240,200	67,700	1	—	—
1893-94	14,340,000	70,500	6	—	2
1894-95	17,365,900	83,000	3	—	9
1895-96	18,701,000	88,850	—	—	8
1896-97	21,823,000	93,750	6	—	3
1897-98	21,838,000	100,050	7	6	—
1898-99	23,780,000	106,390	3	4	—
1899-'00	26,594,000	110,640	2	2	1
1900-01	28,791,900	114,880	2	6	1
1901-02	30,875,500	118,625	3	6	—
1902-03	31,255,500	122,500	2	2	—

* Also under Naval Defence Act an additional sum of £10,000,000, spread over seven years.

In the following year 1903-04 three ships (the last of the *King Edwards*) were provided for. The total number of battleships designed for the British Navy by Sir William White was therefore 48. There were in addition 26 armoured cruisers—making a total of 74 armoured ships, and about as many protected cruisers, including some for Colonial service.

XIV.

THE WATTS ERA.

SIR William White was succeeded by Mr., afterwards Sir Philip Watts, who came to the Admiralty from Elswick, where he had been Chief Constructor. He came with the reputation of " putting in plenty of guns," and his appointment was favourably received, both inside the Navy and outside.

The armoured cruisers *Duke of Edinburgh* and *Black Prince* were the first ships for which he was personally responsible.

Details of these :—

> Displacement—13,550 tons.
> Length (between perpendiculars)—480ft.
> Beam—73½ft.
> Draught—(maximum) 27½ft.
> Armament—Six 9.2, 45 cal., ten 6-inch, 50 cal., twenty-two 3-pounders. Torpedo tubes :— Three submerged (18in.).
> Horse-power—23,500 = 22.3 knots.
> Coal—(normal) 1,000 tons, (maximum) 2,000, also 400 tons of oil.

The former ship was laid down at Pembroke and engined by Hawthorn; the latter was built and engined by the Thames Iron Works. In the matter of armament and its arrangement the ships were to some extent cruiser versions of the *King Edward* ; but equally, in the adoption of a number of single gun-houses for big guns, and the jump from two to a larger number of big guns, the

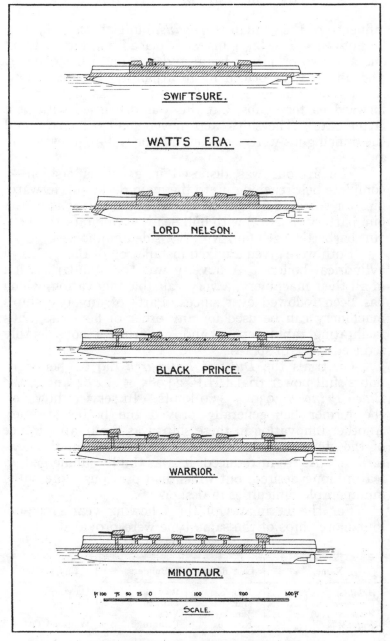

SWIFTSURE.

— WATTS ERA. —

LORD NELSON.

BLACK PRINCE.

WARRIOR.

MINOTAUR.

SCALE.

PRE-DREADNOUGHTS OF THE WATTS ERA.

influence of the Chilian *O'Higgins*, built at Elswick, may be noticed. The big guns were placed one forward and one aft, two on either beam and two on either quarter. The 6-inch were placed in an armoured battery below. As originally designed, right ahead fire was given to the forward battery guns, but this was dispensed with at a latter date. The ships were never good sea boats, and the 6-inch guns were soon found to be well-nigh useless in any sea.

The armour was disposed in generous fashion—a complete belt reaching up to the main deck, 4in. forward, 6in. for some 260ft. amidships, and 3in. aft of that. A 6in. battery (K.N.C.) with bulkheads surmounts the belt. 7in. barbettes with 6in. K.C. flat-sided gunhouses.

Both were given a mixed installation of Babcock and cylindrical boilers. A novelty was the standardisation of all their machinery, a very valuable innovation, which has been followed ever since. Parts of any one ship's machinery can be used for any other of her class, thus facilitating rapid repairs and requiring a considerably reduced stock of spares.

On trials the *Duke of Edinburgh* did on her eight hours' full power trial I.H.P. 23,685 = 22.84 knots, the *Black Prince* 23,939 = 23.6 knots. In service, however, the former has generally proved the better steamer. Another innovation in these ships was the re-appearance of the stern torpedo tube, first introduced in the *Centurions*. As re-introduced it was built submerged, a feature long desired, but which had previously presented innumerable difficulties in design.

For the Estimates of the following year (1903-04) four more ships of the same type were provided—

Name.	Laid down.	Builders.	Engines by
Achilles	Feb. '04	Elswick	Hawthorn
Cochrane	Mar. '04	Fairfield	Fairfield
Warrior	Jan. '04	Vickers	Vickers
Natal	Nov. '03	Pembroke	Wallsend Co.

In these the defect of the low 6-in. battery of the *Black Princes* was anticipated, and instead of ten 6-inch guns, four 7.5 were mounted in gun-houses on the upper deck amidships.   Yarrow and cylindrical boilers mixed were installed.   Otherwise no change was made.   On trial the *Achilles* reached a maximum of 23.27, the other three ships all made their contracts or over.

These four, generally known as the *Warriors*, proved to be the finest cruisers as sea-boats ever built for the British Navy.   They have always proved most remarkably steady gun platforms.   Shooting from them is invariably good—they have always been near the top of the list in gunnery returns.   For a single ship in a single commission good shooting is attributable to causes other than the ship ; but with four ships and different crews at different times the effect of the design is obvious.   Apparently the extra weight on their upper decks is responsible ; for their dimensions are identical with those of the unsatisfactory *Black Princes*.

In all these ships, as in the *Devonshires* which preceded them, raking masts and stumpy funnels were introduced.   The latter proved most inconvenient for navigating purposes, and in 1911 all the *Warriors* had their funnels considerably heightened.

In these four latter the " dove-cot " platform fire-controls first appeared; they were fitted also to the three latest ships of the *King Edward* class.

The main defect of all six is the trivial anti-torpedo armament.   The 3-pounders are perfectly useless against destroyers.   Incidentally it may be noticed that the class signalled the scientific placing of such guns for control purposes.   In the *Warriors* some guns were mounted on turret tops also, this being with a view to their survival after an action.   It was contended that an actual hit was extremely improbable on any anti-t.b. guns, but that shells bursting underneath might easily disarm them. Hence the search for an armoured base.   This idea seems to have originated in the German Navy, though the Germans never adopted the turret-top position.

The Estimates (1904-05) provided for two battleships and three armoured cruisers.   The latter of these,
the *Minotaur* class, were "improved *Warriors*" ; but,
as a matter of fact, except for a larger armament, they
proved somewhat inferior to their immediate predecessors :—

Details are :—

    Displacement—14,600 tons (as against 13,550).
    Length (between perpendiculars)—490ft., (over
      all) 525ft.
    Beam—74½ft. (but a foot more in *Shannon*).
    Draught—(maximum) 28ft. (but a foot less in
      Shannon).
    Armament—Four 9.2, 50 cal., ten 7.5, fourteen
      12-pounders, five 18in. tubes (submerged).
    Horse-power—27,000 = 23 knots.
    Coal—(normal) 1,000 tons (950 only in *Shannon*) :
      (maximum) 2,000, also 400 tons oil.

The 9.2 were placed in double turrets fore and aft.
For those of the *Minotaur* electric manœuvring was substituted for the usual hydraulic.   The 7.5's are disposed
in ten single gun houses on the upper deck, *Warrior*
fashion.   The armour belt is of the same maximum
thickness, but only 3in. for 50ft. from the bow.   Thereafter
it thickens gradually for the next 75ft., then reaches its
maximum.   Vertical armour above the main deck was
given up in order to allow for the increased weight of
armament and its protection—a total of 2,073 tons.
The *Minotaur* has Babcock, the other two Yarrow large-
tube boilers.   No cylindricals were fitted ; the opponents
of the water-tube system having lost their influence by
1905, when the ships were laid down.

None of them steamed up to expectations on trial,
although they developed considerably more than the
contract horse-power.   The *Minotaur* just made her
speed, the *Defence* just failed to reach it, the *Shannon*
failed by half-a-knot.   This last ship had been varied
from the others with an idea that a new form of hull would

produce better speed—an unfortunate surmise. Shortly after completion all had 15ft. added to their funnels. The increased draught added to their power somewhat, but did not materially better their speeds.

Further details of these three ships are :—

Name.	Laid down.	Built at.	Engined by.
Minotaur	Jan. '05	Devonport	Harland & Wolff
Defence	Feb. '05	Pembroke	Scott S. & E. Co.
Shannon	Jan. '05	Chatham	Humphrys

All were completed in 1908. Average cost, £1,400,000 per ship. In them solid bulkheads first appear, their engine-rooms having no water-tight doors.

The battleships of the same programme (1904-05) were the *Lord Nelson* and *Agamemnon*.

Details are :—

> Displacement—16,500 tons.
> Length (between perpendiculars)—410ft., (over all) 445ft.
> Beam—79½ft.
> Draught—(mean) 27ft.
> Armament—Four 12-inch, 45 cal., ten 9.2, 50 cal.,fifteen 12-pounders, sixteen 3-pounders, five submerged tubes (18in.).
> Horse-power—16,750 = 18.5 knots.
> Coal—(normal) 900 tons, (maximum) 2,000 tons ; also 400 tons oil.

The *Lord Nelson* was built and engined by Palmer, the *Agamemnon* by Beardmore and engined by Hawthorn. The former was given Babcock, the latter Yarrow boilers. Both on trial easily exceeded the contract speed, and proved abnormally handy ships. They cost £1,500,000, or only a little more than the *Minotaurs*.

The *Nelsons* are often counted as "Dreadnoughts"; but their only claim to the position is they do not happen to carry any 6-inch guns. Actually they are nothing but improved *King Edwards*, bearing to those ships very much the same relation as the *Warriors* to the *Black Princes*. Their comparatively slow speeds and their mixed armaments entirely differentiate them from the swifter "all-big-gun" ship which followed, and, for that matter, caught them up.*

The *Nelsons* were never really successful ships outside the points alluded to above. Eight of their ten 9.2's were placed in twin turrets, and in many circumstances two 9.2 so mounted proved very little superior in efficiency to a similar single gun in an isolated gun-house.†

In the matter of protection the *Nelsons* far exceeded the *King Edwards*. In place of a 9in. belt amidships they were given a 12in. one, while the 8in. and 6in. strakes above of the earlier ships became a uniform 8in. The bow belt forward was also augmented to 6in. on the water-line, surmounted by 4in., instead of a belt uniformly increasing from 2in. to 6in. further aft. But none of this made them "Dreadnoughts," and the absence of "Dreadnought" features relegated them to the second line very soon after they were completed.

In these ships the tripod mast, the idea of which dates back to the *Captain* era, re-appeared. The *Nelsons* were given as mainmasts the first of those modern tripods which have characterised every British capital ship since built till the *Lion* as altered.

The idea of the tripod mast is that if one leg chance to be shot away, the other two will keep the mast up. Whether battle will bear this out is another matter. Generally speaking ideas abandoned by our forefathers have failed to live long if resuscitated.

In the 1902-03 and 1903-04 Estimates provision was made for four vessels each year of a new type, known

---

* The *Nelsons* were delayed in completion, as the 12-inch guns made for them were appropriated for the *Dreadnought*, in order to ensure rapid completion of that ship.

† To some extent this is probably true of slower firing of larger guns. The only warships with single 12-inch—the Italian *Victor Emanuele* class—have generally achieved almost as many hits at target practice as the *Brins*, with two pairs of 12-inch. Improved mountings have since appeared, but certain advantages still seem inevitable to the single gun. Its disadvantage lies, of course, in much extra weight, and to-day in the space question also.

BLAKE AND TROMP. PERIOD OF THE DUTCH WARS.

BATTLESHIPS OF THE WHITE ERA AT SEA.

THE "FOUDROYANT"—ONE OF NELSON'S OLD SHIPS.

BATTLE OF TRAFALGAR. 1805.

THE END OF AN OLD WARSHIP.

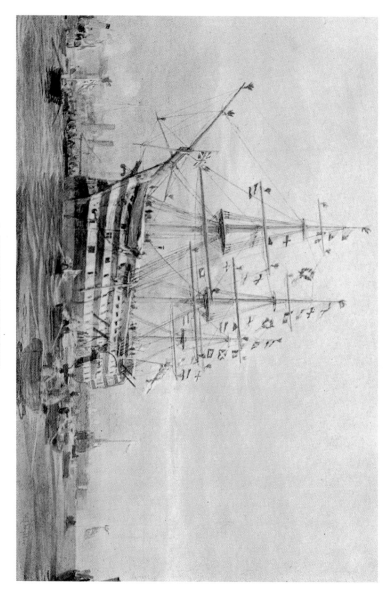

A TRAFALGAR ANNIVERSARY.

THE OLD "INVINCIBLE." 1872.

BOARDING A SLAVE DHOW.

SECOND CLASS CRUISER OF THE NAVAL DEFENCE ACT ERA, NOW CONVERTED INTO A MINE-LAYER.

WHITE ERA BATTLESHIPS OF THE MAJESTIC CLASS.

EARLY TYPE OF "27 KNOT" DESTROYERS.

DREADNOUGHTS ANCHORING—1912.

"INDEFATIGABLE" AND "INVINCIBLE."—1911.

EARLY "30 KNOT" DESTROYERS.

SUBMARINES LEAVING PORTSMOUTH HARBOUR.

HMS New Zealand ready
for launching
W L Wyllie

BATTLE CRUISER "NEW ZEALAND" ON THE STOCKS—1912.

as "Scouts." These were the *Adventure* and *Attentive* (Elswick), *Forward* and *Foresight* (Fairfield), *Pathfinder* and *Patrol* (Laird), *Sentinel* and *Skirmisher* (Vickers-Maxim). One was awarded each year to each of the firms mentioned, but all were actually laid down between June, 1903, and January, 1904. The first four to be given out to contract were originally named *Eddystone, Nore, Fastnet,* and *Inchkeith.*

These vessels came to be built owing to an appreciation of the fact that destroyers had altogether lost their original rôle and had become torpedo-boats, pure and simple. The "Scouts," though from three to four times the size, were the old "catchers" re-introduced. They compared with these as follows :—

	Average Displacement.	Average Designed Speed.	Armament.
"Scouts" .	2850	25	12 to 14—12 pdr., 2—14in. tubes
Halcyons ..	1070	18.5	2—4.7, 4—6pdr., 5—18in. tubes

A $1\frac{1}{2}$ deck on slopes amidships was provided for the "Scouts," which incidentally were designed for ten 12-pounders only. By the year 1912 it became abundantly clear that, like their predecessors the "catchers," they were doomed to pass quickly into the "little use" category on account of their weak armaments and small sea-keeping capacity.

TORPEDO CRAFT.

It has already been mentioned that Sir William White's period of office saw the coming of the destroyer. The origin of this craft is to be found in a public agitation, which arose out of the tremendous attention paid to torpedo boats by the French, who were then our most likely enemy, and who had an overwhelming superiority in torpedo craft.

Some years before a type of craft, the torpedo gunboats already referred to, which were first known as

U

" torpedo boat catchers " and subsequently as " catchers " had been introduced. It soon, however, became very clear that they were little likely to achieve this end, and the doctrine that " the torpedo boat is the answer to the torpedo boat " was being steadily preached. At that time (1892) the then insignificent navy of Germany was in possession of eight very large torpedo boats, which were known as " division boats." Austria also had one or two fast craft, capable of dealing with torpedo boats. Upon these existing lines a new type of craft was developed for the British Navy. The first two to be built were the *Havock* and *Hornet*, which were launched in 1893. In substance they were very large torpedo boats of about 250 tons displacement, designed by Messrs. Yarrow. Their speed of 27 knots was well in excess of that of any existing torpedo boat, and it was confidently expected that they would easily run down and destroy any such. In addition to what was then the very considerable armament of one 12-pounder and three 6-pounders, they were also fitted with torpedo tubes.* The original idea of this was that when hostile torpedo boats had been annihilated by them, the destroyers could be used as torpedo boats in case of need.

In 1894 the *Havock* and *Hornet* were used in manœuvres and tested by being made to lie by for twenty-four hours in the Bay of Biscay. They underwent the test very well, and to this is probably attributed a realisation of the fact that in them a more or less really effective sea-going torpedo boat had been evolved. A large number of duplicates were ordered ; at first of 27 knots. Later this was increased to 30, and in a few boats to a little more.

The whole of these boats were nothing but enlarged editions of existing torpedo boats, and some of them proved rather weak for the service demanded of them. In the year 1902 and onwards, therefore, a type of better sea-going qualities was demanded, and the River class,

---

* They had a bow tube besides broadside tubes. This bow tube was soon done away with and a couple of 6-pounders substituted.

which totalled about 35 boats, began to be built. A feature of the River class was that they were a blend of the early torpedo gunboats of the Rattlesnake type, with the later and heavier torpedo gunboats. There was a reduction of speed to $25\frac{1}{2}$ knots, with a view to securing better sea-going qualities. On account of their slow speed the River class are verging on the obsolete to-day, but the high forecastle first embodied in them has never been departed from, and the very latest types of destroyers are nothing but swifter and larger editions of them.

It is interesting to note that here again to some extent the Germans led the way. German destroyers had the North Sea to consider, whereas all early British destroyers were built with a view to being used only in the Channel. Consequently and naturally enough the Germans were the first to perceive the necessity for a high forecastle.

The submarine also appeared in the pre-Dreadnought era, but the boats of that time were of such a primitive type that they need hardly be specially mentioned. They will be found alluded to in a later chapter.

END OF THE PRE-DREADNOUGHT ERA.

So ended the pre-Dreadnought era. It was characterised by a multiplicity of types which had included :—

First class battleships.
Second class   ,,
Fast intermediate ,,
First rate armoured cruisers.
Second rate   ,,   ,,
First class protected cruisers.
Second class   ,,   ,,
Third class   ,,   ,,
Scouts.
Torpedo gunboats.
Sloops.
Gunboats.
Destroyers.
Torpedo boats.
Submarines.

Although the whole of these types were not all building or provided for at any one and the same time, yet towards the end of the period there was a general feeling that too many types of ships were in use. Reductions in this direction were announced, at first indicating that in future programmes provision would be made only for :—

" Armoured ships."
Destroyers.
Submarines.

Contemporaneously with this came Admiral Fisher's famous " scrap-heap policy," whereby some eighty vessels of one kind and another were struck off the effective list, and either sold or relegated to subsidiary service.

The ships removed included all battleships and armoured cruisers of earlier date than the *Trafalgar*, several ships of the *Apollo* class, all earlier protected cruisers, some of the " P " class, and the bulk of the small fry in the way of sloops and gunboats.

This action aroused a certain amount of criticism on the grounds that the clearance was excessive. As some of the ships were subsequently restored to the active list, something is undoubtedly to be said for that point of view ; especially as no steps were taken to replace the scrapped cruisers. On the other hand, most of the ships removed were of trivial fighting value ; though here again the zeal of the reformer somewhat overlooked the fact that the police duties rendered by the small fry had been valuable.

In connection with this policy some of the outlying naval bases were done away with, and there commenced a " reorganisation " of the Fleet which has continued intermittently from that day to this ! Certain other considerable changes affecting the *personnel* will be found dealt with in a later chapter.

XV.

THE DREADNOUGHT ERA.—(WATTS).

A NEW era in battleship design, not only for the British Navy, but for the navies of the entire world, was opened with the advent of the *Dreadnought*. As has been seen, it was in a way led up to by previous designs, notably the *Lord Nelson* class. The essential point of difference, however, lies in the fact that whereas the *Lord Nelson* carries heavy guns of two calibres, in the *Dreadnought* the main armament is confined to one calibre only. The advantages of this on paper are not particularly great, but for practical purposes, such as fire control and so forth, the superiority to be obtained by a uniformity of big gun armament is tremendous.

As the historical portion of this book indicates, the " Dreadnought idea " has been a fairly regular feature of British Naval Policy, but in this particular case the inception would seem to have been due to accident and circumstance rather than to any settled policy.

Immature and abortive attempts to realise something of "the Dreadnought ideal" had taken place in the past. The earliest ship claimed to represent the Dreadnought ideal is the U.S. *Roanoake*, built at the time of the Civil War. This was a high freeboard ship, fitted with three turrets in the centre line. A few years later something of the same sort found expression in the four-turreted British *Royal Sovereign* and *Prince Albert*, though these were merely coast defence ships. Still later in the *Tchesma* class, Russian, and in the *Brandenburg* class of the German Navy, six big guns were installed as the primary armament. Both these two ideas were laughed out of existence; and it became a settled fashion to carry four big guns, two forward and two aft.

Matters were at this stage when Colonel Cuniberti, as he then was, Constructor to the Italian Navy, conceived the idea of a ship carrying a considerable number of big guns, and embodying in herself the power of two or three normal battleships. This design was considered altogether too ambitious for the Italian Navy; but permission was given him to publish the general idea, subject to official revision. It first saw the light in "*Fighting Ships*," in 1903, and is now so historically interesting that I here reproduce the article in full, the original being long since out of print :—

"Admiral Sir John Hopkins, late Controller of the British Navy, in his admirable article, 'Intermediates for the British Fleet,' published in the last edition (1902) of this Annual, asks what results it would be possible to obtain in the British Navy by extending the ideas of the two Italian Ministers of Marine, Admiral Morin and Admiral Bettolo, which were translated into fact in the *Vittorio Emanuele III* (12,625 tons), so as to arrive at the much greater tonnage of recent British battleships, in the same manner as the ideas that found concrete form in the projected vessels of the *Amalfi* class were amplified and realised in the Italian battleships alluded to and regarding which, even now, so many doubts are expressed as to such realisation being practicable.

"To proceed from 8,000 to 12,000, and from 12,000 to 17,000 tons of displacement, constitutes not only a problem of naval architecture, but also involved high considerations of quite another nature, such as the special functions of the Fleet, so as to harmonise with the political objects of any given maritime Power, the geographical position of that Power, the state of its finances, etc., etc. So that not only does the answer to such a question entail a certain amount of difficulty from the constructive point of view, but before the answer can be seriously considered it is absolutely necessary to determine exactly what end this ideal British battleship is to serve; for it is not to be imagined that we are going merely to enlarge the *Vittorio Emanuele* until we arrive at a displacement equal to that of the *King Edward VII* For example, putting an extra 4,000 tons on board will produce a vessel that will perhaps be a little steadier in heavy weather than the original ship.

* * * * *

"In Britain are to be found naval experts of the highest possible order, and they will have their own ideas as to what type of vessels best fulfil the needs and ideals of the British Fleet, so that it would almost appear a presumption on my part to offer suggestions for any Navy other than the Italian. But in deference to the courteous interrogation of Admiral Hopkins I may be permitted to point out that from the purely human point of view there are two leading methods by which one can strike to the ground one's opponent, either by gradually developing the attack and disposing of him little by little, or, on the other hand, killing him at one blow without causing him prolonged suffering. In like manner there are two distinct modes of sending an enemy's ship to the bottom.

"Let us take, for example, a human combat. The first —the most commonly used, and the most practical in the majority of cases—has as its basis the progressive dismemberment of the enemy.

"Two mortal foes place themselves on guard at a distance; they begin with exceptional strokes, with feints, with opportune advances and retreats, never coming to close quarters for a deadly blow until the capabilities of the enemy, both offensive and defensive, are well tested, and until some fortunate stroke, even although not actually deadly, has considerably weakened the foe, has rendered his defence less able, and has somewhat demoralised him. Covered with blood, stunned, mutilated, and hardly capable of remaining on his feet, then comes the moment when his adversary closes in upon him and delivers the final and mortal blow. And we may almost imagine we hear the beaten one, with thick and choking voice, repeat the terrible words of Francesco Ferruccio at the battle of Gavinana : ' Maramaldo, thou but killest a man already dead ! '

"Similarly, two opposing ships, with but slight difference in their powers, will commence their combat at a great distance, utilising their evolutionary abilities and their speed in prudent manœuvres, seeking to gain as much advantage as possible from their offensive powers, and attempting to place every obstacle in the way of the antagonist utilising powers in either direction. The discharge of projectiles will commence in earnest, greatly assisted by the rapid loading of which the guns of medium and small calibre are now capable. What results can reasonably be expected from the discharge of the smaller guns at such great distances is hard to say ; nor can the slender expectation of, let us say, chancing to hit the captain of the opposing ship in the eye with a lucky shot, at all justify such a waste of ammunition. Gradually nearing one another, the ships manœuvring less freely, hits will become more dangerous ; the boats that were not set adrift before the action began will be alight and burning fiercely ; the cowls of the wind trunks, the funnels, and the masts will be in fragments.

"The crew, wounded and reduced in numbers, will have lost their calm, and consequently the firing will have become wilder ; finally, one of the two antagonists will get in a lucky shot that will disable the other. She will speedily become unmanageable, and her enemy will as speedily close into within the thousand metres which will permit of a torpedo being launched with every chance of success, or the battle may be concluded by a final rush and the point of the ram.

"As the wounded hull sinks slowly beneath the waves, the flag which had put such heart into the crew, and the sight of which had spurred them to fight to the last, may well seem as it disappears to repeat to the enemy these sad words, " Thou slayest but one already dead."

"Four ships in place of two, eight in place of four, will repeat in a perhaps more complex action the same phases of attack, and the same foolish waste of ammunition, which in these days causes the greatest preoccupation of those who, having to design warships, must decide on the quantity of ammunition and projectiles provided for each different calibre of the armament.

* * * * *

"There is, however, another method of fighting and sending your enemy to the bottom ; but it is one that is capable of adoption only by a Navy at the same time most potent and very rich.

"Let us imagine a vessel whose armour is so well distributed and so impervious as to be able to resist all the attacks of an enemy's artillery with the exception of the projectiles of the 12-inch guns. Such a ship could approach her enemy without firing a shot, without wasting a single round of ammunition, absolutely regardless of all the scratchings that her antagonist might inflict on the exterior of her armour plates.

"And as to-day the belts of fighting ships are generally of such thicknesses that, when we leave the results of the proving ground and come to the conditions of actual combat, we find that it would be more than difficult to penetrate them with 6-inch guns, we see at once that it would be useless to equip our contemplated ship with such artillery.

"Further, if this ideal vessel which we have imagined to be so potently armoured is also very swift, and of a speed greater than that of a possible antagonist, she could not only prevent this latter from getting away, but also avail herself of her superiority in this respect for choosing the most convenient position for striking the belt of the enemy in the most advantageous manner.

"For this swift vessel a numerous and uniform armament of 8-inch guns, such as was contemplated for the

Amalfi class,* would appear to be sufficient, if we had only to consider the penetration at right angles of modern belts, especially if capped projectiles are adopted.

"If, however, the hit is an oblique one, and the distance is considerable, it appears necessary that we should adopt the calibre of 12-inch if we want to be absolutely certain of sinking the adversary, striking him *only* on the belt. But the loading of such guns is as yet very slow, although it has been greatly improved of late. Besides, the number of hits that one can get in on to the belt itself is small. From this it appears that in our ideal and intensely powerful ship we must increase the number of pieces of 12-inch so as to be able to get in at least one fatal shot on the enemy's belt at the water-line before she has a chance of getting a similar fortunate stroke at us from one of the four large pieces now usually carried as the main armament.

"We thus have outlined for us the main features of our absolutely supreme vessel—with medium calibres abolished—so effectually protected as to be able to disregard entirely all the subsidiary armament of an enemy, and armed only with twelve pieces of 12-inch. Such a ship could fight in the second method we have delineated, without throwing away a single shot, without wasting ammunition. Secure in her exuberant protection, with her twelve guns ready, she would swiftly descend on her adversary and pour in a terrible converging fire at the belt.

"Having disposed of her first antagonist, she would at once proceed to attack another, and almost untouched, to despatch yet another, not throwing away a single round of her ammunition, but utilising all for sure and deadly shots. A large and abundant supply of 12-inch projectiles and ammunition can be provided, in addition to the belt and guns contemplated, out of the 4,500 tons of

* The vessels of the *Amalfi* class designed by Col. Cuniberti in 1899 were of 8,000 tons displacement; they were to have been armed with twelve 203-m/m (8-inch), twelve 76-m/m (12-pounders), and twelve 47-m/m (3-pounders). The armour belt was 152-m/m (6 inches) thick, as also was the armour of the battery and of the turrets. The engines were to be 19,000 H.P., and the speed with 15,000 H.P. was to be 22 knots.

increase of displacement that will be disposable in the enlargement of the *Vittorio Emanuele III* to become the national British type of vessel in place of the *King Edward VII.*

"It will be necessary to defend our '*Invincible*' with a thick complete belt of twelve inches, and a battery also protected with the 12-inch armour (for the redoubt must be thus defended as well as the water-line, so as to eliminate the perils of the first system of attack sketched out, of progressive damages being adopted against her) ; and at the same time she must be armed with twelve pieces of 12-inch, arranged as in the *Amalfi* class or in the *Vittorio Emanuele III*, so as to be able herself to attack in the second method that has been out-lined, that is to say, the system of the stronger, of the better defended, and most certainly that of the richer. But when a certain number of such colossi of 17,000 tons —six, for example—had been constructed, it is more than probable that the adversary would do his utmost to prevent their getting near him, and, fearful of the fatal result of so unequal a combat, would seek to betake him-self elsewhere immediately on the appearance of the famous *Invincible* division.

" In that case the command of the seas, or a deluded belief that they have such command, will remain with these *Invincible* ships, even although they may be of slow speed ; but to stop at this point would be too little and unworthy of the Navy of the richest and most potent Power in the world.

"For this squadron or division, however ' invincible,' will not be really and truly *supreme* if it cannot also catch hold of the enemy's tail. The bull in the vast ring of the amphitheatre deludes himself with the idea that because he is more powerful than the agile toreador he therefore has absolute command of the scene of the combat ; but he is too slow in following up his adversaries, and these almost always succeed in eluding his terrible horns.

"We must, therefore, come to the conclusion that the type of vessel will not be absolutely *supreme* and worthy of such a nation unless we furnish it with such speed that it can overtake any of the enemy's battleships and oblige them to fight. It is, then, possible to give to a vessel of 17,000 tons displacement—

Protective armour of 12ins.
Twelve guns of 12-inch calibre.
An abundant supply of ammunition, and
A very high speed, superior to that of all and existing battleships afloat.

"It has been said and written—indeed, repeatedly written—that the *Vittorio Emanuele III* was a practical impossibility. But before long she will be actually in the water, and facts already show how vain were the suppositions and criticisms of such croakers.*

"But it has also been asserted that in the case of this vessel surpassing the contemplated speed of $21\frac{1}{2}$ knots on trial and attaining that hoped for of 22 knots, such would only prove that that particular tonnage of displacement especially lends itself to obtaining a form of hull with which we can realise a very high speed, and more so than with larger ships. This, however, is not quite exact. The law which governs the speed and displacement, other things being equal, is well known to all naval constructors, who have by heart the rule that whilst the displacement increases as the cube of the dimensions, the resistance, on the other hand, at a given speed does not increase in the same proportion as the displacement. The pith of the kernel lies in utilising the most opportune dimensions, or, rather, let us say, in adopting the special form of hull most adapted to those dimensions, more than in the actual amount of the displacement itself.

"The amount of the displacement, however, is intimately bound up with the question of the defensive and offensive powers that it is wished to give to a ship ;

---

* The *Vittorio Emanuele* proved a most successful ship, answering all expectations of her. One of her chief novelties was the employment of a special girder construction, and the scientific reduction of all superfluous weights upon a scale never before attempted. Though apparently lightly built the ship was found to be abnormally strong.

so that once the particular objectives of the Italian
Navy had been laid down, and thereby the defensive and
offensive power sought for decided on, the question
resolved itself into harmonising them with a form of hull
of the greatest possible efficiency, and this worked out
at 12,600 tons.   Nor does it appear that the problem could
have been satisfactorily solved with a vessel of less displacement, as in that case it would have been impossible
to realise the required power, while with a greater displacement the ship would have been incapable of obtaining the desired speed.

"In the same manner the defensive and offensive
power of the projected ships of the *Amalfi* class was har-
monised with a form of hull of such high efficiency that
it would have been possible to obtain a speed of 23 knots
and probably more ; but the statement that the problem
could not have been solved with a displacement of much
less or much greater tonnage than that projected, is not
to be taken as insisting that the solution must be interpreted in a too absolute manner, asserting that the speed
of 23 knots could not be efficiently obtained save with a
displacement of from 8,000 to 9,000 tons, for this would
be inexact.

* * * * *

"If now the question be put—Is it possible for some
naval architect to design a special form of hull having
a displacement of 17,000 tons, and with which we can
realise a very high speeed—twenty-four knots, for
example ?

"'Without doubt,' will answer all practical naval
constructors.

"If we go further, and ask—Is it possible for him at
the same time to arm such a vessel with twelve pieces of
12-inch ?

"'Without doubt,' will answer but a certain number
of such experienced men.

"But if we go still further, and demand, finally—Is
it also possible for him to protect such a ship with 12-inch
armour ?

"'Without doubt,' will answer only one here and there who may have already made researches in that direction.

"And as the solving of such a problem necessitates many and many a calculation, and no amount of discussion or argument on the matter could in any way be conclusive unless based on definite plans and figures, these lines might well conclude here.

"But, in deference to the courteous inquiry of Admiral Hopkins, this brief article must not be allowed to close in a manner so indefinite.

"I would, therefore, say frankly at once that the designs for such a vessel have already been worked out, and that its construction seems quite feasible and attainable. Following up the progressive scale of displacement from 8 000 to 12,000 tons, and then on to 17,000 tons, a new *King Edward VII.* has been designed, 521½ft. (159 metres) in length, with a beam of eighty-two feet (twenty-five metres), and mean draught of 27ft. (8.5 metres) ; with the water-line protected with 12-inch plates, and the battery similarly armoured ; having two turrets at the ends, each armed with a pair of 12-inch guns, and two central side turrets high up (similar to the two with 8-inch guns in the *Vittorio Emanuele III.*), also each armed with two pieces of 12-inch, and four turrets at the four angles of the upper part of the battery, having each one 12-inch gun.

"This vessel has no ports whatever in her armour ; she carries no secondary armament at all, but only the usual pieces of small calibre for defence against torpedo attack.

"The speed to be realised, as proved by the tank trials, is twenty-four knots."

The idea was at first received with derision and scepticism, which lasted until, in the Russian-Japanese War, it was announced that the Japanese had laid down two battleships, the *Aki* and *Satsuma*, which " were to be more or less on the lines of the ship projected by Colonel

Cuniberti." Contemporaneous with this the United States authorised the building of the *South Carolina* and *Michigan,* which carry eight 12-inch guns, so disposed as to be available on either broadside.

Both these ideas were public property before the British *Dreadnought* was laid down. She was, however, built with such rapidity that she was completed long before any other vessel of the type.

In the design for a new type of British capital ship, a great many ideas were considered and rejected. Eventually, however, it was decided to equip the *Dreadnought* with five turrets so disposed that eight guns were available on either broadside and six guns available ahead or astern. The designed speed of the ship was twenty-one knots.

Together with this type of ship, another type, somewhat more resembling the Cuniberti ideal, was laid down. Three ships of this class, the *Invincible* class, were designed for a speed of twenty-five knots, and given big guns so disposed that eight guns were available on either broadside and six big guns ahead or astern.

The *Dreadnought* was officially laid down in December, 1905, and completed ten months later. Actually, however, materials for her were collected months beforehand, and the rate at which she was built,* like the secrecy with which her building was surrounded, consisted in great measure of a theatrical display, very impressive to the general public at the time, but to-day generally regarded as " unfortunate " on account of the foreign attention thus attracted. But, while the previous chapter is clear proof of the futility of any real secrecy about the "Dreadnought idea," so far as the British Navy was concerned, it likewise serves to refute a charge which has been made to the effect that the " secrecy policy " induced foreign nations to build Dreadnoughts also. The most that can be said is that had the

---

* The false impression that a British battleship could be built in about a third of the time that German ships take to construct had far more to do with subsequent shipbuilding reductions than any deliberate ignoring of naval needs, such as those responsible were accused of.

Dreadnought been built without so much attention being attracted to her, foreign nations might have been less in a hurry to copy her.   But it is absolutely clear that the all-big-gun ship era had arrived, just as in the past the ironclad era came, or, in earlier days still, the gun and steam eras did.   The actual place of the *Dreadnought* in history is that she marks a wise and rapid recognition of new conditions.

Details of the *Dreadnought* are as follows :—

Displacement—17,900 tons.
Length—526ft. (over all).
Beam—82ft.
Draught—Maximum, 29ft. (normal).
Armament—Ten 12-inch, 45 calibre; twenty-seven 12 pounders; five submerged tubes (18 inch).
Armour Belt—11-in. to 6-in. forward; and 4-in. aft. On turrets 11-inch (K.C.)
Machinery—Parsons Turbine; four screws.
Horse Power—23,000 = 21 knots.
Boilers—Babcock.
Coal—(Normal) 900 tons; (maximum) 2,000 tons; oil fuel also.
Built at Portsmouth; Engined by Vickers.

The *Dreadnought* was unique in every particular. The exact disposition of her big gun armament was only arrived at after a long and careful consultation, and the consideration of a number of alternatives.   It admits of eight big guns bearing in nearly every position, and allows a minimum fire of six in any case.   It is understood that, in addition to the plan actually adopted, in the earliest plan of all (which was merely an adaption of the *Lord Nelson* class), consideration was given to a scheme o' five turrets, all in the centre line, and also to an arrangement whereby the two amidship turrets would be placed *en échelon.*

One of the particular arguments in favour of the plan ultimately adopted was that next to four, eight big guns form the best workable unit for fire control purposes.   It

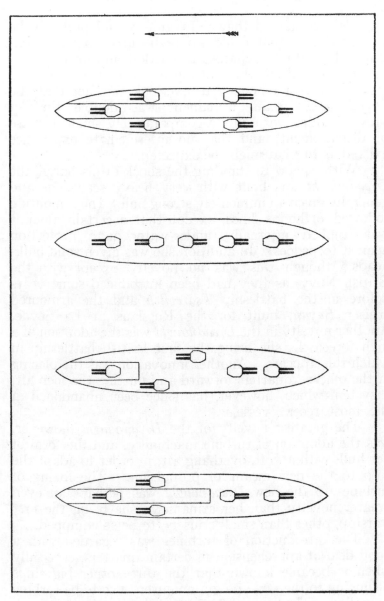

ALTERNATIVE DESIGNS FOR THE DREADNOUGHT.

was also considered that eight guns would probably be the maximum that could safely be fired together continuously, with full charges in battle conditions.

In these days when all big gun armaments are the rule, there is a tendency to overlook the fact that the *Dreadnought's* main armament was double that of previous ships, with only a comparatively small increase of displacement, and that no intermediate experience existed as to what might be expected.

With a view to standing the shock of discharge, the *Dreadnought* was built with very heavy scantlings and generally given an immensely strong hull. The armouring followed orthodox lines, except that a certain amount was applied internally under-water as a protection against torpedoes. In addition she was given solid bulkheads,* though this was no novelty except with the British Navy, as they had been introduced some years before in the battleship *Tsarevitch* and the armoured cruiser *Bayan*, built for the Russians at La Seyne. Another novelty in the *Dreadnought* was the adoption of a high forecastle, she being the first British battleship in which this appears. Another innovation was the placing of the officers' quarters forward and putting the men aft, a system which, however, has since been abandoned in the most recent vessels.

The greatest novelty of the *Dreadnought*, however, was the adoption of turbine machinery, and the form of her hull, with a 3oft. overhang aft, in order to adapt the ship to the new means of propulsion. The fitting of turbines to the new *Dreadnought* was perhaps an even greater novelty than her armament, she being the first warship, other than small cruisers, to be so equipped.

The introduction of turbines was regarded with a good deal of apprehension in certain quarters, especially when it became known that the three other big ships belonging to the same programme were also to be turbine propelled. The type selected for all was the Parsons with

---

* They first appeared, as already recorded, in British cruisers of the *Minotaur* class. Their safety record is to be found in the survival of the *Pallada* at Port Arthur ; their inconvenience in the fact that in the *Neptune* they were abandoned.

four shafts. The wing shafts of the *Dreadnought* have each one high pressure ahead and one high-pressure astern turbine. The amidship ones are fitted with three turbines each—one low pressure one ahead, and one low pressure astern, and one turbine for going astern. Each turbine has 39,600 blades.

On her first trials the *Dreadnought* exceeded her designed speed for short spurts by three-quarters of a knot, but on the eight hours' run barely succeeded in making a mean of twenty-one knots. Shortly afterwards she fell a little below this, but at a later date picked up again, and on more than one occasion since she has easily made twenty-two knots or over. Such early difficulties as occurred were due to the fact that her engine-room complement were at first necessarily unfamiliar with working so large an installation. The total cost of the *Dreadnought,* which belongs to the 1905-06 programme, was £1,797,497, and save that her draught somewhat exceeded anticipations, the ship was a success in every way, proving a remarkably steady gun-platform.

The Committee which sat on the *Dreadnought* design was by no means entirely unanimous as to what sacrifice should be made for speed. The *Dreadnought* herself, despite a considerable increase of speed as compared with the battleships that preceded her, did not obtain that speed by the sacrifice of any battleship qualities, but almost entirely on account of the substitution of turbines for reciprocating engines. To that extent, therefore, though nearly as fast as the armoured cruisers of a few years before, she may be said to have developed entirely along normal lines, rather than on those laid down by Cuniberti.

The appended table and diagrams indicate how the original Cuniberti idea compares with the first results obtained. It will be noticed that, except in the case of the *Invincible* type (and there only at a sacrifice of armour and armament) was, however, anything like the Cuniberti speed attempted. It should be stated that in the Cuniberti ship the peculiar " girder construction " of his

ORIGINAL DREADNOUGHT DESIGNS.

	Normal Displacement. Tons.	Armament.	Belt in.	Des'd. Speed. Knots.	Laid Down.
Cuniberti (as built)	17,000	12-12in., 18-12 pdr	12	24	pro. 1903
Satsuma Design	19,250	12 or 10-12in., 12-4·7	9	20	—
Satsuma	19,250	4-12in., 12-10in., 12-6	9	20	1905
S. Carolina, pro	16-17,000	8-12in., (or 4-12in., 8-10in.), 30-14 pdr.	10	18-20	—
S. Carolina	16,000	8-12in., 22-14 pdr.	12	18½	1906
Dreadnought, 1st Design	?	10-12in.	..	..	—
Dreadnought (as built)	17,900	10-12in., 27-12 pdr	11	21	1905
Invincible	17,250	8-12in., 16-4in.	7	25	1906
Nassau (as " S ")	?	8-11in., 12-6in., 10-24 pdr.	?	19½	1906
Nassau	18,500	12-11in., 12-6in., 10-24 pdr.	9¾	19½	1907

Note.—The Nassau was delayed a year owing to alterations in design.

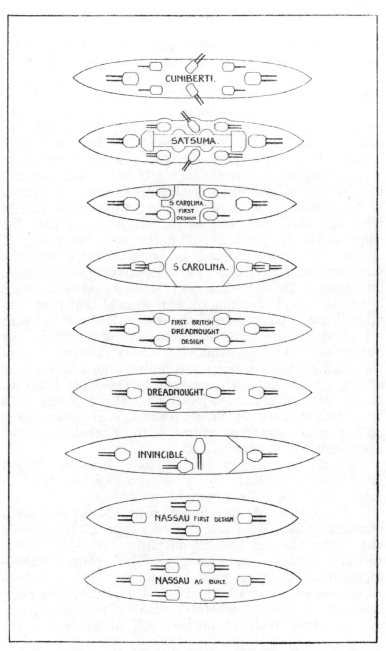

ORIGINAL DREADNOUGHT DESIGNS.

Vittorio Emanuele was obviously contemplated. This construction, which admits of far lighter scantlings than usually employed, has not been attempted in any other Navies, and a corresponding extra dead-weight results.

Coming to details, there is uncertainty as to the exact original design of the *Satsuma*; but a uniform armament of big guns was certainly the first to be projected. It is not clear whether it was abandoned from a preference for a numerically larger but mixed battery; or with a view to utilising such guns as were most likely to be available for early delivery. Japan was then at war, and there was the natural anticipation that the ships might be wanted before the war was over. It should, on the other hand, be borne in mind that the *Kashima* and *Katori*, of 16,400 tons, carrying four 12-inch, four 10-inch, twelve 6-inch, and twelve 14-pounders, with 9-inch belts and 18.5 knots speeds were at that time held up in England on account of the war. Hence it has with some considerable show of reason been argued that the *Satsuma* and *Aki* are nothing but normal developments of the *Kashima* design, bearing just the same relation to it as the British *Lord Nelsons* bear to the *King Edwards*. It was also practically admitted by the Japanese at a later date that for diplomatic reasons, in accounts of the contemporary armoured cruisers of the *Tsukuba* class, the armaments* were exaggerated.

Be all these things as they may, however, Japan is obviously entitled to some considerable share in originating the " Dreadnought movement."

The claims of the United States Navy rest on a stronger basis. The *South Carolina* type, all big guns in the centre line, all bearing on either broadside, was a distinct advance and novelty. The actual chronological date of laying down goes for nothing ; the ships were designed and authorised long before they were commenced. No secrecy whatever was observed about them, and a strong body of opinion will always credit the

---

* These were announced as intended to carry four 12-inch and eight 10-inch, besides smaller guns. The 10-inch proved later on to be mythical.

United States with being the first Navy that definitely adopted the " all-big-gun idea." It is interesting to note (see table) that at one stage a mixed 12-inch and 10-inch armament was regarded as a possible alternative.

It has been claimed, either by those responsible for the *Dreadnought* herself, or by others professing to speak for them, that the *Dreadnought* was evolved entirely independently of Cuniberti's ideal. It is practically impossible to say definitely how far there can be any truth in this. In all Admiralties, ships are, as a rule, designed as " projects " long before they see the light (some never see it at all, as witness the sea-going masted turret-ship of his design referred to by Sir Edward Reed in some remarks quoted on an earlier page !). The first British all-big-gun ship design (see diagram) is a lineal enough descendant of the *King Edward* and *Lord Nelson*, just as Cuniberti's is a descendant of the *Vittorio Emanuele*.

The Cuniberti design appears, however, to have been submitted as early as 1901. In any case, to Cuniberti belongs the first clear exposition of the idea, while the ridicule with which it was at first received indicates the general novelty.

Germany is also a claimant to having evolved Dreadnoughts with the " *S* " type, intended to have been laid down in 1906, to follow the *Deutschlands*. These ships can hardly have been designed much later than 1904. When first heard of they were reported to carry four big gun turrets, of which two were placed on either side amidships. Six big guns was the first reputed armament, later each turret was to carry two guns.

The absurd secrecy with which subsequent German designs have been shrouded was not then in evidence ; and all the indications are that the *Nassau*, as originally contemplated, was to have been a four-turret ship—the two extra 11-inch being Germany's equivalent for the four 12-inch, four 9·2, of our *King Edwards*. This would perhaps accord Germany a priority in actually adopting the principle of an increased number of heavy guns.

All of which suffices to indicate that the adoption

of more than four big guns had little or nothing to do with the somewhat theatrical building of the original *Dreadnought*.

On the other hand (with the possible and doubtful exception of the *South Carolina**) it appears clear that the *Dreadnought* was the first ship in which the all-big-gun principle was adopted as a technical asset in gun-laying over and above guns *qua* guns. After four, eight was the " tactical unit " of guns, promising results altogether out of proportion to anything that six, or for that matter, ten (in proportion) could achieve.

It may not be too much to say that what Cuniberti " saw as through a glass darkly," the *Dreadnought* translated into fact, and that she was the first battleship avowedly so designed.

" Fire control " was a new thing in 1905.   No navy, save the British, had considered it to any appreciable degree.   The *King Edwards* had taught that control of two calibres from one position was a practical impossibility.   Mixed calibres were damned accordingly, and there was no outlet but the *Dreadnought*.

But for Cuniberti she might, and possibly would, have remained a theoretical desirability for several more years.   The measure of his genius may be the demonstration that such an ideal ship could be built.   It is to be argued that he did nothing more than put into practical shape what already existed as a hypothesis.   Even so, however, to him belongs the honour of indicating that the step from theory to practice was possible ; and on that account alone he deserves to go down to posterity as the actual creator of Dreadnoughts.

In the other three ships of the 1905-06 programme, however, a high speed was accepted as the governing factor.   The ships as built were designated " armoured cruisers," and in so far as the Japanese were known to be building armoured cruisers carrying battleship guns, that designation was legitimate.   For that matter, there also existed a paper by Professor Hovgaard, of the

* American scientific gunnery rather post-dates the *South Carolina* design.

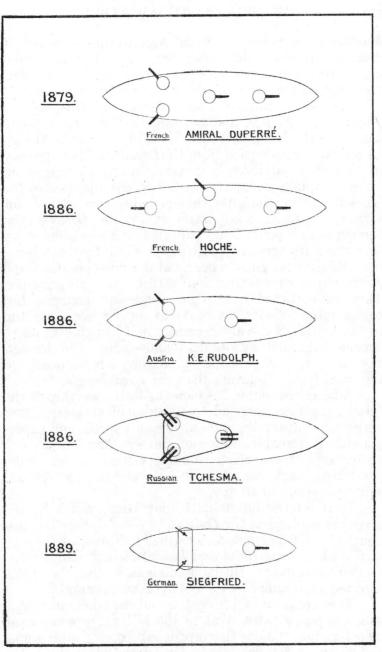

1879.   French. AMIRAL DUPERRÉ.

1886.   French. HOCHE.

1886.   Austria. K.E.RUDOLPH.

1886.   Russian. TCHESMA.

1889.   German. SIEGFRIED.

EARLY EXAMPLES OF WING TURRETS.

Massachusetts School of Naval Architecture, in which it was tentatively laid down that the ideal armoured cruiser of the future would be a battleship in armament and armour, increased in size, to obtain greater speed.

The three companion ships to the *Dreadnought*—the *Invincible, Inflexible*, and *Indomitable*—adhered no more closely to the Hovgaard ideal than to the Cuniberti one. In principle they varied from the *Dreadnought* design only in that they sacrificed a certain amount of armour in order to obtain a greater speed. By the adoption of the échelon system, the same broadside-fire was secured for them (on paper, at any rate) as for the *Dreadnought*, though with a turret less. In practice it has been found that there are very few positions in which they can bring more than six big guns to bear, but this must be considered as an error of construction rather than of principle. They have turned out to be wonderful steamers, but considerably inferior sea-boats to the *Dreadnought*, and in the British Navy are generally likely in the future to become regarded as obsolete long before the former. For all that, they probably approximate more nearly to the warship of the future than the *Dreadnought*.

Admiral Bacon, in his views as to the warship of the future, generally inclined to the idea of very large and very swift ships, relying on armament, speed, and super-scientific internal sub-division rather than on armour protection. These ships would act more or less independently, each, as it were, representing a divided squadron group of to-day.

It is interesting to note that Italy, which in the seventies evolved in the *Duilio* and *Dandalo* the " Dreadnought " of that period, eventually developed a very similar idea in the *Italia* and *Lepanto*, which had no side armour whatever. In later designs a thin belt was reverted to, and finally the old cycle was resumed.

This result was brought about by the quickfirer, which appeared as a rival to the hitherto predominant monster gun. To-day the torpedo is becoming paramount, and a danger to a fleet in close order at almost any range

—hence the Bacon ideal.   It remains to be seen whether the future will produce any analogy to the cycle of the quickfirer of the eighties.

Details of the *Invincible* type are :—

> Displacement—17,250 tons.
> Length (over all)—562ft. (*p.p.*, 530ft.).
> Beam—78½ft.
> Draught—29ft.
> Armament—Eight 12-inch, XI., 45 calibre, sixteen 4-inch (model 1907) ; three submerged tubes.
> Armour Belt—7-inch, reduced to 4-inch at the ends.
> Machinery—Parsons Turbine.
> Horse Power—41,000 = 25 knots.
> Boilers—(*Invincible* and *Inflexible*)   Yarrow, (*Indomitable*) Babcock.
> Coal—(Normal) 1,000 tons, (maximum) 3,000 tons ; oil fuel also.
> Builders—(*Invincible*) Elswick, (*Inflexible*) Clydebank, (*Indomitable*) Fairfield.
> Engined—(*Invincible*)   Humphrys,   (*Inflexible*) Clydebank, (*Indomitable*) Fairfield.

As originally designed, the anti-torpedo guns of these ships would have been the same as the *Dreadnought's*, but, having been completed nearly two years later and a new pattern 4-inch quickfirer having been invented in the interim, they were fitted with these guns.   The trial results were as follows :—*Invincible*, 26.6 knots ;   *Inflexible*, 26.5 knots ;   and *Indomitable*, 26.1 knots ;   the designed horse power being considerably exceeded in every case.   After they were commissioned and had shaken down, these trial speeds were considerably exceeded, and at one time and another they all did well over 28 knots ; the *Indomitable* having made a record of 28.7.

The fuel consumption of these ships is naturally enormous.   The *Indomitable*, in crossing the Atlantic at full speed, burned about 500 tons of coal a day, as well as about 120 tons of oil. As steamers they are to be considered remarkably successful. The average cost of construction was about £1,752,000, which works out at at little under £102 per ton.

Towards the close of the year 1911 the official designation of " armoured cruiser " for them and similar ships was abandoned, and the term " battle cruiser " substituted. No further secret was made of the fairly obvious fact that they were designed as " fast battleships," intended to engage and hold a retreating enemy till such time as the main squadron could come up.

Curiously enough, for some while, though every nation started building *Dreadnoughts*, Germany alone proceeded to build *Invincibles* also. In 1911 Japan ordered a ship of fast battleship type ; but, generally speaking, foreign nations have abstained from embodying this portion of the Cuniberti ideal in their designs.

The programme for the years 1906-07 had been originally intended to include the building of four armoured ships, presumably one *Dreadnought* and three *Invincibles* ; but the Liberal party, which had just come into power, modified this to three battleships of an improved *Dreadnought* type. This action led to a popular agitation which ultimately eventuated in the provision of no less than eight armoured ships in the estimates of three years later.

The three ships which followed, the *Dreadnought*, the *Bellerophon, Téméraire,* and *Superb,* are some seven hundred tons heavier, but otherwise differ only in minor details. For the one heavy tripod of the *Dreadnought,* two were substituted, and the 4-inch anti-torpedo gun was also mounted. In the next year the *St. Vincent* class, a group of similar type, but increased by 650 tons, were provided. The anti-torpedo armament is carried to 20 guns in the *St. Vincent* class, which are 10ft. longer than their predecessors, and carry fifty-calibre big guns in place of the forty-five calibre pieces of the earlier ships.

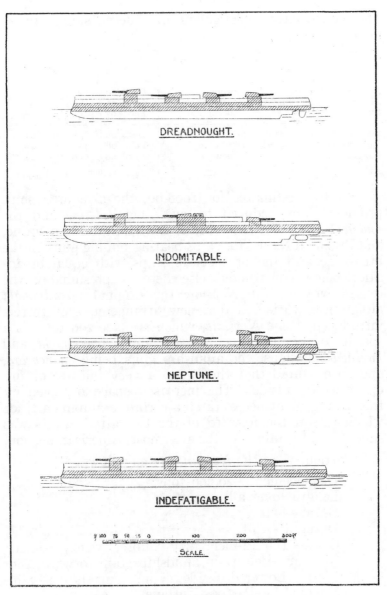

DREADNOUGHT.

INDOMITABLE.

NEPTUNE.

INDEFATIGABLE.

SCALE.

DREADNOUGHTS.

The constructive particulars of these ships are as follows :—

Name.	Built at	Machinery by:	Laid down	Completed.	Trials.
Bellerophon	Portsmouth	Fairfield	Dec., '06	Feb., '07	21.9
Téméraire	Devonport	Hawthorn Leslie	Jan., '07	May, '09	——
Superb ...	Elswick	Wallsend Co.	Feb., '07	June, '09	——
St. Vincent	Portsmouth	Scott Eng. & S. Co.	Dec., '07	Jan., '10	21.9
Collingwood	Devonport	Hawthorn, L.	Feb., '08	Jan., '10	22
Vanguard .	Vickers	Vickers	April,'08	Feb., '10	22.1

In the Estimates for 1908-09, the armoured ships provided were reduced to two, the *Neptune* and the *Indefatigable*. Provision in the United States, Argentine, and Brazilian Navies for ships bearing ten big guns on the broadside and the prospect of ships with equal broadsides being constructed elsewhere is presumably the reason why in the *Neptune* the original *Dreadnought* design was varied, and a new arrangement of turrets introduced. The *Neptune*, which is of 20,200 tons, is a species of compromise between the *Dreadnought* and *Invincible* designs, the amidship guns being *en échelon,* and so mounted that they give a very full arc of fire on either broadside. The increased space occupied by this arrangement necessitated a certain cramping aft, for which reason the forward of the two after turrets was superposed to train over the aftermost, American fashion.

Particulars of the *Neptune* are as follows :—

Displacement—20,200 tons.
Length (over all)—546ft.
Beam—85ft.
Draught—29ft.
Guns—Ten 12-inch, fifty calibre, twenty 4-inch.
Armour—Belt 12-in. amidships, 6-in. forward, 4-in.
    aft. Lower deckside, 9¾-in. Turrets, 12—8-in.
Machinery—Parsons Turbine.
Horse Power—25,000 = 21 knots.
Boilers—Yarrow.

Coal—(Normal) 900 tons, (maximum) 2,700 tons ; oil fuel also.

Built at Portsmouth Dockyard.

Engined by Harland and Woolf.

On trial she developed at three-quarter power I.H.P. 18,575, with a speed of nineteen knots, and at full power 27,721, with 21.78 knots. Her best maximum spurt speed was 22.7—that is to say, about one and three-quarter knots over contract.

In the *Neptune* the original *Dreadnought* practice of mounting the anti-torpedo armament on top of the turrets was entirely abandoned, and these guns were placed inside or on top of the superstructure in three main groups.

The number of torpedo tubes was reduced to three, the reason for this being partly to save space and also to take advantage of improved methods for securing rapidity of fire. In the *Neptune* the possibility of aero craft first received consideration, the upper deck being built sufficiently thick to be proof against bombs dropped from aloft.

The *Neptune* was one of the cheapest ships ever built for the British Navy, her cost working out at a little under £87 per ton.

The other ship of the same programme was the *Indefatigable*, an improved *Invincible*. She represents an increase of nearly 2,000 tons over the type ship, with an increase in length of 18ft. and a foot more beam. Save for the addition of four more anti-torpedo guns the armament remains the same, but an extra inch is added to the belt. The principal improvement achieved in her is that the two amidship turrets are much less crowded up than in the type ship, thus securing a considerably better range of fire.

Although the horse power is proportionately less than that of the *Invincibles*, the better lines of the ship have made her even more speedy. She easily exceeded her designed speed on trial, and has reached as high as 29.13 knots.

The cost of construction was £1,547,426, which works out at about £82 10s. per ton, as against the average £120 per ton that the *Invincibles* cost to build. She is the cheapest ship yet built for the British Navy.* (1912).

Details of the *Indefatigable* are :—

Displacement—19,200 tons.
Length—578ft.
Beam—79½ft.
Draught—27¾ft.
Guns—Eight 12-inch, fifty calibre, twenty 4-inch.
Armour Belt—8-in. amidships, diminished to 4-in. at the ends.
Machinery—Parsons Turbine.
Horse Power—43,000 = 25 knots.
Boilers—Babcock.
Coal—(Normal) 1,000 tons, (maximum) 2,500 tons ; oil fuel also.
Built at Devonport Dockyard.
Engined by J. Brown & Co., of Clydebank.

Two other battle-cruisers almost identical to the *Indefatigable,* the *Australia* at Clydebank, for the Australian Navy, and the *New Zealand* at Fairfield, a gift from New Zealand to the British Navy, were launched in 1911.

The programme for 1908-09, consisting as it did of only two armoured ships, and the fact that the corresponding German programme was increased by one capital ship, bringing the total to four, brought the naval agitation to a head. Meetings demanding eight "Dreadnoughts" were held all over the country, with the result that the British programme for 1909-10 rose to four armoured ships with four other "conditional" ships. The ships of the former programme were the *Colossus, Hercules, Orion,* and *Lion,* and the first two of these were laid down some months before the usual date, the *Colossus* being commenced in July instead of at the end of the year.

---

* It should be remembered that alterations were made in the *Invincible* class in the course of construction, and this probably helped to swell the cost.

The " conditional " ships were all eventually laid down in April of the following year. They were the *Monarch, Conqueror, Thunderer,* and *Princess Royal.*

Under this programme there were no less than three distinct types of ships. The first two, the *Colossus* and *Hercules,* are practically sisters of the *Neptune,* but of 400 tons greater displacement. They differ in appearance in having but one tripod mast instead of two. This, like the *Dreadnought's,* is placed abaft the foremost funnel. The *Colossus* was built and engined by the Scott Shipbuilding and Engineering Co., commenced in July, 1909, and completed two years later. The *Hercules,* built by Palmer's, followed a month later in both cases. The first is fitted with Babcock, and the second with Yarrow boilers. A point of minor interest about these two ships is that whereas the anti-torpedo armament of the *Neptune* is in three groups, that of the *Colossus* and *Hercules* is in two groups only, the mounting of small guns between the échelon turrets being done away with.

The other two types of the 1909-10 Estimates, are the ships generally known as "super-Dreadnoughts."

SUPER-DREADNOUGHTS.

The most obvious feature of the so-called " super-Dreadnoughts " is the introduction of the 13.5-inch gun, particulars of which will be found at the end of this chapter. This gun was experimented with with a certain amount of secrecy, and was for a long time officially designated as the 12-inch " A," although practically everybody knew that it was really a 13.5. It was only rendered possible by recent improvements in gun-mountings and gun-construction. It is not very appreciably heavier than the latest type of 12-inch, as mounted in the *Colossus,* and its adoption was not so much a matter of obtaining an increased range and penetration, as of securing the tremendously increased smashing power of the heavier projectile.

Somewhat less obvious to the general public, but really of a great deal more far-reaching importance, is

Y

the "Americanising" of British naval design exhibited in
all the "super-Dreadnoughts." Though differing in
detail, the arrangement of the armament in all the
"super-Dreadnoughts" followed the American centre-
line system, an interesting indication of the progress of
the United States Navy from the days, not so very long
ago, when American warship design was more or less
a *pour faire rire* !　It is none the less interesting from
the fact that in the earliest designs, in all ships carrying
more than two turrets, the centre line was the only
arrangement ever built or even considered.　Yet when
an increased number of turrets came into being, the
American Navy was the only one which followed the
original practice.　In all other Navies ideas of the
period 1870-1880, when strong end-on fire was considered
an all-important essential, influenced design.　America
alone appreciated the prophecy long ago made by Admiral
Colomb to the effect that whatever else might temporarily obtain, broadside to broadside would always be
reverted to for battle, on the grounds that thus, and thus
only, could the maximum number of guns be utilised.

It is proper here to remark that though the Americans adopted the centre line from the outset for practical
reasons, this disposition became more or less a necessity
when 13.5's came in, owing to the infinitely greater strain
on the structure.　This has been occasionally used as an
argument against American influence having made itself
felt, but the balance of evidence shows that even had the
13.5-inch not appeared, the centre line system would have
figured in the Navy.　The original centre-line idea disappeared because the échelon system looked so superior.
The échelon system of the 1875-85 era, however, died out
in its turn on account of certain practical disadvantages.
It was resurrected when these had been forgotten in the
lapse of years ; but the disadvantages entailed in firing
across a deck soon made themselves felt again once the
system was reverted to.

One of the earliest advocates, if not the first of
modern advocates of the centre-line in England was

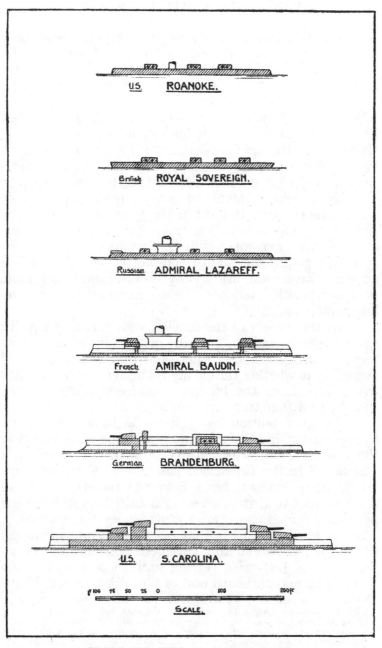

U.S.   ROANOKE.

British ROYAL SOVEREIGN.

Russian ADMIRAL LAZAREFF.

French AMIRAL BAUDIN.

German BRANDENBURG.

U.S.   S. CAROLINA.

ft 100 75 50 25 0   100   200ft

SCALE.

CENTRE-LINE SHIPS OF VARIOUS DATES.

Admiral Hopkins. Discussing the original Cuniberti ideal, Admiral Hopkins pointed out that although for an absolute right-ahead or astern fire wing-turrets gave an advantage, a very slight yaw entirely altered the proportion, and that circumstance in which the enemy was dead right-ahead necessitating such a yaw were likely to occur very rarely indeed in war. He leaned, therefore, to the opinion that a fewer number of guns all in the centre line would be equally as efficacious, practically, as a larger number disposed partly in wing turrets.

The échelon system, of course, renders practically no assistance here, the arc of the guns firing across the deck being necessarily restricted, even with the best échelon arrangement. While, therefore, the échelon system is good for absolute end-on, or for more or less absolute broadside firing, any intermediate and more probable position renders it less efficient than a centre-line arrangement.

Another defect of the échelon system is that with it, except exactly end-on, one side of the ship is necessarily more efficient than the other, and that this is reversed according to whether the enemy is ahead or astern, twenty five per cent. of the big-gun armament being affected thereby in a four turreted ship.

Though attention never seems to have been drawn to the matter, it is a fact worthy of some attention that the *Von der Tann*, which is to be regarded as Germany's " answer " to the *Invincibles* has (like all German* ships on the same system) her échelonned turrets exactly in reverse order to British ones. All British ships have the port turret foremost ; all German ones the starboard. The net result of this is that (as the diagram indicates) there are two worst and two best positions for either design. An *Invincible* getting and keeping a *Von der Tann* upon her starboard bow or port quarter would have

---

* In the Chinese ships *Ting Yuen* and *Chen Yuen*, built in Germany in 1882, with big guns *en échelon*, the former had the port big guns foremost, the latter the starboard ones—presumably an appreciation of and an attempt to overcome the inherent defect of the échelon system—the two ships being intended to fight in company, and so have one of the two always in the best fighting position were the enemy anywhere on the beam or quarter,

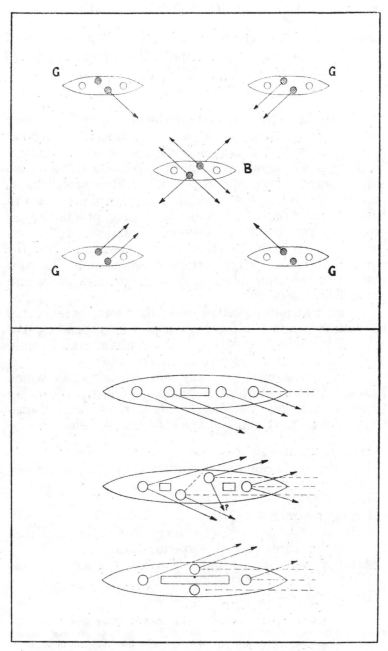

DIAGRAM TO ILLUSTRATE WEAK POINT OF THE ÉCHELON SYSTEM.

a twenty-five per cent. superiority over her, while, supposing the German type to maintain a position on her starboard quarter or port bow she would be to the same extent over-matched, and to a certain extent " in chancery."

With the centre line system, the imposition of fighting one side rather than the other is not imposed, and over-hauling or being overhauled causes no disadvantage. Nothing is lost, save in the almost hypothetical case of two ships engaging exactly end-on—a condition which in no case would endure for more than a very short space of time, to say nothing of the fact that practically all gunnery errors being of " elevation " and not of " direction," a ship adopting the end-on position offers the equivalent of a vertical target of some 6oft. to 7oft. instead of the equivalent of 3oft. or so that she would present broadside on.

The centre-line system may, therefore, be expected to endure against all other dispositions pending the appearance of some fresh condition of affairs which would cause the old end-on idea to be reverted to*.

The *Orion* was the only one of her class which belonged to the normal Estimates, 1909-10, the other three—*Conqueror, Thunderer, Monarch*—being " contingent ships." Details of the class are as follows :—

Displacement—23,500 tons.
Length—(between perpendiculars) 554½ft. ; (over all) 584ft.
Beam—88½ft.
Draught—(mean) 27¾ft.
Armament—Ten 13.5-inch, forty-five calibre ; sixteen 4-inch ; three 21-inch torpedo tubes.
Armour Belt—12—4-inch. Turrets, 12-inch.
Machinery—Parsons turbine.
Horse-power—27,000 = 21 knots.

* The torpedo, for example, may possibly bring about something of the sort by a state of speed and accuracy which leads to heavy or anticipated heavy long-range losses from it in fleet actions. To offer only one-fifth or so of the target would then be a serious consideration.

Boilers—Babcock.
Coal—(nominal) 900 tons ; (maximum) 2,700 tons ;
oil, 1,000 tons.

NAME.	BUILDER.	ENGINED BY
Orion	Portsmouth	Wallsend Co.
Conqueror	Beardmore	Beardmore.
Thunderer	Thames I.W.	Thames I.W.
Monarch	Elswick	Hawthorn.

The *Orion* was laid down in November, 1909, the others in April, 1910.

The *Orion* was the first of these ships to be commissioned, and her gunnery trials were watched with great interest. Few details of them transpired, save that part of the secondary battery was injured by blast. After commissioning, the *Orion* was sent for a voyage across the Bay of Biscay, and attracted much attention by rolling very heavily, this being attributed to the fact that her bilge keels were not large enough,—not to any general structural defect.

An interesting feature of the *Orion* type is that in it provision first appears for the protection of boats in action.

Belonging to the same programme (1909-10), the first belonging to the normal Estimates and the second to the " contingent," are the battle cruisers *Lion* and *Princess Royal*. A great deal of secrecy has been observed about these ships, but their main details are approximately as follows :—

Displacement—25,000 tons. Full load, 26,350 tons.
Length—(water-line), 675ft. ; (over all) 690ft.
Beam—86½ft.
Draught—(maximum), 30ft.
Armament—Eight 13.5 inch 45 calibre, twenty 4-inch, three 21-inch torpedo tubes.
Armour—Belt, 9—4-inch.
Machinery—Parsons Turbine.
Horse-power—(as designed) = 28 knots.

Boilers—Yarrow.
Coal—(normal) 1,000 tons, (maximum) 3,500 tons ; oil also.
Lion—Built at Devonport ; engined by Vickers.
Princess Royal—Built at Vickers' ; engined by Vickers.

The *Lion* was laid down in November, 1909, and launched in the following year. The *Princess Royal* was laid down in April, 1910, and launched a year later. Both were arranged to be completed during 1912.

The *Lion* was somewhat delayed owing to slight repairs being required to her turbines. In addition, the authorities very wisely did not " hurry " her—hurrying ships to fit an exact official date having done more mischief than anything else in the past.

The *Lion* did her trials early in 1912, and reached a maximum of 31.7 knots by patent log, with a mean of 29 knots at full power and 24.5 or so at three-quarter power. For her trials the *Lion* burned coal only, and this at the seemingly enormous rate of 950 tons a day, which worked out at approximately about a ton and a quarter per mile. This consumption, heavy though it seems, really pans out at about the usual " ton a mile," as the ship developed horse-power far in excess of the contract. At the same time it necessarily draws attention to the enormous increase in coal stores required for supplying modern warships. It is unfortunately by no means clear that the question of the very great increase in coal required for modern warships has been thoroughly realised by the authorities. The amount provided may be said to be what ships needed in the pre-Dreadnought era. It is now an open secret that at the time of the " war scare " with Germany in 1911, the British Home Fleet was unable to proceed to sea owing to a shortage of coal supply, many ships being a thousand tons short and no proper arrangements for rapid remedy existing. This state of affairs, at one time alleged to be merely a newspaper *canard*, is not likely to occur again ; but it is an indication of how difficult it is adequately to realise

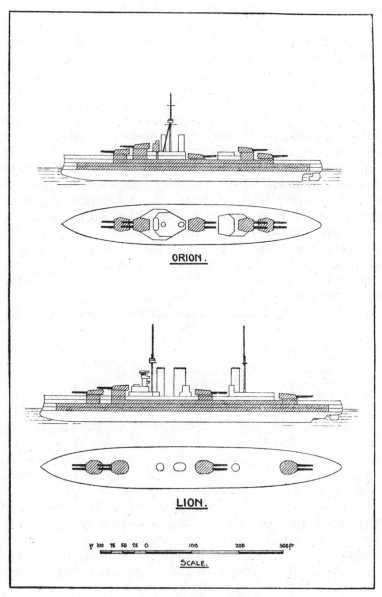

ORION.

LION.

ft 100 75 50 25 0   100   200   300 ft.

SCALE.

SUPER-DREADNOUGHTS.

the problem of coal supply to ships of ever-increasing horse-power.

During the *Lion's* trials it was found that the heat from the fore funnel was so great that the fire-control station (then carried on a tripod mast placed immediately over the forward funnel) was so intense as to render that position practically impossible. On the navigating bridge also, instruments were badly affected by the heat. The ship was consequently further delayed in order to effect essential modifications. These included the abolition of the tripod mast, shifting the fore funnel back a long way, and enormously increasing the height of all funnels.

The principal item of the Estimates of 1910-11 was five armoured ships. Of these, four, the *King George V* Class are slightly improved replicas of the *Orion*, while the remaining vessel, the *Queen Mary*, is a very large battle-cruiser.

Ships of the *George V* Class are as follows :—

Name.	Built at	Machinery by
King George V.	Portsmouth Y.	Hawthorn.
Centurion	Devonport Y.	Hawthorn.
Ajax	Scotts	Scotts.
Audacious	Laird	Laird.

The over-all length is increased to 596ft., and the horse-power to 31,000. All were laid down during 1911, with a view to launching during 1912 and completion in 1913. The displacement of these ships is 25,000 tons odd.

The *Queen Mary*, laid down at Palmers' early in 1911, and engined by Clydebank, is generally reported to have a displacement of 28,850 tons, and an over-all length of 725ft., with an armament and armour as the *Lion*. Her horse-power is put at 80,000 nominal, with forty-two Yarrow large tube boilers.

The 1911-12 Estimates provided for five further large armoured ships, which represent a slight increase in dimensions over their predecessors.

The names selected for these were, for the battle-

ships, *Benbow, Delhi, Marlborough,* and *Iron Duke* ; for
the battle-cruiser, *Tiger.*

The cruisers of the super-Dreadnought era have
been developments of the *Bristol* Class, but with a uniform armament of eight 6-inch guns.

For 1912-13 the Estimates provided for four capital
ships, the usual twenty destroyers, and a new type of
warship designated as "lightly armoured cruisers." These
last alone presented any particular novelty. Only very
meagre details concerning them have transpired, but it
is abundantly clear that they are a species of armoured
Scout or " destroyers."

The destroyers of the period have not materially
differed from their predecessors of the Dreadnought era,
save for the adoption of two 4-inch guns in the armament, instead of one.

Submarines and aerial craft are dealt with in a
separate chapter.

* * * * *

At the time of writing (1912) the " super-Dreadnoughts " may be described as the " last word " in naval
architecture ; though—failing war—still larger ships may
be depended on to follow them.

For what it is worth, however, it may here be put on
record that junior opinion in the Navy is becoming
opposed not only to " super-Dreadnoughts " but to
Dreadoughts in any shape or form. Hardly any naval
officer under the rank of Commander, and an ever-increasing percentage over that rank, is to be found who
is not more or less convinced that the days of the Dreadnoughts and " super-Dreadnoughts " may be nearly
numbered, and that we may possibly be even now on
the verge of some as yet indeterminate revolution in
naval construction as great as any that the "fifties" saw.

As yet no very clear argument can be produced.
Only vaguely as yet is it put forward that with torpedo
range what it is, the big ship's chance against torpedo
craft is practically relegated to not being found, and " not
being found " depends mainly upon the " super-Dread-

nought " being screened with very numerous smaller craft. When Lord Charles Beresford put it on record that a hundred anti-torpedo attack guns would be useless in a battleship, he spoke for all progressive naval ideas. A destroyer may be hit and hit vitally, but it is hard to imagine a hit which will stop her drifting within easy range of her quarry before going down. If hostile destroyers get in, the only real chance of big ships is to sweep their decks with the modern variant of " case shot " and so kill their crews, a difficult proposition at the best owing to the small amount of time available. The proposition is rendered tenfold harder by the certainty that attack, if it comes, will not come from one quarter only, but from several. Consequently to preserve the Dreadnoughts an ever increasing number of auxiliaries are demanded. Of these no Navy can be said to have a sufficiency. Hence it is argued that a destroyer attack is bound to succeed sooner or later, while even did a sufficiency of small craft exist the big ship has to be so nursed and protected that her sphere of usefulness is enormously reduced. Submarines also are a deadly danger.

On the other hand it is argued that, given sufficient bulk to the big ship, torpedoes are likely to be relatively harmless to her; it is also asked how can the small craft protect their own big ships and also search out and attack the enemy's mastodons ?

There, till war proves something more definite one way or the other, the matter must be left. The big ship has been doomed so often, and so often adapted itself to changed conditions, that it may well do so again, despite the seemingly heavy odds against it.

PROTECTED CRUISERS OF THE DREADNOUGHT ERA.

The original conception of the Dreadnought era was " nothing between the most powerful armoured ships and torpedo craft," though so far as second class cruisers were concerned the last of these had been laid down in 1901.

The persistence with which Germany continued

yearly to build small protected cruisers, eventually, however, began to cause some perturbation; and in the 1908-09 Estimates five protected cruisers of the *Bristol* class were provided for. These were the *Bristol* (Clyde-bank), *Glasgow* (Fairfield), *Gloucester* (Beardmore), *Liver-pool* (Vickers), *Newcastle* (Elswick). The designed dis-placement was 4,820 tons, length 453 feet over all, beam 47 feet, and mean draught $15\frac{1}{4}$ feet. Armament two 6-inch, ten 4-inch, and two submerged tubes. A speed of 25 knots was expected from 22,000 horse power. On trials all exceeded 26 knots. All were fitted with Yarrow boilers, also turbines of the Parsons type, except in the *Bristol*, in which Curtiss type turbines were installed.

For 1909-10 four more similar ships were provided— the *Weymouth* class. Displacement rose to 5,250 tons, and a uniform armament of eight 6-inch was substituted for the mixed armament of the *Bristol* class. These four " Town " cruisers were the *Weymouth* (Elswick), *Yar-mouth* (London and Glasgow Co.), *Dartmouth* (Vickers), and *Falmouth* (Beardmore). All were given Yarrow boilers and Parsons turbines except the *Weymouth*, which was supplied with Curtiss turbines.

The Estimates of 1910-11 contained three cruisers, the *Chatham, Dublin,* and *Southampton,* of the same type, but with a displacement increased by 200 tons. Three more, the *Birmingham, Nottingham,* and *Lowes-toft,* figured in the Estimates of 1911-12.

The 1912-13 Estimates saw no more of these cruisers being provided for, but they heralded the appearance of eight vessels of a new type officially described as " lightly armoured cruisers." At the time of writing these vessels have not been laid down, nor have any particulars about them been published. It is, however, generally known that they will be a species of armoured Scouts. In 1907 the practice was instituted of building a Scout or two a year, those constructed to date being the *Boadicea, Bellona, Blanche, Blonde, Active, Amphion,* and *Fearless,* all of which are unarmoured, and so more or less compelled to fight modern destroyers on equal terms.

DESTROYERS IN THE DREADNOUGHT ERA.

The Dreadnought era, while simplifying types of big ships, saw the early institution of two distinct types of destroyers, plus an experimental vessel which was not duplicated. The original staple idea of Dreadnought era destroyers was to build very fast ocean-going destroyers for fleet work, and smaller craft, " coastals," for local duties. A considerable flourish of trumpets accompanied the announcement of this decision, which, however, was in no way really novel. It merely reproduced in destroyers the long exploded idea of sea-going and coast-defence ironclads.

Of these boats the first instalment amounted to a total of eighteen ; the most important being the experimental boat *Swift*, which was given a displacement of 1,825 tons, and so might just as well have been designated a fast small cruiser. The horse-power provided was no less than 30,000, the speed 36 knots, though on trials she once reached nearly 39 knots. Armament four 4-inch, two 18-inch tubes. Cost about £280,500.

It is interesting to note that in 1885 a precisely similar idea found vent in a *Swift* (afterwards re-named t.b. 81) of 125 tons against the 40 to 65 tons that was then normal for torpedo boats. It was nine years before anything else of the same size was built.

The first standard destroyers of the era were the " Oceans " (often known as " Tribals "). These averaged 880 tons, 33 knot speed with oil fuel only. Between 1906 and 1910 altogether a dozen were built. The armament given to the five first was five 12-pounder, and two 18-inch tubes ; in later boats two 4-inch, 25-pounder were substituted for the five 12-pounders.

The " coastal destroyers," which have since lost that name, and are now known as first-class torpedo-boats, were built in groups of twelve for three years ; the first batch averaging 225 tons, and later boats about 260 tons. In all the armament is two 12-pounder and three 18-inch torpedo tubes ; speed 26 knots. Parsons turbines in all, and oil fuel instead of coal,

In 1908-09 there came a revulsion of official feeling against both types, and an attempt to evolve a species of intermediate was made. It was held that the Oceans were exceedingly costly; also somewhat fragile. The new boats, the *Beagle* class, averaged 900 tons instead of the thousand tons that the latest Oceans were getting to. Armament was reduced to one 4-inch, 25-pounder, and three 12-pounders, with the usual two 18-inch torpedo tubes. Speed was cut down to 27 knots. Oil fuel was done away with, and coal reverted to.

The 1909-10 programme provided for 20 destroyers of the *Acorn* class. These are slightly smaller than the *Beagles*, armed with two 4-inch and two 12-pounders, but with oil again instead of coal only.

On account of considerable agitation in Parliament as to the small number of modern British destroyers, the construction of all this class was accelerated by a few months, and with a single exception they were completed in June, 1911.

Up till this time considerable latitude had been given to contractors for destroyers. In the 1910-11 programme the *Acheron* class, an Admiralty design, was given out for fourteen of the boats, which, except that they had two funnels instead of three, closely corresponded with the destroyers of the preceding year. In the other six boats the firms of Thornycroft, Yarrow, and Parsons were given some internal freedom of design with two boats each, and an increased speed was obtained with all.

For 1911-12 boats a similar principal was followed, and there was also still further acceleration. These latest boats are somewhat faster than heretofore, and an interesting innovation in the case of one of them—the Thornycroft type—is the appearance of the Diesel engine for propulsion instead of steam. More or less contemporaneously with this the Yarrow firm in the *Archer* and *Attack*, their special destroyers, evolved a system of super-heated steam, which led to a very considerable increase in speed, as compared with older

methods. A conflict between steam and " gas engines "
for destroyers is, therefore, a probable feature of the
early future ; but it may be unwise to place too much
reliance on the fact that a similar conflict with motor
cars ended in the practical extinction of steam, for all
that the probabilities point in that direction. The
superior convenience of the Diesel engine whether for
destroyers or larger ships is obvious, but there are undoubtedly still certain practical difficulties which cannot
be ignored.

GUNS OF THE WATTS ERA.

The principal guns of the Watts era are as follows :—

Calibre in.	Length in cals.	Weight tons.	Weight of projectile lbs.	Maximum penetration A.P. capped against K.C.	
				at 5000 yds.	3000 yds.
				in.	in.
13.5	45	80	1250	22	26
12	50	58	850	19	24
12	45	50	850	17½	22
9.2	50	30	380	10	13
9.2	45	27	380	8¾	11¼

It may be noted that the 12-inch, 45 cal. (as mounted
in the original *Dreadnought*) is quite capable of penetrating
anything in existence at most ranges, and the 12-inch,
50 cal. anything likely to exist. The main advantage of
the 13.5 is the superior weight of the projectile and the
better capacity of its shell.

Modern progress in gunnery is remarkably demonstrated by a comparison between the 13.5 of the Barnaby
era and the same calibre of the Watts era.

Calibre in.	Length in cals.	Weight tons.	Projectile lbs.	Maximum penetration A.P. capped against K.C. at		Corresponding value in K.C. of belt of ship carrying
				5000 yds.	3000 yds.	
13.5	30	80	1250	9	12	9
13.5	45	67	1250	22	26	12

From which it will be seen that armour has in no way kept pace with the gun, except in so far as that in the conditions which obtained with the old 13.5 a range of 3,000 yards was considered an outside limit, 9,000 yards is now held in the same or even less estimation.

Along such lines progress has been practically nullified during the last twenty years. But the limit of vision has now been reached, and increased gun-power cannot, practically speaking, any longer be met by range. Whence the argument of many that (failing the production of some armour altogether superior to anything now existing) the armoured ship is closely approaching the status of the armoured soldier of the Middle Ages. A precisely similar remark, however, was first made in 1887*, and proved an incorrect prophecy. To-day, therefore, those best able to judge are extremely careful about prophecying.

TORPEDO PROGRESS.

The principal feature of the last few years has been the steadily increasing efficiency of torpedoes, mainly by the adoption of improved engines. For many years 2,000 yards had been the maximum torpedo range. About 1904 an 18-inch Whitehead with 4,000 yards range and a maximum speed of 33 knots came into service. This was presently improved upon by torpedoes of 7,000 yards range. The exact range of the latest type Hardcastle torpedo—so called after its inventor, Engineer Commander Hardcastle—is a matter of uncertainty, but it is supposed to be capable of about 7,000 yards at 45 knots, and up to 11,000 at 30 knots. As a torpedo would take about 5½ minutes to travel this distance, it is obviously unlikely to be able to anticipate the position of a single enemy sufficiently to ensure hitting her, except by pure chance. On the other hand, if a fleet be fired at, hits with a torpedo are almost as likely as hits from a gun, and it seems impossible that the old idea of ships fighting in line can possibly survive, and Admiral

---

* Something of the same kind was also observed about 1870 or earlier, when a Whitworth gun punched through a 6-inch iron plate !

Bacon's theory that for the squadron of the past there will have to be substituted the isolated monster ship of the future seems the only reasonable one, despite all the protests against " mastodons."

With the improvement of torpedoes, especial atten- tion has been devoted to under-water protection against them. One form of this, the solid bulkheads of the original *Dreadnought*, was, after a time, partially aban- doned owing to its extreme inconvenience. Another form of protection adopted in all Dreadnoughts is a certain amount of internal armour, an idea first evolved in France for the battleship *Henri IV.*, which was laid down in July, 1897. Experiments with a view to testing the efficiency of this device were not very promising. An improvement on the system was effected by M. Lagane, of La Seyne, in the Russian *Tsarevitch* in 1899. This ship was actually torpedoed in the Russo-Japanese War, but unfortunately she was not hit on the specially- protected portion, so no experience was gained of the war utility of the system. While it is believed by some that the modern system is proof against half a dozen torpedoes, others are extremely sceptical as to whether any real immunity is afforded. War alone can tell. The most that can be prophesied is that the next naval war will see the torpedo accomplish either a great deal or a great deal less than is generally assumed. A paradoxical position; but so things are! No one can predict with any more certainty.

NAVAL ESTIMATES OF THE WATTS ERA.

Financial Year.	Amount.	Personnel.	Ships provided.			
			Battle- ships.	Battle- cruisers.	Armoured cruisers.	Prot. cruisers.
1902-03	31,003,977	122,500	2	—	2	—
1903-04	35,709,477	127,100	3	—	4	—
1904-05	36,859,681	131,100	2	—	3	—
1905-06	33,389,500	129,000	1	3	—	—
1906-07	31,472,087	129,000	3	—	—	—
1907-08	31,419,500	128,000	3	—	—	—
1908-09	32,319,500	128,000	1	1	—	5
1909-10	35,142,700	138,000	6	2	—	3
1910-11	40,603,700	131,000	4	1	—	3
1911-12	44,392,500	134,000	4	1	—	3
1912-13	44,085,400	136,000	3	1	—	—

Later in 1912 the sum of £1,000,000 was handed to the Navy out of the Budget surplus. This sum, the "supplementary estimate," was allotted in order to set off a corresponding German increase.

The decrease of 1905-1908 is probably directly responsible for the increase 1910-1912 ; owing to the fact that the British decrease was met by a corresponding rise in German expenditure. It is the fashion now-a-days to deplore the sums spent on naval armaments, while little or nothing is said about the military estimates.

On the face of things, this ever-increasing naval outlay looks likely to lead to ultimate financial ruin. This, however, is really a somewhat superficial view, and mostly nothing but a modern equivalent to that " Insular Spirit " which has been referred to in previous pages.

Compared to the national interests at stake, the increase regarded as an insurance is more apparent than real. It is, if anything, a smaller percentage on national existence; also over a period of a hundred years it is far less than the corresponding increase in the Civil Service Vote, which lacks any claims to be considered an "insurance." The entire amount spent in shipbuilding is expended in the country, and about 70 per cent. of it goes in direct payment to "Labour": which is probably a larger percentage than would be achieved were the same sum spent in any other way whatever.

The " ruinous competition in naval armaments " so prated on by certain publicists is really little better than an idle phrase so far as the British nation is concerned; and there is no real reason to regard future increases with apprehension.

XVI.

SUBMARINES.

THE submarine as anything of the nature of a practical arm made its first appearance as a " submarine torpedo boat," useful merely for harbour defence. As such it was eagerly embraced by the French Navy, and had a considerable vogue therein, besides being a commonplace in the United States long before the British Admiralty accepted it as serious in a way.

As a matter of fact, till the invention of the periscope enabled it to see where it was going when submerged, the submarine was little if anything but a paper menace. The periscope altered all this.

The first submarines for the British Navy figured in the 1901-02 Estimates. Five copies of the American *Holland* were laid down at Barrow, the first being launched in October, 1901. These boats were of 120 tons submerged displacement, and used merely as instructional or experimental craft almost as soon as completed.

They were followed immediately by the " A " class, totalling thirteen boats in all. Displacement submerged, 207 tons. Those numbered from five to thirteen were given sixteen cylinder surface motors of 550 horse-power in place of the 450 horse-power twelve cylinder ones of the earlier boats. In 1904 A1 was lost with all hands under tragic circumstances off Spithead, being run down by a merchant steamer. This disaster led to the installation of double periscopes in later types. A3 was lost off Spithead in 1912, being run down by the *Hazard*, very near where A1 was lost. The B class which followed numbered eleven boats, of which B1 was originally known as A14.   The remaining B class belong to the 1904-05 Estimates.   The submerged displacement in these rises to 313 tons, and the surface speed to thirteen knots, instead of eleven and a half, though, owing to improved lines, the horse-power was little increased.

New boats, completed in 1906 and later, though identical with these, were known as the C class, and totalled thirty-eight altogether.   One, C11, was lost at sea from a collision.

In 1907 the earliest boat of a new type (D Class) was put in hand.   Displacing 600 tons submerged, she practically doubled her predecessors.   Her surface speed rose to sixteen knots with 1,200 horse-power.   Three instead of two torpedo tubes were fitted, also wireless telegraphy was experimentally adopted in her.

By the end of 1911 eight boats of the D class had been launched.   It was originally intended to build a total of nineteen of this class, but meanwhile an improved boat of the E type was evolved.   The E class are 177ft. long, with a submerged displacement of 800 tons or thereabouts, and four 21-inch tubes.   They are fitted with wireless.   Their special feature, however, is the fitting of guns, as a regular and integral part of the design.

The first submarine to mount a gun was D4, in which a special 12-pounder was experimentally mounted, so that it could be housed when the boat was submerged ; for later boats two guns were decided on.

At the time of writing (1912) very little is definitely known about the E class.   According to some accounts a surface speed of eighteen knots is hoped for, though fifteen knots is more generally accredited.   In all, heavy oil Diesel motors are definitely adopted.

Guns for submarines were expected to appear sooner than they actually did.   At an early stage it was foreseen that, once radii developed, submarines were likely enough to find themselves in contact with hostile submarines and need something to attack them with.   The original idea of the submarine as " the weapon of the

weaker Power " soon went the same way as a similar idea
about torpedo boats at their first inception.

In torpedo-boats it was at once self-evident that
—whatever the value of the torpedo boat—the stronger
Power was able to build far more than the weaker, and
to annihilate accordingly.

For a time the submarine seemed to defy this law.
It was fatuously hoped that " submarines cannot injure
hostile submarines " ; and that the " torpedo boat is the
answer to the torpedo boat " would not have as sequel
" the submarine is the answer to the submarine."

The submarine with guns has now knocked on the
head all ideas and theories of that sort, and definitely
placed underwater craft on the same footing as others.

It may well be in the womb of the future that submarines to-morrow may be what the ironclad was
yesterday or the day before. The submarine battleship
may appear and render obsolete the " Dreadnought " of
to-day ! But nothing can alter the cardinal fact that,
given equal efficiency, the Power with most such craft
must win, and that, given an inferior efficiency, defeat
may be looked for as the natural corollary on lines
entirely unconnected with whether the " capital ship "
is of a type that floats only or one that can be submerged
at will.

Tactics may alter, the means may alter, and the
most obvious instruments of naval strategy may do the
same. But nothing whatever can affect the bedrock
truth that, given equal efficiency, " numbers only can
annihilate." Given the " equal efficiency " nothing else
really matters !

If the creators of weapons keep themselves to date,
if those who supply them see to it that the supply is
sufficient, if those who work the weapons are efficient,
the part of those in chief control resolves itself into
little save achieving victory with the minimum of loss.
The day may yet arrive when someone discovers that a
good deal of what has been written about the genius of
various famous admirals of the past, is verbiage rather

than fact, that they were a part of one great whole, rather than the sole controlling organisation—at any rate, once battle was engaged.

In the future, if the submarine " Dreadnought " becomes an actuality, this is probably likely to be so to a greater extent than anything which obtained in the past. So far as we can to-day conceive of such future fights, much of the battle, at any rate, will entail more or less blind work under the surface, individual enemies engaging one another, the leader compelled to rely more and more upon the efficiency of his individual units and less upon his own tactical combinations.

Of course things may turn out otherwise. Inventions yet undreamed of may come to the fore, and the nether waters present no greater obstacle to regular operations than the surface does to-day. Plunging may offer no salvation to a beaten enemy. We can only make idle speculations now.

Yet, however things may shape, success or failure, victory or defeat must assuredly depend in a great measure on the makers of the weapons and the efficiency of those who work them—the tools, on the reliability of which every admiral must trust for victory.

XVII.

NAVAL AVIATION.

THE aeroplane idea is so old that we find it in Greek mythology, and it is consequently of unknown antiquity. Hundreds of years before Christ there were hoary old legends of Dædalus and Icarus, who made wings for themselves and flew. Icarus flew too high, the sun melted his wings, with the result that there happened to him what happens about once a week to aviators to-day, he fell and died. Contemporary with these legends, are legends of floating rocks which spurted out fire— stories which sounded inestimably silly till steamships came along. We may imagine prophets able to look ahead and to invest their day with visions of the future. Equally we can discard prophets and imagine a civilisation long since dead which knew all about flying and steamers, and survives in legend only.

The latter alternative is really the more reasonable of the two. While imagination can do a very great deal and exaggerate to any extent, it must have a base to work on. It is easier to believe in some long gone and extinct civilisation which destroyed itself in the air, than to believe that pure imagination accounts for the flying stories of long ago. Africa is full of traces of vast cities older than any history, telling of past civilisations of which nothing is or ever will be known. Also there is practically no known age in which anything but the motive power stood between aeroplane theories and their realisation.

* Dean Swift, in " Gulliver's Travels," described almost exactly the moons of Mars long before their existence was ever suspected.

In support of the theory that men flew before to-day there is the following :—Somewhere about the year 1100, that is to say, back in the reign of King Stephen, a French historian relates the appearance of " as it were, a ship, in the air over London." It anchored, and the citizens of London got hold of the anchor. The airship sent a man down to free it, and the citizens of London caught him and drowned him in the river. The rest of the aviators then cut the rope and sailed away.

This incident is mentioned so baldly and casually and so much mixed up with ordinary petty chat of the era (chat which proves to have been quite true), that it takes far more faith to accept it as " pure lies " than to accept it as fact more or less.

These legends cannot be disregarded lightly. They one and all give priority to the aeroplane—the " heavier than air " vehicle. Once in a way the " lighter than air " idea got a casual look in ; but it was not till the end of the eighteenth century that it got into the regions of practical politics with the French Montgolfiers. But there were people who invented elementary aeroplanes, long before Montgolfier.

From the end of the eighteenth century until to-day the Montgolfier idea of " lighter than air " has got little further. The shape has altered ; instead of hot air, hydrogen gas is now employed ; and by means of motors the balloon no longer drifts before the wind. But progress is terribly slow. That it is so, is a very important thing to recognise, as slow development is by no means a reason for ignoring an invention. Sometimes it is quite the opposite.

It will probably be a good many years before it is definitely settled whether the " heavier than air " or " lighter than air " principle is the better for Naval purposes, though there are not wanting enthusiasts who decry the " lighter than air " machines altogether.

This is probably a grave mistake, brought about by the fact that practical balloons existed long before practical aeroplanes, and dirigibles made flights before

ever aeroplanes rose off the earth.   Yet the dirigible
is in a far more elementary stage than the aeroplane is.
Not only is the aeroplane a much older idea in the
theoretical direction, but being very much smaller it on
that account has very possibly developed more quickly.

The world has been building ships for thousands of
years, yet it has only recently developed *Lions* and
Olympics, and both are still developing and likely to do
so for some time to come.   Row-boats, however, arrived
at perfection a good thousand years ago.   That is to say,
there has been no alteration or improvement in them
at all commensurate with the alterations that have taken
place in big ships during the same period.

Something of the same sort is quite possible with
aeroplanes.   It is already comparatively easy to forecast their eventual form without much danger of being
proved a false prophet later on.   We may safely say that
they will become capable of much higher speeds than at
present ;   also (which is perhaps more important) *slower*
speeds ;   and that all existing troubles with stability will
eventually be overcome.   But experiments made with
birds indicate that the run which an aeroplane has to take
before it can rise occurs in much the same proportion
with birds ;   and so there are few, if any, practical men
who now expect to see future aeroplanes capable of rising
vertically from the ground, or hovering in the air except
under such conditions as any bird can hover without
inconvenience.

The possibilities of the dirigible, on the other hand,
no man can foresee.   The gasbag that can be brought to
the ground by a single bullet hole in it, is a very different
thing from the possibility of airships of the future which
may be a mile or two long, divided into innumerable compartments, filled with non-explosive gas such as is sure to
be discovered sooner or later.   Two miles seems an extraordinary length to-day, but a ship ten miles long would
only be something like the ratio of the early dirigible
to the future ones compared to the ratio Dreadnoughts
bear to the first ships built by men.

On the water, bulk is limited by the depth and size of harbours, but in the vast regions of the air there are practically no limitations whatever, and there is virtually nothing to limit size, save the building of land docks on open plains into which airships could descend for purposes of repair and so forth. Consequently those who hastily assume from a few accidents that the " lighter than air " craft has no future are probably making a great mistake ; at any rate, so far as naval work is concerned. Certain definite uses are apparent even now to those who think and ignore commercial rivalries.

It has been wisely laid down that aeroplanes for naval purposes must be capable of rising from and descending on the water. The Curtiss was the first successful hydro-aeroplane, but since then floats have been fitted to various other types with equal success. It is doubtful whether naval aeroplanes will be carried on shipboard like boats, although this is by no means impossible. It will, however, be more convenient for a variety of reasons to use them like submarines with their own special depot ships.

The main naval use of aeroplanes would be for scouting purposes. How near they would be able to approach a hostile fleet is a question not likely to be solved until the day of battle. The question of their being hit is secondary to the question of their being upset, owing to tremendous concussion of heavy gun fire. The idea of aeroplanes dropping bombs down the funnels of warships can be dismissed as the entirely fanciful dreams of people who know nothing whatever about aeroplanes or the mathematical problems involved. Judging by recent experiments, dropping bombs anywhere upon a moving ship would be impossible, except at ranges where the aviator would at once be brought down by rifle fire. A far more likely and useful service would be the destruction of the enemy's aeroplanes. For this purpose a special gun, firing a species of chain shot, has already been suggested, and the naval aeroplane of the future is certain to carry a gun of some kind. The off-chance of doing a certain amount of damage to a hostile ship by dropping a bomb upon it, is nothing compared to the importance of destroying the enemy's aeroplanes.   This last seems likely to be all-important.

The duties of naval airships will be of a different nature.   Already a point kept in view in their design is ability to " keep the air " for a considerable period, and with what are in these days " large airships " of the Zeppelin type (to which the ill-fated Naval Airship No. 1 *Mayfly* belonged) there seems no reason why an airship should not be kept in the air for three or four days already.

The fuel problem is not very difficult, because a great deal can already be done without the use of the engines, or with only partial use of them.   It is also more than probable that with a view to further economy some kind of sails, combined with sea-anchors, will be evolved, whereby the ship might become able to sail in the air nearly as well as the old three-deckers, or, at any rate, as well as the masted ironclads, sailed in the water.   The difficulty of " keeping the air " is the inevitable leakage of gas, but as leakage nowadays is infinitesimally less than it once was, the assumption is that as the years go on it will eventually be reduced to almost a minus quantity. Gales will be met by " bulk " and efficient anchors, on the principle that the gale which swamps a fishing-boat or blows over a haystack has no effect on a Dreadnought or a cathedral.

Ability to keep the air will enable all Fleets to be accompanied by airships, which would detect mines and submarines, and with their ability to adapt their speeds at will, the presumption is that they would be able to destroy submarines by bombs without much trouble.

A further and very important duty would be the detection of torpedo attacks at night.   Experiments carried out in Austria some few years ago with a captive balloon proved conclusively that except in cases of thick fog any vessels in motion are easily detected at a distance of ten or twelve miles.   It is not merely the telltale flames in the funnels which betray attacking vessels ;

their wakes are always clearly visible, and as a general rule the vessels themselves, no matter how dark the night.

Bomb-dropping from an airship will be a more serious matter than from aeroplanes, as so much more in the way of explosives could be carried. The chance of being hit, however, would probably be so much greater that it is unlikely that any airships would be risked for such purposes. Nor is it very probable that naval airships will for some time to come attack each other, if they can possibly avoid it, the reason being that for a good many years they will be comparatively few in number, and the attack would have, in most cases, to be delivered in the presence of a fleet, which would make the attack, to say the least of it, very hazardous.

Eventually, of course, aerial Dreadnoughts fighting each other are probable enough ; but " the Trafalgar of the air " is unlikely to be witnessed within the lifetime of most or any of us now living. Nor is it likely that aerial Dreadnoughts will replace Dreadnoughts of the water, although as years go on they may cause profound modifications in design in order to allow of mounting guns for vertical fire.

We are in the presence of the introduction of a " new arm." But between what a " new arm " can actually accomplish, and what enthusiastic inventors say it will do, there is always an enormous gap. Inventors, when they come to prophesying, are always one of two things —asses, or prodigious asses ! France—once the second Naval Power in Europe—became of little or no account because it took the submarine at the enthusiastic inventor's face value, and neglected the present and immediate future.

The present stage of aerial progress (1912) in the British Navy is briefly to be summarised as follows :—

1. A naval airship was built in 1909-1911. It proved a total failure. A fresh one is now under construction. Its success or failure must depend on whether it is designed by aerial experts working upon known

possibilities, or (like No. 1) partly designed by nava
officers whose ideas of the possible are obsessed by ideas
of what would be far more useful could it be constructed.

2.   In 1911 four naval officers were appointed to
learn aeroplane work.   Since then others have been
appointed also.   Others, again, have qualified privately.
In 1912, the Royal Flying Corps was established—both
naval and military aviators becoming " wings " of the
same body—an excellent principle, but one necessarily
experimental so far as practical work is concerned.

XVIII.

AUXILIARY NAVIES.

N O account of the British battle fleet would be complete without reference to the various auxiliary navies, which, though none of them possess any very serious fighting value, yet all possess potentialities for the future which can with difficulty be computed.

The auxiliary navies may be divided into two main sections—(1) those which are direct branches of the British Navy, and (2) those which belong to the semi-independent colonies.

Of the former, the principal is the Royal Indian Marine, which consists of a number of armed troopships. Of these the chief are the *Northbrook*, launched at Clydebank in 1907, 5,820 tons, 16 knot speed, and an armament of six 4-inch and six 3-pounders. The *Dufferin*, which was launched in 1904, is of 7,457 tons, has a speed of 19 knots, and an armament of eight 4-inch and eight 3-pounders. The *Hardinge*, launched 1900, is of 6,520 tons, 18 knot speed, and carries six 4.7-inch guns as well as six 3-pounders and 4 Maxims.

There are three older troopships, the *Minto* (1893), the *Elphinstone* (1887), and the *Dalhousie* (1886). These are supplemented by ten small steamers and nine small mining vessels.

The germ of this fleet was created in the early seventies when the breastwork monitors *Abyssinia* and *Magdala* were sent out for the defence of Indian harbours. These were small predecessors of the *Devastation*, very similar to the home coast-defence monitors of the *Cyclops* class, and carried four 18-ton muzzle-loading guns.

About the year 1888 some new torpedo boats (Nos. 100-106) were lent for the Indian Marine service. These, with their names and numbers, were as follows :—
Baluch: (100), *Ghurka* (101), *Kahren* (102), *Pathan* (103), *Maharatta* (104), *Sikh* (105), and *Rajput* (106). The two earliest numbers were built by Thornycroft, and were of 92 tons ; the others were built by White, of Cowes, and were of 95 tons displacement.

In the years 1890-91 two torpedo gunboats, *Plassy* and *Assaye*, of the *Sharpshooter* class, were launched at Elswick for the Indian Marine, in which they remained until withdrawn in the early years of the present century.

On a similar footing to the Royal Indian Marine are the flotillas, mostly consisting of river gunboats, maintained in North and South Nigeria and in Central Africa, and the gunboats on the Nile under the Egyptian Government.

The Colonial Navies are on a different standing. First place in their formation belongs to Australia. The monitor *Cerberus*, practically a sister of the *Abyssinia* and *Magdala* already mentioned, was launched at Jarrow in 1868 for Victoria. This vessel (which still exists as a drill ship) is of 3,480 tons, armed with four 18-ton muzzle-loaders, and protected with an 8-inch belt.

In 1884 Australia's local defence was re-inforced with four gunboats as follows :—The *Protector*, of 920 tons, carrying one 8-inch and five 6-inch guns, for South Australia. She, as well as the others, was built at Elswick. For Western Australia a similar vessel of 530 tons, named the *Victoria*, was built, armed with one 18-ton muzzle-loader. The *Gayundah* and *Paluma*, also of the same type, carrying one old 8-inch and one 6-inch, were built for Queensland. Their displacement is 360 tons each.

From that time onward the Australian Navy occasionally sent a few officers and men for training in the British Navy.

Towards the end of the eighties interest began to

be taken in Australian naval defence, and five cruisers and two torpedo gunboats were ordered for local Australian service while borne on the Royal Navy List. Of these vessels the five cruisers were the *Katoomba* (ex *Pandora*), *Mildura* (ex *Pelorus*), *Ringarooma* (ex *Psyche*), *Tauranga* (ex *Phœnix*), and the *Wallaroo* (ex *Persian*), all 2,575 vessels of the old *Pallas* class, of which, at the time of writing (1912), the *Philomel* still exists. These ships had a designed speed of 16.5 knots, a protective deck, and an armament of eight 4.7-inch and some smaller guns.

The torpedo gunboat *Boomerang* (ex *Whiting*) and *Karrakatta* (ex *Wizard*) belonged to the *Sharpshooter* class, and were lent under the same conditions as the cruisers.

In the course of time all of them wore out and were eventually recalled.

Coincident with this the Australians commenced to have a revived interest in Imperial defence, and in the year 1905-6 Australia and New Zealand contributed £240,000 to Imperial naval defence, and a project was put forward for the building of eight destroyers and four torpedo gunboats for Colonial Defence purposes.

A few years later this project took a more definite shape, and about the year 1910 the battle-cruiser *Australia*, a sister of the *Indefatigable*, was ordered. As part of the same programme, three protected cruisers of the *Dartmouth* type, the *Melbourne*, *Sydney*, and *Brisbane*, were also ordered. Previously to this, three destroyers of the *Paramatta* type had been commenced, and in 1911 three more were ordered, thus forming a nucleus of a serious Australian Navy.*

New Zealand's interest in the Imperial Navy may be said to have commenced about the year 1900. It eventuated in paying for the battleship *New Zealand*† of the *King Edward* class, which was laid down in September, 1903. An old gunboat of the *Magpie* class was purchased,

---

* Of these, the third in either case, was built or put together in Australia.
† Now re-named *Zelandia*,

re-christened the *Amokoura*, and used for training purposes, while to replace some old torpedo boats, which
had been sent to New Zealand about the same time as
similar boats went to Australia, three destroyers of the
Paramatta type were ordered. Finally, an offer from the
New Zealand Premier to supplement the Dreadnought
efficiency of the British Navy culminated in the battle-
cruiser *New Zealand*, which was offered to be provided
about the same time or a little before Australia offered
a similar vessel.*

The Dominion of Canada has always maintained a
certain number of small vessels for Customs duties or
fishery protection, also for service on the Great Lakes.
In 1909 the question of a Canadian Navy became insistent, and two old British cruisers—the *Niobe* of the
Diadem class and the *Rainbow* of the *Apollo* class—were
purchased as training ships for the Canadian Navy. A
project was also brought forward for the creation of
Canadian dockyards and building therein four second-
class cruisers of the *Dartmouth* class and six destroyers,
though to date (1912) none of these ships have materialised, and the Canadian Navy is still very much a
project in the air.

Newfoundland has a naval reserve, trained over
many years in the drill-ship, which is ex H.M.S. *Calypso.*

The whole subject of Colonial Navies is somewhat
involved, owing to the question as to how far they should
be under the orders of and part of the British Navy,
liable to be used when and where required for Imperial
needs, and how far they should be regarded as merely for
local defence. It has been argued from one point of view
that Colonial Navies acting on their own responsibility
might create undesirable Imperial complications—as for
instance, Australia with Japan, or Canada with the
United States. On the other hand it is argued that it
would not be possible to arouse Colonial enthusiasm for
a Colonial fleet which was not always on the spot, despite

* In May, 1912, the *New Zealand* was definitely handed over to the British
Navy. The *Australia* still remains a Commonwealth ship.

any strategical grounds that might exist for its being elsewhere. New Zealand, in May, 1912, negatived this by presenting her battle-cruiser to the Imperial Navy for use where most needed, but generally speaking Colonials think first of local defence.

These two divergent points of view, which are certainly extremely delicate, may be said to be still *sub-judice*, but in the year 1911 the following agreement, which is of the nature of a very judicious compromise, was drawn up :—

1. The naval services and forces of the Dominions of Canada and Australia will be exclusively under the control of their respective Governments.

2. The training and discipline of the naval forces of the Dominions will be generally uniform with the training and discipline of the fleet of the United Kingdom, and by arrangement, officers and men of the said forces will be interchangeable with those under the control of the British Admiralty.

3. The ships of each Dominion naval force will hoist at the stern the white ensign as the symbol of the authority of the Crown, and at the jack-staff the distinctive flag of the Dominion.

4. The Canadian and Australian Governments will have their own naval stations as agreed upon and from time to time. The limits of the stations are as described in Schedule A (Canada) and Schedule B (Australia).

5. In the event of the Canadian or Australian Government desiring to send ships to a part of the British Empire outside of their own respective stations, they will notify the British Admiralty.

6. In the event of the Canadian or Australian Government desiring to send ships to a foreign port, they will obtain the concurrence of the Imperial Government, in order that the necessary arrangements with the Foreign Office may be made, as in the case of ships of the British Fleet, in such time and manner as is usual between the British Admiralty and the Foreign Office.

7. While ships of the Dominions are at a foreign

port a report of their proceedings will be forwarded by the officer in command to the Commander-in-Chief on the station or to the British Admiralty. The officer in command of a Dominion ship so long as he remains in the foreign port will obey any instructions he may receive from the Government of the United Kingdom as to the conduct of any international matters that may arise, the Dominion Government being informed.

8. The commanding officer of a Dominion ship having to put into a foreign port without previous arrangement on account of stress of weather, damage, or any unforeseen emergency, will report his arrival and reason for calling to the Commander-in-Chief of the station or to the Admiralty, and will obey, so long as he remains in the foreign port, any instructions he may receive from the Government of the United Kingdom as to his relations with the authorities, the Dominion Government being informed.

9. When a ship of the British Admiralty meets a ship of the Dominions, the senior officer will have the right to command in matters of ceremony or international intercourse, or where united action is agreed upon, but will have no power to direct the movements of ships of the other service unless the ships are ordered to co-operate by mutual arrangement.

10. In foreign ports the senior officer will take command, but not so as to interfere with the orders that the junior may have received from his Government.

11. When a court-martial has to be ordered by a Dominion and a sufficient number of officers are not available in the Dominion service at the time, the British Admiralty, if requested, will make the necessary arrangements to enable a court to be formed. Provision will be made by order of his Majesty in Council and by the Dominion Governments respectively to define the conditions under which officers of the different services are to sit on joint courts-martial.

12. The British Admiralty undertakes to lend to the Dominions during the period of development of

their services, under conditions to be agreed upon, such flag officers and other officers and men as may be needed. In their selection preference will be given to officers and men coming from, or connected with, the Dominions, but they should all be volunteers for the service.

13. The service of officers of the British Fleet in the Dominion naval forces or of officers of those forces in the British Fleet will count in all respects for promotion, pay, retirement, etc., as service in their respective forces.

14. In order to determine all questions of seniority that may arise the names of all officers will be shown in the Navy List, and their seniority determined by the date of their commissions, whichever is the earlier, in the British, Canadian, or Australian services.

15. It is desirable in the interests of efficiency and co-operation that arrangements should be made from time to time between the British Admiralty and the Dominion for the ships of the Dominions to take part in fleet exercises or for any other joint training considered necessary under the Senior Naval Officer. While so employed the ships will be under the command of that officer, who would not, however, interfere in the internal economy of ships of another service further than is absolutely necessary.

16. In time of war, when the naval service of a Dominion or any part thereof has been put at the disposal of the Imperial Government by the Dominion authorities, the ships will form an integral part of the British Fleet, and will remain under the control of the British Admiralty during the continuance of the war.

17. The Dominions having applied to their naval forces the King's Regulations and Admiralty Instructions and the Naval Discipline Act, the British Admiralty and Dominion Governments will communicate to each other any changes which they propose to make in these Regulations or that Act.

The Schedules A and B defined the stations of Canadian and Australian ships respectively. These stations cover the territorial and contiguous waters in each case. The agreement generally seems framed in an exceedingly able and statesmanlike spirit, designed so far as may be to avoid any possible friction or misunderstanding in the future, and in preparation for the day when the Imperial British Fleet shall be something very much more than a dream or just a fancy.

This chapter merely records the birth of something the end of which none can foretell. It may be the first hint of a great world-wide English-speaking confederation : it may be the swan song of the British Empire. But it is probably one or the other in full measure.

XIX.

GENERAL MATTERS IN THE LAST HUNDRED YEARS.

SINCE the Great French Wars the British Navy has altered out of all recognition in its *materiel* ; but changes in the *personnel* are often considerably less than appears on the surface.

To take matters in the same order as they are taken in Chapter VIII., uniform has, of course, long established itself. It has done so with a formality which, in the view of many, has " established the régime of the tailor rather than the sailor." Within the last few years a slight change for the better has occurred ; but of the greater part of the period so far as concerns purposes for which uniform was first introduced—the sailor and tailor exchanged places. Much has been written about admirals and captains whose ideas of naval efficiency were limited by " spit and polish,"* but " spit and polish " at its worst was never so bad as that tailoring idea which was the ultimate result of George II. admiring the costume of the Duchess of Bedford.†

The mischief is popularly supposed to lie with naval officers. Actually its roots lie with officials, who have piled regulation upon regulation, and the Vanity of Vanities is to be found so far back as the days of the great St. Vincent and his recorded orders about officers' shoe-laces. Lesser lights than he, being in authority, blindly imitated. And so the uniform fetish grew and prospered.

* See page 61. No less a man than Sir Francis Drake appears to have invented " spit and polish."

† See page 137.

This is not to be taken wholly as a condemnation—
for all that a system which made one of the most important duties of a lieutenant to be the carrying round
of a tape measure with a view to ascertaining whether
every man was " uniform " within a fraction of an inch
may seem more suggestive of comic opera than of naval
efficiency.　Within reasonable limits, conformity has
many virtues ; and a man slovenly in observing uniform
regulations is likely enough to be slovenly in things of
greater moment.　Like most bad things in the Navy, the
principle was ideal : only the carrying of it too far was
at fault.　There is not the remotest reason to believe
that a Navy not in uniform would be as efficient as one
in uniform—all the probabilities are that it would be
less so.　The man who invented the saying that " a
pigmy in uniform is more impressive than a giant in
plain clothes " was making no idle statement, but stating
a general verity.　The trouble is solely in the difficulty
that has ever been experienced in striking a common-
sense mean—a difficulty created by the first mediocrity
who tried to stand in St. Vincent's shoes, and who
lacked the brain to realise that what St. Vincent had
started with a definite Service object in view, he—the
unknown mediocrity—had merely lost in the *means*.
An example once created had to be followed.　The hardships of conformity—of which overmuch is heard nowadays—are actually trivial, on account of the custom.
The mischief lies not in the conforming, but in the waste
of time of those who are made responsible for that
conformity.

In essence, modern uniform is simple enough : that
the various ranks should be noted by special insignia is
obviously desirable.　For officers, the distinguishing
sleeve-marks are :—

Admiral　Vice-Admiral　Rear-Admiral　Commodore　Captain　Commander　Lieutenant　Lieutenant　Sub-Lieutenant

The system for the supply of the *personnel* is to-day altogether different from what it was a hundred years ago. Till comparatively recently future deck officers were taken very young, passed into the Service as Naval Cadets, and thence promoted up to Midshipmen, etc., while Engineers and officers of the other civilian branches joined later in life.

More or less contemporaneously with the Dreadnought era this was altered by the " New Scheme of Entry," also known as the " Selbourne Scheme," after the then first Lord of the Admiralty, but really the creation of Admiral Fisher, the Sea Lord who was the moving spirit at the Admiralty at that time.

Few schemes have been more virulently criticised— few, in some cases, more unfairly. Like nearly all Admiral Fisher's innovations, the scheme was better on paper than in fact. Like all his other schemes it was carried through at far too great a pace for the ultra-conservative moods of the British Navy, which has ever resented anything but the most gradual of changes. On the other hand, it is too often forgotten by critics that a great agitation on the part of naval engineer officers, backed by very considerable shore-influences, was then in existence. Something had to be done, and done quickly. Of Admiral Fisher it may ever be said that he acted where others merely argued.

Under the New Scheme, the deck-officer, the engineer, and the marine-officer were all to enter as cadets at a very tender age, undergo a common training, and be specialised for any Branch at option or at Admiralty discretion later on.

Whatever may be said against the New Scheme : it was magnificent on paper. Engineer officers had first come into the Navy as mechanics to work an auxiliary motive-power in which no " seamen " had much faith. From that humble beginning the status of their Branch grew and grew, till both motive-power and the existence of nearly everything on ship-board depended on the engineers. At the same time the official status of the

Branch remained practically in the same stage as it did
when the first few " greasers " were entered. The deck-
officer was (nominally, at any rate) drawn from the
aristocracy ; the engineer officer from the democracy in
a great measure. In so far as this obtained, " social
war " was added to the real issue. It was obvious that
this state of affairs was detrimental to naval efficiency.
Something had to be done.

Admiral Fisher cut the Gordian knot in his own
fashion. In substance his Scheme provided that future
engineer officers were to be drawn from the same class
as deck-officers—to gild the pill, marine officers were
flung into the same melting pot. He might have done
better : but far more conceivably harm might have been
perpetrated.

As an argument behind him, he had Drake and
Elizabethan conditions, the history of the days when
every man was made to " sail his ship and fight it too."
The U.S. Navy had already plunged on a somewhat
similar experiment. When the Russo-Japanese War
came, the Japanese, in the middle of a life-and-death
fight, suddenly granted executive rank to their engineer
officers—i.e., that right to control and punish their own
men which British marine officers have always had.

The Scheme met its first rock in the Marines. For
three hundred years or thereabouts the " Sea Regiment"
has been afloat as a thing apart. The " leather-necks "—
as the sailors call them—have built up their own traditions. They have ever remained a force apart from both
Army and Navy, belonging to both and yet to neither.
The record of the Marines is such that when, recently,
it was proposed that they should have a regimental
colour with their battles emblazoned on it, the idea had
to be abandoned because there was not room on the flag
for their services !

Any attempt to interfere with the continuity of
such a corps was fore-doomed to failure from the first.
The Marines resisted being turned into sailors just as
they would have resisted being turned into soldiers.

They stood out uncompromisingly for being " the Sea
Regiment." The expected happened. By 1911 this part
of the New Scheme was practically shelved, and the
most unique body of men in the world was left to carry
out its own traditions.

In the matter of future engineers, snags were struck
likewise, but here a more or less unreasoning conservatism
on the part of parents played its full part. The average
parent objected to his son becoming an engineer specialist
over old-time reasons. A further and weightier objection
was, and continues to be, raised by engineering experts,
who argue that engineering is a life profession, not to
be picked up efficiently by casual specialization.

The matter is still under discussion, and its verifica-
tion or otherwise rests with the future. As to the first
point, a serious effort to overcome it was made early in
1912 by the promulgation of an order that New Scheme
officers, specialised for engineering, would be eligible for
the command of submarines equally with deck-officers.

The importance of this particular point is great ;
for by the end of 1911 it was generally accepted that
the motor warship would at an early date in the future
replace the steam-driven one ; and so the " sail-his-ship-
and-fight-it-too " theory found a new interpretation.

As regards the rank and file of the Navy, the difference of a hundred years has been so great and so commented on that to-day we perhaps tend to make it seem
far greater than it really is. It is to be doubted whether
the " prime seaman " has altered to anything like the
extent imagined. We are all too prone to forget that in
the days of the Great French Wars all the crews were
not jail-birds, pressed-men, and riff-raff. The leaven of
the mass were the " prime seamen," who, in their own
way, were as well trained for the naval service as are
the bluejacket of to-day.

Since then the " prime seamen " have had many
vicissitudes. So long ago as the time of the Crimean War
men of ten years' continuous service were in existence,
but whatever the " paper " value of this force may have

been, the extracts given in Chapter X. make it abundantly clear that the " prime seaman " was in practice very scarce. It is long since then that the long service system was built up.

Under this every bluejacket was a " prime seaman " either in *posse* or in *esse*. He was entered for a period of ten years, with option to re-engage for a further ten years at slightly increased pay and a pension on retirement. At a later and comparatively recent stage this total of twenty years got increased to twenty-two years. The prospects were improved to the extent that the best men of the Lower Deck upon reaching Warrant Rank were able, towards the close of their careers, to reach the rank of lieutenant on the Active List. In a word, the idea of a Navy consisting entirely of " prime seamen " was more or less actually reached.

This system had, however, one drawback. It was relatively speaking very expensive. When the Fisher revolution took place Economy was very much the motto of the day. It was pointed out that outside the Royal Naval Reserve, consisting of merchant seamen, no effective reserve existed. It was further pointed out that on board a modern battleship there were many duties which could just as well be performed by partially trained or even untrained men as by skilled men.

Out of these two points (according to some critics), by using the first as a cloak for the economy of the second, a certain retrograde movement was established in the institution of the Short Service System. Under this the old time " landsman " was revived under another name. Under the Short Service System a man could enter the Navy for five years, receiving ordinary pay for ordinary duties, but without prospects of promotion or pension, except in so far as he might afterwards be utilised for reserve purposes.

How far this scheme made for efficiency is a moot point, but it certainly led to economy. As certainly it was bitterly resented by the men of the Navy. The views of the officers on the subject of " ticklers "—as

Short Service men were termed afloat—were less decided. Some considered the scheme an abomination ; others thought it very satisfactory.

With so conservative an institution as the British Navy, it is yet too early to give a definite decision one way or the other on the subject. But it is worth noting that no one seems to have remarked on the fact that it was a tentative return, under modern and peace conditions, to what obtained in the days of the Great French Wars, and then at least satisfactorily answered requirements.

No one really knows, and no one can do more than surmise, what will be required for manning the Fleet in the next great war in which the British Navy is engaged. It is generally assumed that in the present century the re-institution of the press-gang would be quite impossible owing to public opinion.

Public opinion, however, is a variable quantity, and with a Navy in desperate plight for men there is no saying definitely what might or might not happen, either publicly or *sub rosa*. It is generally agreed on all hands that, large as the trained *personnel* of the British Navy is, it might prove totally inadequate in a big naval war. In such case extra men would have to be found—sentiment or no sentiment. The Short Service System, despite all its drawbacks, may yet prove a loophole to avoid the horrors of the press-gang of the old days ; and much which on the face of it to-day is obviously unsatisfactory may in the future prove foresight of an unexpectedly high order.

It only remains to add that nothing of this sort has ever been advanced in extenuation by advocates of Short Service, who have confined themselves entirely to the obvious point of economy and the more or less debatable point of an efficient reserve.

To-day, of course, the crews do not find their ships a prison ; but it is a moot question whether they are relatively much better off than in Nelson's day. A great deal of leave is given—far more, indeed, than is

represented by philanthropic agitators—but it is mainly
of the nature of " short leave." This—in these days of
travel—means very little relatively, since it rarely allows
of a trip home. For good or ill, the bluejacket of to-day
is a " home-bird " ; consequently, what a hundred years
ago would have represented " ample liberty," to-day
appears much on all fours with the old time confinement
to the ship. Modern facilities for travel have swallowed
up most of the difference ! This is among the matters
not understood by the Powers That Be. The perspective
has changed ; and Service Conditions have not been
accommodated to the alteration.

Food remains a source of naval grievance to-day
almost as much as in the days of the Great Mutiny.
That it does so is mostly an inherited tradition of the
past ; for both quality and quantity are now excellent.
An impression prevails, however, that were messing
provided by the Admiralty on non-profit lines instead
of by contract, " extras " would either be cheaper, or
that what are now " canteen profits " on them would
be more available than they are at present. There is
little reason to believe that this is so. Like the purser
of a hundred years ago, the modern contractor probably
does not make a tenth of the profit that he is legendarily
supposed to make, nor is there any clear proof that
things could be materially bettered, except in details
which have little or nothing to do with the main point.

When all is said and done, the bluejacket of the
Twentieth Century has always been fed as well or better
than his brother in civilian life, and his growls upon the
subject of messing do not demand any very serious
attention. Just as the Great Mutiny of 1797 brought
about an attention to details of uniform, regulations and
things of that sort which have ever since endured, so it
perpetuated a corresponding impression that an official
eye must ever be directed to keeping messing more or
less up to the mark. And that eye has never slumbered.

In Chapter VIII. a page is devoted to surgery in
the Great War Era. Here, as in some other matters,

progress may be more real than imaginary. Now, as then, the Navy offers little in the way of lucrative inducements to a good surgeon. In one sense it offers less than it did ; for, though exceptions can be found, the general naval conception of the doctor is still the old-fashioned notion of someone to cure the sick man rather than the more modern idea of preventing the man from becoming sick.

The problem it must, however, be admitted is a difficult one in many ways. In peace conditions the medical staff is rather too large than too small ; for all that, for modern war conditions it is probably hopelessly inadequate.

It is more or less accepted that in modern battle the wounded must lie where they fall. Theoretically at any rate, this is mitigated by certain instructions in First Aid, and the furnishing of hypodermic syringes to one member of each gun's crew for use on the badly wounded. The days when lint was forbidden as a useless extravagance, and sponges were restricted for the sake of economy, have indeed gone, just as surely as has the old-time surgeon who, unable to afford his own instruments, had to borrow from the carpenter an ordinary saw to amputate a limb ! But—relatively to shore-practice of equal date—the naval medical service is not much less hampered than it was a hundred odd years ago ; and the next great naval war is likely enough to see as much superfluous agony (relatively speaking) as the last ! The true position of the surgeon in a warship is not recognised ; the official duties of a doctor are officially purely " curative," never, or very rarely, " preventive." Some or most of this is due to the prevalence of old-fashioned obsolete ideas in high quarters ; but some also is to be laid at the door of the " Churches," and their fancy for differentiating between diseases. The matter is not one that admits of further discussion here ; but the enforcement upon naval surgeons (who have to deal with large bodies of men crowded into spaces necessarily favourable for contagion) of conditions which, rightly or wrongly, are deemed to be for the public's ultimate welfare on shore, are a terrible menace to naval efficiency.

After the Great Mutiny of 1797 the pay of the men was approximately trebled. Although " extras " have since been added, the normal pay has remained to all intents and purposes stationary, while if qualifications be taken into account it has actually decreased, since the " ordinary " of to-day is called on to do just about what the " able seamen " of a hundred odd years had to do.

The respective rates are :—

	1797 per week.	1912 per week (minimum).
Ordinary seamen	6/6	7/7
Able seamen	8/4	9/11

Since the cost of living has certainly gone up at least twenty per cent. in the interim, and since the normal increase is undoubtedly under that, a *prima facie* case is certainly made out for those who contend that the British sailor is, if anything, worse paid than he was a hundred years ago.

The board and lodging which he obtains of course adds to the actual total ; but the fact remains that the board and lodging labourer of to-day, who takes no risks of his life, is now as much ahead of the sailor as he was behind him in 1797. And " uniform " means a heavy extra expense for clothing.

In 1912 the men of the Navy definitely asked for a twenty per cent. increase of pay. It amounted to nothing but an adjustment of 1797 conditions to modern ones. They did not obtain it—unasked for off-chances of " Democracy on the Quarter Deck " were given instead.

There at the moment the question remains. It has to a certain extent been obscured by question of naval punishments ; about which a good deal of nonsense has been written by people who in some cases should know better.

Naval punishments are severe ; but discipline necessitates punishments, and these have been regularly toned down to the spirit of the age. The real and genuine grievances of to-day are almost identical with the genuine grievances of which the " prime seamen " complained in 1797:—pay, leave, and the treatment of men who happen to come into the hands of the ship's medical staff through no fault of their own.

At the time of writing (1912) a Commission is enquiring into punishments, and further reductions in them to suit modern ideas are probable ; but it is by no means certain that any advantage in efficiency will be acquired therefrom. Naval Discipline—no matter how harsh—is a tricky thing to tamper with. The highest possible ideal of Discipline was reached by the Japanese, who, previous to the war with Russia, ran their Navy on " the honour of the flag " lines ; and presumably had some similar system in the Army. In what is certainly the most patriotic land of our era this succeeded in peace time. Yet in the attacks on Port Arthur, when a great assault was made, when the time came to cease bombarding the hostile position, the guns were turned on the possible line of retreat, ensuring that for a man to retire was more dangerous to him than to go forward. In the case of the Japanese it was perhaps an unnecessary precaution, but it was borrowed from old-time precautionary usage in Europe.

Every system of discipline is based on the fact that either sooner or later there will be some man who will be frightened enough to turn tail, and lead others to follow his example, unless there is something still worse to stop him. On this foundation stone the most seemingly trivial items of discipline are based.

No normal man *when it comes to the point* cares to risk his life or limbs. Here and there an individual of the " don't care " order is to be found ; but generally speaking he is an anomaly. In the ordinary way the

A2

safest assumption is that he will think more of his skin than anything else—and on this theory all systems of discipline are founded. All rely on the ultimate fact that " it is worse to go back than to go forward." The curse of the present age is the semi-educated humanitarian who criticises the *means* (often crude enough) without taking the *end* into proper account. At the other extreme are those who, though familiar with the story of the Russian sentry regularly placed to protect a favourite flower which had died two hundred years before, understand that there is a *reason* for everything, but fail to realise fully that conditions change.

Many works have been written on the tactical and strategical superiority of those who have led British Fleets to victory ; but in the great majority of cases there is little to show that the majority of our admirals were really more clever than many of their opponents. He would be a bold man who set out to prove in black and white that Collingwood had more brain than Villeneuve, or would have done better than that unlucky admiral had they changed places with each other. Nor would he have much more luck in attempting to prove that at any era in history British sailors were really braver than French ones.

In one critical period of English history Drake appeared—and the most lasting sign of " how he did it " was " spit and polish " ! In another dark time came St. Vincent—and his sign manual was " tailoring " and " routine." In yet another critical hour came Nelson, who supplied enthusiasm by his care for the health of his men. But it was Nelson who went out of his way to congratulate St. Vincent on hanging mutineers out of hand on a Sunday instead of keeping them till the Monday ! These three great men knew what they relied upon.

The real secret of British naval success has surely lain in the possession of naval architects able to create the kind of ship best calculated to stand hammering, and hard-hearted folk in authority who created a discipline which, however unreasonable some of it may now seem, ensured victory.

Superior British courage then, as now, was a pleasing topic for the music hall or its equivalent ; but the real driving power of the British battle fleet was " discipline." Those who to-day would amend or alter even the most seemingly ridiculous anomalies of discipline will do well to ponder and walk warily, lest they upset greater things than they wot of—lest they damage the keystone embodied in the crude words of that unknown stoker who said : " It's just this—do your blanky job."

THE END.

NETHERWOOD, DALTON & CO., RASHCLIFFE, HUDDERSFIELD,

Index.